GLOBAL MONETARY ECONOMICS

EMIL-MARIA CLAASSEN

Oxford University Press

Oxford University Press, Great Clarendon Street, Oxford OX2 6DP

Oxford New York

Athens Auckland Bangkok Bogota Buenos Aires Calcutta
Cape Town Chennai Dar es Salaam Delhi Florence Hong Kong Istanbul
Karachi Kuala Lumpur Madrid Melbourne Mexico City Mumbai
Nairobi Paris São Paolo Singapore Taipei Tokyo Toronto Warsaw

and associated companies in
Berlin Ibadan

Oxford is a registered trade mark of Oxford University Press

Published in the United States by
Oxford University Press Inc., New York

Published in the United States
by Oxford University Press Inc., New York
© Emil-Maria Claassen 1996
First published 1996

British Library Cataloguing in Publication Data
Data available

Library of Congress Cataloging in Publication Data
Claassen, Emil Maria, 1934–
Global monetary economics / by Emil-Maria Claassen.
Includes bibliographical references and index.
1. International finance. 2. Foreign exchange. I. Title.
HG3881.C565 1996 95-49774
332'.042—d20

ISBN 0-19-877465-6 (Pbk)

10 9 8 7 6 5 4 3

Printed in Great Britain
on acid-free paper by
Bookcraft (Bath) Ltd., Midsomer Norton, Avon

To my wife Florence
and my children Yann, Matthias,
Raphael, Lisa, and Thomas

PREFACE

Traditional textbooks on international monetary economics are concerned with the issues of exchange rates, balance of payments, and internal and external adjustment mechanisms. The present book also addresses these issues, but it stresses the fact that, for the last twenty years, the world economy has been operating under a regime of floating exchange rates. Therefore, a greater emphasis is placed upon exchange rates than is traditionally the case.

Part I deals exclusively with floating exchange rates. It conceives the exchange rate—together with the interest rate—as decisive for the expected returns on domestic and foreign financial assets. Any disequilibrium in the market for financial assets in an open capital account economy is eliminated by a change in the exchange rate. This financial approach constitutes the LM-side of the macroeconomic determination of the exchange rate. It is applied to small open economies and to currency areas.

Part II is concerned with the macroeconomic determination of the real exchange rate, which, furthermore, is relevant for floating and fixed exchange rate regimes. The exchange rate is not only a relative price of domestic and foreign financial assets, but also a relative price of domestic tradable goods either with respect to foreign goods ('external relative price of domestic tradable goods') or with respect to nontradable goods ('internal relative price of domestic tradable goods'). Any disequilibrium in the market for domestic goods—which is the IS-side of the macro model—is eliminated by a change in certain macro variables, among which the real exchange rate also figures. Like the interest rate, the exchange rate is both a monetary phenomenon (LM) and a real phenomenon (IS).

Part III is concerned with stabilization policies. It deals with the adjustment mechanisms for the trade balance, the current account balance, and the balance of payments under both exchange rate regimes. The field of internal and external adjustment policies is not only restricted to industrialized countries and to monetary unions, it is also extended to developing countries and to former socialist countries.

Usually an author is obliged to thank many of his fellow economists. I break with that tradition: I must thank my students from various countries. As everybody knows, research and teaching are interconnected. Many pitfalls and inconsistencies were necessarily discovered when the book's various models were presented to classes, before being discussed among professionals. The students served, in effect, as a laboratory for improving the first draft. I would also like to thank my family. Parts of the book were written during numerous weekends and vacations. My wife and children had to endure an overworked husband and a preoccupied father.

CONTENTS

LIST OF FIGURES

List of figures in boxes

LIST OF TABLES

LIST OF BOXES

INTRODUCTION: THE PRESENT EXCHANGE RATE SYSTEM IN THE WORLD ECONOMY

The actual international monetary system is a long way from being a 'pure float'. In industrialized countries there is either a managed float or a fixed, but adjustable, peg as in the European Monetary System. In developing countries an increasing tendency towards more flexible exchange rates can be observed. However, it is still too early to talk about tendencies for post-socialist countries. Initially, all the countries had a successful stabilization policy operated with a fixed exchange rate. Later, some left the fixed peg while many others drifted towards a managed float.

1.1. The Foreign Exchange Rate

Nominal and Real Exchange Rates

A large part of this book is concerned with the analysis of nominal and real exchange rates. If price levels were stable, any change in nominal variables would be identical to a change in the corresponding real variables and the distinction between the two types of magnitudes would become redundant. But in our real world, price levels are not stable. With monetary 'instability', the evolution of nominal income, nominal wages, nominal interest rates, or nominal exchange rates is less important, or not important at all. What matters for economics in general, and for individual decision-making in particular, is the evolution of real income, real wages, real interest rates and real exchange rates as defined in Table 1.1.

The definition of the real exchange rate is slightly more complicated than that of the other real variables, and it is probably for that reason that the notion of the real exchange rate is less familiar in public debate. Since the foreign exchange rate is the relative price of two national currencies—traditionally it is the domestic currency price of a foreign currency unit—the definition of the

Table 1.1. Nominal and real variables

Variables	Nominal	Real
Income	Y	$y = Y/P$
Wages	W	$w = W/P$
Interest rate	i	$r = i - \pi$
Exchange rate	E	$e = EP^*/P$
Real depreciation under fixed exchange rate	$\dfrac{dE}{E} = 0$	$\dfrac{de}{e} = (\pi^* - \pi) > 0$
Real depreciation under floating exchange rate	$\dfrac{dE}{E} > 0$	$\dfrac{de}{e} = \left(\dfrac{dE}{E} + \pi^* - \pi\right) > 0$

real exchange rate has to take two price levels into account, namely the domestic price level (P) and the foreign one (P*).

The main emphasis of this book is on real exchange rates just as a book with a different title would emphasize real income, real wages, and real interest rates. That statement may be taken by the reader as a matter of course. What he or she may not immediately accept is the additional statement that the analysis of the real exchange rate concerns not only the regime of floating (nominal) exchange rates ($\frac{dE}{E} \neq 0$) but also the system of fixed exchange rates ($\frac{dE}{E} = 0$). Thus, a real depreciation (see Table 1.1) can be brought about by a domestic inflation rate (π) which is lower than the foreign one (π^*). Under a floating exchange rate system, it can be realized by a nominal depreciation if it is assumed, for instance, that the inflation rates of the two countries are identical.[1] Part I is only concerned with the regime of floating exchange rates. The other two parts deal with both exchange rate regimes.

(N−1) Independent Exchange Rates

In an economy with n goods, there are $(n-1)$ independent relative prices to be determined. In the world economy with n currencies, there are $(n-1)$ independent exchange rates to be determined. The total number of exchange rates is $n(n-1)/2$, or even $n(n-1)$, rates if a distinction is made between the purchasing and the selling prices of foreign exchange. When the $(n-1)$ independent exchange rates are known, the values for all other (cross) rates can be derived.

In Fig. 1.1 we assume a world of three currencies, namely the US dollar, the French franc, and the German mark. There are two independent exchange rates, that is, the FF/DM rate and the DM/$ rate. Consequently, the dependent (cross) rate, FF/$, is derived from (FF/DM)(DM/$).[2]

The $(n-1)$ problem raises the question of the consistency of exchange rate targets within any international monetary system. Assume that there are only two currencies. There is thus only one exchange rate. The fundamental

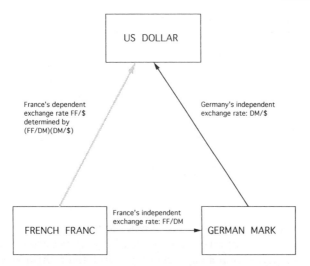

Fig. 1.1. Three currencies and two independent exchange rates

There are three currencies and two independent exchange rates which in the above example are the rate of the French franc/German mark and the rate of the German mark/dollar. The third exchange rate, the rate of the French franc/dollar, can be derived from the first two.

question of any monetary order is to know the rules by which this single exchange rate is determined by the *two* countries.

The first possible rule is a freely floating exchange rate without any exchange rate target on the part of either government. There are neither (by definition) any interventions by the central banks in the foreign exchange market nor any other economic policy (monetary policy, fiscal policy) aimed at influencing the exchange rate indirectly. The passive behaviour by both countries with respect to the exchange rate would be one solution to the $(n-1)$ problem. However, if changes in the exchange rate also imply, in most cases, changes in the real exchange rate, at least for a certain time interval, governments may be tempted by exchange rate targets which could diverge from one another. Such a conflict could emerge even in a system of freely fluctuating exchange rates, since macroeconomic policies other than intervention policies in the foreign exchange market could be used to influence the exchange rate.

If both countries have an exchange rate target, it would be more reasonable to assume that they turn to a managed floating exchange rate system. In a managed float system, and in a fixed but adjustable exchange rate system, a conflict of exchange rate targets between two countries can be solved by international co-operation. Either there will be a compromise on a mutually chosen exchange rate target negotiated between the two countries, or one of the two countries will give up any exchange rate target. The first solution has been practised by the countries of the former European Monetary System (EMS) with respect to their intra-EMS exchange rates, and the second solution is the passive behaviour followed by the USA within the international monetary system. The international monetary system during the Bretton Woods era and afterwards functioned in a very orderly way, in the sense that the USA accepted the exchange rate target of the other countries.[3] When the USA wanted to intervene in the foreign exchange market, it could do so only after consultation with other central banks. Thus, in practice, the United States exercised an attitude of 'benign neglect' with respect to its proper exchange rate.

1.2. Industrialized Countries: Managed Float, Adjustable Peg, and Fixed Peg

The present international monetary system could be considered as the coexistence of three exchange rate regimes (see Fig. 1.2): managed float, adjustable peg, and fixed peg. The managed float concerns the industrialized countries relative to the United States as the centre of the dollar standard. However, the EMS countries play a particular role within the industrialized countries. The intra-EMS exchange rates follow a fixed, but adjustable peg. The third block of countries are the less developed countries (LDCs) and post-socialist countries (PSCs). Even though their exchange rate regimes are very diversified, the predominant feature is a fixed peg in which, for instance, the francophone LDCs peg to the French franc, and other LDCs (e.g. Central American countries) peg to the US dollar.

When the generalized float began in the early 1970s, at the very outset it concerned only the exchange rates of the OECD countries with respect to the US dollar. We have already mentioned that the United States took a predominantly passive role with regard to its exchange rate target while the other industrialized countries did not install freely flexible exchange rates with respect to the US dollar, but used instead the managed float. In the course of the 1970s and, in particular, during the 1980s, the most spectacular examples of managed floating were the ups and downs of exchange rates within the currency triangle of the dollar–yen–deutschmark.

When examining the interventions by EMS central banks in the foreign exchange market (before August 1993), a distinction must be made between those at the margin and the intramarginal ones. The former are compulsory when two currencies hit the limit of the bilateral fluctuation band and they have to be carried out by the central banks using each other's currency. The important interventions in the EMS are intramarginal. According to Giavazzi and Giovannini (1987), Germany very rarely intervened intramarginally in EMS currencies, whereas major intramarginal interventions were undertaken by other EMS countries. Furthermore, when Germany intervened, it did so with respect to the US dollar, and most dollar interventions within the EMS in fact came from Germany (see also Mastropasqua *et al.*, 1988). Consequently, a 'German Monetary Area' emerged, in the sense that Germany, representing all

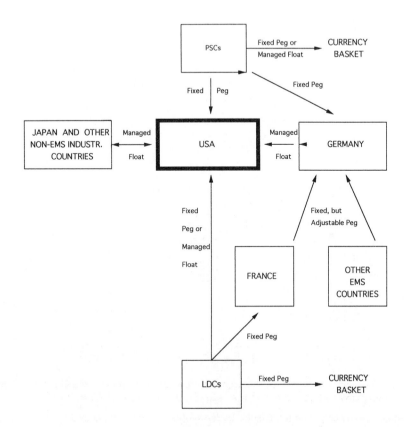

Fig. 1.2. Three dominant exchange rate regimes in the present world economy

The managed float is typical for industrialized countries, except for the fixed but adjustable peg for the currencies within the European Monetary System. The developing and post-socialist countries follow predominantly a fixed peg with respect to a single currency or to a currency basket.

other EMS countries, managed the float of the DM/dollar rate while the other ($n-1$) EMS currencies (plus Austria) were pegged to the German currency and maintained the intra-EMS rates with intramarginal interventions in EMS currencies. This is the reason for putting Germany at the centre of the EMS in Fig. 1.2.

To illustrate the movement of an exchange rate under the regime of the managed float (Fig. 1.3), we have chosen the exchange rate of the German mark with both the US dollar and an average of currencies in terms of the effective exchange rate (EER). The latter is the weighted average of the

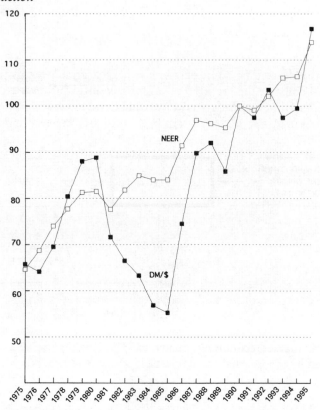

Fig. 1.3. The exchange rate of the German mark with respect to the US dollar (DM/ $) and Germany's effective exchange rate (EER), 1975–95 (1990 = 100)

The effective exchange rate (EER) is the trade-weighted average of the exchange rate of the German mark with respect to the currencies of Germany's most important trading partners. It fluctuated (and appreciated) less than the bilateral exchange rate.

Note: An increase in the exchange rate means an appreciation. Exchange rates are annual averages. The rates of 1995 are those of April.
Source: IMF, *International Financial Statistics*.

country's exchange rates with its most important trading partners. If, for example, Germany had only two trading partners (the USA and France) with equal weights, and the German mark appreciates with respect to the dollar by 10 per cent, while the franc–mark rate remained unchanged, Germany's effective exchange rate would appreciate by 5 per cent. In Fig. 1.3 we have illustrated the (nominal) effective exchange rate of the deutschmark (including more than ten exchange rates), and the (nominal) exchange rate of the German mark with the US dollar. The general trend was a (nominal) appreciation for both exchange rates. However, during the first half of the 1980s, there was a notorious appreciation of the dollar which attenuated the rise of the mark in terms of its EER. As a matter of fact, bilateral exchange rates fluctuate more than the EER does.[4]

1.3 Developing and Post-Socialist Countries

Almost all the developing countries pursue pegged arrangements, mainly to either the US dollar or the French franc as far as a single currency is concerned (see Table 1.2). However, there is an increasing trend towards flexible arrangements. During 1976–89, the proportion of countries relying on a managed float more than doubled and reached one-third of all countries. Simultaneously, the proportion of countries pegging to a single currency fell from 63 to 38 per cent. The countries which maintained a fixed peg are mainly those in Central America and the Caribbean Basin, with respect to the dollar, and the fourteen African countries of the CFA Franc Zone, with respect to the French franc. It is interesting to note that for countries with pegged arrangements there was a slight shift from a single currency peg (in particular with respect to the US dollar) to a currency basket or multi-currency peg. The high inflationary countries of South America are among the countries which have opted increasingly for a managed float (sometimes in the form of a crawling peg).

In our presentation of three dominant exchange rate regimes in the present world economy (Fig. 1.2) we have also mentioned the 'Second World', which consists of the post-socialist countries (PSCs). At the very beginning of their transition to market economies, many of their money markets were still characterized by the internal (or domestic) inconvertibility of their currencies into domestic goods because of price controls and rationing. There was a shortage of goods in the real sector of their economies and, in their monetary sector, an abundance of money (monetary overhang). One condition for establishing 'internal' convertibility was to decontrol prices in the real sector. The other condition consisted of eliminating the monetary overhang in the monetary sector. There were two main alternatives for handling the monetary

Table 1.2. Developing countries' exchange rate arrangements, 1976–89 (percentage of total number of countries)

Classification	1976	1979	1983	1989
Fixed Peg	86.0	75.2	71.7	66.4
To a single currency	62.6	52.1	43.5	38.2
US dollar	43.0	35.0	29.0	23.7
French franc	12.1	12.0	10.5	10.7
Other currency	7.5	5.1	4.0	3.8
To composite	23.4	23.1	28.2	28.2
SDR	10.3	11.1	11.3	5.3
basket	13.1	12.0	16.9	22.9
Managed Float	14.0	24.8	28.2	33.6
Total	100.0	100.0	100.0	100.0
N	107	117	124	131

Note: Based on mid-year classifications, except for 1989, which is based on end-year classification; excludes Democratic Kampuchea, for which no information is available.
Source: Calculated from Aghevli and Montiel (1991).

overhang, either open inflation (as, for instance, in the cases of Poland, Slovenia, and Estonia) or maintenance of the current price level by confiscating some of the outstanding quantity of money (as in the case of the former German Democratic Republic).

Once the internal convertibility was restored, the next step was to introduce external convertibility. In this sequencing, the choice of the exchange rate regime was crucial. In the case of our examples above, Poland chose a fixed peg with respect to the dollar in January 1990, while Slovenia and Estonia pegged to the deutschmark. Other post-socialist countries chose a fixed or crawling peg to a currency basket (as Poland did later in May 1991).

For all types of countries, whether post-socialist, developing or industrialized, the choice of the exchange rate regime (fixed peg versus managed float) is ultimately a choice of the monetary anchor. If a fixed peg is chosen, the exchange rate constitutes the monetary anchor and the quantity of money becomes an endogenous variable, which means that monetary policy is no longer autonomous. On the other hand, if the managed float is chosen, the rate of growth of the quantity of money becomes the monetary anchor, and the exchange rate becomes the endogenous variable.[5]

1.4. An Overview of Exchange Rate Economics

The Basic Model

Fig. 1.4 represents an overview of the financial and macroeconomic approach to the real exchange rate (e). The financial sector is represented by the schedules IRP and LM, which stand for the interest rate parity and the equilibrium condition in the money market, respectively. The analysis of this financial sector is the subject of Part I. It deals predominantly with the regime of floating exchange rates.

By adding the real sector in terms of the equilibrium condition in the market for domestic goods, we are dealing with the real exchange rate either as the external relative price of tradable goods (the IS-schedule for which all domestic goods are tradables), or as the internal relative price of tradable goods (the NN-schedule standing for the equilibrium condition in the market for non-tradable goods). Box 1.1 recalls the two traditional concepts of the real exchange rate by quoting a reputable institution in this field.

The macroeconomic framework of Fig. 1.4, as set out in Part II, refers mainly to floating exchange rates. Under the classical assumption of full employment, the relevant LM schedule is LM(m) where m represents the real quantity of money. Under the oversimplified Keynesian assumption of a constant price level, the corresponding LM schedule is LM(y). The question of external equilibrium (in terms of the trade balance, the current account balance, or the balance of payments) is predominantly the subject of Part III which deals mainly with fixed exchange rates.

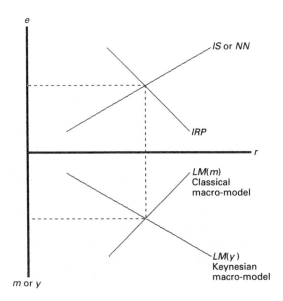

Fig. 1.4. An overview of the macroeconomic determination of the real exchange rate

The financial approach to the exchange rate is represented by the interest rate parity (*IRP*) and the equilibrium condition in the money market (*LM*). We obtain the macroeconomic approach by adding the equilibrium condition for the market for domestic goods (*IS* or *NN*). The real exchange rate is either the external relative price of tradables (*IS*) or the internal relative price of tradables (*NN*).

Box 1.1. Two variants of the real exchange rate

'There are two variants of the real exchange rate. The older variant is the "purchasing power parity" real exchange rate. This compares the domestic price of a representative basket of goods and services with the price of the same basket at world prices converted into local currency. It is, in effect, a measure of overall competitiveness. It can be approximated by comparing changes in consumer prices or changes in labour costs. It does not distinguish between traded and non-traded goods, because it implicitly assumes that their prices move together.

The other variant, which has recently come to be emphasized, compares the price of *non-tradables* in the national economy (typically services and labour, whose prices can be proxied by the GDP deflator) with world prices of *tradables* (foreign wholesale price indexes, for instance, or the import and export price indexes for the national economy). For a small country that cannot affect the world price of traded goods, this variant provides a measure of the changing incentives to move in and out of production and consumption of non-tradable and tradable goods. For instance, a depreciating real exchange rate raises the relative price of tradables, encouraging more production and less consumption of import substitutes and exports. This is the interpretation that is most useful to bear in mind when looking at the effect of changing trade and macroeconomic policies on the structure of incentives and on the current account of the balance of payments.' (World Bank, 1987: 101).

Some readers may be rather surprised at not finding any mention of the existence of the market for foreign exchange in the framework of Fig. 1.4. I do not question the fact that the exchange rate is an outcome of the foreign exchange market. Nor do I dispute the fact that the exchange rate equilibrates the demand and supply of foreign exchange. However, with capital movements dominating 95 per cent of daily foreign exchange transactions, it is no longer appropriate to draw an upward-sloping supply schedule and a downward-sloping demand schedule. These schedules would constantly shift up and down and they would only take into account flow magnitudes of foreign exchange and not stock magnitudes. If there were no capital movements and, thus, no holdings of foreign financial assets, including foreign currencies, except for international reserves held by central banks, the balance of payments would coincide with the trade balance and, under these assumptions, it would be legitimate to operate with the market for foreign exchange. The supply schedule would reflect exports of goods and services, and the demand schedule would reflect imports of goods and services.

Which Exchange Rate is to be Determined?

We must still ask the question which of the variables of the real exchange rate ($e = EP^*/P$) has to be determined by the financial and macroeconomic approach. In a one-country-model, P^* is exogenous and, for simplicity, it could be set equal to one. Consequently, E and P (and, thus, $m = M/P$) remain to be determined. But which E? Under floating exchange rates, only *one single* nominal exchange rate has to be taken into account, since each country disposes exclusively of *one independent* exchange rate. As a rule, the choice of the independent exchange rate coincides with the usual intervention currency (for instance, the US dollar for Germany or the deutschmark for France) of the country concerned. Furthermore, a change in the independent exchange rate of x per cent also implies a change of x per cent in the country's exchange rates with all currencies other than the intervention currency.[6]

However, the choice of the proper E appears to be more complex in a mixed world of floating and fixed exchange rates. Take the case of Germany and France. Assume that France continues to stay within the old margins of plus or minus 2.25 per cent of the French franc with respect to the deutschmark despite the wider bands of exchange rate fluctuations within the new EMS. As far as Germany is concerned, we have to analyse the regime of floating exchange rates, since Germany's independent exchange rate is the mark–dollar rate. Thus, a 10 per cent appreciation of the German mark against the dollar as result of an internal shock in the German economy would also imply a 10 per cent appreciation of the mark against, for instance, the Japanese yen, always under the usual *ceteris paribus* conditions. But it does not imply a 10 per cent appreciation of the mark against the French franc, since France follows the regime of fixed exchange rates—an exogenous variable for Germany.

France's relevant independent exchange rate is the franc–mark rate. The relevant financial and macroeconomic analysis for the French economy is the regime of fixed exchange rates. However, it is true that the above appreciation of the German mark against the dollar would also imply a 10 per cent appreciation of the French franc against the dollar. But this results from the shock in the German economy and, for France, constitutes an external shock coming from outside its economy. To maintain the fixity of its independent exchange rate, it has to tolerate the 10 per cent appreciation of the franc–dollar rate, since, otherwise, it would not be following the rules of the fixed exchange rate of the franc with the mark as the monetary anchor.

What is New about this Book?

As we already mentioned, the emphasis of our analysis is on the real exchange rate under both exchange rate regimes. What is new about this book is its analysis of the special role of the real exchange rate for equilibrating the market for domestic goods. In a small open economy with complete financial integration, the real interest rate is fixed by the 'rest of the world'. A disequilibrium in the goods market cannot be eliminated by changes in the real interest rate. If we also exclude quantity adjustments in the supply of domestic goods to the level of the demand for goods, as in Keynesian economics, the only remaining equilibrium mechanism is that of a change in the real exchange rate.

In the top panel of Fig. 1.5 we have illustrated the supply and demand for domestic goods. The supply (y) is given at the level of full employment, while the demand (y^d) is a decreasing function of the interest rate (r). The equilibrium at point A may be disturbed by a decline in the demand for goods towards y^d_1. This fall could be the outcome of a decrease in consumption ($-\Delta C$) or investment ($-\Delta I$). In the bottom panel of Fig. 1.5, we have reformulated the equilibrium condition for the goods market in terms of $I = S$.[7] In the left-hand panel, the demand shock arises from a change in intertemporal consumption: lower present consumption ($-\Delta C$) and higher future consumption (ΔS). In the right-hand panel, the contraction of demand results from a decline in investment.

The disequilibrium in the goods market—the excess supply of AQ—can be eliminated by various mechanisms. The choice of the adequate adjustment process is the core dispute between Keynesians and the proponents of classical economics.

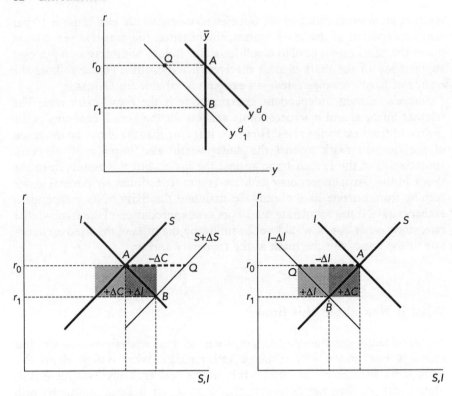

Fig. 1.5. The classical mechanism for avoiding unemployment: real interest-rate mechanism and real exchange-rate mechanism

We assume a fall in the total demand for domestic goods from A to Q which is provoked by a fall in consumption ($-\Delta C$) or investment ($-\Delta I$). The fall in the real interest rate pushes total demand ($+\Delta C$ and $+\Delta I$) back to the level of full employment (point B). To the extent that the concerned country is fully integrated in the world capital markets, the real interest rate cannot fall and it remains at r_0. The real-interest-rate mechanism will be replaced by the real-exchange-rate mechanism and the excess supply of goods (AQ) will be eliminated by a real depreciation.

1. Classical economics stressed the interest rate mechanism (r_1) for insuring full employment. The decline in the interest rate would close the demand gap by increasing consumption ($+\Delta C$) and investment ($+ \Delta I$).[8]

2. The early Keynesians were rather pessimistic about the interest rate elasticity of consumption. The paradox of an increase in savings (i.e. $-\Delta C$) is that there would be an adjustment of production towards point Q (in the top panel of Fig. 1.5), reinforced by the multiplier, since lower production means lower income, and lower income implies lower consumption. As far as investment is concerned, waves of optimism and pessimism about future economic activity would dominate the 'marginal efficiency of investment' more than any change in the interest rate.

3. Assume now that the economy illustrated in Fig. 1.5 is a small open one

with full financial integration whose real interest rate (r_0) is given by the international economy. Furthermore, we look first at a regime of fixed exchange rates. For Keynesians, the adjustment mechanism would be the same as that described above ($A \rightarrow Q$). For the classical economists the general price level will fall, implying a corresponding decline in nominal wages as well, since otherwise the production volume could no longer be maintained at point A. The declining price level would activate the wealth effect—the Pigou effect or real balance effect à la Patinkin—through which consumption would be stimulated so that the economy would move from Q to A.

However, from the point of view of an open economy, the fall in the general price level also means a change in the relative price of domestic goods with respect to foreign goods which signifies, in our case, a real depreciation. Foreign consumption or investment goods have become more expensive than domestic goods. On the demand side for domestic goods, domestic goods are substituted for imported goods; in addition, exports may rise. Consequently, the real exchange rate mechanism ($Q \rightarrow A$) replaces the real interest rate mechanism ($Q \rightarrow B$).

Furthermore, this real exchange rate mechanism operates under both exchange-rate regimes. Under fixed exchange rates, the domestic price level declines. Under floating exchange rates, the exchange rate increases (ΔE). With an unchanged domestic price level the nominal depreciation is equal to a real depreciation.[9]

The role of the exchange rate is as polyvalent as the role of the interest rate. For the real sector of the economy, a disequilibrium in the market for domestic goods can be eliminated by changes in the real interest rate (a closed economy) or by changes in the real exchange rate (an open economy with full integration). This real exchange rate mechanism is valid for the real exchange rate as well as for the relative price of domestic and foreign tradable goods and for the real exchange rate interpreted as the relative price of tradable and non-tradable goods.

In the financial sector, a disequilibrium in the financial markets can be eliminated by a change in the interest rate (in a closed economy) or by a change in the interest rate and in the exchange rate (in an open economy with full integration). In the latter case, the interest rate mechanism assures the equilibrium in the market for domestic financial assets and the exchange rate mechanism brings about the equilibrium in the markets for domestic and foreign financial assets.

In recent literature, the polyvalent nature of the exchange rate is fully disregarded since the main attention is concentrated on the financial sector. Examples are the survey articles on 'Exchange Rate Economics' by MacDonald and Taylor (1992) and Taylor (1995). This omission is rather serious because an important part of the dependance of the financial sector on the real sector is constituted by the expected exchange rate which is like the anchor of the financial determination of the actual exchange rate. To the extent that the expected exchange rate is linked to nominal and real fundamentals, the macroeconomic view is decisive for the financial approach. Another subsequent and serious defect is that this approach does not emphasize the dual nature of the real exchange rate as the relative price of domestic and foreign tradable goods and as the relative price of tradable and non-tradable goods.

Notes

1. Chapter 5 analyses the monetary adjustment mechanism under alternative exchange rate regimes when there is a need for a change in the real exchange rate. It should already be mentioned here that fluctuations in the real exchange rate are far more frequent with floating exchange rates.
2. In the present exchange rate system, the franc–mark rate is fixed, and the mark and the franc are floating with respect to the dollar. A devaluation of the French franc with respect to the German mark also affects the franc–dollar rate since FF/$ = (FF/DM)(DM/$). The devaluation of the French franc means an increase in (FF/DM), while the mark–dollar rate ((DM/$)) remains unchanged. Similarly, a revaluation of the mark with respect to the franc also affects the mark–dollar rate as there is a revaluation of the mark *vis-à-vis* the dollar. Here, the franc–dollar rate remains constant.
3. The devaluations of the US dollar in 1968 and 1971 were only brought about after negotiations with the other important members of the international monetary system.
4. The exchange rate of the domestic currency (e.g. of the deutschmark) with respect to the foreign currency (say, the US dollar) can be expressed in terms of the domestic currency (for instance, 2 DM/1 dollar) or in terms of the foreign currency (0.5 dollar/1 DM). Officially, a change in the exchange rate (for instance, a 50 per cent revaluation of the DM) is measured as 0.75 dollar/1 DM which corresponds to a 33 per cent revaluation in terms of 1.33 DM/1 dollar. For the statistical representation of the real exchange rate as in Fig. 1.3, we shall use the convention that a rise in the exchange rate means an appreciation (it goes up) and a fall stands for a depreciation (it goes down). In our theoretical considerations, the exchange rate represents the inverse relationship.
5. The choice of the nominal anchor concerns an old issue relating to the nominal–real dichotomy of neo-classical general equilibrium analysis à la Patinkin (1965). After solving the equilibrium values for all real variables (including real cash balances), the price level remains undetermined unless one nominal variable is fixed. This can be either the money stock or, in an open economy, the nominal exchange rate and, through this, the price level. See Bruno (1990).
6. Consequently, a change in the nominal independent exchange rate of x per cent would also imply a change of x per cent in the country's nominal effective exchange rate, assuming that there are neither nominal nor real shocks in the other economies which could otherwise have repercussions on the exchange rates of the country concerned. As far as the real effective exchange rate is concerned, it would also change by x per cent provided that the ratio P^*/P remains constant. P^*, which is

exogenous, has to be interpreted now as the weighted average of several foreign price levels.

7. Since $y_d(r) = C(r) + I(r)$, we have $C(r) + I(r) = y$ or $I(r) = y - C(r)$ where $y - C(r)$ is defined as $S(r)$.

8. The y^d schedule could also be interpreted as the IS curve. When there is an IS-curve, there should also be a LM-curve. In the Cambridge tradition where the demand for money was not interest elastic, the LM-schedule would be vertical and coincide with the y line. To the extent that one works with an interest elastic demand function for money, the LM-schedule would be upward sloping and pass through point A. A fall in the interest rate from r_0 to r_1 would only be possible with an expansionary monetary policy shifting the LM-schedule toward point B.

9. As we shall see in Part II, this exchange rate mechanism for equilibrating the market of domestic goods would also function in a Keynesian framework provided that the economy operates under a regime of floating exchange rates.

PART I
A FINANCIAL
APPROACH TO THE
EXCHANGE RATE:
SMALL OPEN
ECONOMIES AND
CURRENCY AREAS

Part I presents a survey of how 'exchange rate economics' has developed over the last twenty years. It is relevant for industrialized countries with highly integrated markets for goods and financial assets. It will be applied to both small open economies and currency areas like the European Monetary System. As far as the integration of goods markets is concerned, the exchange rate is considered as the relative price of domestic and foreign (tradable) goods. The law of one price applies to these goods over the long run. This is also called purchasing power parity. The exchange rate is supposed to move towards this long-run level.

From the point of view of financial integration, the exchange is conceived as the 'relative price' of domestic and foreign financial assets. Financial capital flows between countries are motivated by expected return differentials between domestic and foreign financial assets. These flows dominate the short-run determination of the exchange rate. Expected return differentials push the exchange rate in a direction that tends to eliminate them.

The financial determination of the short-run exchange rate is analysed under two alternative hypotheses. The first one ('the monetary approach') concerns the 'heroic' assumption that individuals are risk-neutral *vis-à-vis* exchange rate changes. From this point of view, the exchange rate will move in a direction that equalizes the return on domestic financial assets and the expected return on foreign financial assets (interest rate parity). The second hypothesis ('the portfolio approach') takes into account the aversion to exchange rate risks. The interest rate parity now has to be modified by a 'currency risk premium'.

2

A MONETARY APPROACH TO THE BALANCE OF PAYMENTS AND THE EXCHANGE RATE: PURCHASING POWER PARITY

Under the regime of fixed exchange rates, the monetary approach represents the most global view of what determines the balance of payments, which itself is a monetary phenomenon, being defined as a change in international reserves held by central banks. A disequilibrium in the balance of payments is provoked by a disequilibrium in the money market. In the present exchange rate system of the industrialized countries, the most representative case of fixed exchange rates is the currency area of the EMS type (fixed, but adjustable exchange rates). Under the regime of floating exchange rates, where the exchange rate is defined as the relative price of domestic and foreign (tradable) goods, the long-run exchange rate tends to the value where the prices of domestic and foreign (tradable) goods are equalized (purchasing power parity). This exchange rate mechanism is shown for a small country with floating exchange rates and for a currency area which, by definition, has a floating rate with respect to the rest of the world.

2.1. A Monetary Approach to Fixed Exchange Rates, a Managed Float, and Currency Areas

The present chapter deals with fixed and floating exchange rates. One of the main issues for the regime of fixed exchange rates is the determination of the balance of payments in terms of its surplus, deficit, or equilibrium. There are three approaches to the balance of payments—the elasticity approach, the absorption approach, and the monetary approach (see Box 2.1). The first two neglect the capital balance—or assume capital immobility—so that the balance of payments coincides with the trade balance.

Box 2.1. The balance of payments: elasticity, absorption, and monetary approaches

The **elasticity approach** asks the question about the impact of a devaluation on the trade balance. This impact depends on the price elasticities of exports and imports. It is a partial approach since the analysis is concentrated on the foreign exchange market whose supply results from exports of goods and services and whose demand is derived from imports of goods and services.

The **absorption approach** is more macroeconomic since it also takes into account the market for domestic goods. Any gap between domestic production and absorption (defined as the demand by residents for domestic and foreign goods) creates a deficit or surplus in the trade balance. Both approaches have to be taken into account for the improvement of the trade balance in terms of expenditure switching (the elasticity approach) and expenditure reducing policies (the absorption approach).

The **monetary approach** represents a global view.[1] It predicts that a disequilibrium in the money market creates a disequilibrium in the balance of payments. The balance of payments is a monetary phenomenon since a deficit or surplus is defined by changes in international reserves held by central banks. These changes in reserves are an outcome of fixed exchange rates, since they are used for maintaining or influencing the exchange rate. International reserves also constitute one element of the counterpart of the monetary base. The causal link between the money market and the balance of payments is the markets for goods and financial assets. Thus, under fixed exchange rates, an excess supply in the money market can provoke both excess demand for domestic goods, with a subsequent trade balance deficit, and excess demand for financial assets, with a resulting capital balance deficit.

The monetary approach is applicable to the contemporary international monetary system, for two reasons. On the one hand, as mentioned in the previous chapter, there is the phenomenon of 'dirty floating'. Countries which have adopted the system of flexible exchange rates in reality pursue the managed float policy. They do not permit a free float, and intervene in the foreign exchange market in order to influence the exchange rate. They have a disequilibrium in the balance of payments by the extent to which the net volume of international reserves held by central banks is modified.

On the other hand, there are currency areas which have a particular type of fixed exchange rate arrangement and, thus, a particular type of monetary integration (see Box 2.2). They are defined as a group of countries with a policy of fixed exchange rates among themselves, but which has floating rates with respect to third countries not belonging to the area. Consequently, a disequilibrium in the balance of payments can emerge among the member countries. One example of such a currency area is the European Monetary System (EMS).

Box 2.2. Different types of monetary integration

Monetary integration and monetary disintegration. The highest degree of monetary integration implies the existence of a single currency in the world economy. The other extreme, representing the lowest degree of monetary integration, is more difficult to define. It could be a world of *n* countries with *n* currencies related to each other by flexible exchange rates. In such a case, a world of *n* currencies with fixed exchange rates would be very close to the hypothetical one-currency world, so that a regime of fixed exchange rates and a regime of flexible exchange rates would reflect the different degrees of monetary integration: the lower the degree of flexibility in the exchange rate system, the higher the degree of monetary integration within the world economy.

Currency areas and monetary unions. A currency area is defined as a group of countries whose exchange rates are fixed with each other, while the group as such has a regime of floating rates with respect to third countries. The degree of monetary integration is low when exchange rates are fixed, but adjustable. It is high when the exchange rates are irrevocably fixed. Furthermore, the integration is higher with a narrow band of fluctuations around the central parity value than with a wider band.

It is questionable whether a currency area with a single currency should be called a monetary union. The term 'monetary union' could be reserved for the crowning achievement of an economic integration process where there are integrated markets for goods and for factors of production (full mobility of labour and capital), where a single currency (or irrevocably fixed exchange rates) exist, and where economic policies are co-ordinated.

2.2. A Monetary Approach for Small Open Economies

Tradable Goods

We shall start with a strict quantity-theoretical model for a small open economy. For the moment, we assume that the world economy has adopted fixed exchange rates. Furthermore, within this world economy, markets for tradable goods and tradable financial assets are highly integrated. Consequently, the 'law of one price' applies for tradable goods and tradable financial assets. These are the essential assumptions of the monetary approach to the balance of payments. In this chapter the exchange rate (E) is conceived as the relative price of domestic and foreign (tradable) goods. An extreme version of purchasing power parity—its 'absolute' version—means that this relative price is equal to one (see Box 2.3).

Box 2.3. Tradable goods

'Tradability' of goods and financial assets means that domestic prices are exposed to international competition. According to purchasing power parity, the domestic prices of goods (P) equal foreign prices (P^*) when the latter are expressed in local currency prices via the exchange rate (EP^*), abstracting from indirect taxes, tariffs, transport costs, and oligopolistic price discriminations. Purchasing power parity assumes fully integrated national goods markets within the world goods market. In a similar way, interest rate parity (which is the focus of the next chapter) constitutes the law of one price (in the sense of a single expected rate of return) for domestic and foreign financial assets and it assumes fully integrated asset markets ('perfect capital mobility' defined as the combination of unrestricted capital mobility and perfect substitutability of domestic and foreign financial assets).

The money market of the small open economy is represented in Fig. 2.1. The initial equilibrium is at the intersection point A of the money supply (M) with the demand for money (M^d). It is assumed that the demand for money is a linear function of the price level (P) and real income (y_0) at full employment (y). The domestic interest rate (r) should be equal to the foreign one (r^*).

We introduce an increase of the quantity of money from M to M_1. Under floating exchange rates, the price level rises to P_2 and the exchange rate to E_2 over the long run according to purchasing power parity.[2] Under fixed exchange rates, the price level will remain at P_0. The excess supply of money AB is used for purchasing goods and bonds. However, domestic prices are linked to foreign prices ($E_0 P^*_0$) so that the excess demand for domestic goods cannot be eliminated by a rise in domestic prices. Similarly, the excess demand for financial assets is not cancelled by a fall in the domestic interest rate. The latter is also linked to the international interest rate (r^*).

Consequently, both types of excess demand switch to foreign markets. Due to the assumption of a small open economy, it is assumed that the huge world

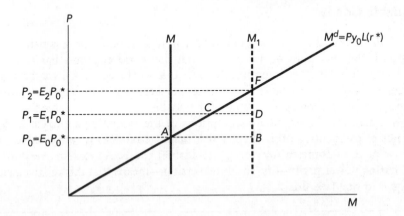

Fig. 2.1. A monetary approach for a small open economy

The excess supply of money is AB. Under floating exchange rates, the domestic price level and the exchange rate rise by BF. Under fixed exchange rates, prices and the exchange rate remain at point A and the excess supply of money creates a deficit in the balance of payments equal to AB.

economy can satisfy both demand components without any change in the foreign prices of goods (P^*) and bonds (r^*). As a result, the excess demand for goods creates a trade balance deficit and the excess demand for financial assets a capital balance deficit:

$$(M - M^d) \qquad = \qquad (A - y_0) \qquad + \qquad (B^d - B) \qquad (2.1)$$

money market	goods market	bonds market
(excess supply of	(excess demand for	(excess demand
money = balance	goods = trade	for bonds = capital
of payments deficit)	balance deficit)	balance deficit)

where M and B are the outstanding volumes of money and bonds, respectively. A stands for absorption and y_0 for a given GDP.[3] Both deficits give rise to the balance of payments deficit which, in turn, is equal to the excess supply of money (AB). The balance of payments deficit is identical to the loss of international reserves held by the Central Bank. Provided that the latter pursues a (non-sterilized) intervention in the foreign exchange market (sale of foreign exchange against domestic currency), the money supply is automatically reduced from M_1 to M.

This example also shows that an autonomous monetary policy is not possible in a world of fixed exchange rates. The monetary shock (M_1) is punished by a loss of reserves. Since the stock of international reserves is limited, the monetary authorities must eventually return to the initial quantity of money (M).

Two other important considerations must be added. If we are in a regime of *managed float*, there will be a mixture of exchange rate depreciation and balance-of-payments deficit. Assume again an increase of the money supply from M_0 to M_1. To avoid the eventual rise of the exchange rate to the level of E_2, the monetary authorities concede a depreciation from E_0 to E_1 and, at point C, they intervene in the foreign exchange market by selling reserves and buying domestic currency (CD) to stabilize the exchange rate at E_1. In this case, the balance-of-payments deficit amounts to CD and the quantity of money will be reduced to point C.

Non-tradable Goods

If the existence of non-tradable goods is also taken into account, a distinction must be made between two domestic goods markets.[4] In equation (2.1) absorption (A) becomes the demand for tradables and non-tradables ($D_T + D_N$) and y has to be interpreted as the supply of tradables and non-tradables ($S_T + S_N$). Consequently, the formula of the monetary approach of the balance of payments has to be rewritten as:

$$(M - M^d) \quad = \quad (D_T - S_T) \qquad + \quad (D_N - S_N) \qquad + \quad (B^d - B) \qquad (2.2)$$

money market	market for tradable goods	market for non-tradable goods	bonds market
(excess supply of money > balance of payments deficit)	(excess demand for tradable goods = trade balance deficit)	(excess demand for non-tradable goods)	(excess demand for bonds = capital balance deficit)

Initially, the excess demand for non-tradable goods is eliminated by the rise in their prices pushing up the general price level, for instance, to P_1 (while E remains at E_0).[5] Consequently, the excess supply of money would only be CD, which generates a lower balance of payments deficit. The subsequent reduction of the quantity of money would be such that the M_1 schedule shifts towards point C.

However, point C is not a situation of permanent monetary equilibrium. At C there is a real appreciation of the domestic currency in terms of the increase in the relative price of non-tradable goods.[6] Consequently, there will be a substitution effect in both goods markets which creates an additional excess demand for tradable goods and an excess supply of non-tradable goods. The excess supply of non-tradables pushes their prices downwards. Consequently, point C moves towards A and the overall cumulative balance-of-payments deficit becomes AB as in the case where there were no non-tradables. Thus, the monetary approach to the balance of payments is useful, regardless of whether there are non-tradable goods or not.

A final remark concerns our quantity-theoretical assumption. If we allow for output expansion, S_T and S_N of equation (2.2) will increase so that the trade balance will be lower. In the very extreme case where there is only an excess demand for goods, and where this excess demand is satisfied by additional domestic production, the excess supply of money would not provoke a balance-of-payments deficit and M^d of Fig. 2.1 would rotate through point B.

Inflation and Growth

The simple quantity-theoretical model of Fig. 2.1 could also be applied to a growing, inflationary economy. The arithmetic is contained in Box 2.4. The equilibrium condition in the money market, $M = Py L(i)$, could be written as $m = y L(i)$ or as $(m/y) = L(i)$ for $m = M/P$. The top panel of Fig. 2.2 describes the demand for real cash balances as a decreasing function of the nominal interest rate for a given real income (y_0). For a growing economy, the desired ratio of real cash balances to real income (m/y)—or the desired ratio of the nominal quantity of money to nominal GDP (M/Py)—has to be shown as a decreasing function of the nominal interest rate. Assuming a given real interest rate (r^*), any increase in the nominal interest rate above r^* means an increase

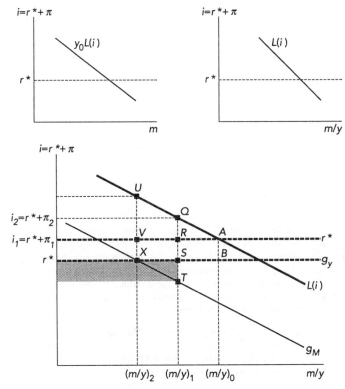

Fig. 2.2. A monetary approach for an inflationary and growing economy.

Demand for real cash balances in an inflationary and non-growing economy. Demand for real cash balances in an inflationary and growing economy. The money growth rate is $UX = QT$ and the real growth rate is $VX = RS$. Under floating exchange rates, the resulting inflation rate is UV. Under fixed exchange rates, the inflation rate is determined by the international economy and is assumed to be QR. The excess supply of money represented by ST creates a deficit in the balance of payments (the shaded area).

in the expected inflation rate, and it is assumed that the expected inflation rate is equal to the effective one. The demand schedule coincides with the equilibrium conditions (*LM*) in the money market.

Box 2.4. A monetary approach in terms of growth rates

Money market:

$$M = Py\, L(i),$$

where $i = r^* + \pi^e$ and $\pi^e = \pi$

It is assumed that the money demand increases proportionately with real income (*y*). The real interest rate (*r*) is given and the expected inflation rate (π^e) is assumed to be the correct one.[7] The counterpart of the money supply (*M*) consists of international reserves (*R*) and domestic credit (*D*) so that

$$R + D = Py \, L(i)$$

By differentiating the last equation, we obtain

$$dR + dD = dP \, yL + dy \, PL + L_i di \, iPy$$

or $(dR/R) \, R + (dD/D) \, D = dP \, yL + (dy/y) \, PyL + L_i \, (di/i) \, iPy$

By dividing the last equation by M or PyL and by writing growth rates in terms of g, we obtain

$$(R/M)g_R + (D/M)g_D = \pi + g_y + L_i \, (i/L) \, g_i$$

where $L_i \, (i/L)$ stands for the elasticity of the demand for money with respect to the interest rate $(El \, L_i)$

$$\underbrace{(R/M) \, g_R + (D/M) \, g_D}_{g_M} = \underbrace{\pi + g_y + El \, L_i \, g_i}_{g_M{}^d} \qquad (2.3)$$

Equation (2.3) represents the equilibrium condition in the money market in terms of the equality between the growth rate of the money supply (g_M) and money demand $(g_M{}^d)$. Equation (2.3) specifies the elements which determine both growth rates. In our geometrical representation (Fig. 2.2), we assume that there is only a once-and-for-all increase in g_M and, thus, in i so that afterwards g_i is equal to zero. Furthermore, monetary policy acts in the form of g_D, while g_R is the reaction of the balance of payments

$$\underbrace{(D/M) \, g_D - [\pi + g_y]}_{\text{excess supply of money}} = \underbrace{- (R/M) \, g_R}_{\text{balance of payments deficit}} \qquad (2.4)$$

The bottom panel of Fig. 2.2 shows the $L(i)$ schedule for a growing economy—or the equilibrium schedule $(m/y) = L(i)$ which is the LM curve. We have added the condition (2.4) of Box 2.4. The initial non-inflationary situation is at point A. The real growth rate (g_y) is measured by the vertical distance between the r^* line and the g_y line. Since there is no inflation, the growth rate of the money supply should be equal to the real growth rate (AB).

The growth rate of the money supply is measured by the vertical distance between the $L(i)$-schedule and the g_M-line which is now the inflationary money supply $(g_M = UX = QT)$. As in Fig. 2.1, we shall look at the inflationary impact of a higher monetary growth rate under floating exchange rates and at the impact of the same policy on the balance of payments under fixed exchange rates. In both cases, the money supply has been increased by the domestic component of the quantity of money $[g_M = (D/M)g_D]$.

Under floating exchange rates, the inflation rate is autonomous and it is equal to $\pi = g_M - g_y$. In terms of Fig. 2.2, the inflation rate is $\pi_2 \, (UV) = g_M \, (UX) - g_y \, (VX)$. From a technical point of view, the equilibrium point is at X, which is the intersection point between the growth rate of the money supply (UX) and the growth rate of the money demand (UX) resulting from the real growth rate (VX) and the inflation rate (UV). Compared to the initial non-inflationary situation at point A, the desired ratio of desired real cash balances to real income has declined from $(m/y)_0$ to $(m/y)_2$. This decline will be realized by a once-and-for-all increase in the general price level which takes place in addition to the continuous inflation rate of π_2.[8]

The inflationary consequences for the determination of the exchange rate are rather evident provided that it is still dominated by the principle of purchasing power parity. To the extent that the foreign price level remains constant ($\Delta P^* = 0$), the once-and-for-all increase in the general price level also produces a once-and-for-all depreciation ($\Delta E = \Delta P$). On the other hand, the domestic currency will be exposed to a continuous depreciation rate of $\Delta E/E = \pi_2$.

Under fixed exchange rates, the inflation rate of a small open economy is exogenous, and is determined by the international economy. We assume that it is $\pi_1 = QR$. In that case, the reduction of the desired (m/y)-ratio is less, that is $(m/y)_1$. Under the hypothesis that the country pursues the same monetary expansion as under floating exchange rates, that is, at the rate of QT, the excess supply of money (in terms of its growth rate) is ST, which provokes a balance-of-payments deficit. This deficit is illustrated by the shaded area representing the deficit as the percentage of GDP. Again, if the loss in international reserves is not sterilized by the central bank, the growth rate of the money supply will be reduced automatically to the rate QS.[9]

2.3. The European Monetary System (EMS): An Example of a Currency Area

The Official Functioning of the EMS

Snake period.   Fig. 2.3 shows the 'snake' period before the establishment of the EMS, the way the exchange rate mechanism of the EMS was officially supposed to function after 1979, and an interpretation of how it has actually been functioning as a German currency area in recent years. The 'snake-in-the-tunnel'-experiment (see the left-hand panel of Fig. 2.3) was actually an attempt to continue the Bretton-Woods system with a selected number of EEC countries. The member currencies were pegged with respect to the dollar and the exchange rate could fluctuate by 2.25 per cent above or below the parity value; under the Bretton-Woods system, the margin was only ± 1 per cent. The bilateral rates between European currencies could therefore oscillate by a maximum of 9 per cent. The snake was considered to be unsatisfactory for two reasons. On the one hand, the bilateral intra-snake margins were thought to be too large. On the other hand, the peg with respect to the dollar could not be maintained for long and was consequently revised too often.

Official view of the EMS.   The EMS was inaugurated in 1979 and replaced the fixed peg to the dollar by a 'managed float'. In addition, the intra-EMS margins were reduced from ± 4.5 to ± 2.25 per cent. Thus, in the new EMS there was more flexibility of the dollar, but less flexibility for the bilateral exchange rates within the EMS.

The Ecu (European Currency Unit) was conceived as the anchor of a symmetrical system (see the central panel of Fig. 2.3). The Ecu is defined as a weighted basket of EEC currencies. Officially, the exchange rates of the currencies of the EMS members were pegged to the Ecu, and the Ecu was floating with respect to the dollar.

The aim of this scheme was for the Ecu to become not only a proper currency, but also an international reserve currency. However, in the event, this proved to be wishful thinking, since the official Ecu still remains nothing but a numéraire. It is true that a certain volume of Ecus was created by the European Monetary Co-operation Fund against the deposit of 20 per cent of the stock of international reserve assets held by the EMS central banks.

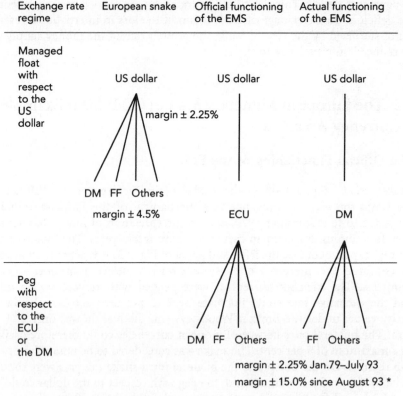

Fig. 2.3. The functioning of the EMS Exchange Rate Mechanism (ERM)

However, central banks did not intervene with Ecus in the foreign exchange markets, since the (private) demand in these markets was not for Ecus, but for existing national currencies.[10]

The Actual Functioning of the EMS—A German Monetary Area

Over time, the EMS came to function as a 'Greater Deutschmark Area'.[11] Germany has, deliberately or not, played the role of the *n*th country in the *n* countries of the EMS plus Austria, and it has mainly been preoccupied with the exchange rate of the German mark with the US dollar (see ch. 1). The other EMS members targeted their exchange rate to the German mark. Consequently, Germany's role within the EMS, i.e. with respect to intra-EMS exchange rates, has been a passive one like the benign neglect of the USA with regard to the $(n-1)$ exchange rates of the international monetary system (the Dollar Standard).

Box 2.5. Germany, the Netherlands, and Austria as the core of the German monetary area

In the past, the Netherlands and Austria have followed a policy of irrevocably fixed bilateral exchange rates with the German mark and have thus pursued the same monetary policy as Germany. In the course of many realignments in the EMS since September 1979, the bilateral exchange rate of the Netherlands (a member of the EMS) with the DM was revised only once by 1 per cent (in March 1983). Austria (not a member of the EMS) maintained a fixed rate of 7 schillings for one mark over the whole period, with a band of ± 0.11 per cent around the par value (instead of ± 2.25 as in the EMS).

Germany, in its role of the *n*th country, provided the monetary anchor of the system. It set the growth rate of the money supply which the others had to follow, for, if they did not, they faced the danger of a realignment in the medium-run. Since Germany withheld itself from any intra-marginal interventions, the burden of intra-marginal interventions, and eventually of adjustments, fell upon the $(n-1)$ EMS members. However, the situation was different when the bilateral exchange rate of an EMS currency (mostly the French franc) with the German mark had reached its margin. Then the German Bundesbank intervened heavily (though the interventions were sterilized), as did the other European central banks (mostly the Banque de France). In many cases, however, this action was the prelude to a realignment which normally took place one or two weeks after the first common marginal interventions.[12]

Only future experience can provide an answer to the question whether the 'new' EMS can still be considered as a currency area. The breakdown of the old system began in September 1992, when Great Britain and Italy left the EMS. A further step towards monetary disintegration took place in August 1993, when the band around the central parity was widened to ± 15 per cent (see Fig. 2.4). However, it should be remembered that a system of floating exchange rates can produce stable exchange rates providing the underlying domestic economic policies remain disciplined and sound. The first stage of Phase III of the future European Monetary Union (irrevocably fixed exchange rates) would be the best example of a currency area. Another would be the second stage of Phase III, when there is only one single currency among the member countries. Box 2.6 illustrates the Maastricht Treaty convergence criteria, under which an EMS country is allowed to enter Phase III. No country has yet met these criteria, neither in 1993 nor in 1994 (with the exception of Luxemburg). Furthermore, the Maastricht Treaty did not take account of the possibility of a wider band of exchange rate fluctuations, which were established in August 1993.

Many member countries may, of course, be suspicious of the monetary hegemony of Germany, because the currency area should operate symmetrically, in the sense that deficit countries must reduce their money supplies and surplus countries must increase theirs. This kind of monetary co-operation is typical for symmetrical currency areas.

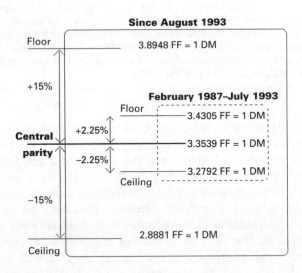

Fig. 2.4. The ERM of the European Monetary System, the example of the French franc and the deutschmark

In the old ERM, the margins of fluctuation around the central parity was ± 2.25%. In the new one, they were enlarged to ± 15%.

Box 2.6. Convergence criteria for joining the European Monetary Union (irrevocably fixed exchange rates), 1993–94

The shaded area represents meeting one criterion. No country met all the criteria in both years, except for Luxemburg in 1994. The best score was realized by Luxemburg and Ireland. The worst countries were Greece, Italy, and Portugal.

	Inflation rate for consumer goods		Budget deficit of the public sector (% of GDP)		Gross debt of the public sector (% of GDP)		Yield on long-run bonds of the public sector	
	1993	1994	1993	1994	1993	1994	1993	1994
Convergence Criteria Countries	2.9	3.1	3.0	3.0	60.0	60.0	9.3	10.4
Austria	3.6	3.0	4.1	4.4	57.0	58.0	6.8	7.0
Belgium	2.8	2.4	6.6	5.5	138.9	140.1	7.2	7.8
Denmark	1.2	2.0	4.4	4.3	79.5	78.0	7.3	7.8
Finland	2.1	1.1	7.2	4.7	62.0	70.9	8.2	8.4
France	2.1	1.7	5.8	5.6	45.8	50.4	6.8	7.2
Germany	4.2	3.0	3.3	3.3	48.1	50.2	6.5	6.9
Great Britain	1.6	1.6	7.8	6.3	48.3	50.4	7.5	8.2
Greece	14.5	10.9	13.3	14.1	115.2	121.3	23.4	20.8
Ireland	1.4	2.3	2.5	2.4	96.1	89.0	7.8	8.1
Italy	4.5	4.0	9.5	9.6	118.6	123.7	11.3	10.6
Luxemburg	3.6	2.2	1.1	1.3	7.8	9.2	6.9	6.4
Netherlands	2.6	2.7	3.3	3.8	81.4	78.8	6.4	6.9
Portugal	6.5	5.3	7.2	6.2	66.9	70.4	12.4	10.8
Spain	4.6	4.8	7.5	7.0	59.8	63.5	10.2	10.0
Sweden	4.6	2.2	13.3	11.7	83.5	93.8	8.5	9.5

Notes: The budget deficit and the gross debt of the public sector include the social security system, but exclude public enterprises.
The convergence criterion for the inflation rate is equal to the average of the three lowest inflation rates plus 1.5 percentage points.
The convergence criterion for the yield on long-run public bonds is equal to the average of the three lowest inflation countries plus two percentage points.
The inflation rate of Germany refers to West Germany. The yield on long-run public bonds refers to one-year treasury bills in Greece and to floating public debt in Portugal.
The limit for the budget deficit ($\Delta D/Y = 0.03$ where D is public debt) is dominated by the limit for public debt ($D/Y = 0.6$). If, for instance, the country has reached its public debt ceiling, its budget deficit has to be zero when growth of GDP is zero.
Source: Deutsche Bundesbank, *Geschäftsbericht 1994*, May 1995, p. 107.

2.4 A Monetary Approach for Symmetrical Currency Areas

Simultaneous Determination of the Price Level and the Exchange Rate

Another application of the monetary approach relates to currency areas. We shall analyse this latter case in terms of a two-country model where the two countries (the home country and the foreign country) form the currency area. The third country is the rest of the world (ROW) to which the currency area is linked via floating exchange rates.

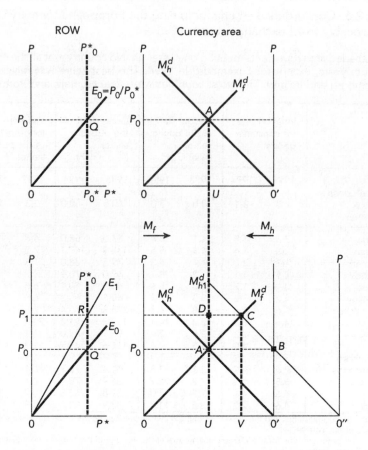

Fig. 2.5. A monetary approach for a currency area

The monetary expansion in the home country amounts to $0'0''$. The new monetary equilibrium in the currency area is at C. Prices and the exchange rate rise by AD. The home country still has an excess supply of money (CD) and a balance of payments deficit (CD). The foreign country has an excess demand for money (CD) with a balance-of-payments surplus.

Fig. 2.5a shows the money market of the currency area (right-hand panel). The total quantity of money is $00'$, which is distributed equally at point U between the home country (M_h) and the foreign country (M_f). The two countries are assumed to be of equal size and to possess identical demand functions for money, M^d_h and M^d_f. The equilibrium price level is at A and the exchange rate with ROW (E_0) is indicated by the slope of the ray OE_0 (left-hand panel).

It is assumed that the initial equilibrium is disturbed because one of the countries undertakes an expansionary monetary policy. Suppose that the domestic country pursues an expansionary monetary policy in the form of an internal credit expansion ($0'0''$ in the right-hand panel of Fig. 2.5b). There will be an excess supply in the domestic money market (*AB*), which causes an excess demand for goods only, since we neglect capital movements.[13] Because full employment is assumed, the additional demand for goods can only be satisfied by foreign markets. However, if the foreign country is also at the threshold of full employment, there will be an increase in prices in both the domestic country and the foreign country. This price increase will be more or less uniform in the two countries because of our other assumptions that markets for (tradable) goods are highly integrated. Despite the equal increase in the national price levels (P_1 at the intersection point *C*), there remains an excess supply of money in the home country (*CD*) and a corresponding excess demand for money in the foreign country (*CD*). The reason for this excess demand is the increase in the foreign demand for money (due to the price increase) which can be only satisfied by a balance-of-payments surplus provided that foreign monetary policy remains unchanged.

The balance-of-payments deficit in the home country (*CD*), and the corresponding surplus in the foreign country, redistribute—via non-sterilized intervention policies—the total outstanding quantity of money $00''$. The quantity of money in the foreign country is $0V$ and that of the home country $0''V$. Since the price level of the currency area has risen from P_0 to P_1, its exchange rate with ROW will increase from E_0 at point *Q* to E_1 at point *R* (purchasing power parity).

The home country ends up with lower international reserves. It will not often be able to pursue an expansionary monetary policy since it loses further reserves each time. Assume, for instance, that there is zero inflation in the currency area, and that the home country raises its monetary growth rate to 10 per cent. Since both countries are of equal size and the real growth rate is zero, the inflation rate within the currency area rises to 5 per cent and the annual depreciation of the currency area against the non-inflationary ROW amounts to 5 per cent. However, the home country continuously loses reserves so that it eventually has to stop its monetary growth. The maintenance of 5 per cent inflation within the currency area and the annual depreciation of 5 per cent against ROW are only conceivable under the assumption that both countries pursue an active monetary expansion policy at the rate of 5 per cent (monetary co-operation).

Multi-period Adjustment of the Balance of Payments

In general, the balance-of-payments adjustment will take place at a decreasing rate over several periods, until the 'full-stock equilibrium' has been reached in the national money markets. Fig. 2.5 was constructed by Claassen (1974) by analogy with Archibald and Lipsey's (1958) representation of the flow-stock demand for money. A stock equilibrium of the demand for money (within a stationary economy) prevails at point *T*, where real national income (y_0) is equal to absorption (A_0) and where real cash balances (m) have reached their

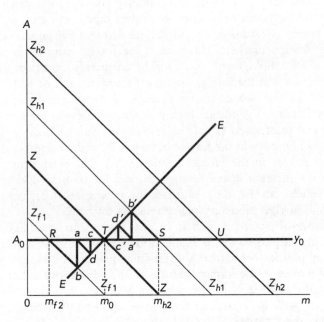

Fig. 2.6. A monetary approach with multi-period trade balance adjustment

For the two countries, full-stock equilibrium is at T. The home country's money supply increases by TU. The currency area's price level rises, reducing each country's real cash balances to m_{h2} and m_{f2}. The home country's stock excess supply of money is TS, which is equal to the foreign country's stock excess demand for money (TR). The flow excess supply of money for the first period is Sa' causing the trade balance deficit $a'b'$. Correspondingly, for the foreign country, the flow excess demand for money is Ra leading to the trade balance surplus ab. The process is completed when point T is reached.

desired long-run level (m_0), which is called full-stock equilibrium. It is supposed that both countries are of the same size, in the sense that they have the same level of income (y_0) and the same full-stock equilibrium level of real cash balances (m_0). The latter assumption is expressed by the expansion line EE, which is assumed to be identical in the two countries. It reflects each country's (identical) preference system with respect to the adjustment speed of actual real cash balances to desired long-run cash balances. Thus, point T is a tangent point of a (not drawn) indifference curve with the budget line ZZ, where the latter indicates a given level of resources equal to $y_0 + m_0$. The indifference curve illustrates the conditions under which the marginal disutility of a reduction in absorption (consumption) in this period is equal to the marginal utility of a permanent increase in real cash balances.

The full-stock equilibrium in the two national money markets (T) is disturbed as soon as the home country increases its quantity of money by TU, and the new budget line becomes ZZ_{h2}. The excess demand for goods in the home country leads to a higher price level in both countries and this reduces real cash balances: in the home country by $SU = Z_{h1}Z_{h2}$ and in the foreign country by $RT = Z_{f1}Z$. The home country has real cash balances of m_{h2} and the foreign country of m_{f2}. The stock excess supply of money in the home country $(m_{h2}m_0)$ corresponds to the stock excess demand for money in the foreign country $(m_{f2}m_0)$ so that there is a stock equilibrium in the money market of the currency area as a whole. A further increase in the price level no longer occurs, because there is monetary equilibrium within the total currency area, although there is sectoral disequilibrium. During the adjustment process, in each period the flow excess supply of cash balances by the home country $(Sa'; a'c' \ldots)$ equals the flow excess demand for cash balances by the foreign country $(Ra; ac \ldots)$.[14] Or, in other words, in each period the excess demand for goods in the home country $(a'b'; c'd' \ldots)$ is equal to the excess supply of goods in the foreign country $(ab; cd \ldots)$. Consequently, there is a continuous redistribution of the real quantity of money from the home country to the foreign country via the trade account of the balance of payments until both countries have reached their full-stock equilibrium at point T.

Inflation and Growth

As in the case of a small open economy (Fig. 2.2), we want to apply the monetary approach to a currency area which is growing and inflationary (Fig. 2.7), even though the common inflation rate might be rather modest, as in the context of the present EMS. We assume again that the two economies are identical, that is, they have the same demand functions for money, $L(i)_h = L(i)_f = L(i)_{ca}$ and the same real growth rates, $g_{yd} = g_{yf} = g_{yca}$ (AB). They differ only with respect to monetary policy where $g_{Mh} > g_{Mf}$. Consequently, the (weighted) average of the growth rate of the money supply within the currency area, g_{Mca} lies between the two national money growth rates provoking a common inflation rate of $FG = UV = QR$. If this inflation rate is different from that of the USA, a corresponding change in the exchange rate of the currency area with the dollar will take place assuming that there is purchasing power parity.

Since the home country has an excess supply of money (ST) and the foreign country an excess demand for money (VX)—so that the money market in the currency area is in equilibrium—the first country will have a balance-of-payments deficit (ST) and the second a surplus (VX). In the absence of any sterilization policies, the home country will reduce its monetary growth to QS and the foreign country will increase its monetary growth to UX.

An essential assumption in our analysis concerns the willingness of the foreign country to tolerate the inflationary impulse coming from the home country. Thus, the foreign country could refuse to increase the money supply by VX when it has a balance-of-payments surplus. Instead, it could sterilize the reserve inflows so as to impose a more disciplined monetary policy on its neighbour. Any surplus country has this power, as it is much easier to operate with a continuous surplus in the balance of payments than with a continuous deficit.

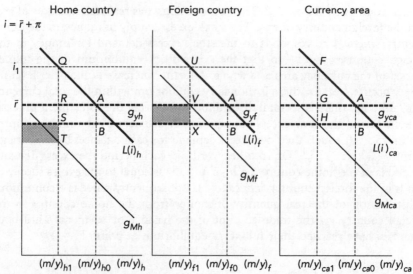

Fig. 2.7. A monetary approach for an inflationary and growing currency area

Both countries are of the same size, have the same behaviour functions, and the same real growth rate (*AB*). The initial monetary equilibrium without inflation is at point *A*, where both countries expand their money supplies at the rate *AB*.

The home country pursues a higher monetary growth rate (*QT*) than the foreign country (*UV*). The weighted growth rate of the currency area is *FH*, giving rise to the inflation rate *FG* = *UV* = *QR*. There is still an excess supply in the home country (*ST*) and a corresponding excess demand in the foreign country (*VX*) provoking a balance-of-payments deficit in the home country and a balance-of-payments surplus in the foreign country (the shaded area).

If the foreign country is a chronic surplus country, its surplus must derive— according to the monetary approach to the balance of payments—from the excess demand in its money market, i.e. from its restrictive monetary policy which, in turn, may be aimed at achieving price stability. This scenario is precisely the historical background for the emergence of Germany as the anchor country of the EMS. First, it—together with Holland and Austria— was always less inflationary than the member countries. Secondly, the member countries began to peg their currencies to the deutschmark. Thirdly, the German mark had gradually acquired the status of an international reserve currency. The case of asymmetrical currency areas—with the hegemony of the anchor country—will be discussed analytically in the next chapter.

Notes

1. The monetary approach was elaborated by Harry Johnson (1968, 1972*a*, 1972*b*) and Robert Mundell (1971). See also Frenkel and Johnson (1976) and Claassen (1976, 1978).

2. In the short run the interest rate parity dominates the exchange rate path with the special feature of overshooting. The relationship $\Delta M \to \Delta P \to \Delta E$ can only be established for the longer run (see ch. 3). The general formulation of the monetary approach to the exchange rate within a two-country framework is based on the equilibrium condition in the money market and on purchasing power parity:

$$M = PL(r, y)$$
$$E = P/P^*$$

P is equal to M/L so that

$$E = P/P^* = M/LP^*$$

P^* is determined in the foreign money market where $P^* = M^*/L^*$. Consequently, the determining factors of the exchange rate become

$$E = P/P^* = (M/M^*)\,(L^*/L)$$

The exchange rate has a *monetary* determinant (the relative money supplies (M/M^*)) and a *real* determinant (the relative demand for real money holdings (L^*/L)). This real determinant is influenced by r, r^*, y and y^*.

3. In the case of a country which is a net creditor or debtor, GDP has to be replaced by GNP and the trade balance would become the current account balance, since GNP = GDP + net interest payments to foreign countries, and trade balance deficit plus net interest payments to foreign countries = current account deficit. We assume other net factor incomes are zero.

4. See on this issue Dornbusch (1973) and Claassen (1974).

5. The price level of tradables (P_T) remains constant since P_T is linked to international prices (P^*_T) via $P_T = E_0 P^*_T$.

6. This specific interpretation of the real exchange rate will be discussed in ch. 5.

7. Strictly speaking, the nominal interest rate is equal to the sum of $r^* + \pi^e + r^*\pi^e$. π^e stands for the protection of the real value of financial assets against inflation and $r^*\pi^e$ for the protection of the real value of the interest payments. Since, at low inflation rates, the term $r^*\pi^e$ is rather small, it is often neglected.

8. If money holdings do not yield an interest, or deposits are not remunerated sufficiently to compensate for the real value loss caused by the inflation, the demand for real cash balances is reduced from m_0 to m_2, creating an excess demand for goods. A jump in the general price level will destroy the unwanted real cash balances of $m_2 - m_0$.

9. Non-sterilized intervention policy means that the central bank does not use other monetary instruments for holding the growth rate of the money supply constant.

10. The intervention mechanism, already mentioned in ch. 1, had been conceived as follows (Ungerer et al., 1986). (1) When a bilateral exchange rate was within the margin, intervention could take place, but it had to be co-ordinated between the two central banks concerned. The aim of these interventions was to bring the bilateral exchange rate back to its central rate. (2) When the exchange rate of an EMS currency with the Ecu diverged from its par value by 75 per cent within the maximum upper or lower level of the margin, the country had to undertake policy measures (interventions or monetary policy measures) to reduce the exchange rate fluctuation. (3) If a bilateral exchange rate hit the margin (necessarily for one country the upper margin and for the other country the lower one),

interventions—called 'marginal' interventions—with EMS currencies by both central banks were compulsory at these margins. These marginal interventions could be financed by the 'very short-term financing facility' which consists of mutual credit lines between member central banks. (4) If, despite heavy marginal interventions, the exchange rate could not be brought back, then, in many cases, a realignment of the parity values had to take place. This realignment was an outcome of multilateral negotiations between the EMS members and the Commission. So, even in this respect, bilateral autonomy of a given exchange rate between the two countries did not exist. In reality, these four provisions applied to the exchange rate mechanism with the deutschmark as the anchor currency, and not with the Ecu.

11. See Dornbusch (1986), Giavazzi and Giovannini (1987*a*, 1987*b*), and Claassen (1989*a*).

12. The gain from Germany's joining the EMS is rather ambiguous. The initial opposition of the Bundesbank to the establishment of the EMS derived from the fear that Germany would lose some of its freedom to carry out anti-inflationary policy, since an accelerated disinflation policy would have imposed an unsustainable strain on other EMS members by requiring too frequent realignments of their bilateral exchange rates. Some authors such as Melitz (1985) argued that the benefit for Germany consisted of the competitive gains (real undervaluation of the German mark) that would result if the high inflation countries became less competitive. However, one of the main political reasons that Germany initiated the EMS was that it was a further step towards political integration for which one requirement was convergence of the EEC inflation rates towards the lowest one, i.e. towards the German rate.

   The gain for other, more inflationary, members is more obvious. Their central banks would gain credibility for their anti-inflationary policy measures when they were linked via fixed exchange rates to the less inflationary country. The gain in credibility is an important matter, since a credible anti-inflationary policy will lower inflationary expectations. Such a reduction is necessary to avoid adverse employment effects (via too high nominal wage adjustment and too high nominal interest rate adjustment). Another reason for increased credibility of the policies of high inflation countries is the extra penalty the member country has to pay when it pursues its former inflation policy, because it suffers a loss in competitiveness (via a real appreciation of its currency). The private sector is aware of the penalty the policy-maker is faced with, and this helps overcome the private sector's mistrust of policy-makers (Giavazzi and Giovannini, 1987*a* and 1987*b*). This point will be analysed in Sect. 9.2.

13. They are taken into account in Chapters 3 and 4.

14. For the home country, the once-and-for-all increase in the price level has reduced its resources to $Z_{h1} = y_0 + m_{h2}$ (point S). The optimum 'consumption' (consumer goods and liquidity services of real cash balances) is indicated by the expansion line *EE*. The country chooses point b' by exchanging Sa' cash balances for foreign goods to the amount of $a'b'$. Similarly, for the foreign country, resources have been reduced to $Z_{f1} = y_0 + m_{f2}$ (point R). The optimum consumption is at point b. The country acquires Ra real cash balances (via reserve inflows) with a trade balance surplus of ab.

3

A MONETARY APPROACH TO THE EXCHANGE RATE: INTEREST RATE PARITY

The simplest version of the financial approach to the exchange rate is the monetary approach. It assumes perfect substitutability of domestic and foreign financial assets. Perfect substitutability for assets means the equality of the rates of return on the various assets. This equality, applied to domestic and foreign financial assets, is called interest rate parity. If their return is measured in units of the domestic currency, the rate of return on (short run) domestic financial assets is the domestic interest rate and the corresponding rate of return on foreign financial assets is the foreign interest rate plus (minus) the expected rate of appreciation (depreciation) of the foreign currency. Any inequality between the two rates of return implies either an immediate movement in the actual exchange rate which changes the expected rate of change in the exchange rate, or an adjustment of the domestic interest rate by domestic monetary policy (exchange rate stabilization policy).

3.1. The Exchange Rate as the Relative Price of Domestic and Foreign Financial Assets

The exchange rate is not only the relative price of domestic and foreign goods,[1] it can also be interpreted as the relative price of domestic and foreign financial assets. The proper financial role of the exchange rate is to equilibrate financial asset markets within an open economy with international capital movements. When international capital flows dominate the foreign exchange market, they become the major determinants of short run movements in the exchange rate. Box 3.1 illustrates the importance of daily transactions in the world's most important foreign exchange markets where financial capital flows make up 95 per cent of the total transaction volume.

Box 3.1. Daily foreign exchange transactions (billion dollars)

Frankel and Froot (1990: 182) report that the daily foreign exchange transactions (adjusted for double counting) in the foreign exchange markets were $ 430 bn. in April 1989. Only 5 per cent of these were between non-financial firms (importers and exporters); 95 per cent of the trading took place among banks and other financial firms. According to the Annual Report of the Bank for International Settlements by April 1992 they had increased to $ 916 bn., which is equivalent to one-third of Germany's annual GDP (and 80 per cent of international reserves held by central banks of the OECD). The foreign exchange transactions by various countries are shown below:

UK	300	Switzerland	68
USA	192	Hong Kong	61
Japan	126	Germany	57
Singapore	76	France	36

Without capital flows—strict capital controls—the exchange rate would cease to be a financial asset price.[2] However, in recent years, full capital mobility, in the sense that there are no exchange controls on capital movements ('unrestricted capital mobility' or 'full capital account convertibility'), has become usual for industrialized countries.

As a financial asset price (equilibrating financial asset markets) the foreign exchange rate has to be interpreted as meaning that a change in the exchange rate is the major factor influencing the expected rate of return on financial assets. Rates of return are the dominant (if not only) incentive for international financial capital flows. Where given domestic and foreign financial assets have the same maturity and are exposed to the same default risk, the return on the domestic asset must equal the expected return on the foreign assets (the assets are perfect substitutes with respect to their returns) or the link could be less strict (i.e. they are not perfect substitutes).

The financial models for determining the foreign exchange rate which assume perfect substitutability, are classified as the 'monetary approach to the exchange rate' shown in Table 3.1. If the financial assets are imperfect substitutes, the determination of the exchange rate proceeds according to the 'portfolio approach to the exchange rate' because investors are exchange rate (or currency risk) averse. Other risks, such as that of future capital controls,

Table 3.1. Financial approaches to the exchange rate

	Monetary approach	Portfolio approach
Capital mobility	Unrestricted	Unrestricted or restricted
Substitutability of domestic and foreign financial assets	Perfect (risk neutrality)	Imperfect (risk aversion)

are also analysed by the portfolio approach. The present chapter deals with the monetary approach while the portfolio approach is the subject of the next chapter.

3.2. Simultaneous Determination of the Exchange Rate and the Interest Rate in Small Open Economies

Uncovered Interest Rate Parity

With perfect substitutability between domestic and foreign financial assets, any return differential between the two types of assets is immediately eliminated by exchange rate movements. Any divergence in the *expected* rates of return gives rise to incipient capital flows. The immediate reactions of the current exchange rate cancel the return differential so that the expected rates of return on domestic and foreign financial assets are equalized (interest rate parity).

Uncovered interest rate parity means that the investor does not protect himself in the forward market against the exchange rate risk as he would in the case of covered interest rate parity. Our investor is simply risk neutral, admittedly a rather heroic assumption.[3] The case of risk protection via the covered interest rate is treated in the next chapter.

Formally, uncovered interest rate parity can be expressed as the equality between the interest rate on domestic financial assets and the expected return on foreign financial assets:

$$i = i^* + (E^e - E)/E \qquad (3.1)$$

where i (i*) stands for the domestic (foreign) interest rate and E^e for the expected exchange rate. If E^e is higher than E, a future depreciation of the domestic currency equal to the expected appreciation of the foreign currency is expected. In the reverse case (E^e is lower than E) a future appreciation of the domestic currency (i.e. depreciation of the foreign currency) is expected.[4]

The financial assets of formula (3.1) refer only to short-term ones. Assume that both types of assets are either three month time deposits or treasury bills with a maturity of three months. The assets have to face the same type of default risk which we assume to be zero. In our example, the expected exchange rate (E^e) is the exchange rate which is now expected to reign in three months time. Correspondingly, the interest rates are three month rates.[5]

The interest rate parity is illustrated in Fig. 3.1. At point A domestic and foreign interest rates are equal ($i_o = i^*_o$). The given expected exchange rate E^e_o is equal to the actual exchange rate E_o. Consequently, neither a depreciation nor an appreciation is expected and the current exchange rate is expected to hold in three months' time. The curve $i^*_o + (E^e_o - E)/E$ indicates the expected return on foreign assets (measured on the horizontal axis) and is a decreasing function of the actual exchange rate (E).

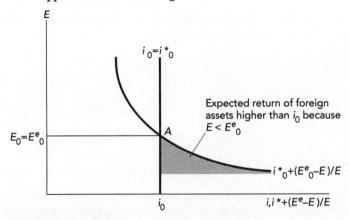

Fig. 3.1. The uncovered interest rate parity

At point A interest rate parity prevails for the special case of $i = i^+$ and $E = E^e$. If the current exchange rate lies below the expected one, foreign assets yield a higher (expected) return than domestic assets, since the foreign currency is expected to be appreciated. There is an infinite demand for foreign assets and the domestic currency will depreciate towards point A, thus eliminating any expected change in the exchange rate.

The shaded area describes those cases where foreign assets yield a higher return than domestic ones (i_o). If for any reason the current exchange rate falls below E^e_o, foreign assets will be more attractive than domestic ones, since the market expects a depreciation of the domestic currency identical to an expected appreciation of the foreign currency. The additional expected return on foreign assets implies an 'infinite' demand for foreign assets.[6] Consequently, the domestic currency must depreciate immediately (point A). In traditional textbooks, this depreciation is described as a result of massive capital outflows, since the return on domestic assets is lower than the return on foreign assets. However, in reality, these capital flows are only incipient ones, because the actual exchange rate adjusts immediately and maintains the same return on domestic and foreign financial assets.[7] It is this movement of the actual exchange rate which equilibrates the returns on domestic and foreign financial assets, and, in this sense, the exchange rate is the relative price of domestic and foreign financial assets.

An alternative formulation of equation (3.1) is:

$$E = E^e/(1 + i - i^*) \qquad (3.1a)$$

Three possible causes of a change in the exchange rate can be derived: a change in i, in i^*, or in E^e. Fig. 3.2 presents the three possible causes of a depreciation. For simplicity, we have drawn the curve of the interest rate parity as a straight line. The initial equilibrium is at point A with $i_o = i^*_o$ and $E_o = E^e_o$.

The case of Fig. 3.2a is that of a fall in the domestic interest rate from i_o to i_1. Domestic assets are less attractive than foreign ones. They become more

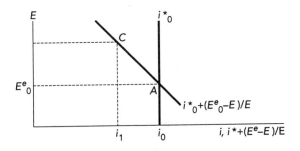

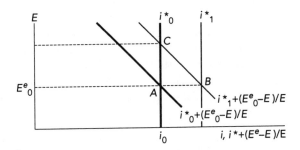

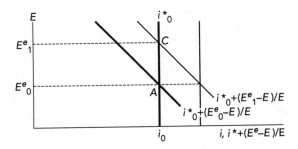

Fig. 3.2. Three causes of depreciation
3.2a. Fall in domestic interest rate
3.2b. Rise in foreign interest rate
3.2c. Rise in expected exchange rate

The initial equilibrium is at point A for all three cases. 3.2a–3.2b Foreign assets become more attractive when the domestic interest falls or the foreign interest rate increases (shifting the foreign-return schedule to the right). The subsequent depreciation (point C) creates the expectation of a future depreciation of the foreign currency. 3.2c An expected depreciation is followed immediately by an actual depreciation (point C).

attractive with a depreciation (point C) which creates the expectation that the domestic currency will appreciate in the future. Or, in other words, foreign assets become less profitable because they are exposed to a future depreciation.[8]

Fig. 3.2*b* concerns the case of an increase in the foreign interest rate from i^*_0 to i^*_1 which shifts the schedule of the expected return on foreign assets to the right through point *B*. As in the former case, domestic assets become less attractive. Again, a depreciation has to take place at the unchanged domestic interest rate i_0 (point *C*) in order to create an expected rate of appreciation of the domestic currency.

Finally, as shown in Fig. 3.2*c*, an 'autonomous' shift in exchange rate expectations, from E^e_0 to the higher expected exchange rate E^e_1, illustrates the crucial role of expectations for the determination of the exchange rate. According to Frenkel (1981*b*), new 'news' about a probable change in the future exchange rate can give rise to a revision of exchange rate expectations. With a zero interest rate differential, an expected depreciation of 10 per cent produces an immediate actual depreciation rate of 10 per cent according to formula (3.1*a*). Expectations can be self-fulfilling (point *C*). In this respect, foreign exchange markets are no different from any other financial asset market, such as the stock market. If there is the general belief that stock prices will fall in the near or distant future, the prices will immediately fall.

The Dominance of Interest Rate Parity over Purchasing Power Parity

Determination of the domestic interest rate.   The monetary approach to the exchange rate with regard to the relative price of domestic and foreign goods (purchasing power parity) and the monetary approach to the exchange rate with regard to the relative price of domestic and foreign assets (interest rate parity) have in common the fact that the exchange rate is determined by the money market. We again assume a disturbance in the equilibrium of the money market resulting from an increase in the quantity of money. Then according to purchasing power parity, the (long run) causal links operate as follows: higher quantity of money → higher domestic price level (of tradable and non-tradable goods) → depreciation of the domestic currency. Under interest rate parity, the (short run) causality is as follows: higher quantity of money → lower domestic interest rate → depreciation.

In order to 'endogenize' one of the three exogenous variables (the domestic interest rate, the foreign interest rate, and the expected exchange rate) of formula (3.1*a*), the domestic money market which determines the domestic interest rate can be chosen using a partial analysis. For a small open economy, i^* has to be considered as given.

The money market determines the domestic interest rate:

$$M = P_0 y_0 \, L(i) \tag{3.2}$$

while the interest rate parity of formula (3.1*a*) fixes the exchange rate. We have shown the money market in the lower panel of Fig. 3.3 and the interest rate

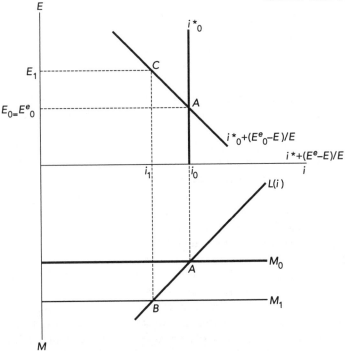

Fig. 3.3. Simultaneous determination of the exchange rate and interest rate

The interest rate parity is represented in the upper panel and the money market in the lower panel. The initial equilibrium is at point A. An expansionary monetary policy lowers the domestic interest rate (point B). Domestic financial assets become less profitable for foreign investors. The subsequent depreciation (point C) creates the expectation of a future appreciation of the concerned currency.

parity in the upper panel. The initial equilibrium is again at point A with $i_0 = i^*_0$ and $E_0 = E^e_0$. We already know from Fig. 3.2a that a lower domestic interest rate (i_1) brings about a depreciation. Fig. 3.3 now tells us the ultimate reason for the lower domestic interest rate. It is the expansion of the money supply from M_0 to M_1 which produces the fall in the interest rate (point B). The depreciation (point C) takes place to create the expectation of a future appreciation of the domestic currency. For foreigners, the expected appreciation renders domestic financial assets once more as attractive as foreign ones.

The determination of the expected exchange rate.   The interest rate parity does not say anything at all about the *absolute level* of the exchange rate. It *assumes* a given level of the expected exchange rate (E^e) which determines the *absolute* level of E, and the interest rate parity indicates the necessary *change* in the exchange rate around the level of the expected exchange rate where the domestic and foreign interest rates are not equal. The anchor of the current exchange rate is the expected exchange rate which, in turn, depends on the fundamental determinants of the exchange rate. One of these is purchasing power parity (PPP).

Looking at the money market, there are short-run and long-run adjustment processes in the case of monetary disequilibrium. The immediate impact of an excess supply of money was a fall in the interest rate and a depreciation of the short-run exchange rate. However, the system will not remain there. The lower interest rate (possibly together with the depreciation) creates an excess demand in the goods market. If we assume a quantity-theoretical (not a Keynesian) framework, prices will rise. It is here that the first important distinction between the short run and long run arises. In reality, we observe that goods prices are sticky. When there is an excess demand for goods, prices do not rise immediately to eliminate the excess demand in the goods market. Prices will gradually increase over a longer time-scale (say of six months to one year) to eliminate ultimately the excess demand.

The different speed of price movements (i and P) is illustrated by Fig. 3.4. In the top panel, we have shown the money market. The initial long-run equilibrium is at point A. The increase of the money supply (from M_0 to M_1) produces an immediate fall in the interest rate (point B). At point B, there is an excess demand for goods, for instance, as a result of the lower interest rate and the depreciation. Since prices are sticky, they rise only step by step. Because the higher price level implies a higher nominal demand for money (a gradual upward shift of the money demand schedule), the increase in the price level is accompanied by an increase in the interest rate.

In this long-term quantity theory scenario, investors may form their expectations on the basis of the exchange rates which emerge in the long run (E_{lt}). This latter may be mainly determined by considerations about purchasing power parity ($E_{lt} = P_{lt}/P^*_{lt}$). The symbol $_{lt}$ stands for the domestic (P_{lt}) and foreign price levels (P^*_{lt}) which will result in the long run.

Consequently, the equation system of the monetary sector can be represented as:

Money market	$P\,y_0\,L(i)$	(3.2a)
Interest rate parity	$E = E^e/(1 + i - i^*)$	(3.1a)
Exchange rate expectations according to PPP	$E^e = \beta\,E_{lf} = \beta\,P_{lf}/P^*_{lf}$	(3.3)

where $\beta \leq 1$. The causal links of monetary expansion are now far more complicated: higher quantity of money → lower interest rate → *expected* and actual depreciation → rising price level → higher interest rate → appreciation.[9]

There are many economists who have shown empirically that purchasing power parity is only valid in the very long run and others who suggest that it does not hold in the long run.[10] The short-run invalidity of purchasing power parity can be explained, from an analytical point of view, by a combination of interest rate parity and purchasing power parity during the whole process of adjustment to a monetary shock. Two elements characterize this adjustment

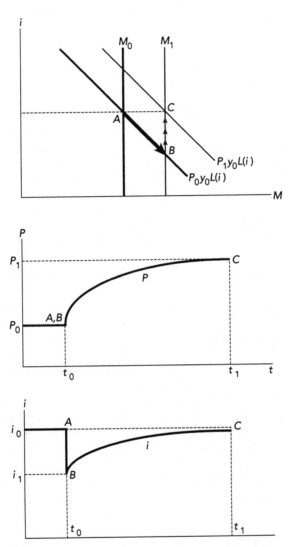

Fig. 3.4. Monetary expansion, interest rate, and the price level

The initial equilibrium is at point A. The immediate impact of monetary expansion is a fall in the interest rate (point B). Afterwards prices begin to move upward implying a rightward shift of the schedule of the demand for money. The interest rate moves toward point C.

process. First, during the adjustment process, interest rate parity dominates over purchasing power parity (the phenomenon of overshooting) so that the law of one price for goods cannot then be valid. Second, the *level* of the long run expected exchange rate can be derived from purchasing power parity

($E^e = E_{1r}$) as one possible benchmark among the various fundamentals of the long-run exchange rate.

The Phenomenon of Overshooting

The phenomenon of overshooting is mostly illustrated for the case of an expansionary monetary policy. The model has been elaborated by Rudiger Dornbusch (1976b). It states that the short-run exchange rate (determined by interest rate parity) overshoots the level of the long-run exchange rate (determined by purchasing power parity). The ultimate reason for the overshooting phenomenon is the fact that adjustment speeds are different in the financial and goods markets. A disequilibrium in the financial markets is eliminated immediately by movements of interest rates and exchange rates. However, a disequilibrium in the goods markets persists for a long time because of price rigidities.

The movement of the domestic price variables (i and P) of Fig. 3.4 is linked in Fig. 3.5 to the interest rate parity in order to show the time path of the exchange rate towards long-run purchasing power parity. The lower panel is a reproduction of the upper panel of Fig. 3.4. The new element (compared with Fig. 3.3) consists of the revision of exchange rate expectations from E_0^e to E_1^e. As already mentioned, individuals are assumed to form their exchange rate expectations on the basis of purchasing power parity. The moment the monetary shock occurs (if it had not previously been anticipated), the interest rate parity schedule shifts upwards. The long-run exchange rate will be E_1 (at point C). Because of the decline in the domestic interest rate from i_0 to i_1, the immediate impact on the exchange rate is E_2 (at point B), overshooting E_1 by E_2E_1. During the subsequent adjustment process (with higher domestic price and interest levels), the interest rate differential diminishes, and this requires a lower expected rate of appreciation. This requirement is realized by the gradual appreciation of the actual exchange rate from point B towards C.

Exchange Rate Stabilization Policies (Managed Float)

Monetary shocks are those which take place in the money market. There is an exogenous change either in the money demand or in the money supply. Usually, the latter case is seen as resulting from an expansionary or restrictive monetary policy. We shall analyse the case of a restrictive monetary policy pursued by the foreign country. For the domestic country, it represents another exogenous monetary shock in the form of an increased foreign interest rate.

As we have already indicated at the beginning of the present chapter (Fig. 3.2b), a rise in the foreign interest rate leads to a depreciation of the domestic currency. The depreciation is necessary to create the expectation of a future

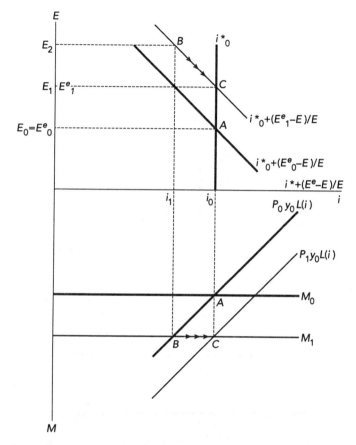

Fig. 3.5. The overshooting phenomenon

The initial equilibrium is at point A. The expansionary monetary policy gives rise immediately to a revision of exchange rate expectations (an upward shift in the foreign-return schedule towards point C). The domestic currency depreciates (point B) above its long-run equilibrium level (point C).

appreciation of the domestic currency, since otherwise domestic financial assets would become less attractive than foreign ones. This depreciation takes place in a freely floating exchange rate regime.

Exchange rate stabilization policies are typical for a managed float. We shall ask the question of what the monetary authorities should do if they want to avoid this depreciation. The answer is that they too have to conduct a restrictive monetary policy as the foreign country does.

In Fig. 3.6, we have plotted the familiar diagram with the interest rate parity in the upper panel and the domestic money market in the lower panel. The initial equilibrium is at point A. The exogenous shock of a higher foreign interest rate, from i^*_0 to i^*_1, shifts the schedule of the expected return of

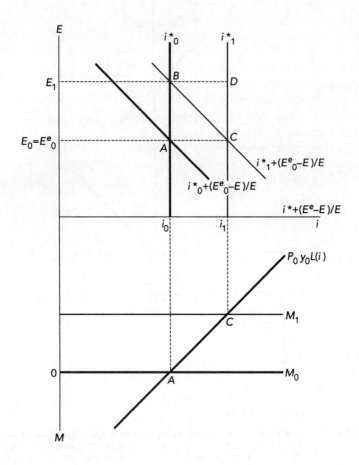

Fig. 3.6. A rise in the foreign interest rate and intervention policy for avoiding the depreciation

The rise in the foreign interest rate provokes an immediate depreciation from A to B. The intervention policy for avoiding the depreciation is only efficient, if it is of the non-sterilized type implying the reduction of the domestic money supply and a corresponding rise in the domestic interest rate (point C).

foreign assets to the right. In a freely floating exchange rate regime, and with an unchanged domestic interest rate at i_0, there would be a depreciation of the domestic currency from E_0 to E_1 (point B). If the monetary authorities want to maintain the exchange rate at E_0, there are various possible ways of achieving this. However, in all cases, they have to move to point C.

Sterilized versus non-sterilized intervention policies in the foreign exchange market.   The first method consists of a direct intervention by the central bank in the foreign exchange market ('intervention policy') by selling foreign exchange in order to prevent the depreciation. However, that policy is still not sufficient, since the return on domestic assets (i_0) is still lower than the return on foreign assets $[i^*_1 + (E^e_0 - E_0)/E_0]$ by the amount AC. Consequently, massive capital outflows will take place.[11]

The intervention policy can avoid the depreciation only if it is of the 'non-sterilized' type (a reduction in the domestic quantity of money). The sale of foreign exchange by the monetary authorities takes place against the purchase of domestic currency, implying an automatic reduction in the monetary base. However, if the monetary authorities have two targets, the maintenance of the exchange rate (E_0) and the maintenance of the money supply (M_0), they will use other instruments of monetary policy (e.g. open market operations) in order to leave the outstanding quantity of money unchanged. Thus, the restrictive impact of the intervention policy on the monetary base is 'sterilized' or 'neutralized' by the expansionary use of another instrument of monetary policy.

In Table 3.2, I have presented the balance sheet of the central bank. Selling international reserves on the foreign exchange market in order to maintain the exchange rate means a simultaneous reduction in the stock of international reserves and currency. However, the fall in the monetary base can be avoided by increasing domestic credits (via the purchase of bonds through open market operations and via additional credit through the discount window).

In particular, in the context of 'perfect capital mobility', which is the assumption behind the uncovered interest rate parity, sterilized intervention policies are doomed to be ineffective. If the money supply is maintained at its original level (M_0), the depreciation may be avoided for only a few days. Massive capital outflows will force the monetary authorities to accept either the depreciation or the reduction in the money supply (M_1 in Fig. 3.6) with the corresponding increase in the domestic interest rate (i_1).[12]

Other instruments of monetary policy.   For the credible pursuit of an exchange rate target, the true choice for a central bank is not between a sterilized and non-sterilized intervention policy, since only the latter is effective. The less

Table 3.2. The balance sheet of the central bank: counterparts of the monetary base

Assets	Central Bank	Liabilities
International reserves		Bank reserves
Domestic credit		Currency
Monetary base		Monetary base

expensive alternative to the non-sterilized intervention policy is the use of other instruments for a direct restrictive monetary policy to reduce the quantity of money to M_1 (Fig. 3.6). Since, in any case, the domestic interest rate has to be raised, the central bank should achieve this by using its conventional monetary policy tools rather than via non-sterilized intervention which implies a loss of international reserves. Otherwise, with an ultimately lower monetary base, the ratio of international reserves to the monetary base will fall instead of rise.

3.3 Simultaneous Determination of the Exchange Rate and the Interest Rate in Currency Areas

A Two-Country Model

As already discussed in Chapter 2, a currency area is presented by using a two-country model. By analogy with the EMS, the domestic country should be the satellite country (France) and the foreign country the anchor country (Germany). The two countries are again identical. In section 2.4 I analysed the *long run* impact of an increase in the money supply on certain key variables in the currency area in terms of purchasing power parity. The price level rose in both countries; the satellite country pursuing the expansionary monetary policy suffered by a deficit in the balance of payments and, correspondingly, the other country had a surplus position; we assumed a symmetrical currency area in which the anchor country (which was the surplus country) did not neutralize the impact of the additional international reserves on its monetary base; the exchange rate of the currency area with respect to the dollar—i.e. the DM-dollar rate of the anchor country and, thus, the FF-dollar rate of the satellite country—reflected the higher price level and the exchange rate was conceived as the relative price of the currency area goods and the American goods.

The objective of the present section is to examine the *short run* effects of an expansionary monetary policy with interest rate parity. As in the old EMS (before August 1993), the exchange rate FF/DM is allowed to fluctuate around the central parity by ± 2.25 per cent, for which the interest rate parity can be applied. The exchange rate is now interpreted as the relative price of French and German financial assets.

The money market of the currency area, M_{ca} and M^d_{ca}, is derived from the two national money markets (see the top panel of Fig. 3.7) where $M_{ca} = M + M^*$ and $M^d_{ca} = M^d + M^{d*}$ (horizontal addition). At the initial equilibrium (point A), we assume identical interest rates ($i_0 = i^*_0$). According to the interest rate parity (in the bottom panel of Fig. 3.7), which is also valid within a currency area for the movement of the exchange rate between the floor and the ceiling, the expected exchange rate must be equal to the actual exchange rate ($E^e_0 = E_0$). We assume that the exchange rate is situated at the central

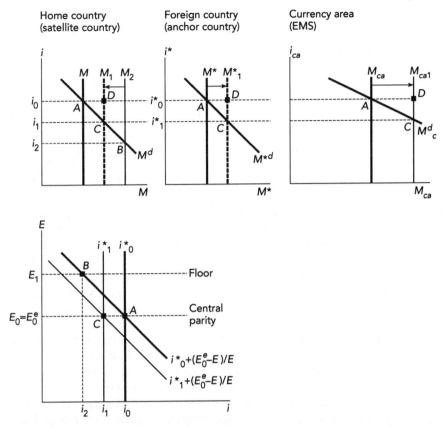

Fig. 3.7. A symmetrical currency area: monetary co-operation by the anchor country

For reasons of internal expansion, the home country wants to reduce its interest rate from i_0 to i_2. If the foreign country's interest rate remains at i^*_0, the home country's currency will depreciate (E_1) according to interest rate parity. It is assumed that E hits the floor of the exchange rate margin and both central banks have to intervene. The home country loses reserves and the foreign country gains them. If the foreign country (which is the anchor country) is co-operative such that it does not sterilize the reserve inflows, its money supply rises to M^*_1. The home country's reserve losses reduce its money supply from M_2 to M_1. There is again an interest rate identity (point C), but at a lower level, and the home country's foreign exchange rate gets back to its central parity level.

parity value. The (identical) interest rates of the currency area are determined by the area's money market.[13]

The short run impact of the monetary expansion by the satellite country on the interest rate of both countries and on their common exchange rate will be analysed under two alternative assumptions with respect to the behaviour of the anchor country. It either co-operates by pursuing non-sterilized interventions on the foreign exchange market (a symmetrical currency area) or it refuses to co-operate (an asymmetrical currency area).

Symmetrical Currency Areas: Monetary Co-operation by the Anchor Country.

Again, as in section 2.4, the home country wants to fight against a recession by reducing its interest rate to the level i_2, which implies an increase of its money supply to M_2. In order to dramatize the impact of this on the exchange rate a little, the home country's exchange rate moves immediately to its floor level (E_1 at point B in the lower panel of Fig. 3.7) according to the rules of the interest rate parity. Both central banks have to intervene: the home country's central bank has to sell foreign exchange (causing a decrease in international reserves) and the foreign country has to buy foreign exchange (causing an increase in international reserves). The deficit country (which is the 'satellite' country) must combine the decrease in its international reserves with a decrease in its money supply ($M_2 \rightarrow M_1$), since it must push its interest rate upwards.

As far as the anchor country is concerned, even though it must intervene in the foreign exchange market according to the rules of the EMS, it is free to decide whether the intervention is to be sterilized or not. If the anchor country follows the 'symmetrical' rules of the game, it has to increase the money supply ($M^* \rightarrow M^*_1$) by not sterilizing its reserve inflows. It co-operates with the satellite country, which wants to achieve a reduction in the interest rate in order to fight unemployment. The final result, for the whole currency area, of the monetary co-operation by the anchor country, would be that the interest rates fell to $i_1 = i^*_1$ and that the exchange rate would be again at E_0 (point C). As a matter of fact, this result would have been achieved less dramatically, and without any movements in international reserves, if both countries had co-operated more directly by decreasing their interest rates simultaneously towards $i_1 = i^*_1$. However, there are important reasons for the anchor country to refuse any monetary co-operation.

Asymmetrical Currency Areas: Monetary Hegemony and Monetary Crises

The only reason of hegemonic behaviour on the part of the anchor country can be found in its role in assuring the overall price stability of the area. If this goal coincides with the plea for internal price stability within the anchor country, conflict could arise in terms of monetary crises for the currency area. In Fig. 3.7, we have shown only the short run effects of a monetary expansion under the assumption of monetary co-operation. However, other effects emerge later from the point of view of the quantity theory of money. The lower interest rate in both countries ($i_1 = i^*_1$ at point C in the top panel of Fig. 3.7) creates an excess demand for goods in both countries which leads to a gradual increase in prices and interest rates so that both countries will end up at point D.

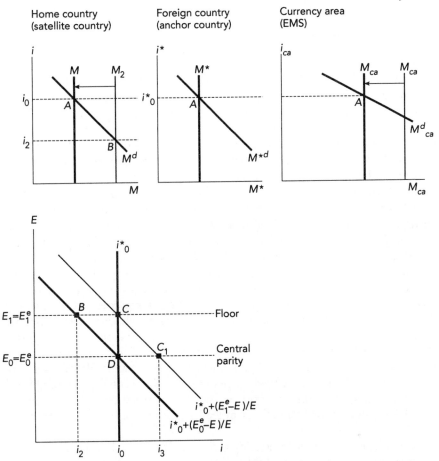

Fig. 3.8 An asymmetrical currency area: hegemonic behaviour by the anchor country

As in Fig. 3.7, the home country wants to reduce its interest rate toward i_2 (point B). The exchange rate rises to E_1 by hitting the floor. Reserves are lost to the anchor country which sterilizes them, since it wants to stick to its interest rate i^*_0. The home country is forced to raise its interest rate, for instance to the initial level i_0. However, the market may expect a realignment of the par value towards E^e_1 (point C) and the home country has to increase i towards i_3 (point C_1).

In order to prevent such an outcome, the anchor country refuses any monetary co-operation. Fig. 3.8 illustrates one possible interpretation of the past crises within the EMS. As in Fig. 3.7, the initial monetary equilibrium of the currency area is at point A with $i_0 = i^*_0$ and $E_0 = E^e_0$ at the central parity value. Also as in Fig. 3.7, the home country expands its money supply with the subsequent decline of its interest rate to i_2 and the depreciation towards the floor (E_1 at point B). Again, interventions by both central banks take place on the foreign exchange market, but now, those of the anchor country are sterilized, with the result that its interest rate remains at the level of i^*_0. Thus, only the satellite country—which is the deficit country—must sterilize in order to bring its interest rate back to a higher level.

Up to now, the scenario has been similar to that of monetary co-operation except for the fact that the anchor country's interest rate remains at i^*_0. However, the interest rate differential (i_2, i^*_0) and the subsequent depreciation of E_1 may trigger expectations about a realignment by pushing the expected exchange rate towards the level E^e_1 (point C), forcing the satellite country to go back to its initial interest rate i_0. However, its exchange rate remains at the floor (point C) so that it has to raise its interest rate to i_3 to regain the central parity value (point C_1). If the market does not believe that the central parity will be maintained—regardless of whether speculators are chartists or fundamentalists[14]—and the expected exchange rate is revised above E^e_1, while the satellite country is again at the floor, the currency area is probably ripe either for a realignment or for wider bands for the exchange rate as in the EMS in August 1993. Whether this action is due to the disciplined anchor country, or to the expansionary satellite country, or to the gnomes of Zurich will always remain a hotly disputed issue—but not for the reader of this book!

Box 3.2 reveals another interesting technical detail which imposes limits on the Bundesbank's ability to sterilize interventions on the foreign exchange market. The absolute maximum lies in the outstanding volume of domestic credit. However, in reality, it is even lower than this since certain domestic credits granted by the Bundesbank to the German banking sector could have a rather long maturity.

As far as the events of September 1992 are concerned, many domestic credits had a maturity of only one or two weeks, so that the Bundesbank did not renew them. The breakdown of the European Monetary System on 2 August 1993 was preceded by a rise in international reserves of DM 52 bn. (see the lower panel of Box 3.2). It was neutralized in the same way as in September 1992, namely in August 93 by a decline in domestic credit of DM 62 billions. The rapid solution of each of the monetary crises was in the interest of the Bundesbank, since it would otherwise have lost the control of the monetary base.

Box 3.2. Technical limits of sterilized intervention policies by the German Bundesbank. Examples: 16 September 1992 and 2 August 1993

Deutsche Bundesbank
First Crisis Episode: Black Wednesday, 16 September 1992
Balance Sheet for 31 August and 30 September 1992 (DM bn.)

	Aug. 92	Sept. 92		Aug. 92	Sept. 92
Reserves	104	181	Monetary Base	284	279
Domestic Credit	237	144	Other	57	46
	341	325		341	325

Second Crisis Episode: Breakdown of the EMS, 2 August 1993
Balance Sheet for 15 July and 7 August 1993 (DM bn.)

	July 93	Aug. 93		July 93	Aug. 93
Reserves	108	160	Monetary Base	264	259
Domestic Credit	236	174	Other	80	75
	344	334		344	334

Source: Monatsberichte der Deutschen Bundesbank, October 1992 and September 1993.

Only time will tell whether both episodes were definite signals for the breakdown of the EMS. In August 1992, Great Britain and Italy left the EMS and in September 1993, the band of exchange rate fluctuations was widened to ± 15 per cent (except for Holland). As Box 3.3 indicates, hegemonic monetary systems can be fallible.

Box 3.3. Fallibility of hegemonic monetary systems: the dollar standard and DM standard

'In 1944, the delegates at Bretton Woods opted for a system based on what came to be called the dollar-gold standard. In 1979, the majority of the European Community chose a system centred on the D-Mark. Signficantly, there seems to have been a post-war need for any formal, monetary system to have a single currency around which others cluster. This is sometimes called hegemony, and the word is not entirely pejorative. Hegemony happens for obvious reasons, but above all because the currency is trusted. As a result, the clustering currencies hope to derive some credibility for their own monetary hopes and ambitions.

And yet the hegemony does not last. Over time, the dollar has gradually become less trusted. For the EMS, the conclusion is less clear-cut, but the double difficulties of 1992 and 1993 have undoubtedly weakened it. And the reason for the fallibility of hegemony is common to both my examples: at a certain point, the hegemonic power develops objectives of its own that conflict with those of the clusterers. For the dollar, it was America's desire to finance its war in Vietnam not by taxation but by borrowing: the result of that was to set off a long and painful inflation that affected the whole world. As for the D-Mark, it was affected by German reunification in 1989, and by the spending programmes and currency convertibility that went with reunification. The result was that German interest rates needed to be higher than would otherwise have been the case—and that change proved painful for all Germany's ERM partners.

For most clusterers and would-be clusterers, the moral of these two episodes is clear: clustering is not for ever. While it lasts, it may be convenient for the clusterers. It may also confer some credibility on them. But these virtues are not theirs by right; they can disappear if the currency at the centre is hit by a shock or by a change in its government's domestic priorities. Since shocks do happen and a country's priorities do change, it is foolish to take a fallible currency and call it a system.' Pennant-Rea (1994).

Notes

1. However, this relative price is equal to one in the extreme version of purchasing power parity (ch. 2).
2. However, a parallel foreign exchange market will emerge in which the exchange rate will diverge from the official one.
3. As we shall see in the Appendix B of ch. 5, the validity of uncovered interest rate parity is strongly challenged by empirical evidence. Nevertheless, it is retained in many models of exchange rate determination on pragmatic grounds, since the models which take the exchange rate risk into account also lack empirical support; see Isard (1991).
4. The above formula (3.1) is derived as follows. An American investor obtains a gross return of $(1 + i) \times 1$ dollar when he holds one dollar in domestic assets. This same dollar could also be invested in German assets. He buys German marks equal to 1 dollar/E and holds German interest-bearing assets which yield a gross return of $[(1 + i^*)/E] \times 1$ dollar. At the end of the period, the investor converts the gross return in German marks back into dollars at an exchange rate which is uncertain and he obtains the *expected* dollar value of the gross return equal to $[E^e(1 + i^*)/E] \times 1$ dollar. The exchange rate mechanism makes the two types of return equal:

$$(1 + i) \times 1 \text{ dollar} = [E^e(1 + i^*)/E] \times 1 \text{ dollar}$$

$$(1 + i)/(1 + i^*) = E^e/E$$

$$(1 + i)/(1 + i^*) - (1 + i^*)/(1 + i^*) = E^e/E - E/E$$

$$(i - i^*)/(1 + i^*) = (E^e - E)/E$$

By neglecting the term $1/(1 + i^*)$, which is near to unity for small values of i^*, we obtain formula (3.1).
5. The interest parity of formula (3.1) cannot be applied to medium and long term financial assets, since their return includes another expected return element, the

expected gain or loss in the capital value. We shall choose the extreme example of perpetual consols. Their market price is equal to the ratio of the annual interest payments to the current long term interest rate. Their expected capital value is again equal to the annual interest payments divided by the expected long term interest rate (i^e). The *expected* domestic return rate on consols would be $i + i/i^e - 1$.

6. Transaction costs are neglected. Taking a risk premium into account, as in the next chapter, there will only be a certain portfolio shift in favour of foreign assets.

7. In a system of fixed exchange rates (like that of the EMS) in which the market expects a realignment of the central parity, there will be massive capital outflows when the government and the central bank hesitate to correct the par value.

8. It should be noted that there is, however, a return differential between domestic and foreign *investors* in the case of $i \neq i^*$. The domestic residents obtain a return of i_1 on domestic assets and a return of i^*_0 on foreign assets minus the expected depreciation rate of the foreign currency (by $i^*_0 - i_1$). In both investment cases, the domestic investor obtains as net return i_1. Foreigners receive the higher return i^*_0: either the interest rate of i^*_0 on their country's assets or the lower interest rate of i_1 abroad plus the expected appreciation rate (by $i^*_0 - i_1$).

9. The reader should not worry about the underdetermination of the above equation system. We are still in the framework of partial macroeconomic analysis.

10. A survey of these empirical studies is contained in Appendix B of ch. 5.

11. The return differential may even increase, if individuals become convinced that the central bank will not take serious action to prevent the depreciation. In that case, E^e_0 will be revised upwards and the new schedule of the interest rate parity (not drawn in Fig. 3.6) may pass through point D.

12. The effects of sterilized and non-sterilized interventions have been analysed by Branson (1979), Marston (1980), Obstfeld (1982, 1983), Tryon (1983), Genberg (1984), and Bordo and Schwartz (1990). The last study analysed the conduct and scale of official interventions by monetary authorities in the United States, Japan; and West Germany since the Plaza Agreement (of 1985) about a managed float. Relative to the trading volume and the stock of internationally traded assets denominated in foreign currencies, intervention was small and sporadic, hence its effects were at best transitory. Useful surveys of the recent literature are in Edison (1993), Dominguez and Frankel (1993), and in Taylor (1995).

As already Mussa (1981) noticed, interventions may have an indirect and durable impact on the exchange rate, if they are able to modify exchange rate expectations. This case implies that the monetary authorities have better information than the public and that they want to reveal this better information through actions in the foreign exchange market.

13. The link between the currency area's interest rate and third countries is established by another interest rate parity which is not illustrated in Fig. 3.7.

14. These types of expectations will be discussed in sect. 4.4.

4

A PORTFOLIO APPROACH TO THE EXCHANGE RATE: INTEREST RATE PARITY WITH RISK PREMIUMS

The monetary approach suffers from its assumption that financial investors are risk neutral with regard to their firm expectations about the future exchange rate. This defect is overcome in the portfolio approach, where the determination of the exchange rate is necessarily more complex. However, interest rate parity could still be used by adding a currency risk premium reflecting the risk aversion and the share of risky assets in the total portfolio. Three additional issues are treated in this chapter, namely: why exchange rate stabilization policies are becoming more effective; how expectations about the future exchange rate are formed; and the existence of another risk premium when there are capital controls.

4.1. Aversion to Currency Risks

Interest rate parity implied perfect substitutability between domestic and foreign financial assets *and* the absence of any foreign exchange controls. One important element of perfect substitutability concerns risk neutrality with respect to exchange rate risks. If individuals are risk averse, they will not consider the return on foreign assets as comparable or substitutable with the riskless return on domestic assets. They will require a higher yield on foreign assets to compensate for their risk aversion (risk premium), or they will hedge against the currency risk in the forward exchange market (covered interest rate parity).

If exchange rate risks are covered, the expected exchange rate (E^e) of equation (3.1) has to be replaced by the forward market rate for foreign exchange rate (F_0)[1]:

$$i = i^* + (F_0 - E)/E \qquad (4.1)$$

Unfortunately, forward rates are very bad predictors of future spot rates.[2] One possible interpretation of this systematic expectation failure is that the unexpected change in the future spot rates is triggered by 'news' which, for expectations between t and $t+1$, becomes known only after time t. This news could take the form of unexpected policy changes, surprising new statistical information, or other unknown events which have exchange rate implications.

The systematic failure of the forward rate as a reliable predictor of future spot rates also has implications for the uncovered interest rate parity. In the absence of any direct recorded data on expected future exchange rates, the uncovered interest rate parity cannot be tested directly. For empirical tests, the forward rate is often chosen as the market indicator for the general state of exchange rate expectations within the economy.[3] Since forward rates are highly unreliable for predicting future exchange rates, predictions of future exchange rates based on uncovered interest rate parity are also highly inaccurate.

An alternative way of handling the systematic bias of the forward rate for future spot rates is to reformulate the uncovered interest rate parity by including a currency risk premium (CRP). The latter is linked to exchange rate risk (or currency risk) which emerges for positions which are not covered by the forward market:

$$i = i^* + (E^e - E)/E - CRP \qquad (4.2)$$

The risk premium enters equation (4.2) as a negative term. The equation again indicates interest rate parity after the risk premium has been subtracted from the level of the foreign interest rate (or from the expected change in the exchange rate). With static exchange rate expectations $[(E^e - E)/E] = 0$, the foreign interest rate is higher than the domestic interest rate by the amount of the risk premium.

By making the right-hand expression of equation (4.1) equal to the right-hand expression of equation (4.2), we obtain:

$$E^e = F_0 + E \times CRP \qquad (4.3)$$

indicating that the expected exchange rate is equal to the forward rate plus the absolute value of the risk premium (i.e. the risk premium in percentage points (CRP) multiplied by the current exchange rate (E)). Equation (4.3) shows that, with aversion to currency risks, the forward exchange rate does not reflect the exchange rate expectations of the market.

4.2. Currency risk premium

Uncovered Interest Rate Parity with Currency Risk Premium

If the assumption of static exchange rate expectations is abandoned and if one assumes instead that the interest rates are identical ($i = i^*$), the risk premium must be equal to the expected rate of depreciation of the domestic currency, which is the same thing as the expected rate of appreciation of the foreign currency. Foreign financial assets yield an expected return higher than domestic ones by $CRP = (E^e - E)/E$.

In Fig. 4.1 we have drawn the uncovered interest rate parity with risk neutrality (dotted line) and with risk aversion (bold line). The vertical (or horizontal) distance between the lines indicates the currency risk premium. Under static exchange rate expectations ($(E^e - E)/E = 0$), the foreign interest rate is higher than the domestic interest rate by the amount of CRP (point B). Where the interest rates are identical, the precise expected rate of appreciation of the foreign currency will be at point C, once again equal to CRP. The mechanism by which this expected change in the exchange rate takes place is either an increase in E^e (by analogy with formula (4.3)) or a fall in E.

The simultaneous determination of the exchange rate and the domestic interest rate is very similar to the determination of the interest parity under risk neutrality, if a constant currency risk premium (CRP_0) is assumed. We shall illustrate this point by the previous example of an expansionary monetary policy which produces the same effects on the economy with risk aversion (Fig. 4.2) as under risk neutrality (Fig. 3.5): a decline in i and an upward revision of the expected exchange rate as result of the future rise in P; a depreciation of the domestic currency over the long run level of E (overshooting), creating the expectation of a future appreciation. However, in contrast to the hypothesis of perfect capital mobility, there always remains a return differential in favour of

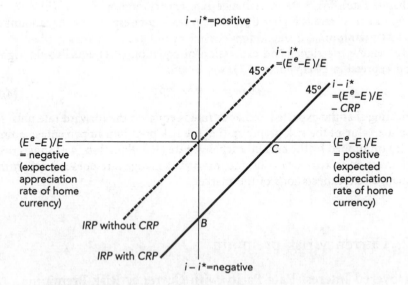

Fig. 4.1. The uncovered interest rate parity with currency risk premium

Aversion to currency risks involves a higher required return on foreign financial assets. Two possible cases are indicated by points B and C. The currency risk premium is either equal to the interest rate differential in favour of the foreign country with static exchange rate expectations (point B) or equal to the expected rate of appreciation of the foreign currency with identical interest rates (point C).

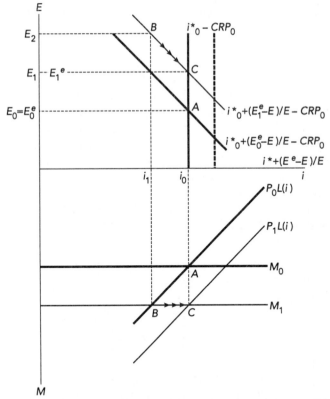

Fig. 4.2. Interest rate parity with risk premium and the overshooting phenomenon

The initial equilibrium is at point A. The expansionary monetary policy (decline of i_o towards i_1) gives rise immediately to a revision of exchange rate expectations (an upward shift of the foreign-return schedule towards point C). The domestic currency depreciates (point B) above its long run equilibrium level (point C).

foreign assets by the amount of CRP_0. The subsequent long-run adjustment process again consists of higher P, higher i and a gradual appreciation of the domestic currency towards point C. At point C, with static exchange rate expectations, the foreign interest rate must be again above the domestic one by CRP_0.

Determination of the Currency Risk Premium

The macroeconomic impact of the expansionary monetary policy will diverge from the above pattern, if the currency risk premium is an increasing function of the holdings of foreign financial assets, and no longer a constant one. It is true that our description of the exchange rate movement does not necessitate a further accumulation of foreign assets provided that capital flows are only incipient capital flows. But, if the flows do happen, an increasing return differential may be necessary.

The (microeconomic) determination of the risk premium is illustrated in Fig. 4.3. We assume that domestic and foreign assets, B and EF, are short-term claims (time deposits, for instance). F represents foreign assets expressed in foreign currency. Furthermore, we assume static exchange rate expectations $(E^e = E)$ so that $(E^e - E)/E = 0$. The total portfolio (W) is composed of both types of assets (principle of risk diversification). The line iA indicates the expected return and the riskiness of various portfolio compositions. When the whole portfolio consists of only the riskless domestic assets $(EF/W = 0)$, the return is Oi and the standard deviation is zero. At the other extreme, the portfolio contains only foreign assets $(EF/W = 1)$ such that the expected portfolio return is Oi^* and the standard deviation is OS_{max}. The indifference

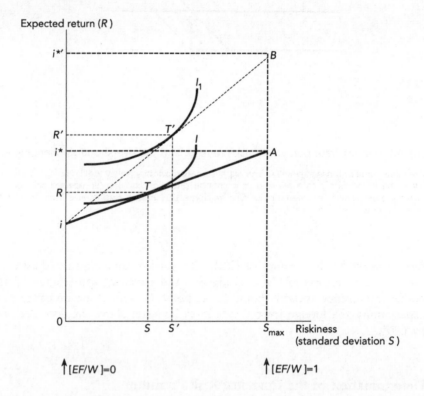

Fig. 4.3. Portfolio selection for domestic and foreign financial assets by a risk-averse investor

The initial optimal portfolio selection is at point T requiring an interest differential of i^*-i by assuming $E=E^e$. A higher ratio of EF over W can only be brought about by the higher foreign interest rate i^* (point T').

curves, I and I_1, show the investor's risk aversion. Welfare rises with a higher expected return and falls with an increase in riskiness. The optimum portfolio selection is at the tangency point T.[4]

With static exchange rate expectations, the market risk premium is $CRP = i^* - i$. However, even with this risk premium, the investor is not indifferent between holding domestic and foreign assets. He chooses a precise diversification of the assets in accordance with his risk aversion (point T).

An increase in the foreign interest rate from i^* to $i^{*\prime}$ raises the expected return. Exchange rate expectations remain static. The return-risk opportunity line rotates to iB and the investor chooses the higher indifference curve I_1 at the tangency point T'. The expected portfolio return increases from OR to OR' and its riskiness from OS to OS'. The fraction of foreign assets at point T' is higher than at point T since a higher standard deviation is only conceivable with a higher share of foreign assets in the total portfolio.

The risk premium (CRP) of equation (4.2) is not a constant, it increases with a rising exposure to the foreign exchange risk illustrated by the ratio EF/W. In Fig. 4.4 we have drawn one possible behaviour pattern for the risk premium as the difference between i^* and i. It does not need to be linear as assumed in Fig. 4.4. The portfolio diversification at point T (T') in Fig. 4.4 corresponds to that at point T (T') in Fig. 4.3.[5]

With imperfect asset substitutability and a variable risk premium, the simultaneous determination of the exchange rate and the domestic interest

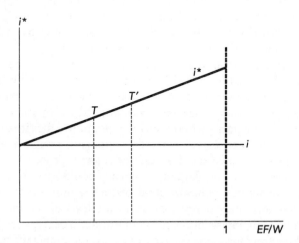

Fig. 4.4. Uncovered interest rate parity with increasing currency risk premium

With static exchange rate expectations a higher ratio of foreign financial assets over the total volume of financial assets can only be realized by a higher interest differential i^*-i, representing an increasing currency risk premium.

rate becomes far more complicated than with risk neutrality or risk aversion with a constant currency risk premium. In the following section and in the Appendix we shall illustrate the main elements of such a model, usually called the portfolio approach to the determination of the exchange rate.

4.3. A Portfolio Model (Reduced Form) and Exchange Rate Stabilization Policies

In the Appendix of the present chapter we have described the portfolio model for the simultaneous determination of the exchange rate and the interest rate. Since it is a rather complicated model, we shall consider here the simpler formulation, or reduced form, of exchange rate determination under imperfect substitutability between domestic and foreign financial assets on the basis of the risk-premium-augmented uncovered interest rate parity of formula (4.2). The determinants of the exchange rate become more explicit by rewriting it as:

$$E = E^e / \left[1 + i - i^* + CRP(EF/W) \right] \qquad (4.2a)$$

Explicitly we have expressed the risk premium as an increasing function of EF/W.

For interpreting formula (4.2a), there are two extreme cases to mention: $i = i^*$ and $E = E^e$. Identical interest rates imply that $E < E^e$. Since foreign assets are risky, they have to yield a higher return rate than domestic assets from the point of view of domestic investors. In fact, they yield a higher expected return in terms of the expectation of a future appreciation of the foreign currency. Furthermore, the difference between E and E^e has to increase with a larger share of foreign financial assets within the total portfolio.

The other extreme case, $E = E^e$, requires that $i^* > i$. Again, the argument is the same. The required higher yield on foreign assets is now obtained by a higher foreign interest rate. We shall continue to consider this particular case in order to analyse exchange rate stabilization policies. In section 3.2 which treated the interest rate parity without any risk premium, the situation of $i^* > i$ was only conceivable with $E > E^e$ since domestic and foreign financial assets were perfectly substitutable (identical rates of return). From a policy point of view, the depreciation of the domestic currency could only be avoided by a non-sterilized intervention policy or other restrictive monetary policies which would bring the domestic interest rate up to the level of the foreign interest rate. Furthermore, any intervention policy of the sterilized type (selling foreign exchange and neutralizing its restrictive impact on the monetary base by other policy instruments) was regarded not only as ineffective for avoiding the depreciation but also as costly by losing considerable amounts of foreign exchange.

This latter policy assessment has to be corrected if one works with the assumption of imperfect substitutability of domestic and foreign financial assets. Assume again that the foreign country—and it may also be the anchor country of a currency area—increases its interest rate. This external shock, even under the risk-augmented interest rate parity of equation (4.2a), would lead *ceteris paribus* to a depreciation of the domestic currency. Assume further that the central bank intervenes in the foreign exchange market: It sells foreign exchange. The private sector possesses more foreign exchange ($E\Delta F$) and less money holdings ($-\Delta M$). On the other hand, for maintaining the initial quantity of money, the central bank pursues an expansionary open market policy by buying domestic bonds (B), and the private sector now has, in addition, less bonds ($-\Delta B$) and more money holdings ($+\Delta M$). Both actions imply that the total portfolio of the private sector remains constant, but its composition has changed: more foreign exchange ($+E\Delta F$) and less domestic bonds ($-\Delta B$) where $E\Delta F - \Delta B = 0$.

Its portfolio has become riskier and the risk premium of formula (4.2a) increases. Consequently, the initial depreciation of the domestic currency (as a consequence of Δi^*) will be reversed. There is no need, for domestic investors, that foreign assets become less attractive through the expectation of a future depreciation of the foreign currency because these foreign assets have already become less attractive via $E\Delta F$ and, by this, via ΔCRP. In the extreme case where $\Delta i^* = \Delta CRP$, the exchange rate would return to its initial level and the sterilized intervention policy would be fully successful.[6]

4.4. Exchange Rate Expectations

Short Run and Long Run

We shall continue with the simpler formulation, or reduced form of the portfolio model (4.2a), by rewriting it as:

$$E_t = E^e_t / (1 + i_t - i^*_t + CRP_t) \qquad (4.2b)$$

Implicitly, for the future, we only took account of one period (t stands for one month, three months, or one year), and not of several periods linking the short run with the long run. E^e_t has to be interpreted as the expected exchange rate for the end of period t, and E_t is the exchange rate prevailing at the beginning of period t.

For the future period $t+1$, the exchange rate at the beginning of period $t+1$, E_{t+1}, will be determined by variables similar to those of formula (4.2b):

$$E_{t+1} = E^e_{t+1} / (1 + i_{t+1} - i^*_{t+1} + CRP_{t+1}) \qquad (4.4)$$

E_{t+1} is clearly the expected exchange rate at the beginning of $t+1$, and it must be consistent with the expected exchange rate E^e_t so that $E^e_t = E_{t+1}$.[7] By replacing E^e_t of formula (4.2b) with E_{t+1} of formula (4.4), we obtain:

$$E_t = E^e_{t+1} / (1 + i_t - i^*_t + CRP_t)(1 + i_{t+1} - i^*_{t+1} + CRP_{t+1}) \qquad (4.5)$$

We can extend the above formula to an arbitrary number of periods which should represent the long run:

$$E_t = E^e_{t+n} / (1 + i_t - i^*_t + CRP_t) (1 + i_{t+1} - i^*_{t+1} + CRP_{t+1})$$
$$\cdots (1 + i_{t+n} - i^*_{t+n} + CRP_{t+n}) \tag{4.6}$$

Formula (4.6) highlights the fact that the actual exchange rate, E_t, is predominantly determined by future events which, by definition, are expected. Or, in other words, the present exchange rate contains all information about the probable future value of the is, i^*s, CRPs, and the long-rate exchange rate E^e_{t+n}, which is the *anchor* of the current exchange rate. It also becomes evident that any new information about the future will be registered immediately by the current level of the exchange rate. Thus, only unexpected news can move today's exchange rate away from yesterday's exchange rate. In this sense, changes in the exchange rate become unpredictable, except for those happy few who have new information but do not transmit it to the public.[8]

Fundamentalists and Chartists

Our monetary and financial analysis of the exchange rate is of the 'fundamentalist' type. Fundamentalists and chartists differ from one another with respect to the type of expectation formation. Fundamentalists look at the macroeconomic fundamentals of exchange rate determination, such as interest rate differentials and purchasing power parity; in the next chapters we shall treat some other fundamentals. Chartists, on the other hand, tend to forecast by extrapolating recent trends if they have 'bandwagon expectations'. If chartists predominate the foreign exchange market, they can exacerbate (or 'destabilize') swings in the exchange rate. The reason is that they will buy on upswings, thus driving the price up, and sell on downswings, thus forcing the price down. In that case the exchange rate deviates from its fundamentals which proves the existence of 'bubbles'.[9]

It is also conceivable, and even probable, that individuals, given short horizons, tend to forecast by extrapolating from recent trends, while, over longer horizons, they predict a return to fundamentals (see Box 4.1). This type of expectation hypothesis can be formalized as follows. Fundamentalists form their exchange rate expectations (E^e) in the following way:

$$E^e = E + a(E_{lr} - E) \tag{4.7}$$

E_{lr} is the long-run exchange rate. In our previous analysis, we derived it from the evolution of the domestic and foreign price levels, as the fundamental determinant of long-run exchange rates according to purchasing power parity. The coefficient a (where $a \leq 1$) indicates the time profile of expectations. If, for instance, we are concerned with yearly forecasts of exchange rates and the economic model predicts a return to PPP after two years, *a* will be 0.5 (assuming additionally that the adjustment process towards E_{lr} is linear).

Box 4.1. Techniques used by foreign exchange forecasting services

The August issues of *Euromoney* present an annual review of foreign exchange forecasting services. Many of them indicate whether they use technical models (i.e. charts) or whether they rely on economic fundamentals.

Year	Number of services surveyed*	Number using only technical models	Number using only fundamentals	Number using both models
1978	23	3	19	0
1981	13	1	11	0
1983	11	8	1	1
1984	13	9	0	2
1985	24	15	5	3
1986	34	20	8	4
1987	31	16	6	5
1988	31	18	7	6

In 1978, only three firms used technical analysis while 19 based their forecast on fundamentals. In 1988 the opposite was the case: only seven out of 31 relied exclusively on fundamentals. The others used either the technical models (18) or even both forecasting models (6).
    *Some services did not indicate the nature of their technique.
    Source: *Euromoney*, August issues and Frankel and Froot (1990): 184. See also Ito (1990).

By contrast, chartists look at the past behaviour of exchange rates and extrapolate the past trend into the future:

$$E^e = E + b(E - E_{t-1}) \tag{4.8}$$

E_{t-1} is the exchange rate of the previous period. Many other past periods may of course be taken into account.

However, as we observed in Box 4.1, traders may use both techniques simultaneously. In combining formulas (4.7) and (4.8), we could establish a weighted average of expectation formation as suggested by Camen and Genberg (1990: 30):

$$E^e = [pE + p\, a(E_{lr} - E)] + [(1 - p)\, E + (1 - p)\, b\, (E - E_{t-1})]$$
$$= E + p\, a(E_{lr} - E) + (1 - p)\, b\, (E - E_{t-1}) \tag{4.9}$$

The weight *p* can be interpreted as the probability that the bubble will burst during the forecasting period. By contrast, the weight $(1 - p)$ indicates the probability that the bubble will continue over the period studied. Thus, if *p* is high, expectations are mainly formed on the basis of fundamentals. In that case, the expected and, by this, the actual exchange rate would mainly reflect its fundamental determinants.

If p equals one, we are in a world of rational expectations. In addition, if expectations are formed without any random forecast error, we are in a world of perfect foresight. All those exchange rate models which work with rational expectations are of the fundamentalist type. It also should be emphasized that exchange rate expectations play an important role under the regime of fixed exchange rates, if the central parity does not reflect any longer the fundamentals of the fixed peg. They can give rise to waves of 'speculation' and to a 'monetary crisis' which may end up with a change of the central parity.

4.5. Capital Controls and Political Risk Premium

At the beginning of the chapter we observed that deviations from the covered interest rate parity were rather insignificant and that they could be explained by transaction costs. According to Dooley and Isard (1980), any larger deviations can only emerge where there are capital controls.

There are two types of risks associated with holding foreign assets, country risks and currency risks. Country risks refer to default risk (indebted developing countries are the most obvious example) and to political risk. The latter is associated with the possibility of future capital controls. In many cases, capital controls also restrict forward transactions.[10]

In this particular case, the covered interest rate parity of formula (4.1) has to be modified by adding a risk premium which we will call the political risk premium (*PRP*):

$$i = i^* + (F_0 - E)/E - PRP \qquad (4.10)$$

It should be stressed that this risk premium refers to the danger of *future* capital controls or to the *future* enforcement of existing capital controls. For this reason, the domestic investor requires a covered return on foreign assets which is higher than the return on domestic assets. He runs the risk of not being able to dispose freely of the funds he has invested abroad. Since capital controls are also implemented with respect to current purchases of foreign exchange, the currency-risk-premium-augmented uncovered interest rate parity of formula (4.2) is affected in a similar way:

$$i = i^* + (E^e - E)/E - CRP - PRP \qquad (4.11)$$

Its interpretation is identical to that of the covered interest rate parity.

4.6. A Synopsis of the Financial Approach

We are now able to classify the types of exchange rate determination under various assumptions regarding the degree of substitutability between domestic

Table 4.1. A synopsis of the financial approach to the exchange rate

Degree of capital mobility	Uncovered transactions in the foreign exchange market	Covered transactions in the foreign exchange market
Risk neutrality		
Unrestricted capital mobility		
The highest degree of financial integration: monetary integration	$E = E^e$ and $i = i^*$	$E = F_0$ and $i = i^*$
Unrestricted capital mobility		
A lower degree of financial integration: perfect substitutability	$E = E^e/(1 + i - i^*)$	$E = F_0/(1 + i - i^*)$
Risk aversion		
Unrestricted capital mobility:		
The lowest degree of financial integration	$E = E^e/(1 + i - i^* + CRP)$	$E = F_0/(1 + i - i^*)$
Restricted capital mobility: Financial disintegration	$E = E^e/(1 + i - i^* + CRP + PRP)$	$E = F_0/(1 + i - i^* + PRP)$

and foreign financial assets and the degree of capital controls. Table 4.1 summarizes the financial approaches to the exchange rate for the different sets of assumptions.

Following van Gemert and Gruijters (1994: 274–6), we have classified the various combinations of substitutability and capital controls into several degrees of financial integration. The highest is that of monetary integration where there are still two currencies, which are linked by irrevocably fixed exchange rates (as in the case of the Austrian schilling/German mark with a band of ± 0.11 per cent). The other extreme is financial disintegration, which is typical when there are capital controls.

4.7. Real Interest Rate Parity

Nominal and Real Exchange Rates

At the end of the present chapter and as a link to Part II which deals with the real exchange rate, we still have to explain the interest rate parity in real terms, i.e. in terms of real interest rates and of the expected change in the real exchange rate. As soon as the general price level is no longer constant, we have to distinguish between nominal and real values. This procedure also has to be applied to the exchange rate. The real exchange rate (e) is defined as:

$$e = EP^*/P \tag{4.12}$$

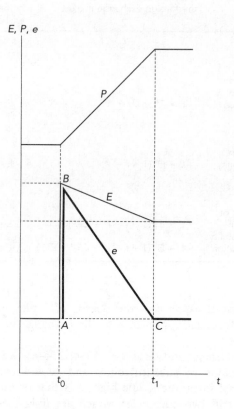

Fig. 4.5. Overshooting and the evolution of the nominal and real exchange rates

The overshooting concerns the nominal and real exchange rates (point *B*). Afterwards a real appreciation (towards point *C*) occurs for two reasons. There is both a nominal appreciation as well as a rise in the price level.

The precise nature of the real exchange rate will be discussed in the next chapter. For the moment, we shall show the evolution of *E* and *P* in our example of overshooting as the immediate reaction of an expansionary monetary policy. Later, we shall relate the real interest differential to the expected change in the real exchange rate.

The evolution of the real exchange rate can be derived from the behaviour pattern of *E* and *P* (Fig. 4.5). Immediately after the emergence of the monetary shock (point *B*), the real depreciation is identical with the nominal depreciation, since the domestic price level is still unchanged; we assume a constant foreign price level (P^*). After time t_0, a nominal appreciation takes place. This also holds for the real exchange rate. However, the real appreciation is very much larger. It has two sources: the nominal appreciation and the rising domestic price level. Purchasing power parity is only realized in the very long run, that is at point *C*, where the real exchange rate has reached its former level.

It is precisely this real exchange rate behaviour which is considered to be a 'disorderly' element in our present exchange rate regime. There are two opposing views on this issue. On the one hand, those economists who only consider the financial sector of the economy regard the exchange rate mechanism as beneficial since it equilibrates the financial markets at all times. On the other hand, those who look at the real sector of the economy are worried about the distortion of relative prices for domestic and foreign goods, which would lead to a misallocation of resources.

However, a counterargument to this latter view does not blame the exchange rate mechanism in itself, but rather the underlying policies which provoke the fluctuation in the real exchange. In our example, it was the expansionary monetary policy which caused the real exchange rate to overshoot. A steady, non-discretionary monetary policy would have avoided the turbulence in the nominal and real exchange rates.

In defense of the present exchange rate regime, we may cite an alternative cause of the excessive fluctuation in the real exchange rate. On the one hand, it was the result of the monetary shock. On the other hand, it could be said to be caused by price rigidities in the goods market for, if they were absent, the price level would move immediately to its new long-run value, the interest rate would be unchanged, and the nominal exchange rate would immediately jump to its long-run equilibrium level so that the real exchange rate would remain unchanged. In this extreme textbook case, we would obtain the 'classical' link between *M* and *E* as:

higher quantity of money → higher price level → nominal depreciation.

However, with price rigidities, the monetary expansion has the following effect during the adjustment process:

higher quantity of money → lower interest rate → nominal and real depreciation → increase in the price level → higher interest rate → nominal and real appreciation.

Thus, the volatility of the real exchange rate can be attributed to discretionary monetary policy and to the price rigidities in the goods markets.

Nominal and Real Interest Rate Parity

The uncovered interest rate parity without any risk premium, described in section 3.2, was expressed in terms of the nominal interest rate (i, i^*) and the nominal exchange rate (E). It can be reformulated in terms of the real interest rate (r, r^*) and the real exchange rate (e) (see Box 4.2).

Equations (4.13) and (4.14) are compared in Fig. 4.6, where the previous example of overshooting is extended. The left panel contains the familiar geometrical illustration of the nominal interest rate parity. The expansionary monetary policy reduces the domestic nominal interest rate from i_0 to i_1. There is a subsequent rise in the price level which is expected as soon as the nominal interest rate falls. This new expected price level has an impact on the revision

---

Box 4.2. Algebraic analysis of nominal and real interest rate parity

The nominal interest rate is equal to the real interest rate (r) plus the expected inflation (π^e). Consequently, the nominal interest rate parity

$$i = i^* + (E^e - E)/E \tag{4.13}$$

can be written as

$$r + \pi^e = r^* + \pi^{*e} + (E^e - E)/E$$

$$r = r^* + (E^e - E)/E \qquad (\pi^e \longrightarrow \pi^{*e})$$

| expected rate of change of the nominal exchange rate | expected inflation differential |

$$(e^e - e)/e$$
expected rate of change
of the real exchange rate

$$r = r^* + (e^e - e)/e \tag{4.14}$$

where e^e is the expected real exchange rate. Thus, the expectation of a real depreciation can result from the expectation of a nominal depreciation which exceeds the expected inflation differential. If the expected nominal depreciation rate is equal to the expected inflation differential, namely $[(e^e - e)/e] = 0$, the real interest rates will equalize. This particular formation of exchange rate expectations uses the purchasing power parity which implies that ex ante real interest rates are equal across countries. This special interest rate parity is called the international Fisher parity.[11]

In order to compare the nominal and real exchange rate determination on the basis of uncovered interest rate parity, we shall rewrite equations (4.13) and (4.14) as:

$$E = E^e/(1 + i - i^*) \tag{4.13a}$$
$$e = e^e/(1 + r - r^*) \tag{4.14a}$$

Assume that the real interest rate differential is zero. In that case, we have $e = e^e$. If there is an (expected) inflation differential, there will also be a corresponding differential in nominal interest rates.

---

of the expected nominal exchange rate (E^e_1) and on the nominal interest rate which is the sum of the real interest rate and the expected inflation. The fall in the nominal interest rate (i_1), which incorporates the expected inflation rate, is smaller than the fall in the real interest rate (r_1). On the one hand, the nominal and real

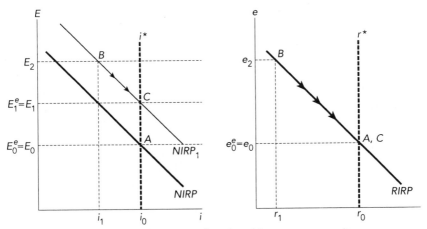

Fig. 4.6. Overshooting and the nominal and real interest rate parity

Numerical example:

NIRP
(1) Point A: $i_0 = i^* = 4\%$
(2) Point B: $i_1 = r_1 + \pi^e = 2\% + 1\% = 3\%$
$i_1 = i^* + (E^e_1 - E_2)/E_2 = 3\% = 4\% - 1\%$
(3) Point C: $i_0 = i^* = 4\%$

RIRP
$r_0 = r^* = 4\%$
$r_1 = 2\%$
$r_1 = r^* + (e^e_0 - e_2)/e_2 = 2\% = 4\% - 2\%$
$r_0 = r^* = 4\%$

interest rates decrease by the same amount. On the other hand, the nominal interest rate is again pushed upwards because of inflationary expectations.

The overshooting of the exchange rate is of the same size for the nominal and real exchange rates (point *B*) because, at the very beginning of the monetary expansion, the price level is still unchanged. Since there will be inflation, at least in the domestic country, the investor now has to calculate the rates of return in real values. For the domestic investor, the real return at point *B* is now r_1, i.e. i_1 minus the expected inflation rate. If the same investor holds foreign assets, he receives the higher foreign real return $r^* = i^*_0$ (there is no inflation in the foreign country), but he has to take into account the expected real depreciation of the foreign currency as a result of the expected nominal depreciation of the foreign currency and as the result of the higher inflation in the domestic country. Thus, for the domestic investor, the real return on domestic and foreign assets will be the same, namely r_1.[12]

At point *B*, the real interest rate differential $(r^* - r_1)$ is higher than the nominal interest rate differential $(i^* - i_1)$. On the one hand, the lower nominal interest rate differential results from the expected inflation in the domestic economy. On the other hand, the expected real appreciation $(e_2 - e_0)$ exceeds the expected nominal appreciation $(E_2 - E_1)$. The subsequent real appreciation is stronger than the nominal appreciation because the movement of the real exchange rate is also determined by the rise in the domestic price level. At the end of the adjustment process (point *C*), we assume that the inflation rate falls to zero.[13]

In the macroeconomic approach to the real exchange rate, one possible illustration of the financial sector—the LM-sector—would be the real interest rate parity of formula (4.14), which stands for the real interest rate parity without any risk premium. If we add the various risk premiums of formula (4.11), that is, currency risk (*CRP*) and political risk (*PRP*), both expressed in percentage points:

$$i = i* + (E^e - E)/E - CRP - PRP \qquad (4.11)$$

and if we replace *i* by $r + \pi$ and *i** by $r* + \pi$, we obtain:

$$r + \pi^e = r* + \pi^{*e} + (E^e - E)/E - CRP - PRP$$

or

$$r = r* + (E^e - E)/E - (\pi^e - \pi^{*e}) - CRP - PRP$$

or

$$r = r* + (e^e - e)/e - CRP - PRP \qquad (4.15)$$

Formula (4.15) stands for the reduced form of the portfolio approach to the *real* exchange rate.[14]

However, both the nominal version (4.11) and real version (4.15) suffer from the constant terms *CRP* and *PRP*. In reality, the risk aversion rises as the foreign asset component (*EF*) of the portfolio (*W*) increases so that *CAP* and *PRP* should be conceived as an increasing function of *EF/W* as we already did in equation (4.2*a*):

$$r = r* + (e^e - e)/e - CRP (EF/W) - PRP (EF/W) \qquad (4.16)$$

In the macroeconomic framework of the determination of the real exchange rate, the financial sector will mainly be represented, for simplicity, by formula (4.15). But the reader should remember that the more appropriate version is that of (4.16).

Appendix: A More General Portfolio Model

Simultaneous Determination of the Exchange Rate and the Interest Rate

Under the assumption of perfect substitutability we had two equations—those of the interest rate parity and of the money market—for determining *E* and *i*. If domestic and foreign financial assets are imperfect substitutes as a consequence of increasing aversion to exchange rate risks when more foreign assets are held, the model of the financial sector has to consist of three markets, namely the market for money (M), the market for domestic bonds (B), and the market for foreign bonds (EF):

Money market
(*MM*-schedule) $M = m(i,\ i^*,\ f)W$ (4.17)

Market for domestic
bonds (*BB*-schedule) $B = b(i,\ i^*,\ f)W$ (4.18)

Market for foreign
bonds (*FF*-schedule) $EF = f(i,\ i^*,\ f)W$ (4.19)

The above formulation is derived from Branson (1979) and Branson and Henderson (1985). M, B, and F are the given stocks of money, domestic bonds and foreign bonds. To avoid the problem of capital gains and capital losses, both types of bonds are short-term ones. $m()$, $b()$, and $f()$ are the demand functions for the three categories of assets as fractions of total financial wealth (W). f represents the expected rate of depreciation $[(E^e - E)/E]$. Because of the wealth constraint

Wealth constraint $W = M + B + EF$ (4.20)

there are only two independent equilibrium conditions which determine E and i.

The portfolio equilibrium is represented in Fig. 4.A1 for a value of f equal to zero (individuals expect the present exchange rate for the future). We have drawn all three equilibrium schedules and not just the two. Their slopes can be explained as follows. Starting from any partial equilibrium point on each schedule, a higher E implies a higher W which increases the demand for each type of assets. The money market will be in equilibrium when i increases as it lowers the demand for money. The market for domestic bonds will be in equilibrium when i falls, because a lower i means a higher price for domestic bonds. However, in the market for foreign bonds, there is an excess supply because a higher E increases the supply (expressed in domestic currency) more than the demand. In order to increase demand, the domestic interest rate has to fall, causing a substitution towards foreign assets. Since the demand for foreign bonds reacts less to a change in the domestic interest rate than the demand for domestic bonds, the slope of the *FF*-line is less than that of the *BB*-line.[15]

We shall again analyse the effect of an expansionary monetary policy on the exchange rate and on the domestic interest rate. The domestic interest rate is now no longer strictly linked to the foreign interest rate (for the case of $f = 0$, i is no longer equal to i^*). The short-run impact of an expansionary monetary policy on the exchange rate operates via the substitution effect (a lower domestic interest rate increases the demand for foreign bonds). We assume that the expansionary monetary policy is effected through open market operations ($\Delta M = -\Delta B$). Consequently, total nominal wealth remains unchanged. In terms of Fig. 4.A2, the *MM*-curve and *BB*-curve shift to MM_1 and BB_1 and the new equilibrium point is at B, where the interest rate has fallen (i_1) and the exchange rate has risen (E_1). The decline in the domestic

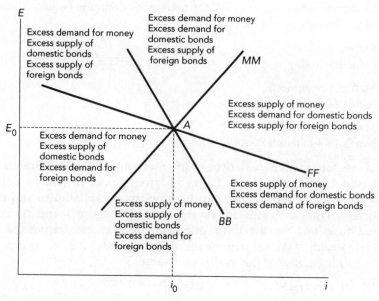

Fig. 4.A1. The determination of the exchange rate and interest rate according to the portfolio model

With static exchange rate expectations the slope of the three schedules can be explained by assuming an increase in E which involves higher wealth. The wealth effect creates an excess demand for money (which is eliminated by a rise in i) and an excess demand for domestic bonds (which is eliminated by a decline in i). With respect to foreign bonds, there will be an excess supply since the value of their outstanding stock increases. The excess supply is eliminated by a fall in i. The interest elasticity of the demand for foreign bonds is lower than that of the demand for domestic bonds.

interest rate increases the demand for foreign bonds. The increase in the exchange rate results from the higher demand for foreign bonds. It is satisfied by an increase in the domestic price of foreign bonds, i.e. by an increase in the exchange rate without any (additional) capital flows, because the stock of foreign bonds remains unchanged (no capital balance deficit). However, their value, expressed in domestic currency, has increased. The subsequent higher share of risky assets among the total portfolio requires a higher risk premium in terms of a higher differential between the domestic and foreign interest rate.[16]

The depreciation of the domestic currency is the immediate effect of the expansionary monetary policy (substitution effect) as described in Fig. 4.A2. We did not take into account the revision of exchange rate expectations according to purchasing power parity. This would shift the three schedules of Fig. 4.A2 upwards. After the immediate depreciation, an appreciation will emerge if $f > 0$ and if two other things occur. First, prices must adjust slowly to an excess demand in the goods market. Under normal conditions there will be a current account surplus (the relative price effect) and a corresponding capital balance deficit. The stock of foreign bonds (F) increases, causing an excess

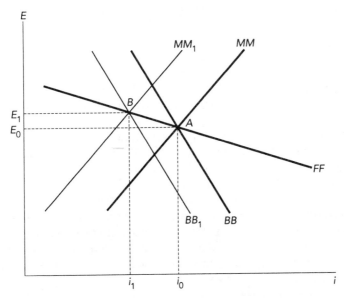

Fig. 4.A2. The portfolio model: the immediate impact of expansionary monetary policy

With open market operations ($\Delta M = -\Delta B$) total financial wealth remains unchanged. The increased stock of money and the reduced stock of domestic bonds shift the MM-schedule and the BB-schedule to the left. At the new equilibrium point B there is a fall in the domestic interest rate and a depreciation of the domestic currency.

supply of foreign bonds and, thus, an appreciation. Second, a wealth effect also occurs when the price level begins to rise, causing the real wealth level to fall. Savings occur so as to re-establish the former level of real wealth. Savings are also used for the purchase of additional foreign bonds (capital balance deficit). This further increase in the stock of foreign bonds is another reason for the future appreciation of the domestic currency.

Thus, we find similar (but not identical) impacts of an expansionary monetary policy on the exchange rate: first a depreciation (as described in Fig. 4.A2) and later an appreciation (which is not shown in Fig. 4.A2), as in the case of uncovered interest rate parity. However, the portfolio approach is richer, since it allows for the repercussions from the real sector (current account surplus) on the financial sector (increase in foreign financial assets) and, hence, on the dynamics of the exchange rate evolution.

Exchange Rate Stabilization Policies

As already explained in section 4.3, sterilized intervention policies can permanently influence the exchange rate under the assumption of imperfect substitutability between domestic and foreign financial assets. The bold lines of Fig. 4.A3a reproduce the portfolio model of Fig. 4.A1. The initial equilibrium is at point A. An external shock occurs in the form of a rise in the foreign interest rate which produces an excess demand for foreign assets and an excess supply of domestic bonds and money at point A. The equilibrium schedules shift to FF_1, BB_1, and MM_1 and the new equilibrium is established at point B, where the domestic currency is depreciated and the domestic interest rate has risen.

The subsequent intervention policy is successful not only for non-sterilized interventions (Fig. 4.A3b where $-\Delta M = E\Delta F$)[17] but also for sterilized interventions (Fig. 4.A3c where $-\Delta M = E\Delta F$ and $\Delta M = -\Delta B$ so that $E\Delta F = -\Delta B$ and $\Delta M = 0$). For both types of intervention, total wealth remains constant. In the first case (Fig. 4.A3b), the decrease in the money supply shifts the MM_1-schedule towards the position MM_2, and the increase in foreign bonds shifts the FF_1-schedule towards FF_2. As far as sterilized interventions are concerned (Fig. 4.A3c), the money stock remains constant. We have the same shift for the FF_1-line as in Fig. 4.A3b. Additionally, the reduction in the volume of domestic bonds shifts the BB_1-line towards BB_2.

We shall look at the latter case in more detail. The intervention operation ($-\Delta M = E\Delta F$) and the open market operation ($\Delta M = -\Delta B$) do not affect total wealth. What is changed by the sterilized intervention policy is the portfolio composition; see Branson (1979) and Claassen (1985). The money stock remains the same, but the private sector possesses more foreign bonds ($E\Delta F$) and fewer domestic bonds ($-\Delta B$). Since, by assumption, the two types of assets are not perfect substitutes, the excess supply of foreign assets drives the foreign exchange rate into an appreciation, and the excess demand for domestic bonds leads to a fall in the domestic interest rate. Thus, an appreciation can be realized by sterilized intervention policies with imperfect substitutability between domestic and foreign financial assets. It is, however, less pronounced than the one shown in Fig. 4.A3b. There are two causes for the decline in the interest rate. On the one hand, there is no decrease in the quantity of money as in the case for non-sterilized interventions. On the other hand, the interest yielding portfolio is exposed to a higher currency risk because there are more foreign bonds and fewer domestic bonds. The higher interest rate differential reflects the higher currency risk premium.

Notes

1. Empirical research has confirmed that deviations from the covered interest rate parity are minimal and are mainly explicable by transaction costs: see Appendix B of ch. 5.
2. See Appendix B of ch. 5.
3. See Isard (1991), MacDonald and Taylor (1992), and Appendix B of ch. 5.
4. On the vertical axis, i and $*$ are the interest rates and R the expected rate of return

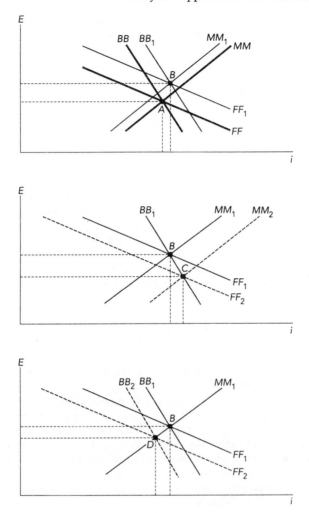

Fig. 4.A3. A rise in the foreign interest rate and intervention policy for avoiding depreciation

Fig. 4.A3a. Rise in the foreign interest rate and depreciation

—The rise in i^* shifts the total system from A to B.

Fig. 4.A3b. Non-sterilized intervention $(-\Delta M = E\Delta F)$ for avoiding depreciation

—Non-sterilized intervention policies operate with a reduction of the quantity of money with the result of an increase in i and an appreciation (point C).

Fig. 4.A3c. Sterilized intervention $(-\Delta M = E\Delta F$ and $+\Delta M = -\Delta B)$ for dampening depreciation

—With sterilized intervention, the fall in B decreases i and the rise in F produces the fall in E (point D).

of the portfolio where $R = (1 - f)i + fi^*$ for $f = EF/W$. The absolute return of the portfolio is RW. Under the alternative hypothesis of risk neutrality, the indifference curves would be horizontal lines and the portfolio choice would consist of the corner solution at point A (the total portfolio consisting exclusively of foreign assets) always assuming $E^e = E$.

5. A higher risk premium can be brought about by a higher i^* (as in Fig. 4.3 and 4.4), or by a lower i, or by the expectation of a future appreciation of the foreign currency. The sign of the risk premium is not necessarily negative as assumed in formula (4.2). In deriving the risk premium, we only looked at the *domestic* investor's risk (for instance, an American investor) when he holds foreign assets (for instance, German assets). But the foreign investor (i.e. the German investor) also requires a risk premium when he holds American financial assets. Thus, the relative strength of risk aversion in the two countries—and also in other countries—is one determining factor of the positive or negative sign of the risk premium. If domestic risk aversion is greater, the sign may be negative. Furthermore, if domestic investors are net lenders and foreign investors are net borrowers, the likelihood that foreigners accept having to pay a risk premium to our domestic investors in the form of a higher foreign interest rate increases.

6. As exposed in the Appendix A, the picture looks by far more sophisticated since there will be an impact on E *and* on i.

7. The end of period t coincides with the beginning of period $t+1$.

8. In this sense, the evolution of the exchange rate follows a random walk. The best forecast for tomorrow's exchange rate would be today's exchange rate. See also Appendix B of ch. 5.

9. 'If the reason that the price is high today is *only* because investors believe that the selling price will be high tomorrow—when 'fundamental' factors do not seem to justify such a price—then a bubble exists. To nonspecialists, the dramatic collapse of the stock market in October 1987 provides all the evidence that is needed to prove the existence of bubbles: otherwise, what event led to a downward revision of the value of the US capital stock by a quarter within hours?' Stiglitz (1990): 13, 16. Bubbles were discussed in the context of rational expectation models by Blanchard (1979) and were applied to exchange rate movements by Dornbusch (1982). A series of articles on this issue can be found in the Spring 1990 issue of the *Journal of Economic Perspectives*, 4.

10. See Claassen and Wyplosz (1985). Besides currency risk, default risk, and political risk, there are many other risks which have to be ignored. Keynes (1923) had already mentioned these in his famous *Tract on Monetary Reform*, 126–7: '. . . the various uncertainties of financial and political risk . . . introduce a further element which sometimes quite transcends the factor of relative interest. The possibility of financial trouble or political disturbance, and the quite appreciable probability of a moratorium in the event of any difficulties arising, or of the sudden introduction of exchange regulations which would interfere with the movement of balances out of the country, and even sometimes the contingency of a drastic demonetisation,— all these factors deter . . . [market participants], even when the exchange risk proper is eliminated, from maintaining large . . . balances at certain foreign centres.'

11. There are a series of econometric studies which show that the equalization of real interest rates across countries is not proved empirically, at least over the short run. See Appendix B of ch. 5.

12. For the foreign investor, the real return on his country's assets is $r^* = i^*$. If he holds the other country's assets, he obtains the lower real return r_1, but an additional return stems from the expected real appreciation of the other country's currency.

13. If the same monetary expansion rate continues in the future, the $NIRP_1$ schedule would shift steadily upwards, while the $RIRP$ schedule would remain unchanged.

14. The Fisher equation of the nominal interest rate had been written as $i = r + \pi^e$. It would be more appropriate to formulate it as $i = r + \pi^e + r\pi^e$. The last term, which is admittedly small and, therefore, often forgotten, expresses the necessity for the nominal interest rate to be increased by $r\pi^e$ in order to compensate the investor for the loss in the real value of the interest payments. Consequently, the nominal interest rate parity of (4.11) should be interpreted as:

$$r + \pi^e + r\pi^e = r^* + \pi^{*e} + r^*\pi^{*e} + (E^e - E)/E - CRP - PRP$$

Both risk premiums, CRP and PRP, imply higher interest payments from holdings of foreign financial assets in order to compensate for the various risks. If the foreign country suffers from inflation, these additional interest payments also have to be protected from the inflation loss so that:

$$r + \pi^e + r\pi^e = r^* + \pi^{*e} + r^*\pi^{*e} + (E^e - E)/E - (1 + \pi^{*e})CRP - (1 + \pi^{*e})PRP.$$

15. Under uncovered interest rate parity (no risk aversion), the two schedules, FF and BB, would coincide since EF and B are perfectly substitutable. Both schedules would be replaced by the familiar schedule of the interest rate parity, provided that the wealth effect ($\Delta W = F\Delta E = 0$) is neglected so that the MM-schedule becomes a vertical line at the equilibrium level of the domestic interest rate.

16. Even though the open market operation ($\Delta M = \Delta B$) does not imply a wealth effect, the depreciation of the domestic currency involves a positive wealth effect since $\Delta W = F\Delta E$. This wealth-value effect will have repercussions on the demand for M, B, and F, which we neglect as second order effects.

   The rise in the foreign exchange rate will be very strong under two conditions. First, if the demand for money has a low interest elasticity so that the expansionary monetary policy reduces the interest rate by a large amount (the MM-schedule shifts a long way to the left). Secondly, if the demand for foreign bonds has a high elasticity with respect to the domestic interest rate, i.e. the substitutability of domestic and foreign bonds is very high (the slope of the FF-curve is very steep). In this case, the fall in the domestic interest rate will induce a significant rise in the demand for foreign bonds and cause a large increase in the exchange rate.

17. The private sector acquires foreign currency from the central bank for buying foreign interest bearing assets ($E\Delta F$), and the central bank receives domestic currency which diminishes the monetary base.

PART II
A MACROECONOMIC
APPROACH TO THE
REAL EXCHANGE RATE

A change in the real exchange rate can take place under both exchange rate regimes, that is, with fixed and floating exchange rates, even though the most frequent fluctuations are observable with floating rates. Part II thus deals with both exchange rate regimes.

The essential feature of the macroeconomic approach is the integration of the financial markets (the LM-side of the model) and the goods markets (the IS-side). The role of the exchange rate becomes 'enriched'. The change in the exchange rate equilibrates not only the financial markets, but also the markets for domestic goods. However, in the short run, it is the LM-sector that is equilibrated, while in the IS-sector disequilibrium is possible. The exchange rate equilibrates both sectors only over the long run.

In the first chapter of Part II, the real exchange rate is defined as the relative price of domestic goods. Domestic goods can be domestically produced tradable or non-tradable goods. Thus, the real exchange rate (e) is both the relative price of domestic tradables with respect to foreign tradables ('external relative price of tradable goods' e_1), the most frequent definition, and the relative price of domestic tradables with respect to domestic non-tradables ('internal relative price of tradable goods' e_2). A further characteristic of the macroeconomic part is the emphasis on both types of relative prices. Each is treated in a separate chapter. In principle, monetary shocks (in the form of expansionary monetary policy) have no long-run impact on these two relative prices, while real shocks (for instance, resulting from fiscal policy) do have similar effects on both types of relative prices.

5

THE NATURE OF THE REAL EXCHANGE RATE (*e*)

A real appreciation or depreciation can take place through a change in the nominal exchange rate or—under the regime of fixed exchange rates—through a change in the domestic price level. With a real depreciation, for example, the latter can mean that domestic tradable goods become less expensive than foreign tradable goods. It can also mean that domestic non-tradable goods become less expensive than domestic tradable goods.

5.1. The Macroeconomic Approach versus the Financial Approach

The macroeconomic approach concentrates on the real sector of the economy represented by the goods market in the simplest version (Chapter 6) and by the goods and labour markets in a more elaborated macro model of an open economy (Chapter 7), where the labour market determines the supply conditions in the goods market. The exchange rate now plays a completely different role. It not only has to be interpreted as the real exchange rate—analogous to any other macroeconomic variables, like real income, real interest rate, real cash balances—but its nature also changes and it now becomes, in addition, a relative price of *goods*.

We actually have two relative goods prices to deal with. One is the relative price of domestic and foreign tradables, which we know already. In the extreme version of purchasing power parity, this relative price is equal to 1. The other is the relative price of tradable and non-tradable goods within the domestic economy (*and* the relative price of both types of goods for the foreign economy) resulting from the distinction between tradable and non-tradable goods. The financial approach conceived the real exchange rate differently again, as the relative price of domestic and foreign assets. The real exchange rate of the latter type had an impact on the real return differential between the two types of assets. The deflator of the nominal exchange rate is the ratio of the two national price levels, where each national price level includes tradable and non-tradable goods.

These various definitions of the exchange rate already show the complexity of its determinants. It is influenced by the financial and macroeconomic conditions of the domestic and the foreign country. Nearly everything in both types of economies has an impact on the exchange rate. This is why there is a lot of confusion about the main determinants of the exchange rate and, in particular, about the interactions between the macroeconomic and financial approaches.

It should be remembered that, like the exchange rate, the interest rate can be interpreted in a variety of ways. It is a monetary phenomenon if it is interpreted as the opportunity cost of holding money (instead of bonds). It is a real phenomenon if it is considered as the rate of return on capital (productivity) and as the relative price of present consumption goods with respect to future consumption goods (time preference). In contrast to the determination of the exchange rate, both of these interpretations of the interest rate are already included in its macroeconomic determination. In the IS-LM model—which is the workhorse of macroeconomics—the monetary aspect is represented by the LM-sector and the real aspect by the IS-sector.

The financial and macroeconomic approaches are still separated with respect to the exchange rate. A first distinction between the two approaches is that financial markets—or incipient and actual financial capital flows—dominate the short-run determination of the (daily, weekly, monthly) exchange rate evolution. 95 per cent of the daily transactions of about one trillion dollars on the world's foreign exchange markets, arise from financial transactions and 5 per cent from foreign trade transactions (see Box 4.1).[1] The financial role of the exchange rate is to equilibrate the expected returns on domestic and foreign financial assets in terms of the interest rate parities of Tables 3.1 and 4.1. In contrast, according to the macroeconomic approach, the role of the (real) exchange rate is to equilibrate—along with other real variables—the goods market, because the real exchange rate is a relative price of goods. Its equilibrium level may serve as the benchmark for the expected exchange rate in one of the interest parity conditions, provided that the participants in the financial markets are fundamentalists and choose one of the macromodels in the following chapters as the one which is relevant for the determination of the fundamental exchange rate. Thus, *the first link between the macroeconomic approach and the financial approach is the fundamental macroeconomic equilibrium exchange rate as the anchor for the exchange rate expectations in the financial markets.*

A second distinction between the two approaches—but also the main criticism of the macroeconomic approach—is that the financial determination of the exchange rate involves a stock approach, and the macroeconomic determination a flow, or balance of payments, approach. Of course, the exchange rate is determined in the foreign exchange market and, at first sight, it is like the price of peanuts in the market for peanuts or the price of steel in the market for steel. The demand and supply of foreign exchange are derived from commercial transactions (trade balance) and from financial transactions (capital balance). The first type of transactions establishes the link between the foreign exchange market and the goods market which is one of the essential domains of the macroeconomic approach. However, financial transactions result from the restructuring of the composition of the stock of financial assets and this is the essential message of the financial, or more precisely, of the portfolio approach. The macroeconomic approach thus has to integrate the portfolio approach as far as financial transactions on the foreign exchange market are concerned.[2] *The second connection between the macroeconomic approach and the financial approach is established by the reduced form of the portfolio approach which consists of the real interest parity under risk aversion.*

There is also a third link between the macroeconomic approach and the financial approach, which operates through the current account balance. The current account is another variable determined by the macroeconomic approach. Except for the case of full capital immobility,[3] the macroeconomic determination of the exchange rate can be accompanied by a surplus or a deficit on the current account, which only reflects a change in net holdings of foreign financial assets.[4] Consequently, this net change in assets has repercussions on the portfolio approach via two channels, namely: the change in the stock of foreign bonds and the change in financial wealth. Both changes will bring about another equilibrium exchange rate according to the portfolio approach. *Thus, the third link between the macroeconomic approach and the portfolio approach consists of changes in net foreign financial assets as a consequence of current account imbalances.*[5]

In the very long run, the macroeconomic approach predicts an equilibrium in the current account and, thus, a real exchange rate level which brings about this equilibrium. A permanent current account deficit (or surplus) would be inconsistent with the country's intertemporal budget constraint. A net debtor country has to reimburse its debts with future current account surpluses or service its interest payments continuously. Since the (main) difference between the trade balance and the current account balance consists of the net interest payments on foreign debt, an equilibrium in the current account implies a trade balance surplus, which is needed to make the interest payments on foreign debt. In principle, this required trade balance surplus necessitates a real depreciation.

5.2. Empirical Measures of the Real Exchange Rate (*e*)

The real exchange rate (*e*) was defined in Chapter 4 (equation 4.12) as the relative price between foreign goods (EP^*) and domestic goods (P)

$$e = EP^*/P \tag{5.1}$$

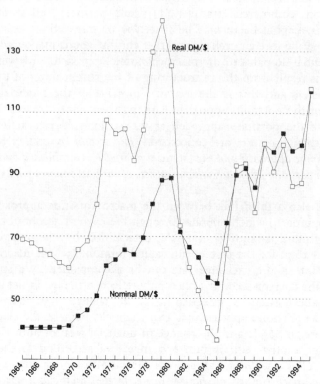

Fig. 5.1a. The nominal and real exchange rates of the German mark with respect to the US dollar (DM/$), 1964–95 (1990 = 100)

Until the mid-1980s the up and down of the real exchange rate was stronger than the movement of the nominal rate. Since then the real exchange rate has been driven by the nominal exchange rate.

Note: An increase in the exchange rate means an appreciation. The 1995 rates are for April.
Source: Calculated from IMF, *International Financial Statistics.*

From an *empirical* point of view, the calculation of the real exchange rate proceeds simply using equation (5.1). There are two practical problems which arise with the correct measurement of the real exchange rate; see Edwards (1989a). On the one hand, the appropriate price index (GDP deflator, wholesale price index, consumer price index, etc.) has to be chosen (see Box 1.1). On the other hand, the choice of the base period ($e = 100$) is also important for deducing the absolute degree of a real overvaluation ($e < 100$) or real undervaluation ($e > 100$). This assumes that the period in which the real exchange rate was at its fundamental equilibrium level is known. This question constitutes one of the main challenges in exchange rate economics.

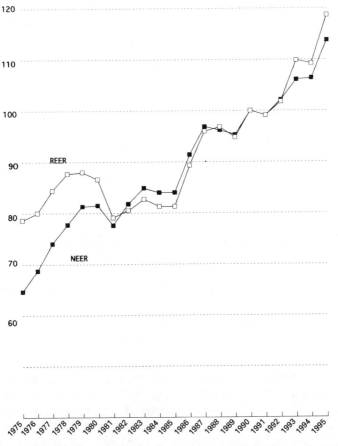

Fig. 5.1b. Nominal and real effective exchange rates (*NEER* and *REER*) of the German mark, 1975–95 (1990 = 1OO)

Over twenty years of floating exchange rates, the German currency followed a path of real appreciation with respect to the nominal and real effective exchange rate. This process was slowed down by the appreciation of the US dollar in 1981–5.
Note: An increase in the exchange rate means an appreciation. The exchange rates are annual averages. The 1995 rates are for April.
Source: IMF, *International Financial Statistics*.

In Fig. 5.1*a* we have calculated the real exchange rate of the deutsch-mark with respect to the US dollar by using the price index of consumption goods. The base period (1990 = 100) has been chosen arbitrarily and the real exchange rate of the year 1990 does not represent, in any case, a fundamental equilibrium value as we shall see in subsequent chapters. If the turbulent years for the dollar 1981–6 are neglected, we observe a steady real appreciation of the German mark by about 60 per cent from the early 1970s to the mid-1990s. For this reason, choosing a base period for the fundamental real exchange rate is already problematical. During the late 1980s and early 1990s the bilateral real exchange rate was quite stable around the level of the mid-1970s. Another interesting factor concerns the high synchronization of the movement of the real exchange rate with that of the nominal exchange rate, at least since the mid-1980s.

Box 5.1. Measuring effective exchange rates

The nominal effective exchange rate (*NEER*) is a weighted average of the domestic exchange rate with n currencies belonging to the most important trading partners of the country. With E_i as the bilateral nominal exchange rate with country i, and with the corresponding trade weight w_i, *NEER* is the geometric average of the n bilateral nominal exchange rates:

$$NEER = E_1^{w_1} E_2^{w_2} E_3^{w_3} \ldots E_n^{w_n}.$$

Analogous to equation (5.1) for deriving the real exchange rate, the foreign price level (P^*) represents a weighted average of the n foreign price levels:

$$P^* = P_1^{w_1} P_2^{w_2} P_3^{w_3} \ldots P_n^{w_n}.$$

P is the domestic price level so that the real effective exchange rate (*REER*) can be written as:

$$REER = [(E_1 P_1)^{w_1} (E_2 P_2)^{w_2} (E_3 P_3)^{w_3} \ldots (E_n P_n)^{w_n}]/P$$

It would be interesting to know whether there were similar real appreciations of the deutschmark with respect to other important currencies. The real effective exchange rate (*REER*) of Fig. 5.1*b* (but only for the period beginning in 1975) reveals a similar pattern. Because the *REER* represents a weighted average of many bilateral real exchange rates of the German mark (see Box 5.1), the real appreciation is smoothed and oscillates less. In the late 1970s and early 1980s the *REER* was quite constant. Between 1985 and 1992 it rose by 25 per cent, while the bilateral real exchange rate with the dollar appreciated by 60 per cent.

In Box 5.2 I have reproduced some recent calculations, by the Bank for International Settlements, of the deviation of the actual nominal exchange rate of some national currencies with respect to the US dollar derived from the *PPP*-value of *E* where $e = EP^*/P$ would be equal to one. The price indices are those of the GDP deflator. In 1960 practically all currencies were heavily undervalued ($e > 1$), while in 1980 many of them were strongly overvalued ($e < 1$). This overvaluation diminished considerably in 1990. One reason for the important discrepancy between actual exchange rates and their *PPP*-values concerns the prices of non-tradable goods, which are represented heavily in the GDP price index but not necessarily linked to international prices as the two following sections will show.

Box 5.2. Bilateral overvaluations and undervaluations of selected currencies with respect to the US dollar: PPP rates ($e = EP^*/P = 1$) and actual exchange rates

	1960			1980			1990		
	PPP	actual		PPP	actual		PPP	actual	
	(1)	(2)	(1)–(2) over (2)	(1)	(2)	(1)–(2) over (2)	(1)	(2)	(1)–(2) over (2)
Germany	3.00	4.17	−28.1	2.37	1.82	+30.2	1.84	1.62	+13.9
France	3.50	4.90	−28.6	5.24	4.23	+23.9	5.82	5.45	+6.9
United Kingdom	0.23	0.36	−37.7	0.49	0.43	+13.3	0.53	0.56	−5.4
Italy	448	621	−27.8	749	856	−11.3	1251	1198	+4.4
Belgium	37.1	50.0	−25.8	36.6	29.2	+25.4	34.7	33.4	+3.8
Netherlands	2.38	3.77	−36.9	2.53	1.99	+27.1	1.91	1.82	+4.9
Spain	31.0	60.0	−48.3	63.6	71.7	−11.2	96.4	101.9	−5.4
Canada	1.07	1.00	+7.4	1.08	1.17	−7.7	1.15	1.17	−1.5
Japan	225	360	−37.4	240	227	+5.7	172	145	+18.8

The actual exchange rates are the annual averages of the nominal market rates. Unlike in Fig. 5.1a, an increase in the exchange rate means a depreciation.

Column [(1)–(2) over (2)] measures the percentage bilateral overvaluation (positive value) or undervaluation (negative value) of the national currency with respect to the US dollar. Thus, in 1960, all currencies (except the Canadian) were undervalued [$e = (EP^*/P) > 1$] and thus had a higher degree of price competitiveness. In 1990 most currencies were overvalued [$e = (EP^*/P) < 1$], indicating a low price competitiveness compared with the USA. However, the degree of overvaluation was relatively modest (except for Japan and Germany) in contrast to the high degree of undervaluation in 1960.

Source: Turner and Van't dack (1993: 75).

5.3. Theoretical Measures of the Real Exchange Rate

The External Relative Price of Tradable Goods (e_1)

From an analytical point of view, the real exchange rate as the relative price between domestic and foreign goods can be conceived of as the combination of two relative prices. The term domestic goods could mean exported goods (exportables) or could refer to internationally non-traded goods. Foreign goods are either imported goods (importables) or internationally non-traded goods. In this section, we shall interpret the real exchange rate as the relative price between importables and exportables. We call this price ratio e_1.

Importables and exportables belong to the category of tradable goods (T). There are two price levels: the absolute price level of domestic tradables (P_T)

and the absolute price level of foreign tradables (P^*_T) expressed in domestic currency (EP^*_T). Their relative price is

$$e_1 = EP^*_T/P_T \qquad (5.2)$$

In the 1960s the purchasing power parity (*PPP*), or the law of one price, was reformulated by Balassa (1964) and Samuelson (1964) in terms of formula (5.2). The law of one price $(e_1 = 1)$ means that $P_T = EP^*_T$ (see Box 5.3) and that national goods markets are fully integrated with one another.

Box 5.3. *PPP*: undervaluations and overvaluations $e_1 = EP^*_T/P_T$

$e_1 = 1$ prices of foreign tradable goods (P^*_T) expressed in domestic currency (EP^*_T) are equal to prices of domestic tradable goods (P_T) : $P_T = EP^*_T$ (law of one price or *PPP*).

$e_1 > 1$ prices of foreign tradable goods (P^*_T) expressed in domestic currency (EP^*_T) are higher than prices of domestic tradable goods (P_T) : $P_T < EP^*_T$ (real undervaluation meaning higher competitiveness).

$e_1 < 1$ prices of foreign tradable goods (P^*_T) expressed in domestic currency (EP^*_T) are lower than prices of domestic tradable goods (P_T) : $P_T > EP^*_T$ (real overvaluation meaning lower competitiveness).

A real undervaluation $(e_1 > 1)$ means that domestic tradable goods are cheaper than foreign tradable goods and indicates an advantage of the domestic economy in foreign trade competitiveness. Domestic tradable goods include exportable goods and import substitutes produced in the domestic economy. Foreign tradable goods are, from the point of view of our domestic economy, the importable goods and the export substitutes of the foreign country. Thus, the real undervaluation implies a relative price advantage for our import substitutes with respect to the imported goods and a relative price advantage for our exportables compared to foreign export substitutes. A real overvaluation $(e_1 < 1)$ means just the opposite and implies a lack of international competitiveness.[6] Box 5.4 indicates the basic tools with which the *PPP* value of the exchange rate could be calculated.

Box 5.4. How to calculate the equilibrium exchange rate $E = P_T/P^*_T$ for Russia

   Directly. The same basket of goods (*T*), say $T_1, T_2, \ldots T_n$ has to be taken for both countries. In each country, the actual price of each good, that is $P_{T1}, P_{T2}, \ldots P_{Tn}$ and $P^*_{T1}, P^*_{T2}, \ldots P^*_{Tn}$, is measured. For simplicity, we choose the simplest formula for calculating the price level which is $P_T = P_{T1} + P_{T2} + \ldots + P_{Tn}$ and $P^*_T = P^*_{T1} + P^*_{T2} + \ldots P^*_{Tn}$. Assume that the domestic country is Russia, whose price level is $P_T = 10,000$ roubles, while the foreign country is the United States with the price level $P^*_T = 100$ dollars. Consequently, the *PPP* exchange rate would be $E = P_T/P^*_T = 10,000/100 = 100$ roubles for one dollar (by assuming $e_1 = 1$).[7]

Indirectly with the unit-labour-cost approach. Prices should reflect marginal cost. With a fixed capital stock, marginal costs are marginal labour costs per unit of output so that $P_T = W_T/MPL_T$ where MPL_T represents the marginal productivity of labour in the tradables sector and W_T the nominal wage. For the foreign country, we have $P^*_T = W^*_T/MPL^*_T$ so that

$$E = P_T/P^*_T = [W_T/MPL_T] / [W^*_T/MPL^*_T]$$

Real wages, i.e. MPL_T and MPL^*_T, should refer to monthly wages in the industrial sector and they should be evaluated in both countries in dollar terms as the numéraire for real wages. Assume that the industrial monthly wage in the USA amounts to $W^*_T = 2,000$ dollars. Since the American nominal wage serves as the measurement of real wages for Russia, we obtain $W^*_T = MPL^*_T = 2,000$ dollars so that $P^*_T = 1$. Consequently, we have $E = P_T = W_T/MPL_T$. Assume that the monthly productivity of the Russian industrial labour force is estimated at $MPL_T = 80$ dollars, while the monthly industrial wage is $W_T = 8,000$ roubles. The corresponding exchange rate would be 100 roubles for one dollar.

If the law of one price does not hold, this means that the domestic and foreign markets for tradables are not fully integrated, and there are two different prices for the same good. This phenomenon could exist both in a system of fixed exchange rates and in a system of floating exchange rates. However, the latter could result in more price inequality if domestic prices are not adjusted immediately to the foreign prices when there is a change in the nominal exchange rate.

In principle, changes in the nominal exchange rate should only involve short-term changes in the real exchange rate. Fig. 5.2 gives examples of a real depreciation and of a real appreciation. A nominal depreciation (a rise from E_0 to E_2) could involve a real depreciation, at least in the time interval $t_0 t_1$ (Fig. 5.2a). Even though the prices of foreign goods (in terms of the local currency) should increase to $E_2 P^*_T$ at the moment the depreciation takes place, they remain at P_{T0}, and adjust only gradually to the higher nominal exchange rate. Consequently, there is also a real depreciation (e_1) at time t_0, which phases out gradually over time. The same phenomenon is illustrated for a nominal appreciation (E_1) in Fig. 5.2b. At point t_0, the nominal appreciation is equal to a real appreciation, and, over time, the real overvaluation disappears step by step.

The Internal Relative Price of Tradable Goods (e_2)

The distinction between tradable and non-tradable goods has a long history. It was used in the German transfer discussion during the 1920s led by Frank Graham (1925) and Bertil Ohlin (1929). Then, the debate focused on the notion of international and domestic goods. In the early 1960s, the Australian economists Salter (1959), Swan (1960), Corden (1960), and Pearce (1961) constructed more rigorous models for the determination of internal equili-

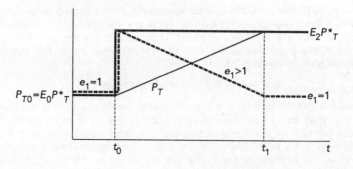

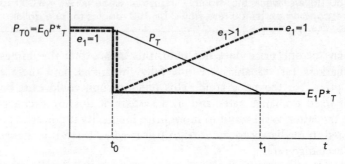

Fig. 5.2a. Real depreciation

—The depreciation from E_0 to E_1 pushes the domestic prices of tradables only gradually to the higher international level. During this time interval of domestic price adjustment, there is also a temporary real depreciation.

Fig. 5.2b. Real appreciation

—In the case of an appreciation from E_0 to E_1 a similar pattern is observed for the real appreciation.

Fig. 5.2. Changes in the nominal exchange rate and the temporary impact on the real exchange rate (e_1)

brium (in the market for non-tradable goods) and external equilibrium (in the market for domestic tradable goods) for a small open economy, sometimes also called the dependent economy.[8] Since the late 1970s, the IMF and the World Bank have used mainly the relative price of tradables and non-tradables as the real exchange rate. While tradable goods are defined as those goods which are exposed to international price competition, non-tradable goods are either not traded physically between countries (housing, construction, certain types of transport, and services such as education, restaurants, hotels, handicraft, commerce) or they have monopoly pricing (public utilities like electricity and transport); see Box 5.5.

Box 5.5. Which goods are non-tradable

'The categories of what is tradable and what is nontradable are not immutable. Technological improvements that reduce transport costs are likely to make more goods tradable. By contrast, increases in protectionism tend to increase the list of nontradable goods.

In practice, then, which goods belong to one category and which to the other? There are hundreds of thousands of goods and services, and we cannot hope to answer this question for each good. But we can try to classify goods into broad categories. One well-known classification used in most countries is the standard industrial classification (SIC) of the United Nations. According to the SIC, goods and services are divided into nine different categories by major industry:

1. Agriculture, hunting, forestry, and fishing;
2. Mining and quarrying;
3. Manufacturing;
4. Electricity, gas, and water;
5. Construction;
6. Wholesale and retail trade, restaurants, and hotels;
7. Transport, storage, and communications;
8. Financing, insurance, real estate, and business services;
9. Community, social, and personal services.

Very roughly speaking, goods included in the first three categories, agriculture, mining and manufacturing, are typically the most tradable, while goods in the other categories are generally assumed to be nontradable.' Sachs and Larrain (1993: 659–60).

With regard to tradables, a distinction can be made between homogeneous and heterogeneous goods. Homogeneous goods are primary products (raw materials and agricultural products) which are exchanged on the world market at a single price. Heterogeneous tradables are subject to product differentiation and apparently similar goods could have some price differences. Goods which are tradable by nature could become non-tradables if their trade is distorted by protectionism (for instance, agricultural products and textiles).

There are important exceptions among the last six categories of non-tradable goods. Thus, for instance, with respect to transportation services, international air travel and shipping are tradable goods. Many financial services have also become internationally tradable with the suppression of capital controls.

The relative price between tradable and non-tradable goods (q) is written as

$$q = P_T/P_N \tag{5.4}$$

where P_N is the price of non-tradables. The link between the real exchange rate (e) and q is derived in Table 5.1. The real exchange rate is the product of two relative prices, e_1 and e_2:

$$e = e_1 \times e_2 \tag{5.7}$$
$$[EP^*_T/P_T] \qquad\qquad [q^b/q^{*b^*}]$$

Table 5.1. The real exchange rate as the ratio of tradable to non-tradable goods

Real Exchange Rate	e	$=$	EP^*/P	(5.1)
General Price Level				
Domestic Country	P	$=$	$P_T^a P_N^b$	
		$=$	$P_T^a P_N^b [P_T^b / P_T^b]$	
		$=$	$P_T^a P_T^b [1/q^b]$	
		$=$	P_T/q^b	(5.5)
Foreign Country	P^*	$=$	P^*_T/q^{*b*}	(5.6)
Real Exchange Rate				
(by combining 5.1 with	e	$=$	$\dfrac{EP^*_T/q^{*b*}}{P_T/q^b} = \dfrac{EP^*_T}{P_T} \dfrac{q^b}{q^{*b*}}$	
5.5 and 5.6)			$= e_1 \quad e_2$	(5.7)
Real Exchange Rate				
(assuming $P_T = EP^*_T$)	e	$=$	q^b/q^{*b*}	(5.8)

where
E = nominal exchange rate
e = real exchange rate
P = general price level
P_T = price level of tradable goods
P_N = price level of non-tradable goods
a = weight of tradable goods within total goods
b = weight of non-tradable goods within total goods
q = $P_T/P_N = EP^*_T/P_N$

The second component (e_2) of the real exchange rate comprises *two relative prices, q* and *q**:

$$e_2 = q^b/q^{*b*} \tag{5.9}$$

For the moment, we assume $q^* = 1$ such that[9]

$$e_2 = q^b \tag{5.9a}$$

If the law of one price for tradable goods holds ($e_1 = 1$), the real exchange rate (e) would coincide with e_2

$$e = e_2 = q^b \tag{5.9b}$$

The link between the nominal exchange rate regime and the real exchange rate (in the sense of e_2) can be highlighted if we write (5.9a) as

$$\begin{aligned} e_2 &= q^b \\ &= (P_T/P_N)^b \\ &= (EP^*_T/P_N)^b \end{aligned} \tag{5.10}$$

A nominal devaluation (ΔE) in a fixed exchange rate regime, or a nominal depreciation in a floating system, involve a type e_2 real depreciation of the same amount under two conditions. The first one assumes that the law of one price is realized immediately [$(\Delta E)P^*_T = \Delta P_T$]. The second assumes a constant P_N.

The real depreciation (of type e_2) produces—as does any change in relative prices—a substitution effect on production and consumption; for the moment we abstract from the income effect for consumers. For producers, it becomes more profitable to shift resources from the non-tradable production sector to the tradable production sector. More exportables and importables will be produced at the expense of non-tradables. The improvement in the trade balance arises when more of the exportables produced are exported, and when importables produced are substituted for imports. A second improvement in the trade balance comes from the demand side. Consumers demand fewer exportables so that more can be exported. They also demand fewer importables so that imports can be reduced.

However, the impact, described above, of a real depreciation on the trade balance, operating through the substitution effect on the composition of production and expenditure is only a necessary, but not a sufficient, condition for improving the trade balance. Since any trade balance deficit corresponds from the macroeconomic point of view to an excess of absorption (residents' demand for domestic and imported goods) over domestic production—as will be illustrated in the following chapters—the most essential, but, in most cases, still insufficient condition for reducing a trade balance deficit consists of a reduction in absorption (or an increase in domestic production). The reader should always remember this caveat against the elasticity approach (the substitution effect of a real depreciation) and the importance of the absorption approach.

Unlike the real exchange rate of type e_1, there is no fundamental benchmark with e_2 against which a real undervaluation (as for $e_1 > 1$ as indicated in Box 5.3) or a real overvaluation (as for $e_1 < 1$) can be identified. Thus, for instance, as illustrated in Box 5.6, the real exchange rate of type e_2 should be at a low level in rich countries (because of a high P_N) and at a high level in poor countries (because of a low P_N). A judgement about the fundamental equilibrium level of e_2 can only be made in terms of an adequate current account and capital account balance. Thus, a country which has a current account deficit may nevertheless have the appropriate level of e_2 if the deficit is financed by sustainable capital inflows. The criterion of sustainability refers to the country's intertemporal budget constraint in terms of which it must be able to reimburse its foreign debt. When the time for reimbursement comes, it is fully conceivable that the adequate level of e_2 may be at another level, in our case, a higher level (real depreciation).[10]

Box 5.6. International purchasing power comparisons in 1985

If a Western citizen travels throughout the world, as a tourist, he purchases mostly non-tradable goods, i.e. services. He takes meals in restaurants, sleeps in hotels, and uses the local transport services. He may begin his travels in his own country by visiting some remote places in the country. He will already observe that these places are rather cheap as far as tourist services are concerned, compared to the capital where he is assumed to live. He continues his travels by flying to Africa. There he may be astonished to find that a tourist's living costs are even cheaper. However, if he does not notice such a theoretically predictable phenomenon, he might leave the country with the firm conviction that the currency there is considerably overvalued. Flying eastwards, he may stop off in Singapore or South Korea, and will notice that these countries are expensive, though not as expensive as Western Europe. He finally arrives in Tokyo and is horrified by the enormous expense of restaurants, hotels, and local transport. He quickly leaves in the direction of Western Europe, stopping in Moscow where he gets himself into a total mess. He could have flown with Aeroflot from Vladivostok to Moscow for only US$7 provided he had exchanged dollars for roubles at the black market rate of 1 dollar for 100 roubles (in early December 1991) and that the travel agency in Vladivostok had treated him like any Russian resident, accepting roubles instead of dollars.

The reason for our tourist's confusion stems from the fact that the level of the real exchange rate must diverge between various groups of countries. Evaluating the foreign price level P^* in US currency (EP^*), and assuming that the prices of tradable goods are equalized in a common currency (US dollar) across countries ($P_T = EP^*_T$), the price levels between countries diverge because of $P_N = EP^*_N$; see Bhagwati (1984). The main reason for this divergence, for instance, between poor and rich countries, is that wages in the production of services are low in poor countries. The United Nations International Income Comparison Project, which the World Bank has helped to support since 1969, is based on the above 'theory of the national price level'; see Kravis and Lipsey (1983), Kravis (1986), and Summers and Heston (1991). For 1985, Summers and Heston (1988) have established the following comparison of national price levels (US = 100):

Selected OECD Countries		Selected Developing Countries	
USA	100.0	Saudi Arabia	104.4
Switzerland	107.1	Taiwan	68.5
Japan	96.6	Israel	67.7
Canada	92.6	Venezuela	67.4
Denmark	84.3	Argentina	51.9
Germany	80.0	Mexico	47.4
Netherlands	78.0	Brazil	43.6
Austria	77.5	Senegal	40.2
France	74.0	Peru	34.0
UK	72.7	Chile	32.8
Belgium	69.3	Chad	31.0
Italy	68.0	Ethiopia	30.1
Greece	58.9	India	27.2
Spain	55.1	Pakistan	26.2
Portugal	43.8	Bangladesh	22.1

Thus, for instance, the purchasing power of one hundred dollars in Bangladesh is nearly five times that of the USA.[11]

The Real Exchange Rate as the Product of Two Relative Prices

The synthesis of the real exchange as the product of the two relative prices (e_1 and e_2) has been already formulated in formula (5.7). Assuming $q^* = 1$, formula (5.7) becomes

$$e = e_1 \times e_2$$
$$= [EP^*_T/P_T]\ q^b \tag{5.7a}$$

e_1 is interpreted as the 'external relative price of domestic tradables' with respect to foreign tradables (EP^*_T/P_T)[12] and e_2 as the 'internal terms of trade' or the 'internal relative price of domestic tradables' with respect to domestic nontradables (P_T/P_N).[13] To what extent does a nominal depreciation have an impact on the real exchange rate? What we do want to show now is the probability that a nominal depreciation will initially cause a real depreciation of type e_1. Later, over time, the real depreciation of type e_1 will gradually be replaced by the real depreciation of type e_2. But, at any given moment, the nominal depreciation always produces (under certain given macroeconomic conditions) a global real depreciation of type e.

In Fig. 5.3 we assume a nominal depreciation from E_0 to E_1. Initially, the law of one price for tradable goods was valid $(P_T = E_0 P^*_T)$. At the time the nominal depreciation occurs, P_T is still unchanged, so that the real depreciation is at the highest rate of type e_1. The real exchange rate of type e_2 is still unchanged. From t_1 onwards, P_T begins to adjust gradually towards $E_1 P^*_T$. Consequently, there is a reverse movement of e_1 (real appreciation of type e_1), but a gradual real depreciation of type e_2. The overall real exchange rate of type

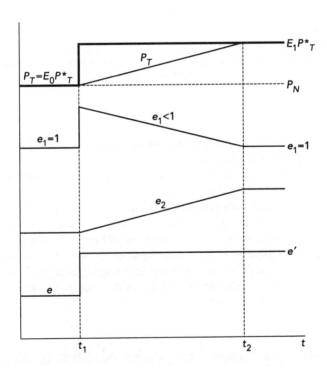

Fig. 5.3. Nominal devaluation and the real exchange rates of type e_1 and e_2

The nominal devaluation from E_0 to E_1 is transmitted fully at time t_1 to the real depreciation of type e_1 since P_T rises gradually only after t_1. The subsequent increase in P_T reverses the initial real depreciation of e_1 but causes a real depreciation of type e_2. At time t_2, the definite real depreciation is of type e_2 provided that P_N remains constant.

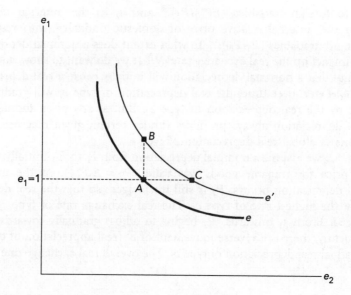

Fig. 5.4. Nominal devaluation and the evolution of the two real exchange rates

Fig. 5.4 represents an alternative geometric exposition of Fig. 5.3. The nominal devaluation AB is identical to the real depreciation of type e_1. The subsequent movement from B to C signifies a real appreciation of e_1 and a corresponding real depreciation of type e_2 by maintaining the overall real depreciation at e'.

e is already depreciated at time t_1 and stays permanently at the higher level e' (provided that P_N remains constant).

Fig. 5.4 describes the same phenomenon in terms of an alternative geometrical technique. The rectangular hyberbola e indicates the initial real exchange rate which is compatible with various combinations of e_1 and e_2. However, the initial situation is at a very precise point, at A where $e_1 = 1$ (*PPP*). The nominal depreciation first produces the real depreciation of type e_1 (point B). Later, the real depreciation of type e_1 is gradually replaced by the real depreciation of type e_2. Finally, at point C, the law of one price is again re-established ($e_1 = 1$), and the real depreciation consists exclusively of the rise in the relative price of tradables with respect to non-tradables.

5.4. The Real Exchange Rate under Alternative Nominal Exchange Rate Regimes

A change in the real exchange rate can take place in a system of floating nominal exchange rates, but also in a system of fixed nominal exchange rates. However, with floating rates, a change in the real exchange rate is far more frequent than under fixed rates, as has been shown by Mussa (1986). In Fig. 5.1*a* we can see that the fluctuation of the nominal exchange rate of the deutschmark with the dollar dominated the fluctuation of the real rate. However, during the regime of fixed exchange rates which prevailed in the 1960s there was a slight real appreciation of the deutschmark in the early 1960s and a slight real depreciation in the late 1960s.

Real Depreciation of Type e_1 under Fixed and Floating Rates

In the top part of Fig. 5.5 we have illustrated the foreign price level (P^*) expressed in domestic currency (EP^*) and the domestic price level (P). Implicitly, both price levels are those of tradable goods since, for the moment, non-tradable goods do not exist. The real exchange rate is equal to the slope of the various $0e_1$ rays. The prevailing real exchange rate is equal to $e_1 < 1$ at point A. The domestic price level of tradables (P_0) exceeds the foreign

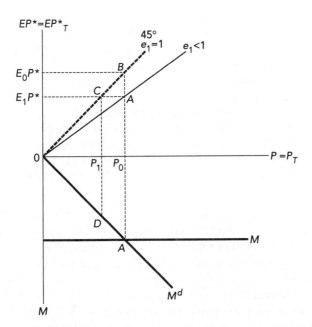

Fig. 5.5. Real depreciation of type e_1 under fixed and floating exchange rates

We assume that there are only tradable goods so that the general price level coincides with the price level of tradable goods. The law of one price is indicated by the slope of the line $e_1 = 1$. The economy is at point A and it has a price level for tradables (P_0) which lies above that of the foreign country expressed in domestic currency $(P_0 > E_1 P^*)$. To become more competitive, a real depreciation has to take place. Under floating exchange rates, the nominal exchange rate has to be increased from E_1 to E_0 (point B). Under fixed exchange rates, the price level has to be reduced (point C) via a lower quantity of money passing through point D.

price level of tradables $(E_1 P^*)$. The real exchange rate which would equalize the two price levels according to the reformulated *PPP* is indicated by the slope of the dotted ray Oe_1 ($e_1 = 1$). The lower panel describes the money market in terms of a given money supply and a money demand which increases with a rising domestic price level. Monetary equilibrium is established at the intersection point A, producing the domestic price level at P_0.

Assume that macroeconomic equilibrium requires that the real exchange rate returns to its *PPP* level ($e_1 = 1$). With flexible nominal exchange rates, the real depreciation is brought about by the rise of the nominal exchange rate (point B) from E_1 to E_0, while the domestic price level remains unchanged (P_0). In the case of a fixed exchange rate regime ($E = E_1$), the domestic price level has to decline from P_0 to P_1 (point C). The fall in the price level can be realized by a restrictive monetary policy which reduces the money supply to point D.

A Real Depreciation of Type e_2 under Fixed and Floating Rates

We shall now assume that $e_1 = 1$. The rectangular hyperbola P_0 in Fig. 5.6 represents a given general price level which can be the result of a different combination of the price level of tradable goods (P_T) and the price level of non-tradable goods (P_N) according to equation (5.5) in Table 5.1. P_0 should be the price level which equilibrates the demand and supply of money. The curve P_0 implies a given quantity of money.

For various reasons (which are explained in the following chapters), a real depreciation should take place in order to make tradable goods more expensive. The initial real exchange rate (q_0) is indicated by the slope of the ray $0q_0$. A real depreciation is indicated by the rotation of the ray $0q_0$ towards $0q_1$. We shall first consider floating exchange rates and then fixed exchange rates.

Floating nominal exchange rates.   There are two possible nominal depreciations which could realize the real depreciation. The first case concerns point B with a nominal depreciation rate of AD/AF (assuming $P^*_T = 1$). At point D, the price level has risen via an increase in P_T. Consequently, there is an excess demand for money which pushes the price level downwards. Since P_T cannot fall because it is linked to EP^*_T ($e_1 = 1$), only P_N can fall. A decline of P_N by the amount BD is necessary to equilibrate the money market. The rate of the real depreciation is higher than the rate of the nominal depreciation. It results from an increase in P_T (via E) and from a fall in P_N.

The second case of the nominal depreciation is represented by point B_1. The nominal depreciation rate is AB_1/AF. Such a higher rate of nominal depreciation occurs when it is assumed that prices of non-tradable goods are rigid downwards. At B_1, the rate of the real depreciation is identical with the rate of the nominal depreciation. However, the general price level (P) has to be higher.

To create an equilibrium in the money market, the supply of money has to increase so that the P_0 schedule shifts through point B_1. In contrast to the first case, the second case of nominal depreciation is inflationary.

I would also like to mention the case where a nominal depreciation-cum-excessive monetary expansion leaves the real exchange rate unchanged. Again, there is a nominal depreciation from A to B_1. However, the money supply is not expanded to an amount which produces the price level at B_1, but to a still higher amount which produces the price level at A_1. In that case, the real exchange rate is not altered. Such a situation could emerge when wage earners in the non-tradables production sector also estimate their real wages in terms of P_T. If they want to maintain their real wages, there will be higher nominal wage claims and the nominal wage costs will increase in the non-tradables sector. The central bank increases the money supply beyond B_1 in order to avoid unemployment.[14]

Fixed nominal exchange rates. In such a regime, the price level of tradable goods is not modifiable and it remains at the horizontal dotted line $E_0 P^*_T$. The

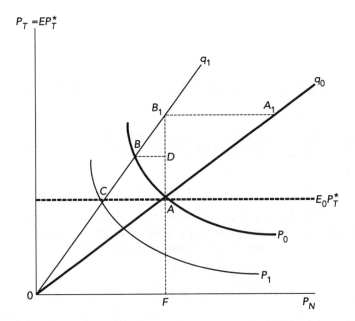

Fig. 5.6. Real depreciation of type e_2 under fixed and floating exchange rates

Assuming PPP ($e_1 = 1$) the slope of the Oq-ray measures the real exchange rate. The rectangular hyperbola P_0 illustrates the equilibrium level of the general price level for different combinations of P_T and P_N. For the real exchange rate q_0, the monetary equilibrium is at point A. The monetary mechanism of a real depreciation (q_1) is as follows. Under floating exchange rates (point B) there is a nominal depreciation of AD and a decline of P_N which ensure that the price at P_0 is maintained. Under fixed exchange rates (point C), P_N has to fall, implying the decline of the price level to P_1 realized by a lower quantity of money.

only chance of bringing about the real depreciation is a deflationary monetary policy which shifts the P_0 schedule towards P_1. This deflationary policy will only induce a fall in P_N since P_T remains constant (point C). Thus, the relative fall in P_N will be greater than the relative fall in P and M respectively. If non-tradable goods make up half of total goods ($b = 0.5$), and a real depreciation rate of 20 per cent is required for q, the general price level has to fall by 10 per cent. The rate of monetary contraction will be lower (10 per cent) than the rate of the real depreciation.

By comparing both nominal exchange rate regimes, the following conclusion about price stability can be reached. The point of departure is the necessity of a change in the real exchange rate—either of type e_1 (Fig. 5.5) or of type e_2 (Fig. 5.6)—which will be analysed in the next two chapters. Comparing point B (floating rates) with point C (fixed rates), point B is realized with a constant price level (P_0) and point C with a variable (decreasing) price level (P_1). Under this particular scenario, floating nominal exchange rates could more easily guarantee price level stability than fixed nominal exchange rates.

Appendix A: The Terms of Trade and the Real Exchange Rate

The relationship between the real exchange rate of type e_1 and the terms of trade $[TOT = P_x/P_m = EP^*_m/EP^*_x = P^*_m/P^*_x = 1/TOT^*]$ has been derived in Table 5.A1.

$$e_1 = TOT^{b^* - a} \tag{5.15}$$

If $a > b^*$ (implying that $b < a^*$), a deterioration in the terms of trade causes a real depreciation. We shall rewrite equation (5.2) in terms of the weighted average of prices for exported and imported goods

$$e_1 = \frac{EP^*_x{}^{a^*} P^*_m{}^{b^*}}{P_x{}^a P_m{}^b} \tag{5.2a}$$

The prices of exported and imported goods are determined in the world market. We assume a shock in the world market which increases $EP^*_x = P_m$ and decreases $EP^*_m = P_x$ where the nominal exchange rate remains fixed. With $a > b^*$ (implying that $b < a^*$), we shall have a real depreciation of the domestic currency.

Table 5.A1. *Terms of trade (TOT = P_x/P_m) and the real exchange rate (e_1)*

Real exchange rate	e_1	=	EP^*_T/P_T	(5.2)
Price level of tradable goods				
Domestic country	P_T	=	$P_x^a P_m^b$	
		=	$P_x^a P_m^b [P_x^b/P_x^b]$	
		=	$P_x^a P_x^b [P_m^b/P_x^b]$	
		=	$P_x [1/TOT^b]$	
		=	P_x/TOT^b	(5.13)
Foreign country	P^*_T	=	P_x^*/TOT^{*b*}	
		=	$P_x^* \, TOT^{b*}$	(5.14)
Real exchange rate (combining (5.2) with (5.13) and (5.14))	e_1	=	$\dfrac{EP_x^* \, TOT^{b*}}{P_x/TOT^b}$	
		=	$\dfrac{P_m \, TOT^b \, TOT^{b*}}{P_x}$	
		=	$\dfrac{TOT^{b+b*}}{TOT}$	
		=	TOT^{b+b*-1}	
		=	$TOT^{b+b*-a-b}$	
		=	TOT^{b*-a}	(5.15)
If $a = b^*$ (implying $a^* = b$)	$e_1 = 1$		A deterioration in *TOT* leaves the real exchange rate unchanged	
If $a > b^*$ (implying $a^* > b$)	$e_1 > 1$		A deterioration in *TOT* causes a real depreciation	
If $a < b^*$ (implying $a^* < b$)	$e_1 < 1$		A deterioration in *TOT* causes a real appreciation	

where
P_x = price level of exportables
P_m = price level of importables
a = weight of exportables among tradables (domestic country)
b = weight of importables among tradables (domestic country)
a^* = weight of exportables among tradables (foreign country)
b^* = weight of importables among tradables (foreign country)
$TOT = 1/TOT^*$

Appendix B: The Empirical Evidence of the Various International Parity Conditions of the Exchange Rate

Purchasing Power Parity (PPP). Until the late 1970s, there was a consensus among the profession that *PPP* would hold. This consensus was particularly strong prior to the recent float beginning in 1973 (see, for instance, Friedman and Schwartz, 1964). The empirical evidence of PPP can be divided into two periods. The first-period tests cover the interwar episodes of floating exchange rates and the recent float from 1973 to about 1978 for which PPP is not rejected. However, the second-period tests going beyond the late 1970s are not supportive of PPP. It should be emphasized that PPP implies a constant real exchange rate, at least for the real exchange rate of type e_1. Consequently, empirical evidence about the validity of PPP has to show that the real exchange rate remained rather stable.

One of the most influential tests was conducted by Frenkel (1976, 1978) who regarded the movement of the deutschmark-US dollar exchange rate over Germany's hyperinflation period of 1920–3. He tested a quantity theoretical (or 'monetarist') model with flexible prices—and not with temporarily rigid prices à la Dornbusch (1976)—which is a rather plausible case for highly inflationary countries. An increase in the money growth rate led to higher depreciation and inflation rates. This PPP view has been confirmed by McNown and Wallace (1989) for some other high-inflation countries. Another support for PPP provided the Canadian float in the 1950s (Choudhry *et al.*, 1991). As far as the recent float is concerned, Hodrick's (1978) test of the deutschmark–US dollar exchange rate for the period July 1972 to June 1975 was also highly compatible with PPP.

In the late 1970s when real exchange rates became highly variable, the doctrine of PPP 'collapsed' (Frenkel, 1981*a*). Dornbusch (1988) showed that PPP was of little empirical use since the real exchange rate fluctuations were persistent. However, recent empirical research on the long run PPP among the OECD countries are again rather optimistic by using longer time series. Flood and Taylor (1995) having tested the whole recent floating period found a strong case for the mean reversion towards long-run PPP; see also MacDonald (1995). Similar results were observed by Lothian and Taylor (1995) who looked even at data covering two centuries and ending in 1990.

Covered Interest Rate Parity (CIRP).   Tests of the CIRP condition are actually tests to find out whether there are barriers to arbitrage across international financial markets. A typical impediment to arbitrage would be capital controls. Deviations from CIRP are often used to indicate the existence and degree of capital controls (Dooley and Isard, 1980; Frankel and MacArthur, 1988). Another measure could be the spread between onshore and offshore interest rates for domestic assets with the same maturity and the same default risk (Claassen and Wyplosz, 1985).

CIRP seems to hold reasonably well. Several empirical studies have shown that there were only minor deviations from CIRP, in particular, when Euro-deposit interest rates were used (Frenkel and Levich, 1975, 1977). These deviations were mainly explicable by transactions costs (Clinton, 1988). However, in periods of turbulence on the foreign exchange markets, a much smaller percentage of these deviations can be attributed to transaction costs.

It should be mentioned that the validity of the CIRP does not depend on the investors' risk neutrality or risk aversion. Furthermore, the holding of *CIRP* does not mean that the forward rate is a good predictor for the future spot rate. Considerable research has been devoted to this issue (e.g. Fama, 1984; Cumby and Obstfeld, 1984; Hodrick and Srivastava, 1986; Taylor, 1987; Kearney and MacDonald, 1992). One possible explanation is that there is a time-varying risk premium that causes the difference between the forward rate and the future spot rate; equation (4.3) in section 4.1 gives some indication for such a wedge.

Uncovered Interest Rate Parity (UIRP). The *UIRP* assumes risk neutrality. The difficulty for testing *UIRP* lies in the estimation of the expected exchange rate. The forward rate cannot be taken because we have seen that it is a very bad predictor for future spot rates. Since other direct measures of exchange rate expectations are not available, one uses the interest rate differential as the point of departure for an optimal predictor of exchange rates by assuming rational expectations. However, all empirical studies rejected *UIRP* (e.g. Cumby and Obstfeld, 1981; Loopesko, 1984).

Even though *UIRP* has been generally rejected, Dornbusch's (1976) over-shooting model which uses *UIRP* and assumes sticky prices, has had some empirical success. Driskill (1981) applied it to the Swiss franc–US dollar rate for the period 1973–7 with largely favourable results. Papell (1988) found equally good empirical evidence for Dornbusch's model by estimating the effective exchange rates of Germany, Japan, the United Kingdom, and the United States for 1973:1 to 1984:4. Smith and Wickens (1990) came to similar results as far as the pound sterling is concerned.

Over the recent float, time series of the major exchange rates have the appearance of random walk (Mussa, 1984). Random walk is inconsistent with *UIRP* (Taylor, 1995). Since *UIRP* has been rejected empirically, the likelihood of randomness of exchange rate changes increases so that 'the predictor of future values of the spot rate is, under the assumption of a random walk, just the current spot rate' (Taylor, 1995: 16). Furthermore, the randomness would be a sign for market efficiency under which an investor could not earn systematic extra profits from speculation. However, this result is only valid if there is randomness of deviations from *UIRP* (see Cumby and Obstfeld, 1981; Levich, 1985). On the other hand, if *UIRP* were valid, the hypothesis of the random walk would be excluded, but foreign exchange markets would still be efficient.

Real Interest Rate Parity (RIRP). Under the assumptions of fully integrated financial markets within industrialized countries and of risk neutrality—which are the hypotheses of the nominal *UIRP* (perfect substitutability of domestic and foreign financial assets)—*RIRP* implies that real interest rates have to be equalized across countries under certain conditions. Empirically, this proposition has been rejected overwhelmingly for the real exchange rate of the United States against other OECD countries (Mishkin, 1984; Cumby and Obstfeld, 1984; Fraser and Taylor, 1990). But this fact is not at all surprising. If the nominal *UIRP* does not hold, why should there be the case that the (uncovered) *RIRP* could be valid?

It should be remembered that there is a compatibility between the nominal *UIRP* and the (uncovered) *RIRP* under the following conditions. Nominal interest rates should take into account expected inflation rates. The inflation rates should be correctly anticipated. And *PPP* should hold. This last assumption has been rather unrealistic since the late 1970s.

Uncovered Interest Rate Parity (UIRP) *with Risk Premium.* The portfolio model (see the Appendix to Chapter 4) can be tested indirectly in the form of the *UIRP* with a varying risk premium. The currency risk premium is the deviation from *UIRP* and it has been conceived as a function of the relative stocks of domestic and foreign financial assets. However, there is no significant empirical evidence that the risk premium rises with an increasing share of risky (foreign) assets. Neither Dooley and Isard (1982) nor Frankel (1982, 1983) who all looked at the US dollar–mark exchange rate nor Rogoff (1984) who examined the Canadian dollar–US dollar exchange rate found a statistically significant relationship. An interesting phenomenon has been documented by Tesar and Werner (1992), namely the empirical regularity that investors in each country tend to hold far more domestic than foreign assets; this is called the 'home country bias'. Both authors argue that the home country bias is too great to be explained by foreign exchange risk.

Another type of analysis was conducted by Meese and Rogoff (1983), who regarded the dollar–mark, dollar–yen, dollar–pound sterling, and the effective dollar exchange rates from March 1973 to June 1981 and who questioned which of the various financial exchange rate models (*PPP, IRP, RIRP,* portfolio model) worked better and whether these models had a better forecasting performance 'out of sample' than alternative models (the random walk model, the forward exchange rate, a univariate autoregression of the spot rate). By using the method of 'rolling regression', their astonishing conclusion was that none of the monetary or financial exchange rate models did outperform the random walk model. This result was a rather devastating shock for all those econometricians who did research on these exchange rate models.

In a second paper, Meese and Rogoff (1984) differentiated their former results—fortunately for the profession—by indicating that the simple random walk model only worked better for a forecasting horizon up to one year. Beyond a year, the financial models outperformed the random walk model. As Salemi (1984) noticed, this result should have been expected. In the short run, the exchange rate reacts as any other price of financial assets to demand and supply, while over the long run, its value may be dominated by fundamental economic factors.

The Collapse of PPP *and* IRP, *or Short-Term versus Long-Term Exchange Rates.* The poor performance of *PPP* since the late 1970s and the poor performance of the various interest rate parities during the recent float—except for the forward rate—may indicate that exchange rates did not reflect 'fundamental' factors as economic theory predicts. We had seen that random walk models could explain short-run fluctuations in the exchange rate better than 'traditional' economic models. However, over the longer run, say beyond one year, 'fundamental' economic analysis may regain its explanatory power.

As we have already emphasized in sect. 4.4, chartists may dominate the expectation formation for exchange rates (non-rational expectations) provoking excessive movements in one direction or the other. However, over a longer time horizon, fundamentalists may become the dominant force bringing the exchange rate back to its level as predicted by economic theory (rational expectations). Frankel and Froot (1986, 1990) have explained the strong overvaluation of the US dollar during the mid-1980s in this way. Taylor and Allen (1992) conducted a survey of chief foreign exchange dealers in the London foreign exchange market. They found that 60 per cent of them considered charts to be as important as fundamentals at the shortest end (one week). For the longest forecast (one year or more), 85 per cent of the chief dealers judged fundamentals to be more important than chart analysis. Studies by Levich and Thomas (1993) and by Menkhoff and Schlumberger (1995) have also shown that, over the short run, there seems to be a persistent profitability of technical analysis which explains the behaviour of chartists, but which casts some doubt on the efficiency of foreign exchange markets.

The lesson from this for model building of the determination of the exchange rate should be that more attention has to be devoted to the fundamental factors which determine the long-term exchange rate, as has also been suggested by the three recent survey articles on 'Exchange Rate Economics' by MacDonald and Taylor (1992), Taylor (1995), and MacDonald (1995). This has already been mentioned for the long-run determination of the nominal exchange rate according to *PPP*. The following chapters of this book are consecrated to the fundamentals of the long-term real exchange rate.

Notes

1. The world's central banks had roughly $1 trillion of international reserves in 1994. But these are stocks, while the daily transactions volumes are flows. Thus, when there is no control of capital movements, a financial attack on an exchange rate can easily exceed the volume of international reserves held by the two central banks concerned with the exchange rate.
2. According to Taylor (1990: 29–31), most macroeconomic models suffer from the neglect of capital movements resulting from stock adjustments. According to the portfolio approach, a change in the international interest differential does not give rise to permanent capital inflows or outflows, but to an once-and-for-all adjustment in desired holdings of domestic and foreign financial assets, as we stressed in the last chapter. This stock adjustment process for capital movements has already been considered by Meade (1951a), in his part III. In his mathematical exposition

(1951*b*: 103), he did not formulate the stock adjustment process of interest rate differentials correctly. The Mundell–Fleming model—Mundell (1961) (but see also Mundell (1968)) and Fleming (1962)—followed Meade's erroneous mathematical exposition and thus abstracted from the stock adjustment implications of a change in the international interest rate differential. Later works, for instance, by Branson (1968) and Kouri and Porter (1974) improved the stock equilibrium constraints on capital movements.

3. In that case, the balance of payments would coincide with the trade balance.

4. Neglecting direct foreign investments which have an impact on the holdings of foreign physical assets, a curent account surplus implies an increase in net foreign financial assets in the case of a net creditor country or a decrease in net foreign liabilities in the case of a net debtor country. A current account deficit means a decrease in net foreign financial assets for a net creditor country or an increase in foreign liabilities for a net debtor country.

5. It should be mentioned that the exchange rate determination according to the portfolio approach also has its drawbacks when it is not linked to the macroeconomic approach. Thus, a disequilibrium in the market for foreign bonds was eliminated by the valuation factor of a given physical stock of foreign bonds $[(\Delta E)F]$, even though changes in the physical volume are also dependent on the capital balance $[E(\Delta F)]$. The current account balance could also be seen as the outcome of stock adjustments. Since, for instance, a current account surplus corresponds to the difference between savings and investment, the determinants of savings and investment are decisive for the size of the current account. Savings decisions result from the speed of adjustment of the actual wealth level to the desired level, and investment decisions are the outcome of the speed of adjustment of the actual capital stock to the desired capital stock.

6. The relative price of tradable goods (e_1) is not identical with the terms of trade (*TOT*). The latter are defined as:

$$TOT = \frac{EP^*_x}{EP^*_m} = \frac{P_x}{P_m} = \frac{\text{domestic price of exportables}}{\text{domestic price of importables}} \quad (5.3)$$

where $P^*_x(P^*_m)$ is the dollar price of exportables (importables) and $P_x(P_m)$ their domestic currency price. As equation (5.3) highlights, the nominal exchange rate has no impact on the terms of trade. P^*_x and P^*_m (and, thus, P_x and P_m) are determined in the world market for exported and imported goods, at least for a small open economy.

The relative price of tradables covers a larger category of goods than *TOT*

$$e_1 = \frac{EP^*_T}{P_T} = \frac{\begin{array}{l}\text{price of foreign tradables, i.e. domestic price of importables}\\\text{and of export substitutes}\end{array}}{\begin{array}{l}\text{price of domestic tradables, i.e. domestic price of exportables}\\\text{and of import substitutes}\end{array}} \quad (5.2a)$$

Under certain circumstances, an improvement in the terms of trade (a rise of *TOT*) could imply a real appreciation (fall in e_1), and vice versa (see Appendix A).

7. According to Koen and Meyermans (1994: 21), there have been several methods used to calculate the *PPP* rate for Russia. The Institute for World Economy and International Relations (IMEMO) computed a *PPP* rate based on the prices of consumer goods (food and non-food) which is published in *Russian Economic*

Trends. For 1993 the *PPP* rate (as an annual average) was 252 roubles to one dollar. Another measure was the comparison of the price of a Big Mac in roubles in Moscow compared to that of a Big Mac in the United States (the average of the prices in New York, Chicago, San Francisco, and Atlanta). For 1993 the *PPP* rate (as an annual average) was 535 roubles for one dollar. Finally, for 1993, the *PPP* rate (as annual average) based on a basket of 19 food items was 171 roubles for one dollar. The actual exchange rate (as a monthly average of 1993) was 969 roubles for one dollar. Thus, the rouble was heavily undervalued according to all three alternative *PPP* measures for 1993.

8. Oppenheimer (1974) documents early writings on models with non-tradable goods.
9. The case of $q^* \neq 1$ is treated in chaps. 7.5 and 9.2.
10. The empirical validity of *PPP* must strictly refer to the test of e_1. A long-run confirmation of *PPP* would imply either that e_1 is equal to one (absolute *PPP*) or $\Delta e_1/e_1$ is equal to zero (relative *PPP*). However, the empirical tests of *PPP* seem to refer to the real exchange rate of equation 5.1; see Box 5.2 and the survey of older and more recent tests in MacDonald and Taylor (1992: 40–2). If we take equation (5.1) as the relevant test for *PPP*, as we did for the calculation of the real exchange rate of the German mark in Fig. 5.1 and Box 5.2, the deutschmark would have become more and more overvalued over a period of more than twenty years despite the continuous current account surpluses. Thus, the validity or invalidity of *PPP* can only be tested on the basis of e_1. If nevertheless equation (5.1) is chosen for the basis of the test, one has to assume that P_N moves in the same direction and by the same rate as P_T, but this seems to be a rather heroic assumption over the longer run. The reader is invited to consult again Box 5.6.
11. Even the price of the consumption of hamburgers eaten at McDonald's should differ in various places. This statement is contrary to the view of *The Economist*, which, since 1986, has regularly published the undervaluation or overvaluation of the US dollar with respect to other currencies on the basis of price comparisons of McDonald's Big Mac hamburgers in various countries. Assume that our tourist visits only those McDonald's situated in the most prestigious avenues of the various capitals. The production cost of a cooked hamburger will be different at each place, because it includes not only the cost of tradable inputs (agricultural input and capital equipment), but also the cost of non-tradable inputs (land and labour). Even if the law of one price holds for the exchange rate of each country, the consumption price of a hamburger expressed in US dollar prices will differ in each capital. It will be lowest in a capital of an African country (provided that its currency is not overvalued) and it may be highest in cities like Tokyo.
12. They are not to be confounded with the terms of trade of n. 6 and the Appendix A.
13. For the empirical measurement of e_1, a useful price index could be wholesale prices or industrial prices. However, they are difficult to use for international price comparison, as their construction varies greatly among countries. See Turner and Van't Dack (1993: 29–30). The appropriate price index for e_2 could be consumer prices, but these exclude important tradable goods like capital goods, and also important non-tradable goods such as government services (education, health . . .). For this reason, a better proxy for e_2 would be the GDP deflator.
14. At point A_1, compared to point A, each price level (P_T and P_N) has increased by the same percentage points and the same is assumed for the wage level in each production sector.

6

THE EXTERNAL RELATIVE PRICE OF
TRADABLE GOODS (e_1)

The proper definition of the real exchange rate e_1 assumes that the prices of domestic and foreign tradable goods can diverge. Assuming full employment, any excess demand for domestic tradable goods can be eliminated by a rise in the real interest rate and by a real appreciation (through the normal exchange rate mechanism or through an increase in the domestic price level). With perfect capital mobility (interest rate parity), the only medium-run adjustment mechanism would work through the real exchange rate. The equilibrium forces in the market for domestic tradable goods are examined in various circumstances, including various types of real shocks (fiscal policy); within the classical and Keynesian framework; for a small and a large country.

6.1. Real versus Nominal Shocks

The determination of the (nominal and real) exchange rate in Part I was carried out through an analysis of the financial sector. A change in the exchange rate was necessary for adjusting the expected return on foreign financial assets to the return on domestic financial assets. The return had to be expressed in real terms when inflation was present. The exchange rate mechanism constituted the equilibrium forces in the financial markets.

The variability in exchange rates was created by monetary or financial disturbances (money supply shocks or portfolio shifts). Nominal shocks hit the nominal fundamentals of the exchange rate and real shocks the real fundamentals. By definition, real shocks emerge in the real sector (i.e. in the goods market), and their origin can be traced to either the supply or the demand side. Supply shocks can be real cost push effects, such as the world wide oil price increases in the 1970s.[1] Demand shocks occur when there is an increase or decrease in autonomous consumption, investment, exports, or government expenditure. Fiscal expansion in the United States and (relative) fiscal contraction in Europe and Japan were the major real shocks of the 1980s.

In the early 1990s Germany's fiscal expansion, which resulted from the reunification, caused the turmoil of Europe's exchange rate mechanism.

By taking real shocks into account, the exchange rate mechanism fills a second role (besides that of equilibrating financial markets). It ensures the equilibrium in the domestic goods market. The exchange rate is thus a key variable which equilibrates not only financial markets but also the domestic goods market. The link between the two markets in terms of the exchange rate is established by the level of the expected exchange rate (E^e and e^e), as has already been mentioned several times. The real exchange rate which equilibrates the domestic goods market is one of the underlying fundamental factors for exchange rate expectations.

The real exchange rate was defined as the relative price of domestic goods (P) and foreign goods (EP^* where $e = EP^*/P$). In the present chapter, it is considered to be of type e_1 (where $e = e_1 = EP^*_T/P_T$). Consequently, we have to assume that all domestic and foreign goods are tradable or, what is a more reasonable assumption, that *domestic prices of traded and non-traded goods move in the same direction*. The real exchange rate of type e_1 could be called the 'external terms of trade'. This however could be confused with the proper terms of trade which are given by the price ratio of exported over imported goods. For this reason, we designate the real exchange rate of type e_1 the 'external relative price of tradables'.

Those macroeconomic models which do not explicitly make a distinction between tradable and non-tradable goods necessarily belong to the kind of exchange rate determination of type e_1.[2] They assume—admittedly implicitly—that *PPP* (in the sense of the law of one price for tradable goods in the world economy) not only holds, but that a change in the relative price of tradables between two countries (in addition to other real variables) is required to equilibrate the market for domestic goods when a real shock occurs.

6.2. The Real Sector of the Economy

The Real Exchange Rate and the Market for Domestic Goods

The real exchange rate ($e = e_1$) represents one important variable in the demand function for domestic goods. The macroeconomic market for goods always refers to that of domestic goods and its equilibrium condition could be formulated alternatively as:

Box 6.1. GDP versus GNP and trade balance versus current account balance

GDP (gross domestic product) is the outcome of location-based—or country-based—factors of production, independent of who the factors belong to. GNP (gross national product) is the product of ownership-based factors of production. Among the factors of production we shall take capital as an example. The country should be a net creditor country with net financial claims on foreign countries equal to F. The net interest income from abroad is rF. Thus,

$$GNP = GDP + rF.$$

The country's 'disposable' (i.e. national) income is that produced at home (GDP) and that earned abroad (rF). From equation (6.1) we know that

$$GDP = A + (X - Im).$$

Putting the value of GDP into the first equation, we obtain

$$GNP = A + \underbrace{(X - Im)}_{\text{Trade Balance (TB)}} + rF$$

$$\underbrace{}_{\text{Current Account Balance (CA).}}$$

The relevant output concept for the domestic goods market is GDP, i.e. output produced by factors of production located in the domestic economy. Consequently, the relevant external balance for the domestic goods market is the trade balance.

   The current account balance not only includes net foreign interest payments, but also workers' net foreign remittances and net foreign aid transfers (or, more generally, net unilateral transfers). The current account balance will be analysed in Part III. It indicates the change in net wealth with respect to the rest of the world ($CA = \Delta F$).

$$
\begin{aligned}
\bar{y} &= D(e) + X(e) \\
&= D(e) + Im(e) + X(e) - Im(e) \\
&= A + X(e) - Im(A,e) \\
&= A + TB(A,e)
\end{aligned}
\tag{6.1}
$$

where

$\bar{y}$ = (given) supply of domestic goods (GDP) (see Box 6.1)
D = demand by residents for domestic goods
X = demand by foreigners for domestic goods (exports)
Im = demand by residents for foreign goods (imports)
A = demand by residents for domestic and foreign goods
    (absorption = $D + Im$)
TB = trade balance ($X - Im$) (see Box 6.1).

In the present chapter we shall gradually introduce other important variables which have an impact on the total demand for domestic goods, first using a classical macro model. At the end of the chapter we also deal with a Keynesian macro model.

The impact of a change in the real exchange rate on total demand for domestic goods runs through two channels. Assume a real appreciation (lower *e* either through lower *E* or via higher *P*) according to which prices of domestic goods are higher than those of foreign goods ($P > EP^*$). Both the demand by foreigners for domestic goods will fall (lower exports) and the demand by residents for domestic goods will fall (lower *D*). More precisely, the latter refers to the demand for import substitutes. There is a lower demand for import substitutes and a corresponding higher demand for foreign goods (higher imports). For the latter reason, absorption is independent of the real exchange rate (assuming that domestic and foreign goods are substitutable).

In Fig. 6.1 we have illustrated the goods market. The given supply of domestic goods is the vertical line $\bar{y}$. The vertical absorption line *A* (where $A = D + Im$) assumes that a rise in *e*, which increases the demand for domestic goods by domestic residents (ΔD), exactly offsets the decline in imports ($-\Delta Im$). The total demand for domestic goods is indicated by the $A + (X - Im)$ schedule. The usual caveat for normal elasticity conditions and the absence of *J*-curve effects (see Box 6.2) also applies.

An 'autonomous' increase in the *demand for domestic goods* (a rightward shift of the $A + (X - Im)$ schedule) brings about a real appreciation which is necessary to equilibrate the market for domestic goods (point *C*). An increase in the propensity to consume domestic goods by domestic residents, an increase in the propensity to

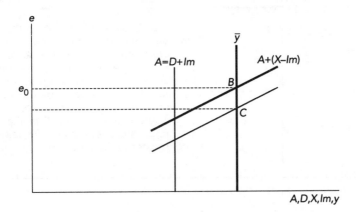

Fig. 6.1. The real exchange rate mechanism for equilibrating the market for domestic goods

The initial equilibrium in the market for domestic goods is at point *B*. An increase in the demand for domestic goods (ΔD or ΔX) shifts the demand locus to the right. The subsequent real appreciation decreases exports and increases the demand for imports at the expense of the demand for domestic import substitutes. An autonomous increase in the demand for imports leaves the demand schedule unchanged ($\Delta A - \Delta Im = O$).

Box 6.2. Devaluation and the J-curve

Imports. Given the domestic price of import substitutes (P_0) and given the foreign price of imported goods (P^*_0), a rise in E from E_0 to E_1 increases the domestic price of imports from $E_0 P_0^*$ to $E_1 P_0^*$. The demand for imports (Q_{im}) decreases which is shown by the proportionate downward shift of the demand schedule. The demand for imported goods falls (and, correspondingly, the demand for import substitutes increases). The shaded rectangular area representing the required foreign exchange for imports shrinks. From the point of view of imports, there is an improvement in the trade balance.

Exports. Given the domestic price of exports (P_0), their price in foreign currency (P_0/E) varies with the exchange rate. A devaluation lowers the foreign price of exports from P_0/E_0 to P_0/E_1 and the demand for exports (Q_{ex}) increases. Export revenues increase with a high price elasticity of the demand for exports, but they decrease with a low price elasticity—as assumed in the illustration by the smaller shaded area—and thus there is a deterioration of the trade balance from the point of view of exports.

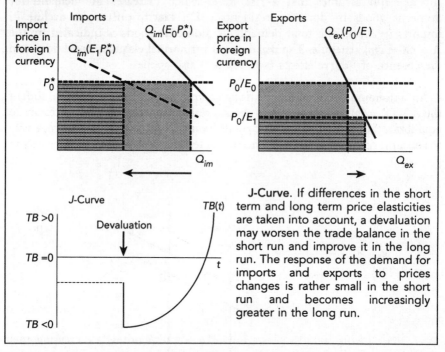

J-Curve. If differences in the short term and long term price elasticities are taken into account, a devaluation may worsen the trade balance in the short run and improve it in the long run. The response of the demand for imports and exports to prices changes is rather small in the short run and becomes increasingly greater in the long run.

invest domestic goods by domestic firms or an increase of public expenditures on domestic goods (or a decrease in the production of domestic goods) all produce a real appreciation which renders domestic goods more expensive relative to foreign goods. Consequently, both the demand by foreigners for domestic goods and the demand by residents for domestic import substitutes fall. We also have the same impact on the real exchange rate if the autonomous shock comes from a rise in the demand for domestic goods by foreigners (exports). In contrast, if the increase in the private demand for consumption or investment goods or the rise in the public demand for goods is exclusively addressed to foreign goods (imports), the real exchange rate remains constant.

However, this statement is only true for perfect capital mobility.[3] In both cases (real appreciation or constant real exchange rate), the demand shock will produce a deterioration of the trade balance which can be easily financed if there is perfect capital mobility. Accommodating capital flows always guarantee an overall equilibrium in the balance of payments. For the opposite extreme hypothesis of capital immobility, any demand shock provoking a trade balance deficit would necessitate a real depreciation provided that the trade deficit is not financed by reserve outflows, something which is conceivable in a managed floating system. Of course, the popular prediction of an expansionary demand shock of the above types would be a (real) depreciation. But different assumptions about the degree of capital mobility affect this popular view.[4]

Fiscal Policy as an Example of Real Shocks (Ricardian Equivalence)

We shall use the case of a budget deficit as an example of a real demand shock in the domestic goods market. We have chosen this particular shock to analyse the *impact of fiscal policy on the real exchange rate*. Unfortunately, at first sight, we have taken a rather controversial example since, under certain assumptions—the Ricardian equivalence theorem—a budget deficit may have no impact at all on real variables, regardless of whether we are in a closed or an open economy. For this reason, we must first discuss the circumstances in which a budget deficit has a real impact on the economy.

In the closed economy literature, there is an on-going debate about whether public debt constitutes net wealth for the global economy. As is to be expected, some economists (e.g. Barro 1974) deny the net wealth aspect and some others argue for it (e.g. Buiter 1985). One of the essential conditions according to which public debt would not represent net wealth concerns the possibility of taxpayers fully discounting their future tax liabilities (which arise to service the debt) so that their disposable permanent income falls. According to this hypothesis, a bond financed budget deficit would imply that private agents react by reducing their consumption and, correspondingly, increasing their savings. In the limiting case the increase in savings could be equal to the amount of the budget deficit. In such a case, a bond financed budget deficit is equivalent to a tax financed budget deficit (Ricardo's equivalence theorem), and its impact on the real macroeconomic variables would be zero, except for the long-run implications of a higher share of government expenditure in GDP; see Box 6.3 and Fig. 6.2.

Applying the Ricardian equivalence theorem to the open economy in terms of equation (6.1) and of Fig. 6.1, an increase in public expenditure on domestic goods ΔG (where $\Delta G = \Delta A = \Delta D$) financed by additional public debt which brings about a reduction in private expenditures of the same size would not involve a real appreciation as predicted in the preceding section (provided that the decline of private expenditures concerns only the outlays on domestic goods). However, there are a couple of reasons why the Ricardian equivalence theorem may not fully hold, and the empirical evidence is also controversial.[5] In the following discussion, we shall assume that public debt is not fully neutral.

Box 6.3. An algebraic formulation of the Ricardian equivalence theorem

Assume an individual whose lifetime consists of two periods, today and tomorrow. His total income is Y_1 (today's income) and Y_2 (tomorrow's income), whose present value is $Y_2/(1 + r)$. During his lifetime he will consume (C) his total income so that:

$$C_1 + C_2/(1 + r) = Y_1 + Y_2/(1 + r).$$

However, his total disposable income streams are reduced by taxes (T) so that his intertemporal budget constraint becomes:

$$C_1 + C_2/(1 + r) = (Y_1 - T_1) + (Y_2 - T_2)/(1 + r).$$

Government also has an intertemporal budget constraint in the sense that today's and tomorrow's public expenditures (G) must equal total tax revenues:

$$G_1 + G_2/(1 + r) = T_1 + T_2/(1 + r).$$

If government increases today's expenditure without increasing today's taxes (today's budget deficit) and without decreasing tomorrow's expenditure, it has to increase tomorrow's taxes [$\Delta G_1 = \Delta T_2/(1 + r)$], which implies a budget surplus for tomorrow. As far as our individual's disposable income is concerned, it will decrease by $\Delta G_1 = \Delta T_2/(1 + r)$. This decrease in disposable income is the same as if ΔG_1 had been financed by ΔT_1 since $\Delta G_1 = \Delta T_1$. This is the essence of Ricardo's equivalence theorem. Additional government expenditure reduces disposable permanent income independently of whether this public expenditure is financed by debt or by taxes: See Fig. 6.2.

The Budget Deficit, the Real Exchange Rate, and the Real Interest Rate

We shall introduce a second variable, the real interest rate, which influences the volume of absorption. Equation (6.1) can be extended to

$$\bar{y} = A(r) + TB(A,e). \tag{6.2}$$

The *IS*-schedule of Fig. 6.3 illustrates the equilibrium in the market for domestic goods.[6] Its positive slope is explained by the fact that a rise in the real interest rate lowers the demand for domestic goods while a real depreciation increases it via a higher demand for (domestic) import substitutes and via higher exports. Any point on the left (right) side of the *IS*-schedule is a situation of excess demand (supply) of domestic goods.

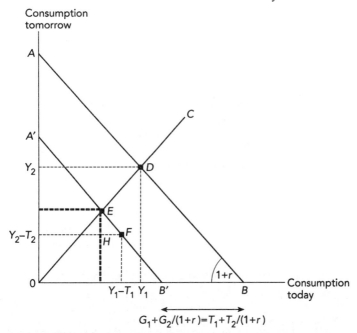

Fig. 6.2. The Ricardian equivalence theorem

Total income (today's and tomorrow's income) is equal to $OB = OA/(1 + r)$. If we assume that today's income is the same as tomorrow's income (point D where $Y_1 = Y_2/(1 + r)$), then by assumption, the individual consumes his total income and his line of intertemporal consumption is OC. His present and future consumption is also at point D.

With taxes, his total disposable income is reduced to $OB' = OA'/(1 + r)$. The distance BB' illustrates government's total expenditures being equal to total tax revenues. If $G_1 = T_1 = G_2/(1 + r) = T_2/(1 + r)$, the individual's disposable income and consumption streams are at point E. However, assume now that, with $G_1 = G_2/(1 + r)$, taxes are lower today (budget deficit) and higher tomorrow (budget surplus). The individual's disposable income is now at point F and his optimal consumption point is at E. Today, he saves FH which permits today's budget deficit to be financed. Tomorrow, he uses his savings for consumption (HE).

A debt financed budget deficit shifts IS toward IS_1. For the moment, it is assumed that the additional government expenditure is used for the purchase of *domestic* goods. Depending on the degree of capital mobility, three alternative equilibrium situations are conceivable from the point of view of the IS-schedule: point B_1 with capital immobility, and points B_2 and B_3 with perfect capital mobility, where B_2 stands for a small country and B_3 for a large country. For the moment, we shall not take into account the monetary sector (i.e. the LM-schedule) which will be added later.

Capital Immobility (point B_1 in Fig. 6.3). When there is complete capital immobility, the domestic economy works like a closed economy. Since the balance of payments coincides with the trade balance, any bond financed

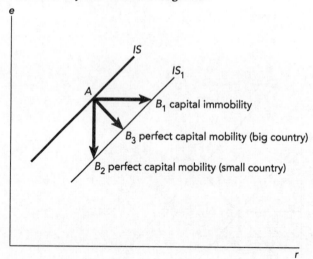

Fig. 6.3. The effects of fiscal expansion on the real exchange rate ($\Delta G = \Delta D$)

The initial equilibrium in the market for domestic goods is at point A. Government increases its expenditures on domestic goods (budget deficit), implying a shift of IS towards IS_1. With capital immobility, the equilibrium in the market for domestic goods is restored by the crowding-out effect of the interest rate mechanism (point B_1). With perfect capital mobility, the equilibrium is brought about by the crowding-out effect of the real exchange rate mechanism for a small country (B_2). For a big country which influences the world interest rate, both mechanisms are at work (point B_3).

budget deficit would be fully financed by domestic savings via a rise in the domestic interest rate (a total crowding-out effect via the interest rate mechanism). The fall in private outlays on consumption and investment is exactly equal to the rise in public expenditure.[7] This model of an economy represents the ideal type of an open economy for the proponents of capital controls (such as Liviatan (1980), Tobin (1982), and Dornbusch (1986)), since real internal shocks would not be transmitted to foreign countries via the real exchange rate.[8] It was also the model which underlay, during the Bretton Woods system, the discussions about the advantages of floating exchange rates, since their advocates disregarded capital movements. In this aspect, the economy works like a closed economy ($TB = 0$).

Perfect Capital Mobility: Small Country (point B_2 in Fig. 6.3).   In a world of capital mobility, the budget deficit will be financed jointly by domestic and foreign savings. According to the hypothesis of perfect capital mobility for a small open economy (which, by definition, has no impact on the real world interest rate), the budget deficit would be totally financed by external savings (i.e. by capital inflows). There must be a real transfer in terms of goods equal to the financial transfer. The real transfer is made possible through a real appreciation of the domestic currency, which includes (under normal elasticity conditions and ignoring short-run *J*-curve effects) fewer exports and more imports. The real transfer via the real appreciation is necessary to equilibrate the market for domestic goods. The excess demand for domestic goods is eliminated by a lower demand by residents for (domestic) import substitutes and by a lower demand by foreigners for domestic goods.

Consequently, the real appreciation creates a total crowding-out effect, not in terms of domestic absorption (which remains unchanged) but in terms of fewer import substitutes demanded by residents and fewer exports demanded by foreigners. This is the traditional result of the old-fashioned Mundell–Fleming model. Through the real exchange rate effect, domestic goods are available for government expenditure via fewer exports and via a switch from import substitutes to imported goods.

Perfect Capital Mobility: Big Country (point B_3 in Fig. 6.3). If the budget deficit takes place in a big country—say the United States—the adjustment process will differ, since a two-country model must now be used: the United States and the rest of the world (ROW). We still retain the assumption of perfect capital mobility. The rise in the US bond financed budget deficit increases the real world market interest rate. Consequently, there is some crowding-out of private expenditure in the United States and some other crowding-out of private expenditure in the ROW, the first creates excess savings in the United States and the second excess savings in the ROW. It follows that the budget deficit is financed partly by domestic savings and partly by foreign savings via capital inflows. The corresponding transfer of goods from the ROW to the United States is realized by the real appreciation of the US dollar which involves a trade balance surplus in the ROW. From the point of view of a two-country model, the former crowding-out effect of net exports (exports minus imports, described for a small country) is actually a crowding-out effect of domestic and foreign private absorption. Furthermore, the change in the real exchange rate equilibrates the markets for domestic goods in the USA and in the ROW.[9]

Consequently, bond financed budget deficits in a large economy like the USA constitute a real shock to the domestic and foreign country; the same reasoning can be developed for an autonomous increase in domestic consumption or investment in the private sector. These real shocks influence the real world market interest rate and provoke a switch of savings in the world economy from the ROW to the United States via capital movements. There must be net trade flows, brought about by a change in the real exchange rate equal to the net capital movements. This change is necessary to equilibrate the national markets for domestic goods. In this sense, the system of flexible exchange rates does not allow macroeconomic independence except in the case of capital immobility. In a two-country model appropriate for big countries, real shocks emerging in one country are transmitted to other countries via the interest and exchange rate mechanisms.

The External Constraint under Capital Immobility

The impact of a real shock on the real exchange rate is different with perfect capital immobility (constancy of the real exchange rate) than with the other extreme possibility of perfect capital mobility (real appreciation). Unfortunately, its impact on the real exchange rate is even more confusing if other factors like the external constraint or the pattern of public expenditure (to be discussed in the following section) are taken into account.

With capital immobility there is an external constraint. It consists of an equilibrated trade balance as long as any movements in international reserves are excluded. In the absence of capital flows, the trade balance coincides with the balance of payments. Thus, a trade balance deficit is identical to a balance of payments deficit. The condition of the external equilibrium has to be added to the condition of the internal equilibrium of the domestic goods market (equation (6.2)):

Internal Equilibrium (*IS*) $\bar{y} = A(r) + TB(A,e)$ (6.2)

External Equilibrium (*TB*) $TB = TB(A,e) = 0$ (6.3)

In Fig. 6.4 we have added the *TB*-schedule to the *IS*-schedule of Fig. 6.3. The negative slope of the *TB*-schedule can be explained as follows. Assume that the economy is at point A. A real depreciation improves the trade balance. The trade balance surplus will be eliminated by a certain fall in the interest rate since the latter increases absorption, i.e. the demand for domestic and foreign goods. Any point right (left) of the *TB*-schedule is a situation of a trade balance surplus (deficit).

It should be emphasized that the external constraint in terms of the *TB*-schedule is relevant for the determination of the real exchange rate only when capital is immobile. With capital mobility, there is no need to stay on the *TB*-schedule.

Types of Government Expenditure

We shall now raise the same question as in Fig. 6.3 with regard to the impact of a budget deficit on the real exchange rate, but now only for the case of a small country. We shall take into account two additional aspects. First, assuming complete capital immobility, we have to consider the movement of the real exchange rate which ensures both internal and external equilibrium. Second, we are now forced to know the category of goods—domestic or foreign goods—on which the additional government expenditure is made, since this question affects the size of the rightward shift of the *IS*-schedule and of the *TB*-schedule. We shall distinguish three extreme cases (Fig. 6.4): (*a*) the additional expenditure is only made for the purchase of domestic goods ($\Delta G = \Delta D$); (*b*)

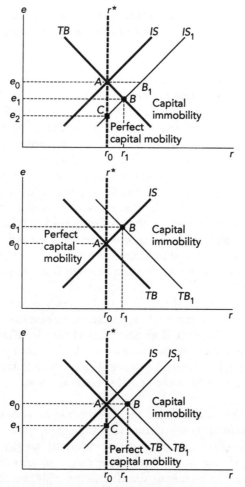

Fig. 6.4. The spending pattern of additional government expenditure (ΔG) and different impacts on the real exchange rate (the case of a small country)

Fig. 6.4a. $\Delta G = \Delta D$

There is only a shift of *IS* to the right. With capital immobility the rise in *r* could eliminate excess demand for domestic goods, but it also lowers imports. The trade balance surplus is eliminated by a real appreciation. Under perfect capital mobility excess demand for domestic goods is eliminated by real appreciation (lower exports and lower demand for import substitutes).

Fig. 6.4b. $\Delta G = \Delta Im$

There is only a shift of *TB* to the right. With capital immobility the trade balance deficit has to be eliminated by real depreciation. Under perfect capital mobility the domestic goods market remains in equilibrium.

Fig. 6.4c $\Delta G = \Delta D + \Delta Im$

Both equilibrium schedules shift to the right. The outcome for *r* and *e* is a combination of Figs. a and b.

the additional government expenditure is made exclusively for the purchase of imported goods ($\Delta G = \Delta Im$); (c) the additional expenditure is made on both categories of goods ($\Delta G = \Delta D + \Delta Im$).

(a) $\Delta G = \Delta D$ (Fig. 6.4a). As in Fig. 6.3, there is only a rightward shift of IS to the position IS_1. With *capital immobility*, the real exchange rate does not remain unchanged (as was the case at point B_1 in Fig. 6.3), but a certain real appreciation is necessary to maintain the external equilibrium (point B). At point B_1 the rise in the domestic interest rate produced a total crowding-out effect on private expenditure in favour of government expenditure. The reduction in private expenditure concerns the decrease of private outlays on domestic and foreign goods. Consequently, at point B_1 there is a surplus in the trade balance. It is true that a trade balance surplus constitutes a less imperative external constraint for the economy than a deficit does. The trade balance surplus is equal to the balance of payments surplus. In a free-floating exchange rate regime, the real exchange rate would appreciate (point B) and the interest rate would rise less, the two mechanisms bringing about internal and external equilibrium.[10]

As far as the assumption of *perfect capital mobility* is concerned (point C in Fig. 6.4a), we observe the same real appreciation as discussed in the context of Fig. 6.3 (point B_2). Since the domestic interest rate is linked to the international one, the crowding-out mechanism works exclusively through the real exchange rate, provoking a trade balance deficit which is the same size as the budget deficit. The trade balance deficit is easily financed by capital inflows.[11]

(b) $\Delta G = \Delta Im$ (Fig. 6.4b). Since the IS-schedule describes the equilibrium condition in the market for domestic goods, the additional demand for imports does not affect the demand for domestic goods. The IS-schedule remains unchanged and the TB-schedule shifts towards TB_1. With *capital immobility* a balance of payments deficit emerges. Given a limited amount of international reserves, this situation is not sustainable. In a situation of freely fluctuating exchange rates, there would be a real depreciation (point B). Since this creates an excess demand for domestic goods (via a higher demand for import substitutes and higher exports), the internal equilibrium is realized by a rise in the interest rate. Here, we are facing the common-sense argument that a budget deficit produces a depreciation. The proper real exchange rate mechanism does not equilibrate the market for domestic goods. Rather, it equilibrates the trade balance under the assumption of capital immobility.

With *perfect capital mobility*, there is no change in the real exchange rate (point A). The budget deficit again provokes a trade balance deficit of the same size financed by foreign credits.

(c) $\Delta G = \Delta D + \Delta Im$ (Fig. 6.4c). We now have a combination of cases (a) and (b). Both schedules shift to the right, that is, to IS_1 and to TB_1. The pattern of the additional government expenditure should be such that we get the precise outcome of Fig. 6.3. With *capital immobility* there is no change in the real exchange rate (point *B*). The rise in the domestic interest rate has two effects. First, it crowds out the private demand for domestic goods by the precise amount of Δ*D*. Second, it also crowds out the private demand for imports by the precise amount of Δ*Im*. Consequently, the interest rate mechanism simultaneously realizes the internal and external equilibrium.

With *perfect capital mobility* (point *C*) the interest rate again remains constant and the whole adjustment burden of equilibrating the market for domestic goods must be carried by the exchange rate mechanism. But the real appreciation is less than in the case of Fig. 6.4*a*, since the autonomous increase in *D* is smaller. Again, the budget deficit must be equal to the trade balance deficit.

Box 6.4 summarizes the present section; see also the Mathematical Appendix. In the case of capital immobility, anything can happen to the real exchange rate. With capital mobility, a real depreciation is completely excluded.[12] In the following sections we shall add the monetary sector. We are concerned exclusively with case (*a*) where Δ*G* = Δ*D*, and the assumption of capital immobility is excluded.

Box 6.4. Fiscal expansion and real exchange rate effects (for a small country)

Pattern of additional government expenditure	Capital immobility: a rise in the real interest rate and	Perfect capital mobility: a constant real interest rate and
(a) Δ*G* = Δ*D*	Real appreciation	Real appreciation
(b) Δ*G* = Δ*Im*	Real depreciation	Constant real exchange rate
(c) Δ*G* = Δ*D* + Δ*Im*	Constant real exchange rate	Real appreciation

---

6.3. The Classical Approach to the Macroeconomic Determination of the Exchange Rate

The Financial Sector of the Economy

There is yet another variable which could contribute to the crowding-out of private expenditure in favour of public expenditure. It is the general price level. It is not only a rising real interest rate, or an appreciating real exchange rate, that would reduce private expenditure on domestic (and foreign) goods, a rising price level would also do so through the 'wealth-saving relationship'. A higher price level reduces wealth via the decline in real cash balances; a lower wealth level increases savings (at the expense of consumption outlays).[13]

This third crowding-out mechanism is a typical equilibrium regulator in classical macroeconomics. The other two, the real interest rate and the real exchange rate described in the previous section, are common to the classical and Keynesian models.

The classical macro model of an open economy with freely floating exchange rates is formulated in Box 6.5, where *RIRP* stands for the real interest rate parity. For the moment, we assume risk neutrality so that $CRP = 0$. We also assume an economy without any inflation so that the real interest rate coincides with the nominal one. There are three variables (e, r, P) to be determined by three equations.[14]

Box 6.5. The classical macro-model for the determination of the real exchange rate (for a small country with perfect capital mobility)

IS	$y = A(r,m) + TB(A,e)$	(6.4)
LM	$m = L(r)$ where $m = M/P$	(6.5)
RIRP	$r = r^* + (e^e - e)/e + CRP$	(6.6)

The easiest way to interpret the determination of the three unknowns is to work with the assumption that $r = r^*$, implying that $e^e = e$. There are now only two variables to be determined, namely m (or P) by the equilibrium condition (6.5) of the money market and e by the equilibrium condition (6.4) of the market for domestic goods.

For the short run—and, in particular, immediately after the emergence of a real or monetary shock—there might be a divergence between the domestic and foreign interest rates. Under these circumstances, the real exchange rate will be determined by *RIRP*. This (financial) equilibrium value of the exchange rate will not necessarily be the equilibrium value for the goods market. Furthermore, the domestic interest rate might not have an immediate impact on m if there is only a gradual adjustment of the price level.

In Fig. 6.5 we have reproduced the *IS*-schedule of Fig. 6.4a, the *RIRP*-schedule of Fig. 4.6 and added the *LM*-schedule in the lower panel. The *LM*-schedule coincides with the demand for real cash balances. Any point below (above) the *LM*-schedule indicates an excess supply (demand) of real cash balances. The initial equilibrium for the real exchange rate is at point A where the financial markets (*RIRP*) produce the same equilibrium exchange rate (e_0) as the goods market (*IS*). The equilibrium in the money market is at point D. We shall again consider a real shock in the form of a budget deficit, but now for both exchange rate regimes—floating and fixed exchange rates.

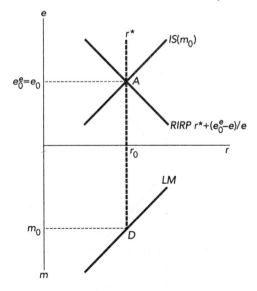

Fig. 6.5. The classical macro-model of the real exchange rate (a small country with perfect capital mobility)

The macroeconomic approach to the determination of the real exchange rate includes the monetary approach in terms of the real interest rate parity (*RIRP*) which assumes perfect capital mobility. The equilibrium value of the real exchange rate is at point A, where $r = r^*$ and where the real exchange rate according to *RIRP* coincides with the real exchange rate as the relative price of domestic goods (*IS*). The monetary equilibrium (*LM*) is realized at point D, where the interest rate gives rise to a certain price level for a given nominal quantity of money ($m_0 = M/P_0$).

Fiscal Policy under Floating and Fixed Exchange Rates

Floating exchange rates. The fiscal shock where $\Delta G = \Delta D$ (Fig. 6.6) shifts the IS-schedule towards the position IS_1 as already explained in previous sections. As far as the long run equilibrium values are concerned, the small open economy is unable to influence the international real interest rate (r^*). Consequently, r_0 is identical to the international real interest rate. The whole adjustment process which equilibrates the market for domestic goods is carried out by the real appreciation (e_2). As long as the decline of e_0 toward e_2 is accompanied by an immediate revision of exchange rate expectations (from $e^e_0 = e_0$ towards $e^e_2 = e_2$), which produces the new $RIRP_2$ schedule, there would be neither short-term fluctuations of r around r_0 nor short-term fluctuations of e around e_2 (point C). If r remains fixed, the monetary equilibrium would be maintained at point D. Thus, the results of Fig. 6.4a are confirmed by the present macroeconomic analysis in terms of the classical model.

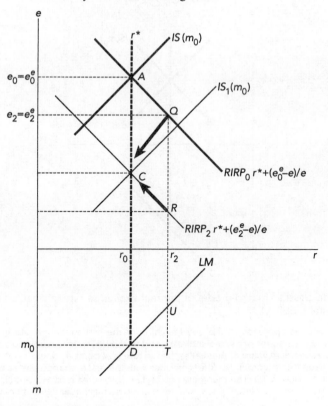

Fig. 6.6. The classical macro-model: fiscal shock (AG = ΔD)

The long-run impact of the fiscal shock (IS_1) is at point C. The monetary equilibrium (LM) remains unchanged (point D). According to RIRP, the short-run run adjustment process for $r > r^*$ begins either at point Q or at the overshooting point R. In both cases, the adjustment converges towards point C.

However, it is highly probable that the short-run adjustment process differs from its long-run path (points C and D). The immediate impact of the fiscal expansion is a rise in the domestic interest rate (r_2). Among the various possibilities for the short-run value of the real exchange rate, we shall choose points Q and R. In both cases, its equilibrium value is dominated by RIRP either with no revision of exchange rate expectations (point Q where $e^e_0 = e_0$) or with their full revision (point R where $e^e_2 = e_2$). The goods market (IS_1) remains in disequilibrium, and so does the money market (LM) at point T. With the higher domestic interest rate, there is an excess supply of real cash balances (TU) which gives rise to an additional demand for domestic goods and bonds, but the inertia in the price level adjustment prevents a rise in P. Consequently, the excess supply in the money market exercises downward pressure on the domestic interest rate—the excess supply of real cash balances spills over to an excess demand for bonds. The subsequent adjustment process will take place either from Q to C under continuous revisions of exchange rate expectations or from R to C for the immediate revision of exchange rate expectations. The latter case stands for the temporary overshooting of the real exchange rate.

The description of the adjustment process assumed floating exchange rates. Short and long run changes in the real exchange rate take place via changes in the nominal exchange rate for a given price level. Fig. 6.7 is a reproduction of Fig. 5.5. In the upper panel, the slope of the Oe_0 ray indicates the initial real exchange rate e_0. The real appreciation (e_2) is brought about by a nominal appreciation $(E_2$ at point $C)$ and the short-run movements of e $(Q$ or $R)$ are identical to movements in E.

Fixed exchange rates. Within the classical model, the change in the real exchange rate can also take place under the regime of fixed exchange rates. With an unchanged nominal exchange rate (E_0) the real appreciation (e_2) is realized by a rise in the price level $(P_2$ at point $B)$. Our fiscal shock now pushes the prices of domestic goods upwards since the excess demand in the market for domestic goods can only be eliminated by an increase in the relative price of domestic goods with respect to foreign goods (via a lower E or a higher P).

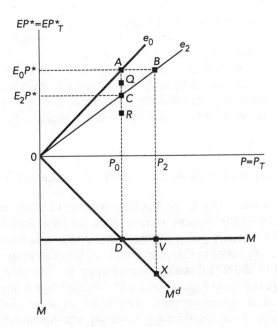

Fig. 6.7. Real appreciation under floating and fixed exchange rates

Under floating exchange rates the real appreciation from e_0 to e_2 is brought about by the nominal appreciation from A to C. Under fixed exchange rates the real appreciation takes place via a higher price level from A to B.

Considering just the long-run equilibrium values (e_2, r_0, and m_0 in Fig. 6.6), the higher price level creates an excess demand for money (*XV* in the lower panel of Fig. 6.7) which has to be satisfied by a higher supply of money (*M*). According to the monetary approach to the balance of payments (see section 2.2), the excess demand for money creates a balance of payments surplus which is identical to an increase in international reserves. With non-sterilized intervention policies for maintaining the fixed exchange rate, the quantity of money increases and the new monetary equilibrium is at point *X*.

Currency risk premium.   Until now we have assumed risk neutrality with respect to the exchange rate risk. The existence of a positive risk premium (*CRP*) in equation (6.6) has to be interpreted as follows. The country has a trade balance deficit provoked by the budget deficit. This trade deficit is financed by foreign investors. Since the latter are risk averse regarding the future evolution of the exchange rate of the domestic currency, they will only hold additional domestic treasury bonds if the return on these bonds is higher than the return on the financial assets of the other country. Thus, for stationary expectations of the future exchange rate $[(e^e - e)/e = 0]$, we have $r - CRP = r^*$; the domestic interest rate must be higher than the foreign interest rate to cover the exchange rate risk of foreign investors who hold domestic assets.[15]

In Fig. 6.8 we have reproduced the upper panel of Fig. 6.6. The new long-run equilibrium position is at point *B*. The interest rate differential $r_1 - r^*$ expresses the currency risk premium for the foreign investors. The adjustment process now runs from *Q* to *B* (gradual revision of the exchange rate expectation) or from *R'* to *B* (overshooting). The ultimate higher domestic interest rate implies a lower real appreciation (e_1), since the interest mechanism contributes equally to the elimination of the excess demand for goods.[16]

Monetary Policy under Floating and Fixed Exchange Rates

Floating exchange rates.   As far as floating exchange rates are concerned, the reader can disregard the present section since we have already treated the impact of an expansionary policy on the real exchange rate within the framework of interest rate parity in Chapters 3 and 4. The main lesson we drew was the explanation of the overshooting phenomenon for both the nominal and the real exchange rates (see Figs. 4.5 and 4.6). We shall repeat this exercise now within the classical macroeconomic framework to show that the partial analysis of Chapter 3 did not miss any other aspects. Again, we shall operate with the interest rate parity with no risk premium.

In Fig. 6.9 we have reproduced the classical macro model of Fig. 6.5. The expansionary monetary policy is indicated in the lower panel by the distance *DF* which represents ΔM. The equilibrium in the money market (*LM*) requires

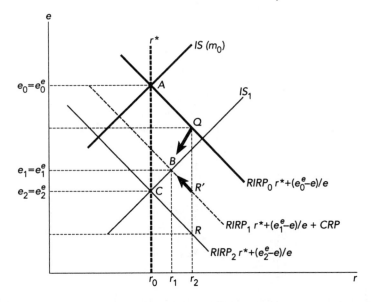

Fig. 6.8. The classical macro-model with currency risk premium: fiscal shock ($\Delta G = \Delta D$)

Unlike in Fig. 6.6, the long-run equilibrium is at point B and not at point C. The higher domestic interest rate (r_1), reflecting the currency risk premium, requires a lower real appreciation since the crowding-out effect also operates via r.

a fall in the interest rate from r_0 to r_1 (point C). Since the domestic interest rate is no longer identical to the foreign one, a real depreciation has to take place according to the interest rate parity (point B), creating the expectation of a future real appreciation of the domestic currency. At point B, situated to the left of the IS-schedule, there is an excess demand for domestic goods which begins to push the price level upwards. Consequently, within the monetary sector, m declines and r rises (a movement from C towards D). The gradual real appreciation is the other consequence (a movement from B towards A). As we know from Figs. 4.5 and 4.6, the real appreciation takes place through a rise in the price level and through a nominal appreciation.

Fixed exchange rates. At first sight, under fixed exchange rates, the nominal shock in the form of an expansionary monetary policy may be feasible within the band of allowed fluctuations of the exchange rate. As we know, fixed exchange rates are flexible within some upper and lower margins which constitute the band. Thus, in the former EMS, the par value could move upwards and downwards by 2.25 per cent. Within this band, the interest rate parity remains valid. Thus, an interest rate differential is conceivable if the necessary changes in the exchange rate take place within the band.[17]

However, the permitted but limited fluctuations around the central par

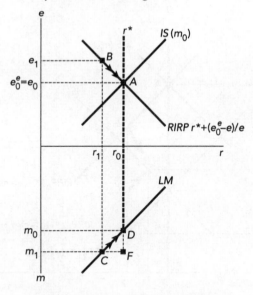

Fig. 6.9. The classical macro-model: monetary shock (ΔM)

The increase in the quantity of money by DF causes the decline of the interest rate to r_1. To render domestic financial assets more attractive, the expectation of a future real appreciation has to arise and this is brought about by a real depreciation (point B). Lower r and higher e provoke an excess demand for domestic goods. Their prices increase gradually, implying that the movements in r ($C \to D$) and in e ($B \to A$) are reversed. The real appreciation is the combined outcome of an increasing price level and of a nominal appreciation.

value refer to nominal exchange rates. The first impact of the expansionary monetary policy is the reduction in the real interest rate to r_1 and a real (and nominal) depreciation to point B (Fig. 6.9). Since the future price level will rise, a revision of the future nominal exchange rate also takes place, which could push the nominal exchange rate toward its floor value. Such a constellation would imply enormous capital outflows, causing large balance of payments deficits and losses in international reserves to maintain the fixed exchange rate. The reserve outflows are the automatic regulator which reduces the quantity of money to its initial level with (in the case of non-sterilized interventions) the consequent re-adjustment of the interest rate towards r_0.

6.4. A Keynesian Approach to the Macroeconomic Determination of the Exchange Rate

The Macro Model

Compared to the classical model, the Keynesian model looks simpler. The assumption of a fixed output is replaced by the assumption of a fixed price level; see Box 6.6. Consequently, any change in nominal variables is identical with a real change. Thus, an increase in the nominal exchange rate (E) coincides with the same increase in the real exchange rate (e).[18] We shall continue with the assumption of perfect substitutability between domestic and foreign financial assets which for a small country means—in the context of Keynesian economics—that the real and nominal interest rates are given within the framework of the interest rate parity.[19]

Box. 6.6. The Keynesian macro-model for the determination of the exchange rate (for a small country with perfect capital mobility)

IS	$y = A(r,y) + TB(A,e)$	(6.7)
LM	$M = L(r,y)$	(6.8)
NIRP and RIRP	$r = r^* + (e^e - e)/e$	(6.9)

Assuming equality between the domestic and foreign interest rate ($r = r^*$), the determination of the macroeconomic equilibrium can be dichotomized. The money market—equation (6.8)—fixes the equilibrium level of income (instead of the price level as in the classical approach) and the equilibrium mechanism of the goods market—equation (6.7)—determines the exchange rate.

The macro model of Box 6.6 is shown in Fig. 6.10. Its upper panel is identical to that of the classical counterpart of Fig. 6.6, though we must again stress that e and r are nominal and real rates. The lower panel illustrates the traditional Keynesian r,y space. For a given interest rate (r_0), LM determines y (point D). The given interest rate is the international one (r^*) so that we have interest rate identity as a special case of the RIRP at point A. At this precise point, the exchange rate as the equilibrium relative price of domestic financial assets (RIRP) coincides with the real exchange rate as the equilibrium relative price of domestic goods (IS).

For purposes of comparison, we have added the IS-LM-diagram of the more familiar Mundell–Fleming model in a box as part of Fig. 6.10. This model always operates with the assumption of interest rate identity in the case of perfect capital mobility. The horizontal r^* line is also often called the schedule of external equilibrium or of balance-of-payments equilibrium. It should be mentioned that the original (or traditional) Mundell–Fleming model disregards interest rate parity. The value of the exchange rate is always determined by the equilibrium mechanism of the goods market (IS).

The Mundell–Fleming model has become the workhorse of international monetary economics all over the world. Being a less sophisticated Keynesian model, it excludes changes in the general price level unlike more elaborated Keynesian models such as neo-Keynesian and new-Keynesian macro models. It is probably for this reason that the popular view of changes in the real

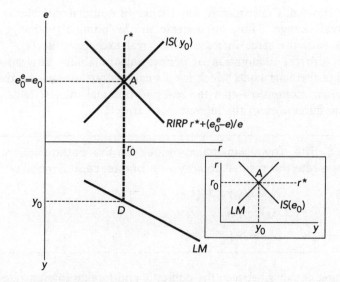

Fig. 6.10. The Keynesian macro-model of the exchange rate (a small country with perfect capital mobility)

The boxed figure represents the traditional Mundell–Fleming version of an open economy. The horizontal r^*-line stands for the external equilibrium schedule of the balance of payments. The upper panel of Fig. 6.10 is identical to the classical case of Fig. 6.5. It is Keynesian since P (or m) is replaced by y (in the lower panel). The financial sector is again the combination of LM and $RIRP$.

exchange rate is considered only in the context of floating exchange rates. This is correct for the simple Keynesian approach, but is erroneous for the classical approach according to which changes in the real exchange rate also take place under fixed exchange rates.

It is precisely for this reason that, within the Keynesian framework, a change in the real exchange rate can *only* be analysed under the regime of floating exchange rates. Furthermore, monetary shocks (monetary policy), and not only real shocks (fiscal policy), will have an impact on the real exchange rate.

Fiscal and Monetary Policy under Floating Exchange Rates

Fiscal Policy. The short- and long-run impacts of a budget deficit on the (real) exchange rate are the same in the Keynesian framework (the upper panel of Fig. 6.11) as in the classical case (the upper panel of Fig. 6.6). Since the reader may be more acquainted with the Mundell–Fleming model which describes the long-run effect, we shall first interpret the results of the model in the box on Fig. 6.11. The expansionary fiscal policy shifts the $IS(e_0)$ schedule towards $IS_1(e_0)$. Since r and y remain at r_0 (due to the assumption of interest rate

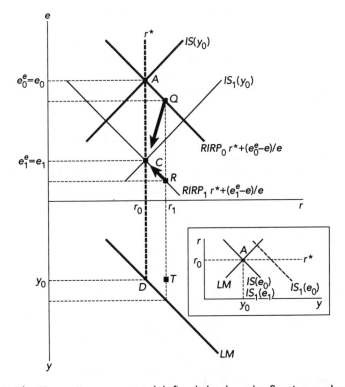

Fig. 6.11. The Keynesian macro-model: fiscal shock under floating exchange rates

In the Mundell–Fleming framework (shown in the boxed figure), the fiscal expansion shifts the $IS(e_0)$ schedule toward IS_1 (e_0). The excess demand for goods is eliminated by the long-run appreciation of e_1 which shifts the IS_1 (e_0) back to IS_1 (e_1). In the short run (Fig. 6.11), the interest rate can rise toward, r_1. The short-run repercussion on e is at Q (a gradual revision of exchange rate expectations) or R (overshooting).

identity) and at y_0 (due to the determination of y by LM), the crowding-out of the excess demand in the market for domestic goods can only be brought about by an appreciation (e_1) which shifts the $IS_1(e_0)$ line back towards $IS_1(e_1)$.

However, our model (Fig. 6.11) also highlights the transition period of exchange rate movements dominated by interest rate parity. With interest rate parity, the domestic interest rate can increase (r_1) under the pressure of the fiscal deficit. If exchange rate expectations are not revised immediately after the fiscal shock occurs, there is only a slight appreciation (point Q) leaving the goods market (IS_1) with excess demand and the money market (LM) with excess supply (point T). An instantaneous reaction to an increase in output (y) is excluded by assuming that producers only gradually adjust output to changes in demand, and that their first adjustment is to reduce inventories. With revisions of exchange rate expectations step-by-step towards the new fundamental exchange rate e_1, the exchange rate movement may follow the path $Q \rightarrow C$.

If the new fundamental exchange rate for the long run (point C) is recognized immediately by financial markets after the real shock occurs, the $RIRP_0$ line shifts towards $RIRP_1$. We again notice overshooting of the exchange rate (point R). As in the classical case, the adjustment of the exchange rate could follow the arrow $R \rightarrow C$.[20]

Monetary policy. The best guide for the long-run impact of an expansionary monetary policy is the Mundell–Fleming model shown in the Box on Fig. 6.12. The *LM*-schedule shifts towards LM_1, and, with rising output and unchanged interest rates ($r_0 = r^*$ at point B), there would be an excess supply in the goods

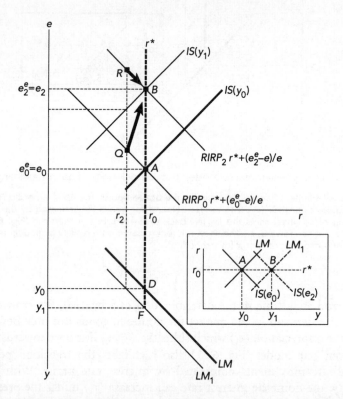

Fig. 6.12. The Keynesian macro-model: monetary shock under floating exchange rates

Within the Mundell–Fleming model (the boxed figure), the long run impact of monetary expansion (a shift of LM toward LM_1) increases income to y_1 creating an excess supply of domestic goods. This excess supply is eliminated by the depreciation of e_2. In Fig. 6.12 the long-run movements are from D to F and from A to B. The short-run adjustment process during which r falls, implies either gradual depreciations (point Q with several revisions of exchange rate expectations) or overshooting (point R).

market $[IS(e_0)]$. Under floating exchange rates, a depreciation (e_2) must take place to equilibrate the goods market at point B $[IS(e_2)]$. Thus, in the Keynesian world with perfect capital mobility and floating exchange rates, an expansionary monetary policy is effective for increasing output (accompanied by depreciation) while an expansionary fiscal policy (accompanied by appreciation) is not.

By taking into account Fig. 6.12, the long-run adjustment process takes place as in the Box of Fig. 6.12. The monetary expansion (LM_1) leads to a higher real income (y_1). The ultimate higher production (y_1) shifts the $IS(y_0)$-schedule toward $IS(y_1)$ and the resulting excess supply of domestic goods (at the interest rate level r_0) can only be eliminated by the depreciation towards point B.

The first short-run effect of the expansionary monetary policy is the lower interest rate (r_2) in Fig. 6.12. On the one hand, according to interest parity, the fall in the interest rate involves a depreciation at point Q. On the other hand, it creates an additional demand for domestic goods through which production (y) will be increased, shifting the $IS(y_0)$ upwards. From the point of view of the domestic goods market, an additional depreciation is needed to increase the demand for domestic goods, since production has risen and the fall in the interest rate will be reversed.

The exchange rate movements are either $A \rightarrow Q \rightarrow B$ with gradual revisions of exchange rate expectations or $A \rightarrow R \rightarrow B$ with an immediate revision of exchange rate expectations $(RIRP_2)$ just after the monetary shock occurs, again involving the overshooting phenomenon.

Fiscal and Monetary Policy under Fixed Exchange Rates

Fiscal policy. For the regime of fixed exchange rates with perfect capital mobility for which interest rate identity $(r = r^*)$ becomes the relevant case,[21] we can again consult the Mundell–Fleming model of Fig. 6.13. An expansionary fiscal policy $(IS_1(e_0)$ in Fig. 6.13*a*) is effective for increasing output (y_1). Since the fiscal deficit with a slight upward movement of the domestic interest rate implies huge capital inflows, gains in international reserves, and the possibility of a subsequent increase in the money supply shift the LM-schedule to LM_1 and point B would be reached.

Monetary policy. An expansionary monetary policy $(LM_1$ in Fig. 6.13*b*) with some slight downward divergence from the international interest rate would provoke large capital outflows, losses in international reserves for maintaining the fixed exchange rate, and finally a return to the initial monetary policy (LM).

Thus, in the Keynesian world with perfect capital mobility and fixed exchange rates, an expansionary monetary policy is not effective for increas-

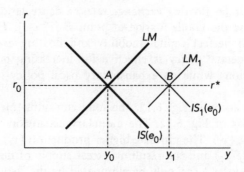

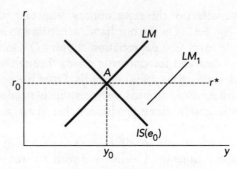

Fig. 6.13. The Keynesian model (Mundell–Fleming): fiscal or monetary shock under fixed exchange rates

Fiscal expansion succeeds in increasing *y* since it is accompanied by a gain in international reserves (via a slightly higher interest rate) and by a corresponding increase in the money supply. Monetary expansion has no impact on *y* because there is a slight fall in the interest rate and a subsequent loss in international reserves.

ing output and an expansionary fiscal policy (accompanied by monetary expansion) is effective. At the end of the presentation of the various macro models, we have illustrated in Box 6.7 some of the bewildering taxonomy of what could happen to the real exchange rate when government increases its money supply or its expenditure (depending on the type of public expenditure, on the degree of capital mobility, and on the underlying and extremely simplified macro models—classical or Keynesian ones—without a labour market).

Box 6.7. The long-run effects of expansionary fiscal and monetary policy under floating and fixed exchange rates: classical and Keynesian models (for a small country with perfect capital mobility)

	Classical model			Keynesian model		
	e	E	P	e	E	y
Expansionary fiscal policy ($\Delta G = \Delta D$)						
Floating rates	–	–	0	–	–	0
Fixed rates	–	0	+	0	0	+
Expansionary monetary policy (ΔM)						
Floating rates	0	+	+	+	+	+
Fixed rates	0	0	0	0	0	0

6.5. Fiscal Policy in a Large Country (the USA)

The most remarkable case of divergence from purchasing power parity over the recent period of floating rates is the real appreciation of the US dollar during the first half of the 1980s (see Fig. 6.14). This period witnessed a major real shock: the formidable US debt financed budget deficit, which was accompanied by fiscal contraction in Europe and Japan. The excessive real appreciation of the dollar cannot be considered as a rational bubble, but rather as a reflection of a change in the fundamentals as far as the divergent fiscal policies (coupled with divergencies in tight monetary policies) are concerned.

The real exchange rate of Fig. 6.14 is the effective one, representing the weighted average of the nominal exchange values of the currencies of the most important industrial countries with the US dollar. The nominal effective rate is adjusted for changes in the consumer price indexes of the countries concerned.[22] There were some similar movements between the budget deficit and the real exchange rate, less pronounced for the late 1970s and more accentuated for the 1980s.

If the budget deficit occurs in a large country—say the United States—the adjustment process will differ, since the world interest rate will be affected. Consequently, a two-country model has to be used: the United States and the rest of the world (ROW). Here we only discuss perfect capital mobility. For this reason there is no external constraint. We assume that $\Delta G = \Delta D + \Delta Im$ or $\Delta G = \Delta D$.

The rise in the US bond financed budget deficit increases the real world market interest rate. There is some crowding-out of private expenditure in the United States and some other crowding-out of private expenditure in the ROW, the first creating excess savings in the United States and the second excess savings in the ROW. It follows that the budget deficit is financed partly by domestic savings and partly by foreign savings via capital inflows. The

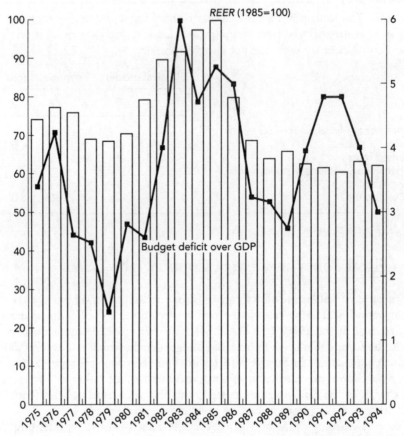

Fig. 6.14. United States: budget deficit and real effective exchange rate (*REER*), 1975–94

Note: An increase in *REER* means an appreciation.
Source: IMF, *International Financial Statistics.*

corresponding transfer of goods from the ROW to the United States is realized by the real appreciation of the US dollar, which, within the US economy, involves a lower demand for American products and a higher demand for foreign goods. From the point of view of a two-country model, the former crowding-out effect of 'net exports' (described for a small country) is actually a crowding-out effect of domestic and foreign private absorption. Furthermore, the change in the real exchange rate equilibrates the markets for domestic goods in both the USA and in the ROW.[23]

Choosing the classical macro model (Fig. 6.15), an expansionary fiscal policy [IS_1 (m_0) as a result, for instance, of $\Delta G = \Delta D$] in a large country now provokes three crowding-out effects, namely a reduction in the demand for

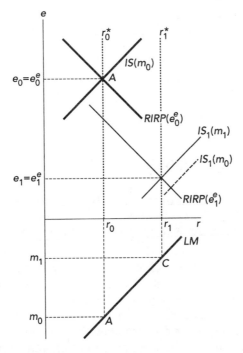

Fig. 6.15. Expansionary fiscal policy in a large country (classical macro-model)

Assuming perfect capital mobility, the expansionary fiscal policy ($\Delta G = \Delta D$) produces a rise in the world interest rate and a real appreciation (point C). Both reduce the demand for domestic goods. A third crowding-out effect results from the decline in m (wealth effect on consumption).

domestic goods through the real interest rate mechanism (r^*_1), through the real exchange rate mechanism (e_1), and through the price level mechanism (m_1). The third stems from the disequilibrium in the money market. The rise in the national and international interest rates reduces the demand for real cash balances. Lower real cash balances via the rise in the national price level increase savings and decrease consumption (the wealth effect). Consequently, as far as the real variables are concerned, the final equilibrium may be situated at C [$IS_1(m_1)$]. Lower real cash balances shift the $IS_1(m_0)$-schedule to the left through point C.

We have also added the real interest rate parity. We assume that real exchange rate expectations are revised correctly, at the very beginning of the real shock, from $e^e_0 = e_0$ to $e^e_1 = e_1$. The evolution of the nominal and real exchange rates must be almost identical. From the point of view of a two-country model (see Mathematical Appendix B to the present chapter), the rise in the international interest rate reduces the demand for real cash balances in both the domestic and foreign countries. Consequently, the price level increases in both countries. If they rise by the same percentage, there is no need for the nominal and real exchange rates to diverge.

If bond financed budget deficits lead to a real appreciation, continuously increasing budget deficits involve a continuous, on-going, real appreciation over time. Consequently, the continuous increase in the US budget deficit in the early 1980s could explain the trend in the US real exchange rate (Fig. 6.14).[24]

6.6. Exchange Rate Stabilization Policies

Nominal versus Real Exchange Rate Stabilization Policies

There are two important guidelines for exchange rate stabilization policies.

Symmetrical shocks.   When shocks, either monetary or real, are common to the whole world economy and hit all countries with the same intensity, the exchange rate system will not be affected since all domestic variables are influenced in the same way. There is no need for an exchange rate stabilization policy since the exchange rates do not move. We shall use two examples.

First, if we assume that all countries have the same inflation rate, then they pursue the same anti-inflationary policy by squeezing the growth rate of the money supply (monetary shock). In principle, nominal and real exchange rates remain unchanged (provided that the adjustment process over time is also identical for all countries). The floating exchange rate system works like a fixed exchange rate system when common shocks are assumed.

The same is true for real shocks. If we assume that all countries have opted for the same fiscal policy (either a balanced budget or the same budget deficit as a percentage of GDP), then if they change their fiscal stance in the same direction and with the same intensity (real shock), the nominal and real exchange rates will not be affected, as we shall see in the final section of this chapter. Again, the floating exchange rate system works like a fixed exchange rate system.

Two conclusions can be drawn from these considerations: first, if shocks are provoked by policy actions (monetary and fiscal policy), a floating exchange rate system will be a stable one provided that there is international policy co-ordination which results in the convergence of macro policies; and second, a fixed exchange rate system can only work effectively under the above rules of policy co-ordination.

Asymmetrical shocks.   Exchange rates respond to asymmetrical monetary and real shocks in the world economy. This is when exchange rate stabilization policies may become relevant for carrying adequate macro policies.

Here, it is possible to ask the question whether a real shock could be avoided by an adequate monetary policy, assuming a classical macro model and perfect capital mobility. Take the case of a small country which pursues an expansionary fiscal policy (bond financed budget deficit) that produces a real appreciation. In Fig. 6.16 the nominal and real exchange rates appreciate by moving from A to B. To avoid the two appreciations, the central bank could simultaneously follow an expansionary monetary policy which would maintain the nominal and real exchange rates at point A at time t_0. However, after t_0, the evolution of the nominal and real exchange rates will be E' and e', respectively (as we know from Fig. 4.5). After the monetary adjustment process has come to an end, the real exchange rate will again be at level B. Consequently, real shocks cannot be avoided by producing adequate nominal shocks through monetary policy. Over the long run, monetary policy can only influence the nominal variables. Our example of an expansionary monetary policy has produced, in addition, a higher price level (P').

To avoid the ultimate real appreciation, the country could simply be advised

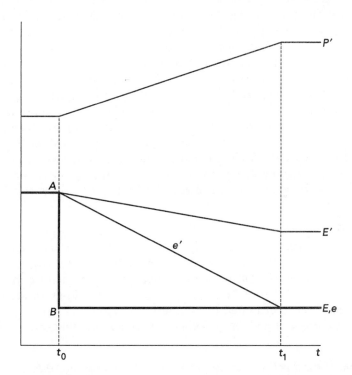

Fig. 6.16. A monetary policy reaction for accommodating real shocks

The economy has pursued an expansionary fiscal policy with the result of a nominal and real appreciation ($A \rightarrow B$). Its monetary authorities try to counterbalance this exchange rate movement by an expansionary monetary policy which immediately provokes a nominal and real depreciation of the overshooting type ($B \rightarrow A$). Due to the subsequent rise in the general price level (P'), the real exchange rate (e') will return to its former appreciated level.

against following an expansionary fiscal policy. However, what should be the recommendation if the fiscal shock happens outside the country?

Real Exchange Rate Stabilization versus Real Interest Rate Stabilization (Two-Country View)

How could the rest of the world have reacted to the real shock brought about by US fiscal policy in the early 1980s? In particular, would appropriate exchange rate management have avoided the tremendous fluctuations in the real exchange rate of the US currency over the 1980s?[25] Proper real exchange rate management can only be conducted by influencing the real fundamentals of the exchange rate, and the proper policy tool would be fiscal policy. In what follows we shall concentrate on possible fiscal policy reactions (Corden, 1986).

Fig. 6.17 illustrates the fiscal policy reactions of the rest of the world, which we shall call Europe (standing for all other OECD members). The European fiscal policy parameter is the size of Europe's budget deficit (BD/GDP). The real exchange rate of European currencies is represented by e, where an increase in e signifies a real depreciation of European currencies, which is equivalent to a real appreciation of the US dollar. The trade-off line T describes the results of our theoretical arguments (with perfect capital mobility). An increase in Europe's bond financed deficit implies a real appreciation of Europe's currencies provided that the additional government expenditure is not exclusively spent on imports.[26] The T_0-line is constructed for a given US budget deficit $[BD/GDP]^{us}_0$. The initial situation may be shown by point A. A US expansionary fiscal policy $[(BD/GDP)^{us}_1]$ shifts the T_0-line to the position T_1. There can be three fundamentally different fiscal policy reactions by Europe.

No fiscal policy reaction (point B in Fig. 6.17).   On the one hand, there is a real appreciation of the US dollar, which corresponds to a real depreciation of Europe's currencies (e_1). On the other hand, there is an increase in the real world market interest rate from r_{w0} to r_{w1}. The real shock inside the US economy has been transmitted to Europe in the form of a real depreciation of Europe's currencies and an increase in the real world interest rate.

Expansionary fiscal policy reaction for reasons of real exchange rate stabilization (point C in Fig. 6.17).   The real exchange rate would remain unchanged between the two areas (e_0) as long as Europe expands in line with the United States by raising its budget deficit from BD_0 to BD_1. However, there would be a still sharper rise in the real world interest rate (i.e. from r_{w1} to r_{w2}). In both parts of the world, the budget deficits are completely financed by internal savings via the additional increase in the real interest rate. Consequently, the

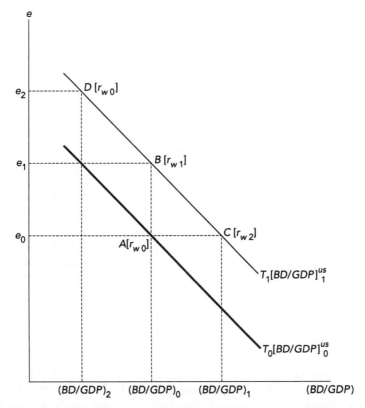

Fig. 6.17. Real exchange rate versus real interest rate stabilization

The line *T* describes the causal relation between higher (European) budget deficits and real appreciation (of the European currencies with respect to the dollar). The initial situation is at point A. A higher American budget deficit shifts T_0 towards T_1 and point A towards B. If Europe wants to stabilize the real exchange rate, it also has to pursue an expansionary fiscal policy, which results in a higher world interest rate (point C). If Europe wants to stabilize the interest rate, it has to pursue restrictive fiscal deficits at the cost of a still higher real depreciation of its currencies (point D).

real exchange rate remains unchanged (a case of symmetrical real shocks within the world economy).

Restrictive fiscal policy reaction for reasons of real interest rate stabilization (point *D* in Fig. 6.17). If the Europeans are annoyed about the rise in the real interest rate (while considering the real depreciation of their currencies as conducive to employment creation), they can only reduce the real interest rate by a contractive fiscal policy. Provided that they want to re-establish the initial real interest rate at r_{w0}, they have to reduce their budget deficit by an amount that compensates for the increase in the US budget deficit, so that the real interest rate in the world capital market remains constant. The increased availability of savings as a consequence of lower European budget deficits is used to finance fully the US budget deficit (assuming perfect capital mobility). In the American economy there is a still stronger excess demand for American goods, and in the European economy there is a large excess supply of European goods. The corresponding trade transfer of goods from Europe to the United States can only be realized by a still stronger real appreciation of the dollar, that is, by a still stronger real depreciation of European currencies.

It is now interesting to observe what actually happened on the fiscal side in Europe in the early 1980s. The trend was more in the direction of a restrictive fiscal policy (especially for the United Kingdom, Japan, and West Germany). Consequently, the relevant evolution of the real exchange rate was that between points B and D on the T_1-line. Thus, Europe's fiscal policy intensified the size of the change in the real exchange rate. Whether this policy was consciously carried out for reasons of real interest rate stabilization or for reasons of public debt consolidation remains an open question. It is probable that both reasons played a role, despite the tremendous repercussion of the European restrictive fiscal policy on the real exchange rate between the United States and Europe.

Fiscal Policy Co-ordination

When fundamentals change, as in the case of the new fiscal policy mix between the United States and the rest of the world, then the real equilibrium exchange rate also changes. In the case of real shocks, no reasonable ground can be found for proposing exchange rate management and, thus, for any exchange rate co-ordination.

If more real exchange rate stability is wanted, the only way to achieve it is to co-ordinate fiscal policies among countries. This means that fiscal policy autonomy is sacrificed to an exchange rate target. In the real world, such a plea for international fiscal policy co-ordination must remain a vain hope, since it would imply fiscal convergence—all countries together pursue, with the same rhythm, either expansion or contraction. Furthermore, as we have shown, fiscal convergence implies a sacrifice of real interest rate stability, since more real exchange rate stability implies more real interest rate instability. Thus, world-wide fiscal expansion raises real interest rates and world-wide fiscal contraction lowers them.

Instead of more real exchange rate stability, real exchange rate flexibility could also be defended if changes in the real exchange rate are an outcome of justifiable real shocks in the world economy. Max Corden (1986) made this point. Real shocks are justifiable when they result from the adjustment of actual stocks to desired stocks. A fall in the savings ratio represents the case where the actual wealth ratio exceeds the desired one. An increase in private investment is the adjustment of the actual capital stock to the desired stock. A large decline in savings or large rise in investment has effects on the real interest rate and the real exchange rate similar to those of large budget deficits—the real interest rate rises and the real exchange rate appreciates. Thus, the real exchange rate instability has to be compared with the gains from stock adjustment.[27]

A case against exchange rate management must be made in the presence of asymmetrical real shocks. The shock of divergent fiscal policies to the world economy over the 1980s illustrates this. In a world of capital mobility, a bond financed budget deficit will be financed to a large extent by foreign savings. To ensure the real transfer in the form of more traded goods available, the real exchange rate generally has to appreciate (as long as the additional public expenditure also affects the purchase of domestic goods). This real appreciation is nothing more than a reflection of the change in the real fundamentals of the exchange rate. Exchange rate management of the non-sterilized intervention type and, *a fortiori*, international co-ordination of such intervention policies, would be a nuisance to the international monetary system (and over the long run, it could only change the nominal exchange rate). Consequently, if any international co-ordination takes place to avoid the real shock, it could only be at the level of fiscal convergence—a hopeless hypothesis in the present circumstances. A recent example against fiscal convergence is given by Germany, which had to pursue fiscal expansion as a result of its reunification.

Mathematical Appendix: Fiscal Policy and the Real Exchange Rate in Small and Large Countries (the Classical Model)

A. Budget Deficit (dG) and Impact on the Real Exchange Rate (de) in a Small Country (Fig. 6.4)

Internal Equilibrium (*IS*) $\bar{y} = A(r) + B(A,e,G) + G$ (6.2a)

External Equilibrium (*TB*) $B = B(A,e,G) = 0$ (6.3a)

A stands now for *private* absorption, B for the trade balance, and G is government expenditure. The first equation is relevant for perfect capital mobility, and both equations must be used under capital immobility.

Perfect capital mobility: (6.2a) where $r = r^*$

$$B_e \, de + B_G \, dG + dG = 0$$

$$B_e \, de = - (1 + B_G) \, dG$$

$$\frac{de}{dG} = - \frac{1 + B_G}{B_e} \leqslant 0$$

where $B_e > 0$ and $0 \geqslant B_G \geqslant -1$.

For $\Delta G = \Delta D$, $B_G = 0$ and $de/dG = -(1/B_e) < 0$.

For $\Delta G = \Delta Im$, $B_G = -1$ and $de/dG = 0$.

Capital immobility: (6.2a) and (6.3a)

IS $A_r\, dr + B_A\, dA + B_e\, de + B_G\, dG + dG = 0$

where $dA = A_r\, dr$

$A_r\, dr + B_A\, A_r\, dr + B_e\, de + B_G\, dG + dG = 0$

TB $B_A\, dA + B_e\, de + B_G\, dG = 0$

$B_A\, A_r\, dr = -B_e\, de - B_G\, dG$

TB into IS $-(B_e/B_A)de - (B_G/B_A)dG - B_e\, de - B_G\, dG + B_e\, de$
$+ B_G\, dG + dG = 0$

$(B_e/B_A)\, de = [(B_A - B_G)/B_A]\, dG$

$$\frac{de}{dG} = \frac{B_A - B_G}{B_e} \leqslant\, \geqslant 0 \text{ where } B_A < 0$$

For $\Delta G = \Delta D$, $B_G = 0$ and $de/dG = (B_A/B_e) < 0$.

For $\Delta G = \Delta Im$, $B_G = -1$ and $de/dG = [(1 + B_A)/B_e] > 0$.

B. Budget Deficit (dG) and Impact on the Real Exchange Rate (de) under Capital Mobility in a Large Country (Fig. 6.15)

Goods Market (IS) $\bar{y} = A(r,m) + B(A,e,G) + G$ (6.4a)

Money Market (LM) $m = L(r)$ (6.5)

Before differentiating the two equations, we have to find the value for r which is determined in the world markets for goods and money. The world variables are designated by an asterisk.

World Goods Market (IS*) $y^* = A^*(r,m^*) + G^*$ (6.4b)

World Money Market (LM*) $m^* = L^*(r)$ (6.5b)

IS* $A^*_r\, dr + A^*_{m^*}\, dm^* + dG = 0$

LM* $dm^* = L^*_r\, dr$

LM^* into IS^* $\quad A^*_r\, dr + A^*_{m^*}\, L^*_r\, dr + dG = 0$

$$(A^*_r + A^*_{m^*}L^*_r)\, dr = -dG$$

$$dr = -\ \frac{1}{A^*_r + A^*_{m^*}\, L^*_r}\ dG > 0$$

where $A^*_r < 0$, $A^*_{m^*} > 0$, $L^*_r < 0$ and where $-1/(A^*_r + A^*_{m^*}\, L^*_r) = \Omega > 0$ so that $dr = \Omega\, dG$.

We now differentiate equations (6.4a) and (6.5).

$IS \quad A_r\, dr + A_m\, dm + B_A\, dA + B_e\, de + B_G\, dG + dG = 0$

where $dA = A_r\, dr$

$LM \quad dm = L_r\, dr$

dr is equal to $\Omega\, dG$.

LM into $IS \quad A_r \Omega\, dG + A_m\, L_r \Omega\, dG + B_A\, A_r \Omega\, dG + B_e\, de + B_G\, dG + dG = 0$

$$B_e\, de = -\ (A_r + A_m L_r + B_A A_r)\ \Omega\, dG - (1 + B_G)\, dG$$

$$\frac{de}{dG} = -\ \frac{1 + B_G}{B_e} - \frac{(A_r + A_m\, L_r + B_A\, A_r)\ \Omega}{B_e} \leqslant 0$$

provided that $-\ (A_r + A_m\, L_r) > -\ (B_A\, A_r)$.

For $\Delta G = \Delta D$, $B_G = 0$ and

$$\frac{de}{dG} = -\ \frac{1}{B_e} - \frac{(A_r + A_m\, L_r + B_A\, A_r)\ \Omega}{B_e} \leqslant 0$$

For $\Delta G = \Delta Im$, $B_G = -1$ and

$$\frac{de}{dG} = -\ \frac{(A_r + A_m\, L_r + B_A\, A_r)\ \Omega}{B_e} \leqslant 0$$

Notes

1. Or according to de Grauwe and Fratianni (1985) the increase in taxes on labour income, such as social security contributions and personal income taxes, in Europe in the 1970s.
2. In the existing literature the majority of macroeconomic models are of this type. They can be classified as the IS-LM approach to open economy macroeconomics. As we shall see in ch. 7, when taking non-tradable goods into account, the IS sector has to be split into two markets, namely the market for tradable goods and the market for non-tradable goods.
3. Defined as perfect substitutability of domestic and foreign financial assets which implies the absence of any capital controls.
4. With perfect capital mobility the size of the real appreciation depends on the relative importance of $(\Delta D + \Delta X)/(\Delta D + \Delta X + \Delta Im)$.

5. Theoretical reasons are, for instance, that life is finite and its duration is uncertain; furthermore, there may be divergent discount rates for the evaluation of Treasury bonds and tax liabilities. An overview of the theoretical and empirical issues is contained in the Spring 1989 volume of the *Journal of Economic Perspectives*. The book by Frenkel and Razin (1987) for an open economy also represents an interesting contribution to this debate, since they assume only a certain degree of public debt neutrality.

6. Absorption A of equation (6.2) also includes government expenditures (G).

7. Note that with Ricardian equivalence, this switch would take place without any rise in the interest rate.

8. Furthermore, capital controls would minimize or nullify the impact of capital flows on the volatility of exchange rates.

9. The case of imperfect capital mobility (in the sense of imperfect substitutability between domestic and foreign financial assets) would produce a higher real US interest rate and a lower real appreciation of the dollar. The reason is that with imperfect capital mobility, the domestic real interest rate can rise by much more than the foreign one (or, more precisely, by much more than the real interest rate parity condition without currency risk premium would predict). Consequently, more domestic excess savings are available, fewer foreign excess savings are necessary, and it follows that capital inflows are lower. Point B_3 could also be interpreted as the higher domestic interest rate for a small country with imperfect substitutability of assets. Foreigners hold more financial assets of the domestic economy and, due to the increased currency risk, they require a higher domestic interest rate than the foreign one.

10. In the traditional Mundell–Fleming model (which is a Keynesian approach which we will be presenting later), the trade balance is not interest elastic. The *TB*-schedule would be a horizontal line at the level e_0 and B_1 would be the point of internal and external equilibrium. The assumption of a horizontal *TB*-schedule implies that the rise in the interest rate only reduces those private expenditures which are spent on domestic goods—which is rather unlikely.

11. $\Delta G = \Delta D$ means that government increases its demand for domestic tradables. If, for instance, the economy is in a regime of fixed exchange rates, the real appreciation will take place through an increase in P_T where $P_T > E_0 P_T^*$ (domestic tradables are more expensive than foreign tradables). Here we shall anticipate some results of the next chapter on non-tradables so that the reader can see some connections between the present chapter and the following one. ΔG can be spent on domestic tradables (ΔD_T) or on non-tradables (ΔD_N). P_T will rise as in the above example, but P_N will also rise. Furthermore, as will be explained in the next chapter, there is a real appreciation of type e_2 if $\Delta P_N > \Delta P_T$.

12. With Ricardian equivalence, the rise in the domestic real interest rate (capital immobility) would be excluded. However, under both assumptions about the degree of capital mobility, a change in the real exchange rate is still highly probable as long as the pattern of additional government expenditure (ΔD and ΔIm) is not the same as the pattern of the reduced private expenditure ($- \Delta D$ and $- \Delta Im$).

13. The ultimate target of savings is to establish a certain desired wealth level. The target applies when actual wealth is below desired wealth. An increase in the general price level decreases real cash balances, widens the gap between actual and desired wealth and gives rise to additional savings. The 'wealth-saving relation-

ship' is an essential element of the Chicago School elaborated by Lloyd Metzler (1951), Don Patinkin and Robert Mundell. See Niehans (1978).

14. With the assumption of capital immobility, equation (6.6) has to be replaced by equation (6.3).

15. In ch. 4, the sign of the currency risk premium was different, because we were looking at a domestic investor holding foreign assets. We now assume that the domestic country is a net borrower and the foreign country a net lender. See also ch. 4, n. 5.

16. In contrast to Fig. 6.6, the higher level of the domestic interest rate involves a fall in the demand for real cash balances. The decrease in m produces a third crowding-out effect: lower $m \rightarrow$ lower demand for domestic goods (wealth effect) $\rightarrow$ lower rate of the real appreciation.

17. Exceptions to this 'fixed' exchange rate mechanism are, for instance, the Netherlands and Austria. Both countries have imposed 'voluntarily' a margin of $+/-$ 0.11 per cent with the German mark since the early 1980s to achieve the same credibility as the Bundesbank. See again Box 2.5.

18. The Keynesian model for open economies under fixed and floating exchange rates was developed by James Meade and later, within the *IS-LM* framework, by John Fleming and Robert Mundell; see footnote 2 in ch. 5.

19. As in the classical model, if capital immobility is assumed, equation (6.9) has to be replaced by the external equilibrium condition (6.3). Furthermore, the case of the currency risk premium can be incorporated in a way similar to the classical model.

20. However, the real appreciation is not required if there is a combination of expansionary fiscal and monetary policy. The monetary expansion increases y which would satisfy $\Delta G = \Delta D$. In terms of the box of Fig. 6.11, the *LM*-schedule would shift to the right and intersect the $IS_1(e_0)$ schedule at the level of r^*. With respect to Fig. 6.11, the *LM*-schedule shifts downwards producing a higher y for the interest rate r_0. The $IS_1(y_0)$ schedule shifts back to $IS(y_0)$; however, real income is higher than y_0. The additional production satisfies the additional public expenditure.

21. We shall ignore the upper and lower exchange rate margins around the central parity value between which the exchange rate is allowed to fluctuate.

22. The movements of the nominal and real effective exchange rates were rather similar, which means that there was only a slight inflation differential between the USA and the other countries.

23. The case of imperfect capital mobility (in the sense of imperfect substitutability between domestic and foreign financial assets) would produce a higher real US interest rate and a lower real appreciation of the dollar. The reason is that, with imperfect capital mobility, the internal real interest rate can rise by much more (currency risk premium) than the external one. Consequently, more domestic excess savings are available, fewer foreign excess savings are necessary, and it follows that capital inflows are lower, as shown in Section 6.3 (Fig. 6.8).

24. See Branson (1986), Frenkel (1986), and Dornbusch (1986). Tight monetary policy in 1980–1 and relatively loose monetary policy in 1985 could have played an additional role.

25. See Fig. 5.1a for the sharp fluctuations in the real exchange rate of the dollar with respect to the deutschmark.

26. The slope of the *T*-schedule is mainly determined by the degree of capital mobility, by the composition of government expenditure on domestic and foreign goods,

and by the elasticity of the trade balance with respect to the real exchange rate in the case of limited capital mobility.

27. 'When Japanese savings are being transferred to the United States in order to finance tax cuts or private investment in the United States, the process might be regarded as optimal. Hence the much misaligned current account "imbalances" may be optimal. There are gains from trade in financial assets against goods, as there are in goods-goods trade. The Japanese want to export more goods and import more bonds in return, and the Americans want to trade in the opposite direction.' Corden (1986: 429).

7

THE INTERNAL RELATIVE PRICE OF
TRADABLE GOODS (e_2)

An additional interpretation of the real exchange rate concerns the relative price of domestic non-tradable goods (or the internal relative price of tradable goods). In order to work with a manageable macro model, it is assumed that domestic and foreign tradables are perfect substitutes. Thus, any excess demand for domestic tradables (which involved a real appreciation in the former chapter) will be satisfied now by imports without any change in e_1.

The existence of non-tradable goods implies the inclusion of a second domestic market for goods. It is now an excess demand for non-tradable goods which provokes a real appreciation so as to render non-tradables more expensive than tradables. Again, within a classical model, the real appreciation can take place under floating exchange rates (nominal appreciation) and under fixed ones (an increase in the domestic price level of non-tradables). In contrast to the long-run evolution of e_1, which tends towards unity, e_2 could underlie a continuous change within the context of a growing economy in the sense that, for instance, non-tradables become steadily more expensive than tradable goods.

7.1 The 'Dependent' Economy

Two Markets for Domestic Goods

The *external* relative price of domestic tradables is the ratio of the foreign price of tradables with respect to their domestic price, both expressed in a common currency unit [$e_1 = EP_{T^*}/P_T$], i.e. in domestic currency. The *internal* relative price of domestic tradables is the ratio of the domestic price of tradables with respect to the domestic price of non-tradables [$e_2 = q^b = (P_T/P_N)^b = [(EP_T^*/P_N)^b]$], implying that $e_1 = 1$ (purchasing power parity or law of one price).[1]

We shall work with a quantity-theoretical macro model for a small open economy. The real sector (or *IS*-sector) represented in the following sections now has two goods markets (the 'Australian model'), the market for non-tradable goods (*N*) and the market for (domestically produced) tradable goods (T). The equilibrium in the first market is called internal equilibrium and the equilibrium in the second market is called the external equilibrium.[2] The formulation of the equilibrium conditions in the real sector of the economy must be different (Box 7.1) from that described in Chapter 6. The term e has to be interpreted as e_2 throughout the whole chapter. We shall first analyse the supply conditions in both markets (S_T and S_N) and then the demand conditions (D_T and D_N).

Box 7.1 The real sector of the dependent economy

Markets for domestic goods	Perfect capital mobility		Capital immobility	
Non-tradables (NN)	$S_N(e) = D_N(e, r)$	(7.1)	$S_N(e) = D_N(e, r)$	(7.1)
Tradables (TB)	$S_T(e) - D_T(e, r) = TB(e, r)$	(7.2)	$S_T(e) - D_T(e, r) = TB(e, r) = 0$	(7.3)

The Labour Market and the Supply of T and N

Since an increase in e (real depreciation) means that T becomes more expensive ($P_T > P_N$), producers will shift resources from sector N to sector T in order to supply more T and less N. Labour is the resource that moves from N to T. Of course, the resource shift will only take place if the real depreciation is considered as a permanent change in the relative price of P_T/P_N. Furthermore, it must be assumed that labour skills are the same in the two sectors. The production factor capital is sector specific and fixed in each sector. Only any new investment would go to sector T.

From the point of view of the firm's demand for labour, the level of labour input is determined by maintaining the nominal wage rate (W) equal to the marginal product of labour (MPL) valued at its market price (P). This traditional formula for profit maximization should hold in both production sectors, T and N:

$$W_T = P_T \, MPL_T \qquad W_N = P_N \, MPL_N \qquad (7.4)$$

With product competition, prices should reflect marginal cost. With a capital stock fixed in both sectors, marginal costs are marginal labour costs, also called marginal unit labour costs:

$$P_T = W_T/MPL_T \qquad P_N = W_N/MPL_N \qquad (7.5)$$

With labour skills the same in T and N, nominal wages are also the same in both sectors ($W_T = W_N = W$),[3] since otherwise labour would move between the two production sectors. Consequently, formula (7.5) becomes simplified as:

$$P_T = W/MPL_T \qquad P_N = W/MPL_N \qquad (7.5a)$$

However, *real wages (represented by the marginal product of labour MPL) are likely to differ because the stocks of capital in T and N differ.*

Equation (7.5a) can also be written in terms of the real exchange rate:

$$P_T/P_N = MPL_N/MPL_T \qquad (7.6)$$

From the point of view of production cost, the real exchange rate has to equal the ratio of labour productivities above. A real depreciation involves a higher ratio of MPL_N/MPL_T which is brought about by the movement of labour from N to T.

In Fig. 7.1a we have illustrated the labour market in terms of equation (7.4) for $W_T = W_N = W$. $L^d{}_T$, measured from left to right, represents the demand for labour in the tradable goods sector. Similarly, $L^d{}_N$, measured from right to left, is the demand schedule for labour in the non-tradable sector. The point of departure is point A at the common nominal wage rate W_0. A rise in P_T—which was our example of a real depreciation—induces firms to hire more workers in the T sector, since $P_{T1} MPL_{T0} > W_0$. The increased demand for labour for the production of tradables $[L^d{}_{T1}]$ will bid up nominal wages throughout the economy because workers are basically the same in both sectors. Firms in the N sector find it less profitable to produce the same quantity as before, since $P_{N0} MPL_N < W$, and they will release labour and reduce production. The new equilibrium is at point B with a higher labour input in the T sector and, correspondingly, a lower labour input in the N sector. Nominal wages have increased towards W_1.[4]

The labour migration from the N sector to the T sector can also be shown by the downward movement along the production possibility curve PP of Fig. 7.1b from A to B. T is the volume of tradables produced and N the volume of non-tradables produced. If the economy is at some point on the production possibility curve, there will be full employment. A higher production of T via a higher labour input implies a fall in the marginal productivity of labour in T; with constant marginal productivity the curve would be a straight line. The slope of the line which is tangent to point A indicates the level of the real exchange rate (P_T/P_N), as will be explained later. Since prices are equal to costs in a competitive economy, the price ratio P_T/P_N has to be equal to the productivity ratio MPL_N/MPL_T according to formula (7.6). A low real exchange rate level implies that the volume of non-tradables (point A) is large and a high level of e means a large volume of tradables (point B).

Demand for T and N and Internal–External Equilibrium

The sensitivity of the demand for N and T to the *interest rate* can be considered as identical for D_N and D_T. As far as a change in the *relative price of non-tradables* is concerned, there is first of all the substitution effect that is

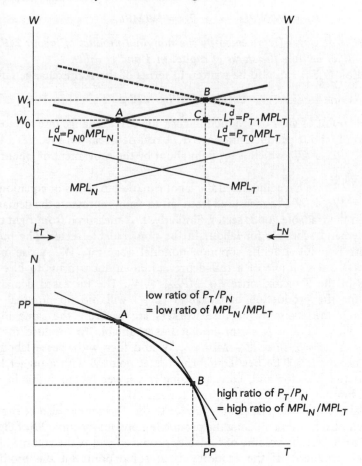

Fig. 7.1. Labour migration from *N* to *T*.

Fig. 7.1a. The labour market for *T* and *N*

The initial equilibrium is at point A. A real depreciation (P_{T1}) increases the demand for labour in *T*-sector. The new equilibrium is at point B with higher labour input in *T*, lower labour input in *N*, and higher nominal wages.

Fig. 7.1b. The production possibility curve

From the point of view of the supply side, the impact of the real depreciation on the production of *T* and *N* is the movement from A to B.

operating. In the case of a real depreciation, domestic tradables become more expensive compared to non-tradables and residents will demand fewer tradables and more non-tradables. The decline in the demand for tradables by residents can affect both types of tradable goods, domestic and foreign (imported) ones. However, assuming $e_1 = 1$, there is no substitution between foreign and domestic tradables because their relative prices do not change (the law of one price for tradables). In addition, because of this assumption, exports also remain unchanged.

In Fig. 7.2, the *NN*-schedule describes the equilibrium conditions in the market for non-tradables (internal equilibrium) according to formula (7.1). Point *A* is one equilibrium configuration of r and e which ensures the internal equilibrium. A rise in r would create a lower demand for non-tradables. There are two reasons why an increase in e would eliminate the excess supply of non-tradables. One is that the supply would decrease since the production of tradables has become more profitable. The other is that the demand for non-tradables would increase since they have become less expensive compared to tradables.[5]

The equilibrium condition in the market for *domestic* tradables (7.2) is less evident after reading Chapter 6. We assume a small open economy which can eliminate any disequilibrium between supply and demand for *domestic* tradables by corresponding foreign trade transactions without any change in relative prices (of type e_1). If the country has an excess supply of *domestic* tradables, exports to foreigners will absorb it. Conversely, an excess demand for *domestic* tradables can be satisfied by additional imports, because domestic and foreign tradables are perfect substitutes under the assumption of the law of one price for tradables.[6]

However, this automatic equilibrium mechanism assumes that the country concerned can easily finance any trade balance deficit in international credit markets (perfect capital mobility). If the access to international credit is restricted, the external constraint can become relevant, so that the country's

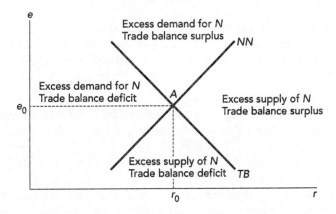

Fig. 7.2. The real sector of the Australian model

NN is the schedule of internal equilibrium and *TB* the schedule of external equilibrium. Assuming capital immobility, the equilibrium real exchange rate is at e_0. With perfect capital mobility, only the *NN* schedule determines the equilibrium exchange rate for a given international interest rate.

trade balance must be equilibrated according to equation (7.3) in Box 7.1. The *TB*-schedule of Fig. 7.2 has to be interpreted differently from that of the former chapter, since *e* is now the *internal* relative price of domestic tradables. Starting from any point on the *TB*-schedule, a real depreciation (in the sense of e_2) does not decrease the demand for imported goods in favour of import substitutes (as in the case of e_1), but instead decreases the total demand by residents for tradable goods (domestically produced import substitutes and imported goods). The subsequent trade balance surplus could be avoided by a fall in the interest rate which stimulates residents' demand for any category of goods.[7]

In summary, under the assumption of capital immobility, where the domestic interest rate is not linked to the international one, equilibrium in the real sector of the economy (goods markets) simultaneously implies that there will be an internal equilibrium (*NN*) and an external equilibrium (*TB* at point *A*). With perfect capital mobility, the market for domestic tradable goods is always in equilibrium, even though it can be accompanied by a trade balance deficit or surplus, since any excess supply of domestic tradables is easily exportable and any excess demand for domestic tradables is satisfied by imports. The market for non-tradables will be equilibrated by movements in the real exchange rate for a given domestic interest rate which is the same as the international one ($r = r^*$).

7.2 Fiscal Policy and the Real Exchange Rate

Public Expenditure on Non-tradables

As in Chapter 6 (Fig. 6.4), we are interested in the exchange rate effect of a bond financed budget deficit.[8] The increase in government expenditure is assumed to be used exclusively for the purchase of non-tradables (such as administration, education, defence, transport, or construction) or tradables.

$\Delta G = \Delta D_N$ (Fig. 7.3).   In Fig. 7.3a, *NN* shifts to NN_1. We shall again consider two alternative situations: that of complete capital immobility (point *B*) and that of perfect capital mobility (point *C*).

The absence of any capital flows means that the budget deficit has to be fully financed by domestic savings. The interest rate mechanism (r_1) ensures its domestic finance via the decline in the private demand for tradables *and* non-tradables. Thus, at the initial real exchange rate (e_0) and the higher interest rate (r_1), there is a disequilibrium between the structures of total demand and total supply of goods: an excess demand for non-tradables (ΔG_N is greater than the interest induced reduction of D_N) and, correspondingly, an excess supply of tradables. The latter could easily be exported, but the former cannot be satisfied by imports. The relative price of non-tradables must rise (e_1) causing

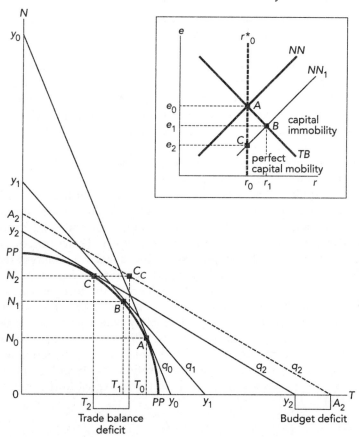

Fig. 7.3. Fiscal shock ($\Delta G = \Delta D_N$) and the structure of production

Fig. 7.3a. Under capital immobility, the private demand for N is crowded out by the rise in r and by the real appreciation involving also a higher production of N. Under capital mobility, the crowding-out effect operates only through e.

Fig. 7.3b. The movement from A to B (capital immobility) or from A to C (capital mobility) on the production possibility curve highlights the shift of resources towards the production sector of N as the consequence of real appreciation. In the case of capital mobility, the production point is C and the consumption point is C_c with a corresponding trade balance deficit.

the substitution effect to operate on both the demand side (lower private demand for non-tradables and higher private demand for tradables) and the supply side (higher supply of non-tradables and lower supply of tradables).

With perfect capital mobility, the domestic interest rate is linked to the international interest rate (r^*_0). The domestic interest rate remains at the level r_0 and the budget deficit will be fully financed by foreign savings (point C). The real appreciation is necessarily higher (e_2) than in the former case of capital immobility. The additional public demand for non-tradables can be satisfied only by domestic production, since the nature of non-tradables means that they cannot be provided through international trade. The interest rate mechanism no longer makes non-tradables available to the public sector via a decline in the private demand for non-tradables. Consequently, the full adjustment in terms of a lower private demand for, and a higher supply of, non-tradables must come from the exchange rate mechanism. Furthermore, the budget deficit will be equal to the capital balance surplus, and the latter to the trade balance deficit (provided that, initially, both balances were in equilibrium).[9]

The above results are summed up in Fig. 7.3b, which is derived from Salter's (1959) exposition of the Australian model and which is often used in the literature on tradable vs. non-tradable goods (e.g. Dornbusch, 1975). The production possibility curve is illustrated by PP. The initial equilibrium point for production and consumption is at A, to which an indifference curve (not drawn) is tangent. The slope of the income line $y_0 y_0$ indicates the relative price $q_0 = P_T/P_N$. The case of the budget deficit with capital immobility is shown by point B. The new income line is $y_1 y_1$, whose slope indicates the new real exchange rate (q_1). Due to the interest rate mechanism, income remains equal to absorption and the production point coincides with the consumption point. For the opposite hypothesis of capital mobility which involves a higher real appreciation (q_2), the production point (C) diverges from the consumption point (C_C). The income line tangent to point C is $y_2 y_2$. In terms of traded goods measured on the horizontal axis, absorption (A_2) exceeds income (y_2) by the amount of the budget deficit which, in turn, is equal to the trade balance deficit (CC_C).[10]

Public Expenditure on Tradables

$\Delta G = \Delta D_T$ (Fig. 7.4).   The bond financed budget deficit is now oriented toward the purchase of tradable goods. The TB-schedule of Fig. 7.4a shifts towards TB_1.

With capital immobility (point B), the rise in the domestic interest rate crowds out private expenditure on tradables and non-tradables. However, there is still an excess demand for tradables and a corresponding excess supply of non-tradables. The substitution effects of a real depreciation on the supply and demand for each category of goods eliminates the sectoral disequilibria.

If perfect capital mobility is assumed, there will be no change in the real exchange rate (point A). The relevant equilibrium schedules are NN and TB_1. The internal equilibrium remains at point A. The additional government demand for tradables creates a corresponding trade balance deficit which is identical to the gap between total absorption and domestic production.[11]

In terms of the production possibility curve PP (Fig. 7.4b), initial internal and external equilibrium is at point A. With capital mobility, the additional

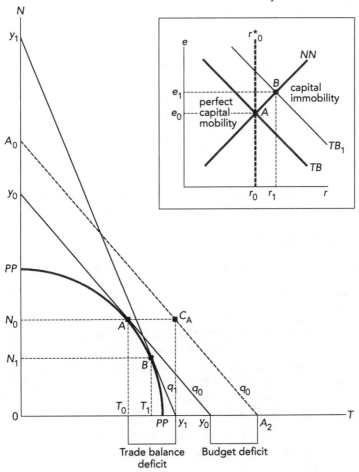

Fig. 7.4. Fiscal shock ($\Delta G = \Delta D_T$) and the structure of production

Fig. 7.4a. The higher demand for tradable goods only affects the TB-schedule. Under capital mobility, the real exchange rate remains at e_0 and the trade balance deficit is financed by capital inflows. Under capital immobility, the trade balance has to be in equilibrium by a rise in r and e.

Fig. 7.4b. Under capital mobility, the production point remains at point A and the consumption shifts toward C_A. With capital immobility, production and consumption move to B. The real depreciation is necessary in order to produce more T at the expense of N.

government demand for tradables will only create a trade balance deficit (AC_A). The production point remains at A and the consumption point shifts towards C_A. The trade balance deficit is equal to the budget deficit ($A_2 - y_0$). With capital immobility, the rise in the interest rate brings absorption back to the domestic product y_1. However, the sectoral disequilibrium—excess demand for tradables corresponds to an excess supply of non-tradables—is eliminated by the real depreciation (q_1). The production and consumption point is now at point B.

It should be remembered that we arrived at identical results in Chapter 6 (see Box 6.4). In that chapter, the real exchange rate was interpreted as the relative price between domestic and foreign tradable goods (which is our type e_1 real exchange rate). Thus, for instance, with capital immobility for a small country, an increase of public expenditure oriented toward more imports necessitated a depreciation in order to equilibrate the trade balance, whereas the real exchange rate remained unchanged when capital mobility was assumed.[12]

7.3 The Classical Approach to the Macroeconomic Determination of the Exchange Rate (the Australian Model and Perfect Capital Mobility)

Up to now we have only described the real sector of the Australian model (see Box 7.1). We have to add the monetary sector to obtain the macroeconomic framework for the determination of the real exchange rate (see Box 7.2). Again, as in Chapter 6, we shall only consider the case of perfect capital mobility for which the real interest rate parity (*RIRP*) has to be used. The money market (*LM*), which determines the price level within the framework of the classical approach, has been formulated for the two alternative exchange rate regimes, namely floating and fixed nominal exchange rates. The definition of the price level in equations (7.9a and 7.9b), that is, $P = (P_T/e)$, is derived from equation (5.5) in Table 5.1.

Box 7.2. A macro-model of the dependent economy (with perfect capital mobility)

NN	$S_N(e) = D_N(e,r,m)$	(7.7)
RIRP	$r = r^* + (e^e - e)/e + CRP$	(7.8)
LM	$m = L(r)$ where $m = M/P$	(7.9)
(a) Floating nominal exchange rates	$M = PL(r) = [P_T/e] L(r) = [EP^*_T/e]L(r)$	(7.9a)
(b) Fixed nominal exchange rates	$M = PL(r) = [P_T/e]L(r) = [\bar{E}P^*_T/e]L(r)$	(7.9b)

The assumption of perfect capital mobility (with a currency risk premium $CRP = 0$) facilitates the macroeconomic determination of the real exchange rate along lines similar to those of the classical *IS-LM-RIRP* macro model of Chapter 6 (see Box 6.5 and Fig. 6.5): $r^* \to r \to P \to e$. With stationary expectations about the future exchange rate ($e^e = e$), the domestic interest rate is identical to the international one; see equation (7.8). The precise level of the demand for real money holdings (m_0) determines the price level for a given nominal quantity of money; see equation (7.9). Any disequilibrium in the market for non-tradable goods—equation (7.7)—is eliminated by movements in the real exchange rate.

Fig. 7.5 illustrates the Australian macro model of Box 7.2. It is identical to the classical macro-model of Fig. 6.5 except for the equilibrium schedule for the market of domestic goods, which now becomes NN instead of IS. The demand and supply of domestic goods are now for domestic non-tradable goods, and not, as before, for domestic tradable goods. Any excess demand for domestic goods is an excess demand for non-tradables. It is eliminated by the real appreciation in terms of the type e_2 real exchange rate. Non-tradables become more expensive than tradables and the substitution effect of the real appreciation lowers the demand for non-tradables and increases their supply.[13]

We shall again analyse the macroeconomic effects of a fiscal shock ($\Delta G = \Delta D_N$) and of a monetary shock (ΔM) under the hypothesis of risk neutrality ($CRP = 0$). There is no need to construct new geometrical figures, since we can use Fig. 6.6 (reproduced as Fig. 7.6) and Fig. 6.9 (reproduced as Fig. 7.7), respectively, in which $IS(m_0)$ has to be replaced simply by $NN(m_0)$ of Fig. 7.5. At the same time, this procedure, as we shall see, *rehabilitates the traditional*

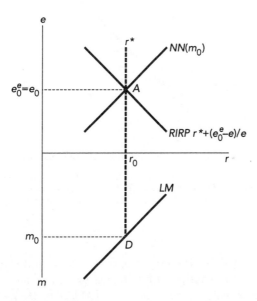

Fig. 7.5. The classical macro-model of the real exchange rate (the Australian model with perfect capital mobility)

The macroeconomic approach to the determination of the real exchange rate includes the monetary approach in terms of the real interest rate parity (*RIRP*), which assumes perfect capital mobility. The equilibrium value of the real exchange rate is at point A, where $r = r^*$ and where the real exchange rate according to *RIRP* coincides with the real exchange rate as the relative price of domestic tradables to domestic non-tradables (*NN*). The monetary equilibrium (*LM*) is realized at point D, where the interest rate gives rise to a certain price level for a given nominal quantity of money ($m_0 = M/P_0$).

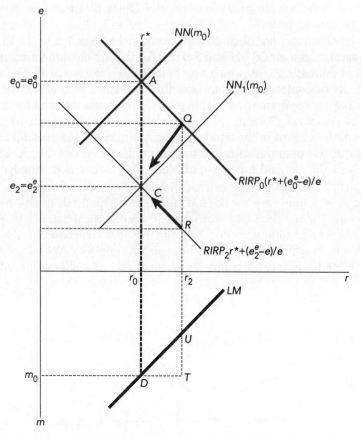

Fig. 7.6. The classical macro-model: fiscal shock ($\Delta G = \Delta D_N$)

The long-run impact of the fiscal shock (NN_1) is at point C. The monetary equilibrium (LM) remains unchanged (point D). According to $RIRP$, the short-run adjustment process for $r > r^*$ begins either at point Q or at overshooting point R. In both cases, the adjustment converges towards point C.

macroeconomic IS-LM-*models for an open economy since the direction of the movement in the real exchange rate provoked by real or monetary shocks is the same for the real exchange rate of type e_1 (IS-LM) as for the real exchange rate of type e_2 (NN-LM).*[14]

Fiscal shock $\Delta G = \Delta D_N$ *(Fig. 7.6).* In terms of comparative static analysis, the domestic interest rate remains unchanged (r_0) and hence so does the real volume of money balances (m_0). The long-run movement of the real exchange rate is that from A to C. The fiscal shock has driven the NN-schedule to the position of NN_1. The eventual revision of exchange rate expectations pushes the $RIRP_0$-line towards $RIRP_1$.

For the short-run adjustment process, the domestic interest rate (r_2) can lie above the international one (r^*). Consequently, according to the interest rate parity, a future depreciation of the domestic currency must be expected. Without any immediate revision of exchange rate expectations, the first exchange rate impact is at point Q. Afterwards, the subsequent exchange rate movement will be from Q towards C, assuming gradual revisions in exchange rate expectations. The other extreme of the short-run adjustment process consists of the correct revision of exchange rate expectations from e_0^e = e_0 to e_2^e = e_2. In that case, the overshooting phenomenon occurs (point R), with the subsequent real depreciation from R to C.[15]

Monetary shock ΔM (Fig. 7.7).   The excess supply of money is equal to the distance *DF* in the lower panel, and pushes the domestic interest rate down to r_1. The interest rate parity requires a real depreciation (e_1 at point B) to create the expectation that there will be a real appreciation of the domestic currency. At point B, with a lower real interest rate and a real depreciation, there is a high

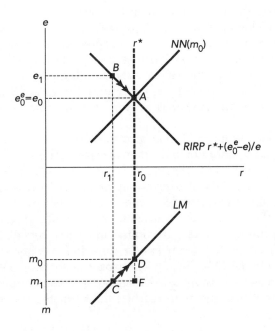

Fig. 7.7. The classical macro-model: monetary shock (ΔM)

The increase in the quantity of money by *DF* causes the interest rate to fall to r_1. To make domestic financial assets more attractive, a future real appreciation must be expected and this is brought about by a real depreciation (point B). Lower r and higher e provokes an excess demand for domestic goods. Their prices increase gradually, implying that the movement in r (C → D) and in e (B → A) reverses. The real appreciation is the combined outcome of an increasing price level and of a nominal appreciation.

demand for tradables and an excess demand for non-tradables which pushes up P_N.

As far as the long-run levels of the real variables (r, m, e) are concerned, they will remain the same as before the emergence of the monetary shock. E rises proportionately to M. The rise in P_T is the same as in E. If P_N rose less than P_T, an excess demand for non-tradables would continue to exist. This excess demand can be eliminated only by a rise in P_N sufficient to re-establish the former real exchange rate at the level e_0.

7.4 Monetary Adjustment under Alternative Exchange Rate Regimes

A permanent increase in the quantity of money is only conceivable under floating exchange rates. With fixed rates, the additional quantity of money will be eliminated through the mechanism of a balance of payments deficit (see the monetary approach to the balance of payments in Section 2.2).

In contrast, real shocks can last under both exchange rate regimes. Taking again the case of a budget deficit which provoked a real appreciation assuming capital mobility for a small country, the real appreciation can be brought about either by a nominal appreciation (floating rates) or by a rise in the domestic price level (fixed rates). We have already shown this monetary mechanism for the type e_1 real exchange rate as far as the classical macromodel was concerned (Fig. 6.7). A similar mechanism is at work for the case of a type e_2 real appreciation.

For given money supply and interest rate, there is only one general price level which realizes equilibrium in the money market. This equilibrium level of P_0 is represented by the *LM*-schedule in Fig. 7.8, which is a reproduction of Fig. 5.6 which showed a real depreciation under alternative exchange rate regimes. The equilibrium value of P_0 can be accompanied by various combinations of P_T and P_N. Any position situated to the right of *LM* reflects an excess demand in the money market. The initial monetary equilibrium is at the intersection point A of the $0q_0$ ray (whose slope indicates the size of the real exchange rate) with the *LM*-schedule. The expansionary fiscal policy involves a real appreciation from q_0 to q_1; see the $0q_1$ ray. The equilibrium value of the price levels of tradables and non-tradables differs in the two exchange rate regimes.

Floating rates (equation 7.9a in Box 7.2).   Under the regime of flexible nominal exchange rates, the general price level remains that of the *LM* line, namely P_0. The domestic price levels for both categories of goods are determined by the intersection point B between the *LM*-schedule and the new $0q_1$ ray. To maintain price stability at P_0, the nominal appreciation rate (E_1) must

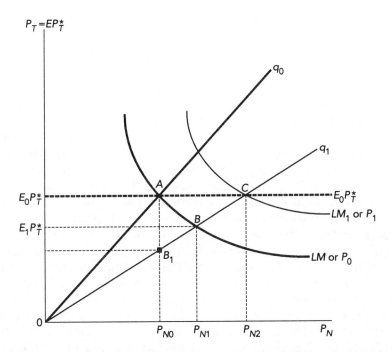

Fig. 7.8. A real appreciation under floating and fixed exchange rates

The initial monetary equilibrium is at point A. A real appreciation takes place (q_1) as the result of an expansionary fiscal policy. Under floating exchange rates, there is either a movement from A to B (an unchanged quantity of money) or from A to B_1 (a lower quantity of money). Under fixed exchange rates, P_N has to increase (a movement from A to C) via a higher quantity of money and, with this, by a higher general price level.

be lower than the real appreciation rate (lower P_T via E_1 and, correspondingly, higher P_N).[16]

Fixed rates (equation 7.9b in Box 7.2). With fixed nominal exchange rates, the domestic price level of tradable goods remains constant at $E_0 P^*_T$. Consequently, the real appreciation must imply a corresponding rise in the price level of non-tradables (point C). However, an increase in P_N involves a rise in P resulting in an excess demand for money at point C (compared to the LM-schedule). According to the monetary approach to the balance of payments (see Section 2.2), the excess demand for money creates a balance of payments surplus (an increase in international reserves held by the central bank), shifting the LM line to the position LM_1.[17]

7.5 The Long-Run Evolution of the Real Exchange Rate

The Long-Run Evolution of the Demand and Supply of N

During the various stages of development in developing countries, and during the growth process in developed countries, the relative price of tradables and non-tradables underlies continuous and systematic changes. In developing countries, tradable goods should be extremely expensive while non-tradable goods should be cheap. Consequently, the *level* of the real exchange rate should be very high: a small quantity of tradables should be exchanged for a large amount of non-tradables. The ultimate reason for this is that capital is scarce and labour abundant. Tradables are produced with more capital and less labour, and non-tradables with much more labour and less capital.

Looking at longer periods of five, ten, or twenty years, services have continuously become more expensive than industrial products in industrialized countries. There are two reasons for this. The first concerns the income elasticity of the demand for non-tradable goods. In the long-run context of a growing economy, this income elasticity is generally greater than one. Individuals increase their expenditure with rising income per capita and spend relatively more on services (including leisure activities) than on industrial goods. Since, by definition, the non-tradable services cannot be imported, they have to be produced by the domestic economy. The demand pressure for both absolutely and relatively more non-tradables increases their relative price and this gives producers an incentive to produce more non-tradables. Consequently, the *level* of the real exchange rate is very low in industrialized countries.

In Fig. 7.9a, we have illustrated a few production possibility curves (*PP*). The growth aspect of our economy shifts the possibility curve more and more in a northeasterly direction over time. We assume the same productivity growth for both production sectors. If the tastes of the individuals are such that they always spend the same percentage on each category of goods, we would have the expansion line *QE* and a constant price of tradables relative to non-tradables. However, with an income elasticity of the demand for non-tradables greater than one, we would have the expansion line *QA*. The slopes of the income lines (*yy*) indicate the relative price P_T/P_N.[18]

The second reason for the continuous rise in the relative price of non-tradables concerns the supply side. A growing economy is not only the result of a rising capital stock, but also of technical progress. As a rule, it is easier to realize technical progress in the industrial sector than in the service sector. Technical progress can mean innovation of products or innovation of production techniques. In the latter case technical progress is translated into lower production costs. If the technical progress is higher in the industrial sector than in the service sector, the implication is that production costs fall more in

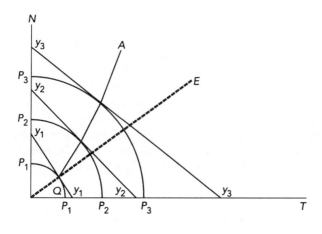

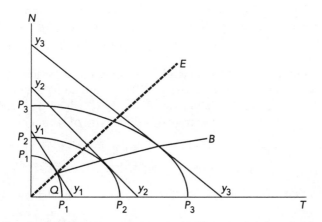

Fig. 7.9. Two cases of real appreciation in a growing economy

Fig. 7.9a. The income elasticity of demand for non-tradables greater than one

The productivity growth is the same in both production sectors. The divergent income elasticities produce the income-consumption path QA.

Fig. 7.9b. Productivity growth with a bias towards tradables

While the income elasticity is the same for both goods, the decrease in labour unit cost is stronger in the production sector of tradables. The relative price of tradables diminishes producing the income-consumption path QB.

the industrial sector than in the service sector. Consequently, from the point of view of supply, the relative price of non-tradable goods rises over time.

In Fig. 7.9b, the non-parallel outward shift of the production possibility curves indicates that, over the long-run growth process, relatively more tradables than non-tradables can be produced. Assuming an income elasticity of the demand for both categories of goods equal to one, the relative price effect arising from relatively lower production costs of tradables produces the expansion line QB (instead of QE). Again, there is a long-run real appreciation in terms of increasing relative production costs of non-tradables.

If demand- and supply-side evolutions are combined it can be concluded that two constantly operating forces produce a continuous real appreciation during the growth process. Both an income elasticity of the demand for non-tradables greater than one and the relative rise in production cost of non-tradables causes the steady price rise of services relative to industrial products. In the remaining three sections we shall focus on the *differentiated productivity growth between the two production sectors* which is the subject of the Scandinavian model.

Productivity Growth and Wage Behaviour

Whether the productivity growth which favours the production of tradables provokes a continuous change in the real exchange rate ($dq/q = dP_T/P_T - dP_N/P_N = \pi_T - \pi_N$), also depends on the nominal wage behaviour in the labour market.

From the point of view of the demand for labour, and according to equation (7.4), the growth rate of nominal wages $[dW/W]$ is limited by the inflation rate (π) and by the growth rate of labour productivity (β where $\beta = dMPL/MPL$ which is the growth rate of the marginal productivity of labour):

$$dW_T/W_T \quad = \quad \pi_T + \beta_T \tag{7.10}$$

$$dW_N/W_N \quad = \quad \pi_N + \beta_N \tag{7.11}$$

Thus, the increase in real wages ($dW/W - \pi$) is equal to the gain in labour productivity (β).

According to Box 7.3, two cases of wage behaviour can be conceived. If the productivity gains are fully transmitted to increases in wages—which is the case with nominal wage differentials (equation 7.12a), there will be no impact on the real exchange rate (the classical model).

Box 7.3 Differentiated productivity growth and nominal wage behaviour

By subtracting equation (7.10) from equation (7.11), we obtain

$$\pi_N - \pi_T \quad \rightarrow \quad = \quad \rightarrow \quad (dW_N/W_M - dW_T/W_T) + (\beta_T - \beta_N) \tag{7.12}$$

Nominal Wage Differentials	No Nominal Wage Differentials
By assuming $dW_T/W_T - dW_N/W_N = \beta_T - \beta_N$ we have	By assuming either $dW_T/W_T = dW_N/W_N = 0$ or $dW_T/W_T = dW_N/W_N = \pi_T + \beta_T$ we have
$$\pi_N = \pi_T \tag{7.12a}$$	$$\pi_N - \pi_T = \beta_T - \beta_N \tag{7.12b}$$
The nominal and real wage differential corresponds to the productivity differential. The inflation differential is zero.	The inflation differential (which is necessary for the real wage differential) corresponds to the productivity differential.

In the second case ('no nominal wage differentials' of formula 7.12*b*), the productivity differential is fully transmitted to product prices with a subsequent real appreciation (the Scandinavian model).

Classical Model. In Fig 7.10 which mainly is a reproduction of Fig. 7.1*a*, the initial equilibrium of the labour market is at point *A* (full employment). The increase in labour productivity is indicated by the dotted lines MPL'_T and MPL'_N. Nominal wages rise from W_0 to W_{T1} in the *T* sector and to W_N in the *N* sector. We assume constant prices for tradable and non-tradable goods, P_{T0} and P_{N0}. The nominal and real wage differential between both sectors is equal to the distance *DC* representing ($\beta_T - \beta_N$). However, this wage differential will not be maintained. With identical labour skills in both sectors, labour migration will take place from *N* to *T* which equalizes nominal and real wages (point *B*). This re-allocation of labour increases output by the triangle *CDB*. The labour movement made the productivity differential between *T* and *N* disappear and the real exchange rate remains unchanged.

However, we wanted to show that, over the long run, there is the likelihood

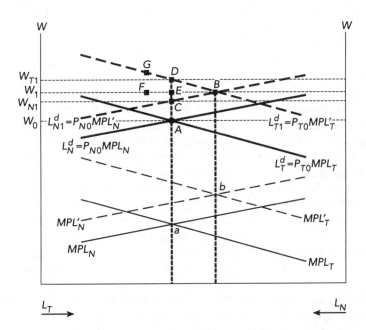

Fig. 7.10. Productivity growth and wage behaviour (classical model)

The initial equilibrium of the labour market is at point *A*. The differentiated increase in productivity pushes wages upwards, in the *N* sector to point *C* and in the *T* sector to point *D*. The subsequent labour migration from *N* to *T* leads to an equalization of wages at point *B*. A real appreciation can only be derived from the two goods markets. At point *B*, there is a rise in the supply of *T* and a decline in the supply of *N*. On the demand side, there is probably a stronger rising demand for *N* than for *T* pushing the prices of *N* upwards. The definite equilibrium point of the labour market will be situated leftwards from point *B*.

of an appreciation in the sense that non-tradable goods become relatively more expensive. For that, we have to look at the supply and demand side in both goods markets. The initial higher labour productivity gains in T and the beginning labour migration from N to T will increase, at least in relative terms, the supply of T and diminish the supply of N. With an unchanged composition of the total demand for goods between T and N, the relative price for N will rise. In addition, with an income elasticity of the demand for non-tradable goods greater than one, the rise in the relative price of N will be stronger. In terms of Fig. 7.10 and assuming floating exchange rates, P_T falls (a downward shift of the L^d_{T1} schedule) and P_N increases (an upward shift of the L^d_{N1} schedule). One possible new equilibrium point in the labour market would be, for instance, E (no labour migration) or F (labour migration from T to N). Under fixed exchange rates and assuming $\Delta P^*_T = 0$, the L^d_{T1} schedule cannot shift downwards and the whole adjustment burden lies on the rise in P_N (upward shift of the L^d_{N1} schedule either through point D or point G).

Scandinavian Model.   Assuming that there is no (positive) inflation rate and that nominal wages are constant, there will be a fall in P_T and P_N (negative inflation rates), but P_T diminishes more strongly than P_N (real appreciation). On the other hand, with positive inflation rates *and* with the same nominal wage increases in both production sectors, π_N has to lie above π_T by the amount of the productivity differential (real appreciation).

This last possibility for wage behaviour is the case of the Scandinavian model.[19] As already mentioned at the beginning of the present chapter, it assumes that the 'exposed' sector (i.e. the sector of tradable goods which is exposed to international price competition) is the nominal wage leader for the 'sheltered' sector (i.e. the sector of non-tradable goods which is protected against international price competition) so that $dW_N/W_N = dW_T/W_T$. Consequently, the inflation differential $\pi_N - \pi_T$ results from the 'structural' component of inflation represented by the growth differential of labour productivity, $\beta_T - \beta_N$ (see equation 7.12b). The change in relative prices [$(dq/q) < 0$] arises from the growth differential of labour productivity.

In order to compare the Scandinavian model with the classical model, we have drawn the labour market conditions in Fig. 7.11 in a similar way as in Fig. 7.10. The only difference with the classical model is that the L^d_{N0} schedule does not shift towards the position L^d_{N1} (point C) but it moves further upwards to L^d_{N2} (point D) such that nominal wages between T and N are equalized (W_2). By definition, there cannot be any labour migration since $W_2 = W_{T2} = W_{N2}$. Unlike the classical model, nothing is said about matching the level and composition of demand with those of production. With the income shares constant in the two productive sectors, the Scandinavian model predicts balanced growth rates for the supply of both tradables and non-tradables. As far as the market for non-tradable goods is concerned, the additional supply is accompanied by an increase in relative prices. This shift in relative price must

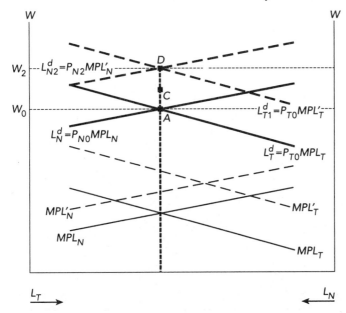

Fig. 7.11. Productivity growth and wage behaviour (Scandinavian model)

Unlike the classical model, the demand schedule for labour in the N sector does not shift from A to C, but from A to D, since wages rise to the level of wages in the T sector. This cost push rise in P_N must be accommodated by an adequate rise in the demand for N, since otherwise a real appreciation will not take place because of an excess supply on the market for N.

lead to a relative decline in the demand for the non-traded goods. Consequently, the decline has to be compensated by a high income elastic demand for non-tradables (Branson and Myhrman, 1976). If that is the case, the rise in P_N is determined by cost push and demand pull forces.[20]

Productivity Growth and Inflation under Fixed and Floating Exchange Rates

The wage behaviour of the Scandinavian model has different implications for the *overall* inflation rate ($\pi = a\pi_T + b\pi_N$)[21] depending on the underlying exchange rate regime. It is more inflationary under fixed exchange rates than under floating rates.

Because of the law of one price, the inflation rate for tradables has to be equal to the foreign inflation rate for tradables under the regime of fixed nominal exchange rates (equation 7.13a in Box 7.4). In the opposite case (equation 7.13b), it can be completely isolated from the foreign inflation rate via an appropriate change in the nominal exchange rate.

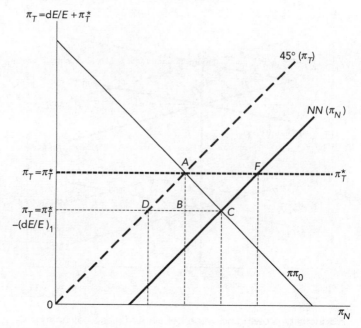

Fig. 7.12. The Scandinavian model under fixed and floating exchange rates

The bias of productivity growth towards tradables and the assumption of identical nominal wage increases in both production sectors imply that $\Pi_N > \Pi_T$. Under fixed exchange rates, this difference is equal to AF implying a higher inflation rate. Under floating exchange rates, the inflation rate remains constant (point C) as a result of a nominal appreciation (AB) and an increase in Π_N (BC).

The horizontal line π^*_T of Fig. 7.12 reflects the given foreign inflation rate for tradables. The $\pi\pi_0$ schedule indicates a given overall rate of inflation (π_0) for which the money market is in equilibrium (in terms of the equality between the rate of growth of the money supply and the rate of growth of the money demand). The inflation rate π_0 can be accompanied by different combinations of π_T and π_N (where $\pi = a\pi_T + b\pi_N$). The initial equilibrium is at point A. The domestic rate for inflation of tradables (π_T) is equal to the foreign rate of inflation for tradables (π^*_T) and is also assumed to be equal to the domestic inflation rate for non-tradables (π_N). Consequently, the real exchange rate remains constant.

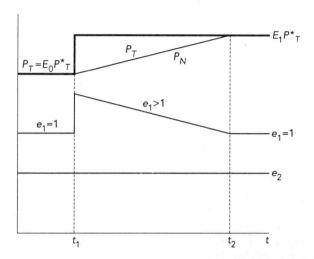

Fig. 7.13. Monetary expansion with a temporary effect on e_1 and no effect on e_2

There is a nominal depreciation from E_0 to E_1. At the very beginning of the monetary shock, the nominal depreciation is equal to the real depreciation of type e_1. Over time prices of domestic goods (P_T and P_N) begin to rise, gradually nullifying the initial real depreciation. Assuming a proportional rise in P_T and P_N, the real exchange rate of type e_2 remains unchanged.

Box 7.4 The Scandinavian model under fixed and floating exchange rates

Real appreciation rate	$-dq/q$	$=$	$\pi_N - \pi_T$	$=$	$\beta_T - \beta_N$ (7.13)
Fixed nominal exchange rates $\pi_T = \pi^*_T$	$-dq/q$	$=$	$\pi_N - \pi_T$	$=$	$\beta_T - \beta_N$ (7.13a)
Floating nominal exchange rates $\pi_T = dE/E + \pi^*_T$	$-dq/q$	$=$	$\pi_N - dE/E - \pi^*_T$	$=$	$\beta_T - \beta_N$ (7.13b)

Assume now a growing economy for which, according to the special wage behaviour of the Scandinavian model (see equation 7.13 in Box 7.4), there must be a continuous real appreciation rate. The line NN, which is parallel to the 45° line, indicates the inflation rate π_N and the 45° line indicates the inflation rate π_T. The *horizontal* difference between the two lines measures the rate of real appreciation ($\pi_N - \pi_T$).

If the country operates within a regime of fixed nominal exchange rates, the real appreciation requires a horizontal movement from A to F. On the one hand, the inflation rate of tradables must be identical in both countries ($\pi_T =$

π^*_T). On the other hand, the real appreciation is brought about exclusively by the rise of π_N at an amount of AF. Consequently, the overall inflation rate (π_0) has to increase. The necessity of a continuous real appreciation implies a higher total inflation rate which can be only realized by a higher monetary growth rate. The $\pi\pi_0$-schedule has to shift rightward and must pass through point F.

In a system of floating nominal exchange rates, the real appreciation can be realized by a movement from A to C. We assume the same monetary growth rate and the same total inflation rate π_0. The real appreciation rate is brought about by the nominal appreciation rate $[AB = -(dE/E)_1]$ *and* by the rise of the inflation rate for non-tradables $[BC]$.

In both exchange rate regimes, the inflation differential, $\pi_N - \pi_T$ is the same since it is identical to the rate of the real appreciation according to equation (7.13). Under floating exchange rates it is DC, and under fixed exchange rates it is AF. However, the overall inflation rate remains constant under floating rates, while it rises under fixed rates.

A Two-Country View

The need for a continuous real appreciation in a growing economy has to be essentially modified in a two-country view of the real exchange rate. In Section 5.3 the real exchange (of the type e_2) had been derived analytically, according to formula (5.8), as follows:

$$e \quad = \quad q^b/q^{*b^*} \tag{7.14}$$

by assuming purchasing power parity

$$P_T \quad = \quad EP^*_T. \tag{7.15}$$

In terms of growth rates, both formulae become, respectively

$$de/e \quad = \quad bdq/q - b^*dq^*/q^* \tag{7.14a}$$

$$\pi_T \quad = \quad dE/E + \pi^*_T. \tag{7.15a}$$

Assuming $b = b^*$, and since $q = P_T/P_N$, we can rewrite formula (7.14a) as

$$de/e \quad = \quad b[(\pi_T - \pi_N) - (\pi^*_T - \pi^*_N)]$$

$$= \quad b[(\pi_T - \pi^*_T) + (\pi^*_N - \pi_N)]$$

$$= \quad b[dE/E + (\pi^*_N - \pi_N)]. \tag{7.16}$$

The evolution of the real exchange rate now depends on the evolution of π_N *and* π^*_N as well as on changes in the nominal exchange rate.

It should be remembered that our above case of a continuous real appreciation was the outcome of a growing economy in which the relative price of non-tradables increased because of lower technical progress in the production sector for non-tradables, combined with the assumption of equal nominal wage increases in both sectors (the Scandinavian model), *and* because of higher income elasticity of the demand for non-tradables. If two countries with only one real exchange rate (equation (7.14)) are considered explicitly, the results of the preceding sections are greatly modified.

If fixed nominal exchange rates are assumed ($dE/E = 0$ in formula (7.16)), a necessary change in the relative price of non-tradables can only be brought about by an adequate change in P_N and P^*_N. Let us assume that the countries are identical with respect to taste, technical progress, and the real growth rate per capita. Consequently, we have the case of $\pi_N = \pi^*_N$ so that $de/e = 0$ according to equation (7.16). A rise in the relative price of non-tradables takes place at the same rate in both countries and the overall inflation rates, π and π^*, must also increase by the same amount since

$$\pi = a\pi_T + b\beta_N \qquad (7.17a)$$

$$\pi^* = a^*\pi^*_T + b^*\pi^*_N \qquad (7.17b)$$

Of course, these higher inflation rates (for $(\pi_T = \pi^*_T) < (\pi_N = \pi^*_N)$) have to be accommodated by higher monetary growth rates.

Consider now the situation where the countries are identical except for their real growth rate per capita. If the domestic country has a higher growth rate than the foreign country, we have $\pi_N > \pi^*_N$ and the domestic currency appreciates in real terms. On the one hand, the domestic country has a higher technical progress in the T-sector than the foreign country. On the other hand, as a result of higher domestic growth, the domestic country's increase in the demand for N is stronger than that in the foreign country.

In this sense, rapidly growing economies are characterized by real appreciations and slowly growing economies by real depreciations. If both groups of countries are linked by fixed nominal exchange rates, the rapidly growing countries have to be more inflationary than the slowly growing ones. Under floating exchange rates, the higher inflation rate of the rapidly growing economies would be replaced by a nominal appreciation rate of $b(dE/E)$ according to formula (7.16), and the total inflation rate would not increase.

7.6 The Real Exchange Rate Mechanism Once Again

Which Real Exchange Rate is Relevant: e_1 or e_2?

In principle, both are relevant. It is true that only e_2 would be relevant if it is assumed that *PPP* is always valid so that e_1, by assumption, always equals one, but that assumption does not reflect reality.

Different kinds of shocks—real, financial, or long-run—can affect the exchange rates differently. The impact of a particular kind of shock may be mainly on one or other of the exchange rates, or it may be on both. In what follows we shall assume, for simplicity, a world of perfect capital mobility.

Financial shocks. A monetary shock in terms of an increase in the money supply provokes a nominal depreciation (Fig. 7.13). With initially rigid prices, this depreciation is also a real one, but only of type e_1. When prices do rise, the rises will be the same for P_T and P_N so that e_2 remains constant and e_1 returns to its initial level.[22]

Real shocks. We shall refer to our—perhaps extreme—example of a budget deficit under perfect capital mobility. Depending on the type of government expenditure, ΔG could affect e_1, e_2, or both as we shall now show (Box 7.5.). ΔG can consist of ΔG_T (additional expenditure on domestic tradables), of ΔG_T^* (additional expenditure on foreign tradables which are imports) and of ΔG_N (additional expenditure on domestic non-tradables). In the present chapter, we assumed that $e_1 = 1$ (so that $\Delta G = \Delta G_T^*$), but we shall now relax that assumption. A real appreciation of type e_1 emerges if $\Delta G = \Delta G_T$ and the same happens for e_2 if $\Delta G = \Delta G_N$. Of course, both real exchange rates will be affected if $\Delta G = \Delta G_T + \Delta G_N$. Only the case $\Delta G = \Delta G_{T^*}$ does not produce any exchange rate effect (under the assumption of perfect capital mobility).

Box 7.5. The impact of real shocks (budget deficit) on e_1 and e_2 (real appreciations) under perfect capital mobility

	Δe	Flexible E	Fixed E
Real exchange rate of type $e_1 = EP^*_T/P_T$			
$\Delta G = \Delta G_T$	$-\Delta e_1 [P_T > EP^*_T]$	$-\Delta E$	$+\Delta P_T$
$\Delta G = \Delta G_T^*$	$\Delta e_1 = 0 [P_T = EP^*_T]$	$\Delta E = 0$	$\Delta P_T = 0$
Real exchange rate of type $e_2 = EP^*_T/P_N$ (assuming $P_T = EP^*_T$)			
$\Delta G = \Delta G_T^*$	$\Delta e_2 = 0 [P_N = EP^*_T]$	$\Delta E = 0$	$\Delta P_N = 0$
$\Delta G = \Delta G_N$	$-\Delta e_2 [P_N > EP^*T]$	$-\Delta E$	$+\Delta P_N$

For $-\Delta e$ we assume that $-\Delta e = \Delta E$ in the case of flexible exchange rates. For e_2 we assume that $e_2 = 1$ before the emergence of the real shock.

With $\Delta G = \Delta G_T$, however, there will also be a real appreciation of type e_2, and with $\Delta G = \Delta G_N$, there will also be a real appreciation of e_1. Assuming that purchasing power parity does not hold, not only does the demand for domestic tradable goods depend on the relative price of domestic and foreign tradable goods (e_1), but the demand *and* supply of domestic tradable goods also depend on the relative price of domestic tradable and non-tradable goods (e_2). In Fig. 7.14, both the *IS*- and the *NN*-schedules are influenced by both relative prices

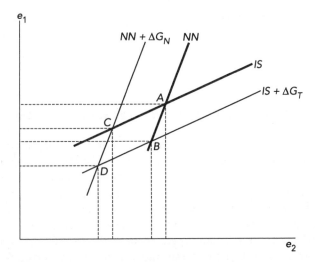

Fig. 7.14. Simultaneous determination of the real exchange rates of type e_1 and e_2

The equilibrium condition in the market for domestic tradable goods (*IS*) also depends on e_2. Similarly, the equilibrium condition for the market of non-tradable goods (*NN*) also depends on e_1. The initial equilibrium is at A. The fiscal shock ΔG_T produces the real appreciation at B. The fiscal shock ΔG_N causes the real appreciation at C.

through cross price elasticities. Thus, for instance, *IS* is more sensitive to e_1 than to e_2. A real depreciation of type e_1 $(P_T < EP_T{}^*)$ creates an excess demand for domestic tradable goods which can be eliminated by a much stronger real depreciation of type e_2 (a fall in P_N). The simultaneous determination of both real exchange rates takes place at the intersection point A.

A fiscal shock resulting from ΔG_T (schedule $IS + \Delta G_T$) provokes a strong real appreciation of e_1 and a slight real appreciation of e_2. Since domestic tradable goods have become very expensive with respect to foreign tradable goods, there is a substitution in favour of both foreign and non-tradable goods which causes the real appreciation of e_2 (point B). Along similar lines, a fiscal shock caused by ΔG_N (schedule $NN + \Delta G_N$) produces a real appreciation which is stronger for e_2 than for e_1 (point C). If both shocks occur, there will be a common real appreciation (point D).

Another important conclusion from Part II was that the change in the real exchange rates could also take place under the regime of fixed (nominal) exchange rates, at least as far as the classical macro model was concerned. With $E = E_0$, a real appreciation of type e_1 was brought about by a rise in P_T, and a real appreciation of type e_2 by an increase in P_N.

Long-run structural changes. In Section 7.5, we dealt with one type of structural change (differential productivity growth in T and N and different income elasticities of the demand for T and N) which concerned only e_2. In the following chapter, we shall treat another long-run phenomenon (changes in wealth as an outcome of current account imbalances) which not only affects e_2 but e_1 too.

Real Exchange Rate Mechanism versus Real Interest Rate Mechanism

At the end of Chapter 1 I illustrated the case of an excess supply in the market for domestic goods—instead of an excess demand as in the present and previous chapters—for which the adjustment mechanism could be conceived in terms of quantity changes (Keynesian) or price changes (classical).

The classical adjustment mechanism for a closed economy consisted of a fall in the real interest rate through which demand was increased to the full employment level. In a small open economy with fully integrated world capital markets, the real interest rate mechanism could not be operated as r was given by the international economy. Consequently, the real exchange rate mechanism had to take over the role of the real interest rate mechanism.

Still in the classical framework, there will be a real depreciation and not a decline in the real interest rate which now pushes up the demand for domestic goods towards the full employment level of production. Under the regime of fixed exchange rates, and if the excess supply of goods is mainly of type T, P_T has to fall with respect to $E_0 P^*_T$ to create an additional demand for domestic tradable goods at the expense of imported goods; additional exports would also push total demand up. Under floating exchange rates, ΔE could bring about the necessary real depreciation by leaving the price level of domestic tradables unchanged.[23]

If the excess supply of domestic goods covers mainly non-tradables, the decline in the real interest rate is again replaced by the real depreciation which is now predominantly of type e_2. Under fixed exchange rates, P_N will fall, thus creating substitution effects on the demand and supply sides (higher D_N and lower S_N). Any remaining excess supply of T would be exported with no change in relative prices under the hypothesis of the 'dependent' economy. Under floating exchange rates, the monetary adjustment mechanism for realizing the real depreciation could be a rise in E only.[24]

Thus, with perfect capital mobility, the real exchange rate mechanism takes over the classical role of the real interest rate mechanism which is mostly relevant for closed economies. In addition, the real exchange rate mechanism is applicable to both floating and fixed exchange rates. In this respect, the nature of the real exchange rate is similar to the nature of the real interest rate. Both assume the function of equilibrating the market for domestic goods under alternative assumptions about the openness of the economy.

However, over the short run, real interest rates can diverge among countries. One example is the real interest rate parity with no risk premium. Any divergence of real interest rates immediately provokes movements in the real exchange rate to equilibrate international financial markets. The change in the domestic real interest rate equilibrates domestic financial markets, while the change in the real exchange rate is necessary to harmonize the real rate of return between domestic and foreign financial assets. Thus, over the short run, the real exchange rate mechanism establishes the equilibrium in the domestic and foreign financial markets, and in its long-run role, it establishes the equilibrium in the market for domestic goods.

Appendix A: An Alternative Version of the Australian Macro-model

Fig. 7.A1 shows another geometrical version of the Australian model as an alternative to Fig. 7.5. It represents an extension of Fig. 7.8. For simplicity, we

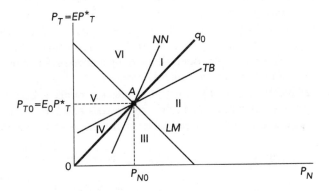

Fig. 7.A1. The Australian macro-model

Equilibrium is at point A with internal equilibrium (NN), external equilibrium (TB), and monetary equilibrium (LM).
I   Excess supply N; TB > 0
     Excess demand M
II Excess supply N; TB < 0
     Excess demand M
III Excess supply N; TB < 0
     Excess supply M
IV Excess demand N; TB < 0
     Excess supply M
V   Excess demand N; TB > 0
     Excess supply M
VI Excess demand N; TB > 0
     Excess demand M

have drawn the equilibrium schedule of the money market (*LM*) as a straight line. The slope of the *NN*- and *TB*-schedules is determined only by the *relative* price effect on the demand and supply of non-tradable goods (*NN*) and the trade balance (*TB*). Tradable and non-tradable goods are treated as gross substitutes. Starting from point *A*, a rise in P_N creates an excess supply of non-tradables (lower demand and higher supply) and an excess demand for tradables (higher demand by residents and lower supply), thus creating a trade balance deficit. To eliminate the disequilibrium, P_T has to increase more in the first case than in the second one.

Fig. 7.A2 describes the effects of a budget deficit assuming perfect capital mobility. The rise in public expenditure on non-tradable goods shifts the *NN*-schedule to the position NN_1. The size of the real appreciation is indicated by the slope of the Oq_1 ray. Under flexible exchange rates, internal equilibrium is at the intersection point *B* of the NN_1-schedule with the *LM*-line. The price level is not modified and monetary equilibrium is at point *B*. The real appreciation has been brought about by a fall in *E* and a rise in P_N. In a fixed exchange rate regime, the general price level has to increase to point *C* and this requires a corresponding increase in the quantity of money. *LM* has to shift to LM_1, which means a new NN_2-schedule (and a new TB_2-schedule).[25] The real appreciation has been brought about by a rise in P_N only.

Fig. 7.A3 illustrates the neutrality of an increase in the money supply (LM_2) for real variables (q_0). In a comparative static analysis, the general price level increases by the same percentage as *E* and P_N. This monetary experiment is of course only conceivable under floating exchange rates. With fixed exchange rates, the system must return to point *A*.

This alternative version of the Australian macro-model is less appropriate for describing the short-run adjustment process to a fiscal or monetary shock since the interest rate parity has not been included as it was with Fig. 7.5.

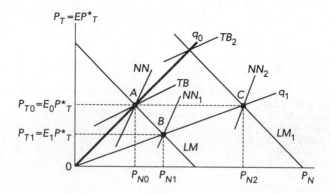

Fig. 7.A2. Fiscal shock ($\Delta G = \Delta D_N$)

The fiscal shock (NN_1) produces the real appreciation q_1. Under floating exchange rates, the new equilibrium is at *B*. Under fixed exchange rates, the new equilibrium is at *C*.

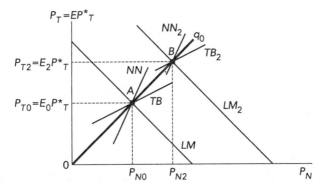

Fig. 7.A3. Monetary shock (ΔM)

The increase in the money supply (LM_2) shifts all nominal variables upwards (point B).

However, Figs. 7.A1–3 provide a more straightforward description of the evolution of the absolute values for P_T and P_N. The figure of the interest rate parity could always be added in terms of the e, r-space.

Mathematical Appendix: Fiscal Policy and the Real Exchange Rate

We shall rewrite the conditions for internal and external equilibrium of Box 7.1 in the following form:

Internal equilibrium (*NN*) $S^N(e) = D^N(e,r) + G_N$ (7.1a)
External equilibrium (*TB*) $S^T(e) - D^T(e,r) - G_T = 0$ (7.3a)

D now stands for *private* demand and G for government expenditure. The above equations are differentiated according to the assumptions $\Delta G = \Delta G_N$ and $\Delta G = \Delta G_T$.

A. $\Delta G = \Delta G_N$ (Fig. 7.3)

Perfect capital mobility: (7.1a) where $r = r^*$

$$S^N_e \, de - D^N_e de = dG_N$$

$$\frac{de}{dG_N} = \frac{1}{S^N_e - D^N_e} < 0 \qquad (A.1)$$

where $S^N_e < 0$ and $D^N_e > 0$.

Capital immobility: (7.1a) and (7.3a)

$$
\begin{array}{ll}
NN & (S^N_e - D^N_e)\, de - D^N_r\, dr = dG_N \\
TB & (S^T_e - D^T_e)\, de - D^T_r\, dr = 0 \\
 & dr = [(S^T_e - D^T_e)/D^T_r]\, de
\end{array}
$$

TB into *NN* $(S^N_e - D^N_e)\, de - D^N_r[(S^T_e - D^T_e)/D^T_r]\, de = dG_N$

We assume that $D^N_r = D^T_r$

$$
\frac{de}{dG_N} = \frac{1}{(S^N_e - D^N_e) - (S^T_e - D^T_e)} < 0 \tag{A.2}
$$

where $S^T_e > 0$ and $D^T_e < 0$. Comparing (A.2) with (A.1), we have (A.2) > (A.1) or, in absolute terms, (A.1) > (A.2). The real appreciation is lower with (A.2) than with (A.1).

B. $\Delta G = \Delta G_T$ (Fig. 7.4)

Perfect capital mobility: (7.1a) where $r = r^*$

ΔG_T has no impact on equation (7.1a), but, under capital immobility, it has an impact on (7.1a) via dr.

Capital immobility: (7.1a) and (7.3a)

$$
\begin{array}{ll}
TB & (S^T_e - D^T_e)\, de - D^T_r\, dr = dG_T \\
\\
NN & dr = [(S^N_e - D^N_e)/D^N_r]\, de
\end{array}
$$

NN into *TB* $(S^T_e - D^T_e)\, de - D^T_r\,[(S^N_e - D^N_e)/D^N_r]\, de = dG_T$

We assume again that $D^N_r = D^T_r$

$$
\frac{de}{dG_T} = \frac{1}{(S^T_e - D^T_e) - (S^N_e - D^N_e)} > 0 \tag{A.3}
$$

Notes

1. Refer again to Box 1.1.
2. The model was elaborated by the Australian economists Salter (1959), Swan (1960), and Pearce (1961) for countries the size of the Australian economy. Later contributions are those by Mundell (1971: ch. 9); Dornbusch (1974; 1980: ch. 6), and (1983); and Edwards (1989a). This model is also called the non-traded goods model or the dependent economy model; see Caves *et al.* (1990: 486). The Scandinavian model is a special case, as we shall see later.
3. Which is the assumption of the Scandinavian model. It assumes that the 'exposed' sector (i.e. the sector of tradable goods which is exposed to international price competition) is the nominal wage leader for the 'sheltered' sector (i.e. the sector of non-tradable goods) such that $W_T = W_N$.
4. The real depreciation was assumed to result from a rise in the exchange rate where $\Delta P_T = \Delta E \times P^*_T$. In this case, the general price level would also increase as did the

nominal wage rate (W_1) in Fig. 7.1a. However, as we already discussed in ch.5 (Fig. 5.6), a real depreciation can also be accompanied by a constant price level if P_T increases *and* P_N decreases. In terms of Fig. 7.1a, we obtain the same labour migration to the T sector at an unchanged nominal wage rate (W_0), if P_T increases less, and P_N decreases so that the new labour demand schedules pass through point C.

5. With respect to the demand side for non-tradables, the real depreciation induces not only the substitution effect in favour of non-tradables (at the expense of tradables), but also the income effect which is negative for the demand of both categories of goods, if real income is measured in terms of internationally traded goods. This is the value standard for small open economies. Total nominal income is $Y = P_T S_T + P_N S_N$. By dividing the equation by P_T and defining real income (y) as Y/P_T, we obtain $y = S_T + (P_N/P_T) S_N$. A rise in P_T lowers y. The substitution effect of a real depreciation increases the demand for non-tradables and its negative income effect lowers it. Consequently, for the positive slope of the NN-schedule, we have to assume that the substitution effect is stronger than the income effect.

6. This is the reason that the model is called the Australian model (a small and dependent economy). In ch. 6, an excess demand for domestic goods which had an impact on the real exchange rate was exclusively an excess demand for domestic tradable goods. This excess demand was eliminated by a real appreciation. Domestic tradable goods were not perfect substitutes for foreign tradable goods. Either P_T had to increase or E had to decrease implying $P_T > EP^*_T$ in order to equilibrate the market for domestic goods. This is not the case in the present chapter which operates under the assumption that $P_T = EP^*_T$.

7. It must also be emphasized that a change in e does not have any direct impact on exports, since only a real depreciation of type e_1 would increase exports. However, since the real depreciation increases the production of tradables and lowers residents' demand for tradables, the remaining gap would be exported.

8. We would also obtain the same exchange rate effect for other types of autonomous increases in expenditure (consumption or investment).

9. Under the hypothesis of Ricardian equivalence, the budget deficit is financed by additional domestic savings, independently of the underlying degree of capital mobility. The interest rate and the trade balance remain unchanged. Since individuals observe a reduction in their permanent disposable income as the result of higher future tax liabilities, they save more and, correspondingly, they reduce their consumption on tradable and non-tradable goods. Even though total expenditure will equal domestic production, there is still an excess demand for non-tradables and an excess supply of tradables. The real appreciation eliminates the disequilibrium in the market for non-tradables (and, with this, that of tradables too).

10. Fig. 7.3b (more than Fig. 7.3a) highlights the production implications of a budget deficit: lower production of tradables and higher production of non-tradables. On the one hand, the shift of resources for production at B or C may depend on the specific time profile of the budget deficit, i.e. whether it is temporary or permanent, whether it takes place at the present or in the future, and, consequently, whether it is anticipated or not (see Frenkel and Razin, 1987). On the other hand, the feasibility of the intersectoral movement of the factors of production depends on the nature of the production function. If labour is the only factor of production

(and, additionally, if there are no labour market rigidities), the resource shift would be easier to realize (Penati, 1987) than in the case of labour plus existing capital under the assumption of a non-growing economy (Obstfeld, 1987). In the case of a growing economy, the increase in the capital stock would go exclusively to the non-tradable goods sector.

11. Taking the case of the Ricardian equivalence theorem, the additional public expenditure on tradable goods via the budget deficit crowds out private expenditure on tradables and non-tradables with no change in the interest rate. Since permanent disposable income decreases as the consequence of higher future tax liabilities, individuals save more and reduce their consumption on tradables and non-tradables. There is still an excess supply of non-tradables (which corresponds to an excess demand for tradables). Both disequilibria are eliminated by a real depreciation.

12. We did not take into account the case of $\Delta G = \Delta D_N + \Delta D_T$ in the present chapter as we did in the previous chapter. If half ΔG is spent on N, and the other half on T, we would obtain results analogous to the case of ch. 6. A more rigorous analysis of the impact of the budget deficit on the real exchange rate can be found in the Mathematical Appendix to the present chapter.

13. In the case of *IS*, the excess demand for domestic goods was for domestic tradable goods. The type e_1 real appreciation lowered the demand by residents for domestic tradables in favour of more foreign tradables (more imports) and it reduced the demand by foreigners for domestic tradables (fewer exports). Remember that, for the present type of the 'dependent' economy, any excess demand for domestic tradables is satisfied by imports without any change in e_1.

14. Of course, the *IS* and *NN* schedules do not coincide. Thus, the steepness of their positive slopes and their positions differ.

15. Taking into account the aversion to the exchange rate risk ($CRP > 0$), the relevant figure would be Fig. 6.8. in which *IS* has to be replaced by *NN*. The final equilibrium would produce a higher domestic interest rate ($r_1 > r^*$) reflecting the currency risk for foreign investors who finance a part of the budget deficit. The adjustment path would be $Q \rightarrow B$ or $R' \rightarrow B$.

16. The case where the real appreciation rate is identical to the nominal appreciation rate is indicated in Fig. 7.8 by point B_1. The absolute price level of non-tradables remains unchanged. Such an outcome is only conceivable with a restrictive monetary policy which shifts the *LM*-schedule through B_1. The real appreciation also changes the composition of domestic goods towards more non-tradables and fewer tradables. There is a lower weight for tradables (a) and a higher weight for non-tradables (b). Since the slope of the *LM*-schedule is equal to $-b/a$, the *LM*-schedules would become steeper, at points B and B_1, respectively.

17. The $P_T P_N$ space of Fig. 7.8 is an alternative geometrical representation of the Australian model as set out in the Appendix to this chapter.

18. The income line is tangent to the production possibility curve and to an indifference curve which has not been drawn.

19. The Scandinavian model was developed by Scandinavian authors like Aukrust (1970), Edgren *et al.* (1973), Branson and Myhrman (1976), and Lindbeck (1979). It is also applicable to other small countries the size of the Scandinavian economies.

20. Recent contributions to the differential productivity growth and the real exchange rate are contained in issue 3 of the new *Review of International Economics*, 2 (1994).

21. Where a is the weight of tradables among total production and b the weight of non-tradables according to the price level definition of Table 5.1.

22. In Fig. 7.13 we did not take into account the overshooting phenomenon according to interest rate parity. If P_T rises more than P_N, there would be also a temporary real depreciation of type e_2.

23. Within the simple Keynesian framework, the analysis is the same as with the classical model under the regime of floating exchange rates. However, *under fixed rates*, P_T is rigid downwards. Consequently, there will be a quantity adjustment. Since a real depreciation is excluded, the production will be adjusted to the lower level of the total demand for domestic tradable goods; see Fig. 1.5.

24. Under fixed exchange rates, the fall in P_T or P_N also implies a downward flexibility of nominal wages, since otherwise there would be a contraction in the supply of domestic goods with subsequent unemployment. This issue will be discussed in the next chapter.

25. Since the demand and supply of tradables and non-tradables only depend on relative prices, a higher general price level shifts the NN_1-schedule upward along the $0q_1$ ray. The TB-schedule moves upward along the $0q_0$ ray at the same time. The real cash balance effect is also excluded because $\Delta m = 0$.

PART III
POLICY ISSUES: EXTERNAL EQUILIBRIUM, INTEGRATION, AND THE SECOND–THIRD WORLD

Although policy issues were not excluded from the two previous parts, these were concerned with the analytical aspect of economic policies. One of our main concerns was the analysis of the effects of monetary policy ('nominal' shock) and fiscal policy ('real' shock) on the exchange rate and other macro variables. Part III deals mainly with the normative aspect of economic policies. What should be done to attain external equilibrium? How do monetary unions work and what should be done to make them function better? What type of stabilization programme should be implemented in developing and post-socialist countries?

Part III deals explicitly with the First, Second, and Third Worlds. Chapter 8 is concerned with the traditional issue of the policy mix for attaining internal and external equilibrium in industrialized countries, since we are assuming that capital is highly mobile. Chapter 9 deals with monetary integration, which, for the moment, is primarily a European policy issue. Chapter 10 tries to apply the general theoretical framework of international monetary economics to macro-economic stabilization issues in developing and post-socialist countries.

8

INDUSTRIALIZED COUNTRIES: INTERNAL–EXTERNAL EQUILIBRIUM

External equilibrium, defined as a balanced current account, can be viewed from two different angles. There is an analytical point of view, according to which a disequilibrium in the current account (equal to a change in net external wealth) over the longer run leads automatically to an external equilibrium via the wealth effect. There is also the policy point of view, according to which the necessary and sufficient conditions for a successful policy mix for attaining internal—external equilibrium concern policy measures in the markets for domestic goods, money, and labour.

8.1 Internal–External Equilibrium

External Equilibrium

External equilibrium can be identified as the equilibrium of the balance of payments, as the equilibrium of the current account, or as the equilibrium of the trade balance. As we have seen in Chapter 2, the problem of an equilibrated balance of payments—defined as an unchanged stock of international reserves held by the central bank—is essentially an issue of the regime of fixed exchange rates (or 'dirty' floating). With respect to the other two balances, the necessity for an external equilibrium can arise under both exchange rate regimes. It emerges for deficit countries mostly when the access to international credit markets is limited ('imperfect capital mobility') or when deficit countries— even in the case of 'perfect capital mobility'—are reluctant to take on more foreign debt.

The current account balance is the trade balance of goods and services $(X-Im)$ plus interest payments (r^*eF^*) on net foreign assets $(F^* > 0$ in the case of a net creditor country) or minus interest payments on net foreign debt $(F^* < 0$ in the case of a net debtor country). I neglect other items like unilateral transfers (e.g. workers' remittances) which can also make the balances differ. In Fig. 8.1 I have reproduced the equilibrium schedules for the trade balance (TB

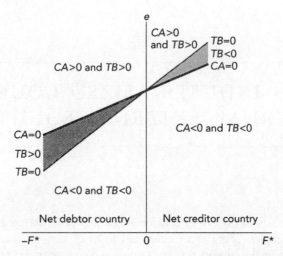

Fig. 8.1. External equilibrium: trade balance versus current account balance

It is assumed that the balances diverge by net interest payments either received from abroad ($F^* > 0$) or transferred to other countries ($F^* < 0$). External equilibrium, in the sense of $CA = 0$, would imply a trade balance deficit in the case of $F^* > 0$, i.e. the interest payments received are used for buying foreign goods. Assuming $F^* < 0$, the external equilibrium in terms of $CA = 0$ is accompanied by a trade balance surplus which is necessary in order to pay the interest service on foreign debt without incurring further net indebtedness.

$= 0$) and the current account balance ($CA = 0$) for both a net creditor country (right-hand panel) and a net debtor country (left-hand panel). The algebraic formulation of both schedules is shown in Box 8.1.

The slope of both schedules must be explained by the relative price effect (de) and by the wealth effect, which is composed of the wealth value effect ($F^* de$) and the wealth volume effect ($e\, dF^*$). If we start from a point on the *TB*-schedule in the right-hand panel and assume an increase in e, there are two opposing forces which act on the trade balance. The relative price effect improves the trade balance (and, thus, also the current account balance too). However, the wealth value effect ($F^* de$) increases absorption and, thus, imports, and it worsens the trade balance (and the current account balance too). The same is true for the interest income value effect ($r^* F^* de$), which pushes imports upwards. We shall assume that the relative price effect is stronger than the wealth value and income value effects so that any point above the *TB*-schedule represents a trade balance surplus ($TB > 0$) and a current account surplus ($CA > 0$). This surplus can be eliminated by an increase in the volume of wealth (dF^*) which increases absorption and, thus, imports.[1]

Box 8.1 External equilibrium: trade balance versus current account balance

Trade Balance ($TB = 0$) $X(e) - Im(A,G,e) = TB(A,G,e) = 0$ (8.1)

$$\text{where } A = A(r,w,T)$$
$$w = m + eF^*$$

Current Account Balance ($CA = 0$) $TB(A,G,e) + r^*eF^* = e\,dF^* = 0$ (8.2)

F^* = net foreign financial assets ('real' bonds promising to pay a unit of foreign output indefinitely)
A = absorption by the private sector[2]
T = taxes
w = real net financial wealth[3]

The two schedules must coincide on the vertical axis since F^* is equal to zero. With increasing F^*, and moving upwards on the CA line, the wedge between the lines representing the trade balance deficit becomes greater. The reason is that—moving up along the CA line—there is a rising interest income from foreign assets which permits a rising trade balance deficit to be financed by the interest payments, even though the current account remains in equilibrium.

The more relevant case of an 'external constraint' is illustrated in the left-hand panel where the country is a net debtor. If the country is below the CA-schedule and it wants to stop its net debt accumulation,[4] it has to choose the current account balance ($CA=0$) as the target for external balance. Achieving this target involves the realization of a certain trade balance surplus—represented by the vertical distance between the CA-schedule and the TB-schedule—which is required in order to honour the interest payments on the outstanding volume of foreign debt when these interest payments are not serviced by taking on additional foreign debt.

In the context of a growing open economy, its 'external constraint' could be defined in a more sophisticated—or even more 'realistic'—way. External equilibrium could be defined as the realization of a certain current account deficit which is *sustainable* by steady capital inflows. If, for instance, the country's current account deficit amounts to 3 per cent of GDP and its sustainable current account deficit is judged to be 2 per cent of GDP, its external disequilibrium could be interpreted as being 1 per cent of GDP.[5]

Internal Equilibrium

Internal equilibrium is defined as the equilibrium in the market for domestic goods; see Box 8.2.[6] In the preceding chapters we operated with two alternative interpretations of the goods market. In one interpretation, there was only one category of domestic goods, tradable goods, and the real exchange rate (of type e_1) had to be conceived as the relative price of domestic and foreign tradable goods (equation 8.3a). The modelling of the domestic goods market was elaborated either according to the classical approach (given real income and variable price level) or the Keynesian approach (given price level and variable real income). In equation (8.3a) (and in (8.3b)), we have used the classical approach. In the other interpretation, if the Australian model is followed, internal equilibrium has to be regarded as the equilibrium condition in the market for non-tradable goods and the real exchange rate (of type e_2) as the relative price of tradable and non-tradable goods (equation 8.3b).

Box 8.2 Internal equilibrium: two types of markets for domestic goods

Market for domestic tradable goods (the traditional approach and the classical model; real exchange rate of type e_1) IS	$\bar{y} = A(r,w,T) + G + TB(A,G,e)$ (8.3a) where $A = A(r,w,T)$ $w = m + eF^*$
Market for non-tradable goods (the Australian approach and the classical model; real exchange rate of type e_2) NN	$S_N(e) = D_N(e,r,w,T) + G_N$ (8.3b)
Money market LM	$m = L(r)$ (8.4)

In the present chapter, we are concerned with two fundamental issues of external equilibrium. The first is an *analytical* one. Any country which has a disequilibrium in its current account balance will accumulate foreign assets or foreign debts. The subsequent wealth effect may enhance automatic mechanisms which bring about an external equilibrium over the longer run without implementing any discretionary policy mix. This issue also involves the macroeconomic determination of the real exchange rate as analysed in the two last chapters, but now considered over the very long run. The second issue is a *political* one which one finds in all textbooks on international economics. We ask about the proper policy mix for realizing internal and external equilibrium for a country which is suffering from a current account deficit.[7]

8.2. The Current Account Balance and Full Stock Equilibrium

Long-Run Evolution of the Real Exchange Rate (e_1 and e_2)

We shall address first the analytical issue which concerns the impact of the current account balance on the long-run behaviour of the real exchange rate.[8] The macroeconomic determination of the real exchange rate outlined in

Chapters 6 and 7 did not take into account the change in the outstanding volume of net external wealth or debt. Neither changes in stocks (wealth) as a result of an imbalance in the current account, nor long-run tendencies towards a full stock equilibrium in terms of a balanced current account ($CA = 0$) were taken into account. This long-run equilibrium in the current account is another concept for the external equilibrium (besides the 'sustainable' account deficit).[9]

Remaining exclusively within the framework of a small open economy with perfect capital mobility, we shall again operate with a real shock in the form of increased public expenditure.[10] If the fiscal shock initially produces a real appreciation and a current account deficit, there will subsequently be a further movement of the real exchange rate. The path of the real exchange rate is a result of the wealth effect created by the imbalance in the current account: current account deficit → lower net external wealth → lower absorption → real depreciation. Furthermore, there are forces in the markets which push the current account into balance over the longer run.

The current account is given by equation (8.2) in Box 8.1, and the market for domestic goods refers to tradable goods (*IS*) or non-tradable goods (*NN*) as indicated in Box 8.2. The domestic real interest rate is equal to the international rate (r^*). We have not added the interest rate parity. We are dealing only with comparative statics. The interest rate parity would be relevant for the transition period.[11]

The equilibrium condition of the goods market (Fig. 8.2) concerns the supply and demand for tradable (*IS*) or non-tradable (*NN*) goods produced by the domestic economy. The downward slope of the schedules must be explained as follows. A real depreciation from any point on the *IS*- or *NN*-

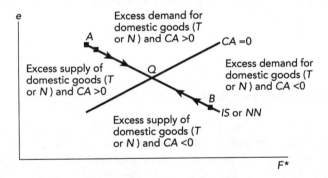

Fig. 8.2. The long-run path towards external equilibrium via changes of external wealth and the real exchange rate

At point *A* there is internal equilibrium and a current account surplus, implying an increase in net external wealth which increases the demand for domestic goods. The excess demand for domestic goods is eliminated by a real appreciation which reduces the current account surplus. The increase in wealth stops at point *Q*, where internal and external equilibriums coincide. The reverse adjustment process would take place at point *B*.

schedule creates an excess demand for three reasons. First, if the rise in e is interpreted as a relative price effect for domestic and foreign goods where domestic goods are either tradables (*IS*) or non-tradables (*NN*), domestic goods become less expensive than foreign goods. The demand for exports and import substitutes rises (*IS*), or, in the case of identical prices for domestic and foreign tradables, the demand for non-tradables increases (*NN*). Second, a rise in e induces a positive wealth value effect ($F^* de$), since $d(eF^*) = F^* de + e\, dF^*$. This wealth value effect produces an increase in the demand for goods by domestic residents. Finally, there is an interest income value effect ($r^* F^* de$) working on the demand for goods in the same direction as the wealth value effect. Consequently, there are three strong elements of a rise in e which create an excess demand for domestic goods, either domestic tradables (*IS*) or non-tradables (*NN*). This excess demand can be eliminated by a fall in the wealth volume ($e\, dF^*$) which exercises a downward pressure on the demand for domestic goods by domestic residents.

The schedule of the current account balance ($CA=0$) is that of Fig. 8.1. We assume a net creditor country.[12] The schedules for internal equilibrium (*IS* or *NN*) and external equilibrium ($CA=0$) coincide at point Q which indicates full stock equilibrium with respect to the wealth level. At any other point on the *IS*- or *NN*-schedules, the current account is in disequilibrium. At point A, the internal equilibrium is associated with a surplus in the current account. The current account surplus is identical to a rise in wealth and implies a higher demand for domestic goods. The excess demand in the domestic goods market is eliminated by a real appreciation which brings about a lower demand for exports and import substitutes. However, there is still a surplus (even though a lower one) on the current account. The simultaneous process of wealth accumulation and real appreciations continues until wealth is adjusted towards Q. The reverse process of wealth decumulation and real depreciations takes place if the initial external disequilibrium is that of a current account deficit (point B).

Comparative Statics of Real Shocks

When the real shock results from a bond financed budget, ambiguous wealth effects may exist depending on the degree of validity of the Ricardian equivalence theorem. Therefore, we shall deal with an expansionary fiscal policy in the form of a tax financed increase in public expenditure ($\Delta G = \Delta T$). As Fig. 8.3 indicates, anything can happen to the real exchange rate during the wealth adjustment process, but in all cases there is a deficit on the current account and a subsequent reduction in wealth.

Let us assume that the additional government expenditure is spent exclusively on domestic goods: domestic tradables (*IS*) or non-tradables (*NN*). Furthermore, the decrease of private consumption as a result of higher taxes

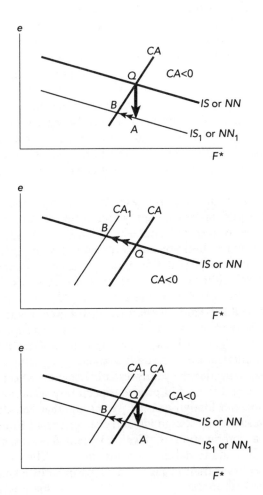

Fig. 8.3. Expansionary fiscal policy ($\Delta G = \Delta T$) and its long-run impact on the real exchange rate

The immediate impact is either a real appreciation or a constant real exchange rate. In all cases, a current account deficit emerges, involving lower net external wealth and an excess supply of domestic goods which is eliminated by real depreciations.

Fig. 8.3a.

Excess demand for domestic goods: shift of the *IS*- or *NN*-schedule.

Fig. 8.3b.

Additional demand for imports: shift of the *CA*-schedule.

Fig. 8.3c.

Excess demand for domestic goods (shift of the *IS*- or *NN*-schedule) and additional demand for imports (shift of the *CA*-schedule).

and lower disposable income should refer exclusively to a reduction in the private demand for domestic goods. Consequently, according to the Haavelmo theorem, there is still an excess demand for domestic goods which explains the downward shift of the *IS*-schedule (or the *NN*-schedule) in Fig. 8.3*a*. The real appreciation (point *A*) eliminates the excess demand for domestic goods via the crowding-out effect (as the result of the relative price effect and of the wealth value effect). The resulting current account deficit decreases wealth and lowers the private demand for domestic goods. We have now an excess supply of domestic goods (moving from point *A* to the left) so that the real exchange rate begins to move in the opposite direction (real depreciation). The new long-run equilibrium is reached at point *B* after a continuous process of wealth decumulation.

We shall now assume the opposite case. The additional public expenditure is used only for the purchase of foreign goods (imports) and the reduction in private expenditure concerns exclusively imports. Consequently, the equilibrium of the market for domestic goods remains at point *Q* (Fig. 8.3*b*), while there is still an additional demand for imports (again as a consequence of the Haavelmo theorem) shifting the *CA*=0-schedule upwards. The immediate impact is an unchanged real exchange rate at *Q*. The current account moves into deficit and wealth begins to decrease. The lower wealth level depresses private demand for domestic goods and creates an excess supply in the market for domestic goods. The exchange rate mechanism (real depreciation) re-establishes the equilibrium in the goods market.

Finally, we shall consider the more realistic situation where the increase in public expenditure and the fall in private expenditure relate to both categories of goods, domestic and foreign ones. If we assume that half the increase, and half the fall, concern domestic goods and the other half foreign goods (Fig. 8.3*c*), we have a combination of Figs. 8.3*a* and 8.3*b*: excess demand for domestic goods and additional demand for imports. The excess demand for domestic goods is lower than in Fig. 8.3*a*. Consequently, a smaller crowding-out effect via the real appreciation is needed. At *A*, there is again a current account deficit with the subsequent wealth adjustment towards *B*.

By looking at the long-run exchange rate level at point *B* in all three panels, compared with the initial long-run exchange rate level at point *Q*, we ultimately obtain a real appreciation for the first and third cases and a real depreciation for the second case. The real appreciation takes place when there is an excess demand in the market for domestic goods and the real depreciation occurs in the opposite case. Wealth has been reduced in all three cases, since there was always a current account deficit caused either by the real appreciation or by the demand shock on imports.[13]

Repercussions on the Financial Sector

The wealth effect which results from the current account imbalance not only affects the market for domestic goods but also the market for financial assets. In our previous example of a current account deficit, net financial wealth decreases ($CA = dw = edF^*$ where $dF^* < 0$). According to the portfolio approach to the determination of the exchange rate (see the Appendix to ch. 4), the portfolio will be reshuffled to give a lower demand for money, and for domestic and foreign financial bonds. The resulting change in the exchange rate may be different from the exchange rate which equilibrates the market for domestic goods (*IS* or *NN*).

In the right-hand panel of Fig. 8.4 we have shown at point Q the given stock of foreign financial assets (F^*_0) valued at the real exchange rate e_0. If e is lower or higher than e_0, the real value component of F^*_0 will decrease or increase according to the line $F^s[F^*_0]$. We assume identical real interest rates for the domestic and foreign countries and static expectations with respect to the exchange rate. Under these heroic assumptions, the demand for foreign assets, $F^d[F^*_0]$, only reflects the wealth value effect: a higher e, which implies an increased value of the portfolio, gives rise to a higher demand for *all three* kinds of assets.

Points Q and B represent two long-run real exchange rates, each of which is characterized by different fundamentals in terms of fiscal stance. It is conceivable that these two real fundamental exchange rates are compatible, over

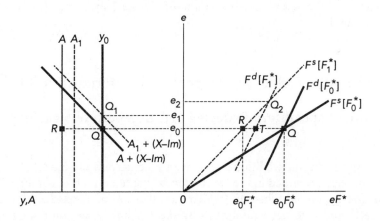

Fig. 8.4. The trade balance deficit and the market for foreign financial assets

The left-hand panel represents the supply and demand for domestic goods. At the equilibrium point Q there is a trade balance deficit of QR. Ignoring interest payments on holdings of net foreign assets, the supply of foreign assets decreases from F^s_0 to F^s_1. The wealth effect reduces F^d and A. According to the financial approach the new exchange rate would be at Q_2 and, according to the equilibrium condition for the market of domestic goods, it would be at Q_1.

the long run, with *PPP.* One has now to differentiate again between e_1 and e_2. e_1 would converge to $e_1 = 1$ according to *PPP,* while e_2 would move from point Q to point B. Another consideration concerns a net debtor country which is assumed to be exposed to the same fiscal shock and which will have the same evolution of its real exchange rate as our net creditor country (see the Appendix to the present chapter). However, the difference between the two is that the long-run external equilibrium ($CA = 0$) for the first one implies a trade balance deficit and for the second one a trade balance surplus. If there are some doubts resulting from news that the country may be less able to honour his debt service in the future, then this country is more vulnerable to possible expected depreciations.

The left-hand panel of Fig. 8.4 represents the market for domestic goods analogous to Fig. 6.1. The real exchange rate which equilibrates the goods market is e_0. Since absorption (A) exceeds domestic production (*GDP* or y_0), the trade balance deficit is equal to QR. Neglecting the receipt of interest payments, the decumulation of net foreign wealth will be $QR = e_0 F^*{}_0 - e_0 F^*{}_1$.[14] The shift of the supply schedule to $F^s[F^*{}_1]$ will be larger than the shift of the demand schedule to $F^d[F^*{}_1]$ since part of the wealth loss, namely RT, is reflected in a lower demand for domestic financial assets.

Even though we have operated with a partial portfolio model—a single market for one type of assets—the excess demand for foreign assets brings about the real depreciation (e_2) at point Q_2. In contrast, the new equilibrium in the market for domestic goods—the wealth effect has shifted the demand schedule to $A_1 + (X - Im)$—would require a lower real depreciation (e_1 at point Q_1). As we have stressed on several occasions, the financial markets dominate the 'short-run' determination of the exchange rate (money and domestic bonds).

8.3. The Policy Mix for Internal and External Equilibrium

Policy Mix: Expenditure-Reducing and Expenditure-Switching Policies

We shall return to our traditional short-run macroeconomic model (Fig. 8.5) which has been developed in the two previous chapters. Internal equilibrium is represented by the *IS*-schedule (which can also be interpreted as the *NN*-schedule)[15] and external equilibrium by the *CA* line. Any point situated to the right of the *IS*- (or *NN*)-schedule represents an excess supply of domestic tradable (or non-tradable) goods. With respect to the *CA* schedule, there is a current account surplus ($CA > 0$) on the right-hand side. Since we assume a net debtor country for which the policy mix is more urgent, external equilibrium in terms of an equilibrated current account balance implies a trade balance surplus being equal to the interest payments to be paid on net external

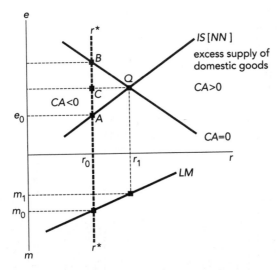

Fig. 8.5. The policy mix for internal and external equilibrium

The initial situation is at point A with a current account deficit. Under perfect capital mobility (r = r*), possible outcomes of the policy mix are A, B, or C. In all three cases, government expenditure is reduced (a lower budget deficit). Point A means that expenditure on imports is curtailed (a downward shift of CA through A). Point B involves the reduction in fiscal expenditure on domestic tradables (IS) or on non-tradables (NN) (an upward shift of IS and NN, respectively), implying a real appreciation. Point C represents a mixture of cases A and B.

Assuming capital immobility, the domestic interest rate is autonomous and can be increased to r_1 by restrictive monetary policy (m_1). Private expenditure is reduced on both imported goods and domestic tradables (IS'), or on tradables and non-tradables (NN). The subsequent excess supply of domestic goods is eliminated by a real depreciation (point Q).

debt to foreign countries.[16] The initial situation is at point A (e_0, r_0) with an internal equilibrium and an external disequilibrium (current account deficit) which is considered as unsustainable.

The policy mix needed to attain internal and external equilibrium depends on the underlying degree of capital mobility and, as usual, we shall treat two extreme cases, with perfect capital mobility and with complete capital immobility. In the lower panel of Fig. 8.5 we have drawn the *LM*-schedule of equation (8.4) by analogy with the classical macro-model of Fig. 6.5 (*IS-LM*) and Fig. 7.5 (*NN-LM*). This curve will be relevant for the case of capital immobility.

Perfect capital mobility. We assume a *small (industrialized) country* with perfect capital mobility. The domestic interest rate (r) corresponds to the international one (r*).[17] At point A, absorption exceeds domestic production, causing the trade and current account deficit. As the left-hand part of Fig. 8.6 indicates, the *trade balance deficit* corresponds to an excess of absorption (A) over GDP (y) and the *current account deficit* to an excess of absorption

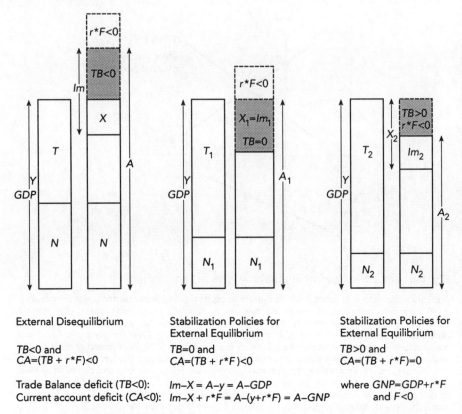

External Disequilibrium

$TB<0$ and
$CA=(TB + r*F)<0$

Stabilization Policies for External Equilibrium

$TB=0$ and
$CA=(TB + r*F)<0$

Stabilization Policies for External Equilibrium

$TB>0$ and
$CA=(TB + r*F)=0$

Trade Balance deficit ($TB<0$): $Im-X = A-y = A-GDP$ where $GNP=GDP+r*F$
Current account deficit ($CA<0$): $Im-X + r*F = A-(y+r*F) = A-GNP$ and $F<0$

Fig. 8.6. Stabilization policies for external equilibrium: expenditure-reducing policies (lower absorption) and expenditure-switching policies (devaluation).

over *GNP* (where *GNP* is equal to *GDP* minus net interest payments to abroad). One policy element consists of reducing expenditures (*A*) to the level of *GDP* for an equilibrated trade balance ($A_1 = GDP$ in the centre part of Fig. 8.6) or even further to the level of *GNP* ($A_2 = GNP$ in the right-hand part of Fig. 8.6) in order to realize a current account equilibrium.

We shall assume that absorption is reduced by a decline in public expenditure (restrictive fiscal policy via a lower budget deficit). Another important element of the expenditure reducing policy concerns the choice of the expenditure category to be reduced. Government can reduce its expenditure on imported goods only (a downward shift of the *CA*-schedule through point *A* in Fig. 8.5) and the internal–external equilibrium would be attained without any change in the real exchange rate.

Another extreme case is at point *B*, where there is a maximum depreciation rate. The reduction in public expenditure is only for domestic goods. *If domestic goods are tradable*, there will be an excess supply in the domestic market for tradables (an upward shift of the *IS*-schedule through point *B*). The high depreciation rate is required for switching domestic expenditure from foreign tradables (less imports) to domestic tradables and for switching expenditure by foreigners to domestic tradables (more exports).

If domestic goods are non-tradable, the reduction in public expenditure on domestic goods creates an excess supply of non-tradables (an upward shift of the *NN*-schedule through point *B*). The real depreciation of type e_2 is required for switching domestic expenditure from tradables to non-tradables (less imports) *and* for switching domestic production from non-tradables to tradables (fewer imports and more exports).

The intermediate, and more realistic case, concerns the reduction in government expenditure on both types of goods: either domestic tradables and imported goods (*IS-CA*), or non-tradable and tradable goods (*NN-CA*), and the intersection point of the new schedules would be at point *C*. At point *A* there is now a disequilibrium in the goods market: an excess supply of domestic tradable goods (*IS*) or an excess supply of non-tradable goods (*NN*) which is eliminated by the expenditure switching policy which results from the rise in *e*.

Capital immobility. This case is representative, for instance, of a *developing economy* which is a net debtor country. In the past it had access to the international credit market, but for reasons which we shall explain in Chapter 10, international credit is no longer available. The point of departure is again point *A*. However, the domestic interest rate r_0 is autonomous and has no relation to the international one, since, for instance, the country's currency is not convertible with respect to the capital account.

Consequently, the country's policy mix in terms of expenditure reducing and expenditure switching policies could also consist now of a restrictive monetary policy (for reducing total expenditure via a higher *r*) and of real depreciation (point *Q*). The restrictive monetary policy has to reduce the outstanding quantity of money. With an unchanged general price level, the real quantity of money is reduced from m_0 to m_1 (the lower panel of Fig. 8.5) and the interest rate rises to r_1. The higher interest rate reduces total expenditure and creates an excess supply of domestic goods as well as a lower current account deficit. The composition of the reduced expenditure has to be altered through a real depreciation in favour of more domestic tradables (*IS*) and, in the case of the *NN*-schedule, in favour of more non-tradables as far as the demand side is concerned. On the supply side it must be altered in favour of the production of more tradables. A summary of the policy mix is contained in Box 8.3.

Box 8.3. Expenditure-reducing and expenditure-switching policies

An alternative geometrical representation of the policy mix is illustrated below. Expenditure or absorption is measured on the horizontal axis. An increase or decrease in expenditure is assumed to affect the purchase of domestic and foreign tradable goods in the case of the *IS*-schedule or the purchase of domestic tradable and non-tradable goods in the case of the *NN*-schedule. Higher expenditure implies a lower real exchange rate to maintain the equilibrium in the market for domestic goods. With respect to the *CA*-schedule, higher expenditure also involves more purchases of imported goods implying a deterioration in the current account balance. A real depreciation re-establishes the external equilibrium.

At point *A* the economy suffers from a current account deficit. Internal and external equilibrium could be realized at point *C*. Expenditure has to be reduced either by a restrictive fiscal policy or by a restrictive monetary policy (higher interest rates leading to lower expenditures) to the extent that the domestic interest rate is not strictly linked to the international one. Simultaneously, a real depreciation is required for switching expenditure from foreign tradables to domestic tradables (in the case of *IS*) or for switching expenditure from tradables to non-tradables (in the case of *NN*).

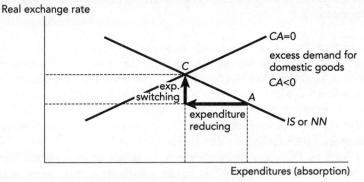

Fig. 8.A. Policy mix for internal and external equilibrium.

Note: If expenditures are only spent on foreign goods, the *IS*-schedule (or the *NN*-schedule) would be horizontal at point *A*. In that case, there is only need for an expenditure-reducing policy. The other extreme case where expenditures are used exclusively for the purchase of domestic goods, the *CA*-schedule would be horizontal at point *C*. In this particular case, the traditional policy mix has to be applied.

Alternative Exchange Rate Regimes

Up to now we have been dealing with the required change in the real variables (absorption-production and their composition, real exchange rate, real quantity of money . . .) required to attain internal and external equilibrium. We still have to describe the necessary monetary adjustment which has to accompany the real adjustments. We shall limit the analysis to the case of perfect capital mobility. We came to the conclusion that, except in some academic cases, for the real sector of the economy, the policy mix required a real depreciation. The monetary adjustment which brings about the real depreciation consists either of a nominal depreciation under floating exchange rates or a fall in the general price level under fixed exchange rates; see Box 8.4.

Box 8.4. Policy mix and monetary adjustment (with perfect capital mobility)

	e of type e_1		e of type e_2	
Money market *LM*	$M = PL(r)$	(8.5)	$M = PL(r)$	(8.5)
Floating nominal exchange rates (M = nominal anchor and E = endogenous variable)	$M = [EP^*/e_1]L(r)$	(8.6a)	$M = [EP^*_T/e_2]L(r)$	(8.6b)
Fixed nominal exchange rates (E = nominal anchor and M = endogenous variable)	$M = [\bar{E}P^*/e_1]L(r)$	(8.7a)	$M = [\bar{E}P^*_T/e_2]L(r)$	(8.7b)

According to Table 5.1, the general price level can be written in terms of the real exchange rate as:[18]

$$\text{for } e \text{ of type } e_1 \qquad P = EP^*/e_1 \qquad (8.8a)$$
$$\text{for } e \text{ of type } e_2 \qquad P = EP^*_T/e_2 \qquad (8.8b)$$

Under floating exchange rates, a rise in e is realized by a rise in E while the money supply is the monetary anchor; for an unchanged M, we shall have an unchanged P.[19] With fixed exchange rates, a rise in e is brought about by a fall in P; the monetary anchor is represented by E and the quantity of money has to fall to bring about the decline in P.

Fig. 8.7 describes the monetary adjustment mechanism under floating and fixed exchange rates for the real depreciation of types e_1 and e_2. The initial monetary equilibrium is at point A. In the first case (Fig. 8.6a), the policy mix requires a real depreciation from $e_1{}^0$ to $e_1{}^1$ (see the increased slope of the $Oe_1{}^1$ ray). With floating exchange rates, the nominal exchange rate moves from A to B with an unchanged monetary equilibrium at A_1 (in the lower panel). Under fixed exchange rates, the price level has to decline from A to C, involving a lower quantity of money (point C_1 in the lower panel).

The monetary adjustment for the real depreciation of type e_2 (Fig. 8.6b) is not exactly the same as e_1. The equilibrium of the money market is represented now by the LM_0-schedule which implies that P_0 is the equilibrium level of the general price level. Under floating exchange rates, the monetary adjustment is from A to B, implying a rise in E *and* a fall in P_N to maintain the price level at P_0; the monetary anchor is again M, which is assumed to be constant. With fixed exchange rates, the whole monetary adjustment burden is carried by a lower P (P_1) for a decline in P_N (movement from A to C), requiring a lower quantity of money (LM_1) which is now the endogenous variable.

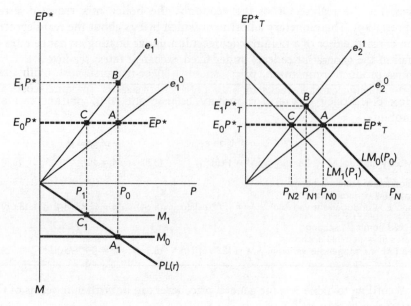

Fig. 8.7. A comparison of real depreciation of e_1 and e_2

Fig. 8.7a. A real depreciation (e_1) under floating and fixed exchange rates

Under floating exchange rates, the monetary adjustment is brought about by a nominal depreciation from A to B. Under fixed exchange rates, the domestic price level has to be reduced ($A \rightarrow C$) by a decline in the quantity of money ($A_1 \rightarrow C_1$).

Fig. 8.7b. A real depreciation (e_2) under floating and fixed exchange rates

Under floating exchange rates, the monetary adjustment is brought about by a mixture of nominal depreciation and decline of P_N ($A \rightarrow B$). Under fixed exchange rates, P has to fall via a decrease in the quantity of money ($A \rightarrow C$).

Policy Mix and Labour Cost Behaviour

As we have seen, a real depreciation can be brought about in both exchange rate regimes: either by the nominal depreciation under floating exchange rates where the nominal anchor is the quantity of money; or by the fall in the general price level through the reduction in the quantity of money under fixed exchange rates where the nominal anchor is the exchange rate peg. However, whether ΔE or $-\Delta M$ results in a real depreciation depends crucially on the wage behaviour in the labour market.

From the point of view of the firms' demand for labour, the level of labour input is determined by making the nominal wage rate (W) equal to the marginal product of labour (MPL) valued at its market price (P). This traditional formula for profit maximization should hold in both production sectors, T and N, as we have already shown at the beginning of the previous chapter:

$$W_T = P_T \, MPL_T \qquad W_N = P_N \, MPL_N \qquad (8.9)$$

Under product competition, prices should reflect marginal cost. With fixed sector specific capital stocks in both production sectors, marginal costs are marginal labour costs, also called marginal unit labour costs.[20]

$$P_T = W_T/MPL_T \qquad P_N = W_N/MPL_N \qquad (8.10)$$

Real depreciation of type e_1 and labour cost behaviour. If the real depreciation is brought about by a nominal depreciation, $\Delta E \times P^*_T$ is not transmitted to P_T (otherwise, e_1 would be equal to unity) so that there is no reason for workers to adjust their wages W_T upwards, even though prices of imported goods have risen.[21] They can still consume more import substitutes whose domestic prices are unchanged.

Under fixed exchange rates, we have again the same initial scenario, namely a reduction in public expenditure on domestic tradables and an excess supply of domestic tradables. The real depreciation is realized by a fall in P_T which has to be accompanied by restrictive monetary policy. Again, as in the case of a nominal depreciation, the fall in P_T leads to a switch in private expenditure from imports to import substitutes and to an increase in exports such that the excess supply of domestic tradables disappears. *The downward adjustment of* P_T *requires a corresponding fall in* W_T *since otherwise real wages would increase with the consequence of unemployment.* A fall in W_T could only be avoided if there is a corresponding increase in MPL_T according to equation (8.10).

In Fig. 8.8 we have illustrated the labour market. Since there is only the production of T, total labour input (L_0) is used exclusively for the T-sector. For reasons of simplicity, we assume a vertical supply schedule of labour. The initial demand schedule for labour is $P_{T0} \, MPL_T$ and the nominal wage rate is at W_{T0} assuring full employment (point A). While the real depreciation under floating exchange rates leaves P_{T0} unchanged (point A), the fall of P_T to the level P_{T1} under fixed exchange rates decreases the demand schedule for labour towards $P_{T1} \, MPL_T$. In order to assure full employment, wages have to fall to the level of W_{T1} (point C). Otherwise, there would be an unemployment level equivalent to AD. The unemployment could only be avoided, if an increase in labour productivity is achieved being equal to the distance AC.

Real depreciation of type e_2 and labour cost behaviour. We now assume that $e_1 = 1$. Under floating exchange rates, there is a rise in P_T ($\Delta P_T = \Delta E \times P^*_T$) *and* a fall in P_N to keep the general price level stable. Again, total domestic production remains unchanged (assuming full employment) while its composition must be modified in favour of T. Assuming homogeneous labour qualifications in T and N, nominal wages are the same in both sectors ($W_T = W_N = W$), since otherwise labour would migrate between the production

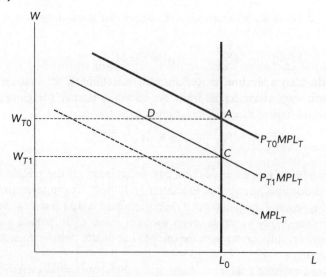

Fig. 8.8. Real depreciation (e_1) and wage behaviour

The initial equilibrium is at point A. Under floating exchange rates, the demand for labour and the nominal wage remain unchanged. Under fixed exchange rates, P_T decreases and the nominal wage has to fall (point C). Otherwise, there would be an unemployment of AD, which could only be avoided in the case of an increase in the labour productivity by the amount of AC.

sectors. However, real wages (represented by the marginal product of labour *MPL*) are likely to differ as the consequence of the different sector specific stocks of capital in T and N. Consequently, using the equations of formula (8.10), we have the inequalities

$$P_T > W/MPL_T \qquad P_N < W/MPL_N. \qquad (8.10a)$$

In the T sector, prices are above marginal cost and in the N sector they are below it. More labour will be drawn from the production sector N to the production sector T, implying a lower MPL_T and a higher MPL_N so that the equalitites of equation (8.10) are again attained.

The above argument can be understood more easily by consulting Fig. 8.9 which is, to a large extent, a reproduction of Fig. 7.1. The initial equilibrium in the labour market is at point A with a low labour input in T and a high labour input in N. The real depreciation is necessary for producing more T with a higher labour input L_T at the cost of the labour input L_N.

Under floating exchange rates, the value component of the marginal product of L_T increases to P_{T1} and, correspondingly, the value component of the marginal product of L_N falls to P_{N1} so that the general price level *and* the nominal wage level remain constant (point B). As far as W_T is concerned, the potential increase in W_T as a result of ΔP_T is compensated by the decline of

MPL_T due to the labour migration to T. Similarly, W_N should fall as the consequence of $-\Delta P_N$, but the rising labour productivity in N compensates the potential decline in W_N.

Under fixed exchange rates, there is a decline from P_{N0} to P_{N2} and, consequently, also a decline in P. The new schedule of L^d_N passes through point C. Both wages have to fall from W_0 to W_2 as they did in the case of the depreciation of type e_1 under fixed exchange rates. With respect to W_N, the large fall in P_N is not fully compensated by the rise in MPL_N. The fall in W_T is uniquely due to the decline in MPL_T.

In the case of downward wage rigidities, unemployment rises by the amount AD. It could be avoided assuming that labour productivity growth is not compensated by increases in the nominal wage rate. In terms of Fig. 8.9a, *both* schedules of the marginal productivity of labour (drawn as dotted lines), MPL_N and MPL_T, have to shift upwards by the distance of BC. Both sectors must have the *same* productivity growth of the amount of BC in order to avoid the unemployment at the wage level W_0.[22]

Equation (8.10) can also be written in terms of the real exchange rate (for $W_T = W_N = W$):

$$P_T/P_N = MPL_N/MPL_T \tag{8.10b}$$

From the point of view of production cost, the real exchange rate has to correspond to the ratio of labour productivities given above. A real depreciation involves a higher ratio of MPL_N/MPL_T which is brought about by labour migration from N to T as illustrated in Fig. 8.9b.

Expenditure-Reducing and Expenditure-Switching Policies Reconsidered

Fig. 8.9b also makes it clear that the policy mix for attaining internal and external equilibrium is necessary regardless of the exchange rate regime. Internal equilibrium concerns the situation on any point of the production possibility curve PP (full employment) and external equilibrium involves either an equilibrated trade balance or a trade balance surplus for equilibrating the current account balance in the case of a net debtor country.

At the initial point A in the labour market, the production point P_A and the consumption (or absorption) point C_A in the lower panel of Fig. 8.9 correspond to a trade balance deficit of $P_A C_A$. If any trade balance deficit is considered to be unsustainable, one indispensable policy tool of the policy mix is the reduction of expenditure from the absorption level A_1 to the *GDP* level y_1 or y_2. The reduction of absorption from A_1 to y_1 implies that only the expenditure on imports is curtailed by $P_A C_A$ and that the consumption point now coincides with the production point P_A. In that special case it is not necessary to use the additional policy tool of a real depreciation.

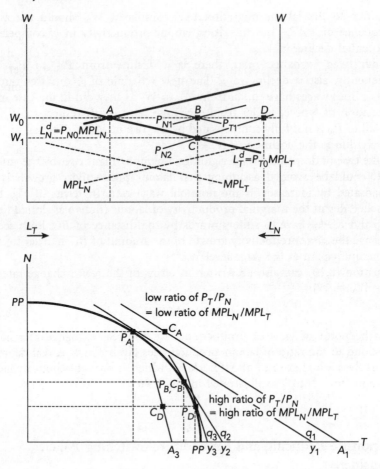

Fig. 8.9. The policy mix for internal and external equilibrium: real depreciation and expenditure-reducing policies plus wage behaviour

Fig. 8.9a. The labour market for T and N

The initial equilibrium is at point A. Real depreciation increases labour input in T and lowers labour input in N. Under floating exchange rates, nominal wages remain constant (point B). Under fixed exchange rates, nominal wages fall (point C).

Fig. 8.9b. The production possibility curve and expenditure-reducing policy

The trade balance deficit is $P_A C_A$. A reduction of expenditure (A) plus real depreciation produce an equilibrated trade balance ($P_B = C_B$) or a trade balance surplus ($P_D C_D$).

However, in all other cases, the reduction of expenditure covers both tradables and non-tradables, so that there is an excess supply of non-tradables which can be eliminated only by a real depreciation. The first case of expenditure-reducing ($A_1 \to y_2$) and expenditure-switching policy ($q_1 \to q_2$)

is the production point P_B, which must be equal to the consumption point C_B. The trade balance is in equilibrium. Provided that a trade balance surplus is needed to balance the current account, both the reduction in expenditure ($A_1 \rightarrow A_3$) and the real depreciation rate ($q_1 \rightarrow q_3$) have to be larger. The consumption point is now C_D, which is inferior to the production point P_D, and the difference represents the trade balance surplus.

Appendix: The Long-Run Evolution of the Real Exchange Rate in the Case of a Debtor Country

We shall illustrate the $IS(NN) - CA$ model for a debtor country for which F^* is negative (the left-hand panel of Fig. 8.A1). The long-run internal and external equilibrium is at Q. The equilibrium of the current account must imply a trade balance surplus. The interest payments on foreign debt ($-r^* e F^*$) are financed by a corresponding trade balance surplus ($X - Im$) which, in the context of a

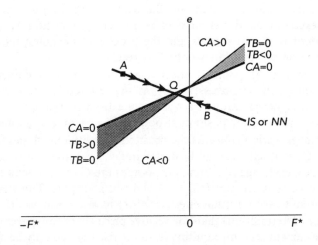

Fig. 8.A1. Wealth adjustment to full-equilibrium (Q) (net of foreign debt)

The economy is assumed to be at point A (internal equilibrium) with a current account surplus. Net foreign debt decreases, creating an excess demand for domestic goods which provokes a real appreciation. The wealth adjustment process stops at point Q where CA = O and where the trade balance surplus finances the interest service on the remaining net foreign debt.

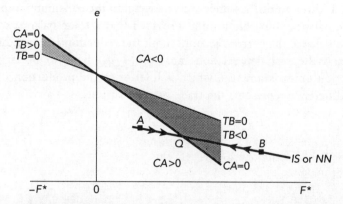

Fig. 8.A2. Wealth adjustment to full equilibrium (Q) (Negatively sloped CA-schedule)

The economy is assumed to be at point B (internal equilibrium) with a current account deficit. Net wealth decreases creating an excess supply of domestic goods which provokes a real depreciation. The wealth-adjustment process stops at point Q where CA = 0 and where the net interest payments on foreign claims finance the trade balance deficit.

debtor country, is also called the 'resource gap', or the 'net transfer of resources' from the debtor country to the creditor country.

If the economy is at point *A*, the internal equilibrium is accompanied by a current account surplus. The net indebtedness of the country decreases, implying an expansionary impact on the demand for domestic goods. The subsequent excess demand is eliminated by the real appreciation. However, the current account is still in surplus and the process of declining indebtedness and real appreciations continues until *Q* is reached.

If the country is at point *B*, the current account is in deficit. Wealth decreases resulting in an excess supply in the market for domestic goods. Equilibrium is achieved through a real depreciation. At point *Q* the country which had the net creditor position at point *B* has become a net debtor.

Our next investigation concerns the possibility of different slopes for the *TB* = 0 and the *CA* = 0 schedules as illustrated in Fig. 8.A2. In contrast to Fig. 8.1, a rise in the real exchange rate from any point of the *CA* = 0 schedule creates a deficit in the current account (*CA* < 0) and not a surplus. The wealth value effect (F^*de) and income value effect (r^*F^*de) have a stronger effect on the trade balance (deterioration) than the relative price effect (improvement). The deficit in the current account resulting from the rise in *e* can only be eliminated by a fall in the volume of wealth which reduces absorption and, thus, imports.

If the economy is at point *A* (internal equilibrium), the current account surplus increases wealth. The higher wealth volume level causes an excess demand in the goods markets and necessitates a real appreciation. Conversely, an internal equilibrium combined with a current account deficit (point *B*) produces a lower wealth volume level, creating an excess supply in the goods market which is eliminated by a series of real depreciations.

Notes

1. In the Appendix we have described the case where both schedules have a negative slope.
2. In contrast to chs. 6 and 7, we now distinguish between absorption by the private sector (A) and absorption by the public sector (G).
3. The definition of wealth concerns net financial wealth, comprising real cash balances (m) and net foreign assets or net foreign debt (F^*). According to Dornbusch and Fischer's procedure (1980: 961), F^* are '"real" bonds promising to pay a unit of foreign output indefinitely.' Its nominal value in domestic currency would be EP^*F^* and its real value is $EP^*F^*/P = (EP^*/P)F^* = eF^*$.
4. Which can be the result of higher foreign indebtedness (capital balance surplus) or of lower international reserves (balance of payments deficit).
5. The 'sustainable' current account deficit could be defined by a net debt/GDP ratio which remains constant ($eF^*/y = $ constant). Consequently, eF^* can rise by the growth rate of GDP.
6. Since for the moment we do not take into consideration the labour market with unemployment, we are not able to specify whether the internal equilibrium is accompanied by full employment or not.
7. This case is also relevant for a net creditor country (the right-hand panel of Fig. 8.1) which is very much below its CA-schedule ($CA<0$) and which could become a net debtor country in some future time. The third issue which is treated in ch. 9 is a *normative* one and it is concerned with the desirability of an external disequilibrium in terms of the trade balance. Such a disequilibrium can represent an optimal shift of resources (savings) among countries and can bring about the optimal specialization between net savers (surplus countries) and net investors (deficit countries).
8. Remember that we already dealt with another issue concerning the long-run behaviour of the real exchange rate with respect to e_2 at the end of the previous chapter. Structural changes (differential productivity growth for T and N and different income elasticities for the demand for T and N) could give rise to continuous real appreciations.
9. However, it should be emphasized that the desirability of a balanced current account is a special case which depends on the underlying propensities to save and to invest. A current account deficit (decumulation of net external financial wealth) can represent the ideal solution for a country provided that its (efficient) investment exceeds national savings and provided that it can be financed by foreign credits. For similar reasons, a current account surplus (accumulation of net external wealth) can be a desirable target when national savings exceed domestic investment. This 'normative' aspect of external equilibrium will be treated at the beginning of the next chapter.
10. It should be remembered that this real shock could also be initiated by an autonomous rise in private investment or private consumption.
11. Even though the model operates explicitly with a wealth variable (w), we did not

incorporate it in the money market of equation (8.4) in Box 8.2 within a portfolio model. The demand for money is not conceived of as a fraction of wealth (see the Appendix to ch. 4). It is based simply on the transactions motive. As we shall see, the size of wealth varies in our *IS–CA* model as a consequence of a disequilibrium in the current account. Consequently, there would constantly be repercussions on the money demand, if the latter were constructed as a desired fraction of wealth. Our interpretation of the money demand based on transactions permits us to work with a reduced model. However, at a later stage, we also take into account the portfolio approach.

12. In the Appendix we have described the case where the country is a net debtor and where the *CA*-schedule can have a negative slope.

13. We arrive at the same conclusions for a country which is a net debtor in the Appendix to the present chapter.

14. The current account deficit will be lower than the trade balance deficit by the amount of the received interest payments.

15. Since *IS* is related to the real exchange rate of type e_1 ($= EP^*_T/P_T$) and *NN* to the real exchange rate of type e_2 (for $q = EP^*_T/P_N$), the position and slope of *IS* are necessarily different from those of *NN*. For economizing on one additional geometrical figure, both schedules coincide for sake of simplicity.

16. Consequently, the *TB*-schedule will be a parallel line below the *CA* line. The *CA*-schedule shifts upwards with a higher net foreign debt position. For similar reasons to those indicated in the former footnote, the *CA*-schedule will not be the same under the alternative hypotheses $e = e_1$ and $e = e_2$. See Section 7.1 and 7.6.

17. We neglect the real interest rate parity since we are simply interested in the final impact of the policy mix for which r is again equal to r^*.

18. In formula (8.8a), all goods are tradable so that P coincides with P_T. In formula (8.8b), $P = P_T/e_2 = EP^*_T/e_2$, where $e_2 = q^b$.

19. Looking at equation (8.5), the demand for real money balances remains unchanged with perfect capital mobility, according to which $r = r^*$. With a constant M, P also remains unchanged.

20. From the point of view of production costs, the real exchange rate of type e_1 and e_2 could be reformulated as, respectively:

$$e_1 = EP^*_T/P_T = EP^*_T(MPL_T/W_T)$$
$$e_2 = q^b$$
where $q = (P_T/P_N) = (W_T/W_N)(MPL_N/MPL_T)$.

21. We assume that $P_T = P$ and $W_T = W$. For the moment we abstract from the existence of N.

22. Another possibility for avoiding unemployment in the case of wage rigidities would be for the anchor currency to be slightly inflationary in terms of P^*_T. ΔP^*_T would be transmitted to a ΔP_T. If the rise in P_T were equivalent to the decline of P_N, which is required by the real depreciation from q_0 to q_1, there would be no necessity for a fall in P_N. The general price level would rise as a matter of course, and an accommodating monetary policy would be required.

9

INTEGRATION: REAL CAPITAL MARKETS AND MONETARY UNIONS

....

After treating financial integration in Part I and commercial integration with respect to tradable goods in Part II, the present chapter analyses two other types of integration, namely: real capital market integration and monetary integration. The welfare gains are shown for net borrowing countries and net lending countries for the first type of integration. However, from an empirical point of view, a high degree of financial integration does not imply necessarily a high degree of real capital market integration.

Monetary integration like that of the future European Monetary Union is conceived in two stages, namely: the introduction of irrevocably fixed exchange rates and the subsequent single common currency. The benefits and costs of both steps are examined. Small countries can gain a higher net benefit than large countries can.

9.1. The Integration of Real Capital Markets or the International Specialization of Savings and Investment

The Desirability of Trade Balance Surpluses and Deficits

If one group of countries has a trade balance surplus, another group must have a trade balance deficit. In Table 9.1 we have listed the surplus and deficit countries since the mid-1970s. The notorious trade balance deficits of the USA were more or less matched by the trade balance surpluses of Germany and Japan. They were moderate in the 1970s and reached extremely high levels in the 1980s. In the early 1990s, a structural change occurred to the German trade balance surplus which diminished as the consequence of Germany's reunification, while the Japanese trade balance surplus continued to increase. The North (industrialized countries) and the South (developing countries) give another picture. Astonishingly, we do not find the result that the North was in surplus and the non-oil exporting South in deficit. Both were in deficit *vis-à-*

Table **9.1.** Trade balance surpluses and deficits in the world economy (US $bn.) 1975–93

Year	USA	Japan	Germany	Developing countries (oil exporting)	Developing countries (non-oil exporting)	Industrial countries
1975	8.9	4.9	16.9	54.4	−37.5	4.3
1976	−9.5	9.8	16.0	65.7	−23.7	−19.1
1977	−31.1	17.2	19.4	60.9	−21.5	−24.7
1978	−33.9	24.3	24.1	45.0	−31.1	−0.2
1979	−27.5	1.7	16.5	115.0	−42.6	−47.9
1980	−25.5	2.1	8.7	171.2	−60.9	−76.9
1981	−28.0	20.0	16.1	122.7	−70.2	−30.8
1982	−36.4	18.1	24.7	61.5	−40.5	−26.3
1983	−67.1	31.5	21.4	42.7	−14.9	−27.6
1984	−112.5	44.3	22.1	51.6	5.7	−50.2
1985	−122.2	56.0	28.6	53.0	−1.3	−45.2
1986	−145.1	92.8	55.7	8.6	4.3	−11.8
1987	−159.5	96.4	70.2	31.2	20.5	−30.1
1988	−127.0	95.0	79.8	20.8	18.5	−10.2
1989	−115.9	76.9	77.7	44.9	5.9	−35.1
1990	−108.1	63.6	71.7	76.2	−16.8	−37.5
1991	−73.6	103.1	22.6	45.8	−28.6	9.5
1992	−96.1	132.4	32.3	37.8	−53.7	44.6
1993	−132.5	141.6	43.1	43.1	−86.7	78.3

Source: IMF, *International Financial Statistics Yearbook.*

vis the oil-exporting developing countries. The oil price shock of 1979/80 had driven the oil-exporting developing countries into huge surpluses and both industrialized and non-oil exporting developing countries into deficits. However, since the mid-1980s when the oil price began to fall, the three groups of countries tended towards equilibrium in their trade balances. Because of the debt problem which emerged in the early 1980s, the non-oil exporting developing countries had to run a trade balance surplus. During the early 1990s, the situation was reversed to a more reasonable pattern where the North run increasing trade balance surpluses and the South, correspondingly, trade balance deficits.

The 'counterpart' of the disequilibrium in the trade balance is the savings–investment gap (see Box 9.1).

Trade balance surplus $\quad X - Im = (S-I) + (T-G)$ $\qquad$ (9.5*a*)

Trade balance deficit $\quad Im - X = (I-S) + (G-T)$ $\qquad$ (9.5*b*)

S and I are private sector savings and investment. A budget surplus $(T-G>0)$ implies an excess of public savings over public investment. Similarly, a budget deficit $(G-T>0)$ implies an excess of public investment over public savings; public savings are defined as the difference between government revenue and government expenditure on consumption goods.

Box 9.1. The algebra of the trade balance

Trade balance surplus according to absorption approach	$y-A$	$=X-Im$	(9.1)
Composition of absorption	A	$=C+I+G$	(9.2)
Combining (9.1) and (9.2)	$y-C-I-G$	$=X-Im$	(9.3)
Definition of savings (T are taxes and $y-T$ disposable income)	$y-C$	$=S+T$	(9.4)
Setting (9.4) into (9.3) (a) Trade balance surplus	$X-Im$	$=(S-I)+(T-G)$	(9.5a)
(b) Trade balance deficit	$Im-X$	$=(I-S)+(G-T)$	(9.5b)

Since deficit countries are often criticized for the bad performance of their trade balance, we shall indicate the circumstances in which a trade balance deficit proves to be a good sign of the health of an economy.

According to equation (9.5b), a trade balance deficit emerges from either a rise in I or a fall in S, assuming a balanced budget for the public sector. If the investment projects are profitable and the volume of domestic savings is insufficient, it is in the country's interest to have a trade balance deficit. A deficit is frequently regarded negatively when it arises from a decline in S and thus a rise in consumption. In this case, it is said that the economy is 'living beyond its production possibilities' (according to Box 9.1, the absorption is higher than *GDP*). However, the ultimate reason for earning income is consumption. Depending on its intertemporal utility function, a growing country may equalize consumption over time (as in the case of the life-cycle consumption hypothesis for an individual) so that it consumes more than its income today and less tomorrow.

Consider now the existence of a budget deficit. Box 9.2 illustrates the American case for which the counterparts of the budget deficit were the trade balance deficit and an excess of private domestic savings over private domestic investments. Thus, the budget deficit ($G - T$) was financed by internal savings ($S - I$) and external savings ($Im - X$). Judgement of the desirability of a trade balance now depends on the pros and cons of the budget deficit. In principle, a bond financed budget deficit is justified if there is an exceptional but temporary rise in public expenditure or an exceptional but temporary fall in public revenue, since changes in tax rates should only be permanent ones.

Box 9.2. The US twin or sibling deficits (US$bn.) 1975–93

'The aim of this paper (*Fiscal Policy and the External Deficit: Siblings, but not Twins*) is . . . to spell out the evidence linking US fiscal policy to the external deficit. The evidence is perhaps best summarized by a 50% rule of thumb—that an increase in the fiscal deficit arising from changes in government spending, in the macroeconomic environment of the 1980s, is likely to have been accompanied by an increase in the external deficit about half as large.' Helliwell (1990: 20).

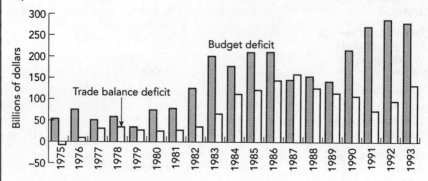

Fig. 9.A. US budget deficit and trade balance deficit, 1975–1993.

Note: We have extended the figure for the early 1990s for which the above rule of thumb is less evident.
Source: IMF, *International Financial Statistics Yearbook.*

External 'Disequilibrium' and Differences in Time Preference

As with individuals, different time preferences for countries lead to net borrowing and lending, and increase the intertemporal welfare of all of them. When capital is not mobile internationally, and assuming for a moment stationary economies with a zero level of investment, each country is forced to consume its income in each period. A country with a high preference for present consumption goods improves the utility level of its intertemporal consumption stream by borrowing in international credit markets when its marginal time preference rate under capital autarchy (and, thus, its domestic interest rate) is above the international interest rate. It will borrow from other countries until its marginal time preference rate is equal to the international interest rate. A trade balance deficit resulting from an increase in imports corresponds to the net amount borrowed abroad. It makes more consumption goods available since the international relative price of present consumption goods is lower. International trade in buying present goods and selling future goods becomes profitable.

The case where the domestic interest rate in the formerly closed economy is above the international rate implies that there are other countries whose time preferences were low when capital was immobile. They prefer to shift part of their present consumption to the furture via lending abroad when the international interest rate is above their marginal time preference rate. Correspondingly, they will have a trade balance surplus in the current period when the international relative price of present consumption goods has risen relative to future goods.

Fig. 9.1 illustrates this situation. The left-hand panel describes the domestic credit market of a closed economy. K^s stands for the supply of credit (positive savings) and K^d for the demand for credit (negative savings). We assume that credit is only demanded for consumption purposes and that there is no investment. In each country there is a group of negative savers with a strong preference for present consumption goods (K^d, K^{*d}) and a group of positive savers with a strong preference for future consumption goods (K^s, K^{*s}). The domestic market interest rate is r'. r'^* is the foreign equilibrium interest rate when the foreign country is a closed economy. The countries differ in terms of their demand schedules for credit, indicating that the home country as a whole has a strong preference for present consumption goods and that the foreign country as a whole has a weak preference for present goods. Total net savings are zero in each country.

When the economy is opened, the world interest rate is r_0 as in the centre panel. ED is the domestic excess demand for savings ($ED = K^d - K^s$) and ES^* ($= K^{*s} - K^{*d}$) the foreign excess supply of savings derived from the right-hand panel. With free capital movements, the interest rates become $r_0 = r^*_0$ and total capital imports for the home country are OE (negative savings) corre-

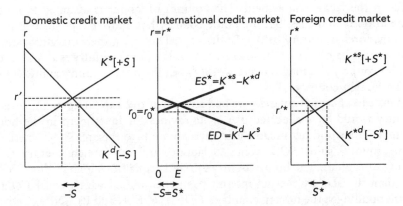

Fig. 9.1. A disequilibrium of the trade balance as a result of differences in time preference

The domestic country has a higher time preference for present consumption goods than the foreign country, since its demand for consumer credit is stronger. Consequently, its interest rate (r') lies above the foreign one (r'^*) when both economies are closed. When both are opened, the international interest rate lies between r' and r'^*. Net savings flow from the foreign country to the domestic country whose consumption is higher than income which results in a trade balance deficit.

sponding to the trade balance deficit. The home country's capital imports are the foreign country's capital exports and the latter has a corresponding trade balance surplus. The surplus reflects the amount of net positive savings (S^*).

Thus, where there are differences in time preferences among countries, free trade in financial assets equalizes the marginal rates of time preference for all countries. Each country which had a formerly high (low) time preference can now have more present (future) consumption goods. The resulting net dissaving and saving are necessarily reflected by an imbalance in the trade account.

External 'Disequilibrium' and Differences in Capital Productivity

If the marginal return on capital diverges among countries, the income in all the countries is increased by capital movements from the low return countries to the high return countries. The former countries now specialize in savings and the latter in investment. World income and that of each individual country will be maximized when the marginal productivity of capital is the same in all countries.

Fig. 9.2 illustrates this income gain for a two-country world. The world capital stock is given by 00^*. The home country's capital stock is measured from point 0 to the right, and the foreign country's capital stock is measured from point 0^* to the left. The marginal productivity of capital schedules, *MPK* and *MPK**, are assumed to be the same in the two countries. However, they differ in the factor endowment. The amount of labour is assumed to be the same in both countries, but the home country has a lower capital stock ($00'$) than the foreign country ($0^*0'$). Under capital autarchy, their marginal rates of return must be different: the interest rate in the home country is r' and in the foreign country r'^*; total income is $ABO'O$ in the home country and $RDO'O^*$ in the foreign country.

If instead of capital autarchy we had a world of free capital flows, the foreign country would have allocated $0'E$ of its savings for investment in the home country. The world net income gain then amounts to the area BQD where the home country gains BQC (going to labour) and the foreign country CQD (going to capital). The home country's GDP is equal to $AQEO$ but its GNP is less than its GDP by the net interest payments abroad which equal $CQEO'$. Correspondingly, the foreign country's GDP is $RQEO^*$, and its GNP exceeds its GDP by the net interest payment receipts of $CQEO'$.[1]

An important implication of the welfare gains from free capital movements are two types of factor income redistribution. This may explain the hostility of trade unions to capital exports and their preference for capital imports. First, there is a loss in world labour income: it is higher with autarchy ($ABr' + RDr'^*$) than with capital mobility ($AQr_0 + RQr^*_0$).[2] Second, labour income (and, thus, the real wage rate) increases in the capital importing

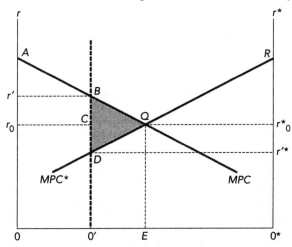

Fig. 9.2. A disequilibrium of the trade balance as a result of differences in capital productivity

Both countries have identical production functions, the same labour input, but different capital stocks when they are closed economies. Consequently, the domestic interest rate (r') as indicator of the marginal productivity of capital (MPC) lies above the foreign one (r'^*). With the financial opening of both countries, the foreign country would have invested $O'E$ in the domestic country and not in its own country. The welfare gain of free capital movements is represented by the shaded area implying a trade balance surplus for the foreign country and a trade balance deficit for the domestic country.

country by $r'BQr_0$ and it (and the real wage rate) decreases in the capital exporting country by $Qr^*_0{}'^*D$.[3]

Real versus Financial Capital Mobility

Real capital mobility means that countries with a high savings rate and a low investment rate export domestic savings to those countries with high investment and low savings. High real capital mobility—or high *real capital market integration*—would imply that a country which wants to invest more than it saves is able to borrow abroad. Statistically, investment would be independent of the level of domestic savings. Imperfect real capital mobility would imply that some investment would not be realized. Upward pressure on domestic interest rates would make investment dependent on domestic savings instead of it being financed by foreign savings.[4]

As Feldstein and Horioka (1980) have shown, investment and saving are not unconnected over the longer run. Despite the globalization of financial markets, i.e. despite the high degree of financial capital mobility (as shown in Chapters 3 and 4), transfers of savings from surplus countries to deficit countries are rather limited. Box 9.3 illustrates one example of real capital mobility. As far as the late 1980s are concerned, the increased savings rate of Japan and the reduced savings rate of the USA allowed the transfer of savings from Japan to the USA. With respect to the developing countries of the Pacific Basin, the four newly industrialized economies (NIEs) experienced a spectacular rise in their savings ratio which pushed them into the position of surplus countries, while the four other Asian developing countries remained modest importers of savings.

Box 9.3. Low real capital mobility

There are three groups of countries shown in this box: namely, two big industrialist countries (USA and Japan), the four new industrialized economies (Hong Kong, Korea, Taiwan, Singapore) and the four Asian industrializing economies (Indonesia, Malaysia, Philippines, Thailand).*I* and *S* refer to the investment and saving rate (as a percentage of *GNP*), respectively; group totals are weighted by *GNP*. The difference between *I* and *S* indicates the current account balance (changes in net external assets). Real capital mobility seemed to be higher in the late 1980s than in the early 1970s and 1980s. Taking the evolution from 1970–2 to 1980–2, the fall in the Japanese investment rate may have been driven by the fall in the savings rate. Similarly, in the four NIEs and the four Asian economies, the rise in the investment rate may have been caused by the rise in their saving rate.

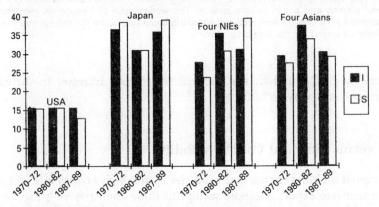

Fig. 9.B. Real capital mobility: USA and Asia
Source: Goldsbrough and Teja (1991).

9.2. A Cost–Benefit Analysis of Monetary Unions with Irrevocably Fixed Exchange Rates

Inflationary Countries: Gradualism versus Shock Therapy for Irrevocably Fixed Exchange Rates

A monetary union is a special case of a currency area. In a currency area, the currencies of the member countries are linked together by fixed exchange rates, while the group as such has a regime of floating rates with respect to third countries. Stage I of a monetary union like the European Monetary Union would be a currency area with 'irrevocably' fixed exchange rates. Stage II means the existence of a single currency. Stage III would mean the crowning achievement of an economic integration process where there are not only integrated markets for goods and factors of production (full mobility of labour and capital), but also where economic policies are co-ordinated.[5] How quickly stages I and II of a monetary union can be achieved and the comparison of the costs and benefits of such a union are the remaining subjects of the present chapter.

The more inflationary countries have an important motive for rapidly establishing a monetary union (for instance, for the currency area of the EMS type) if they want to deflate as quickly as possible without increasing the unemployment rate. This disinflation programme must have a very high degree of credibility and this could be established by irrevocably fixed exchange rates with the anchor currency or by the introduction of a single common currency.

The argument can be presented in terms of the Philips curve as de Grauwe (1992: 134–41) proposed it. In Fig. 9.3a, we have illustrated the rationale for an inflation based on the Philips curve. The inflation is caused by an expansionary monetary policy to create 'money illusion' (erroneous inflationary expectations π^e where $\pi^e < \pi$) on the supply side of the labour market:

$$U = U_n + \beta(\pi^e - \pi) \tag{9.6}$$

Nominal wage claims (based on π^e) are lower than would be justified by the higher future inflation rate (π). Thus, real wages are lower and the demand for labour stronger.[6] If $\pi^e = \pi$, the unemployment rate is at its natural rate U_n (also called the NAIRU—the non-accelerating-inflation rate of unemployment). This condition is realized, for instance, at point A, where $\pi^e_0 = \pi_0 = 0$ for which the long-term vertical Phillips curve holds.

We have also drawn indifference curves (I_1, I_2, I_3) indicating the preferences for the mix of the two evils, π and U.[7] Those indifference curves closer to the origin involve a smaller loss of welfare than those further away. At point A, where there is full employment—defined by the natural rate of unemployment—and no inflation, the government is nevertheless not content with the economic situation as indicated by the indifference curve I_1.[8] It could improve welfare by moving along the short-term Phillips curve, $U = U_n + \beta(\pi^e_0 - \pi)$, from A to the tangency point B. However, point B is not a stable point, since the Phillips curve will shift from B to C as soon as the economic agents have revised their inflation expectations from π^e_0 to π^e_1. The reaction of the authorities would be to inflate more, to π_2 (point D), which would avoid the employment loss of $U_2 U_n$. For them, point C is worse than point D. Over time, the economy ends up at the tangency point F, where the short-term welfare can no longer be increased.

There is some troublesome inconsistency in the government's behaviour, since its long-run situation has become worse (point F compared to point A).

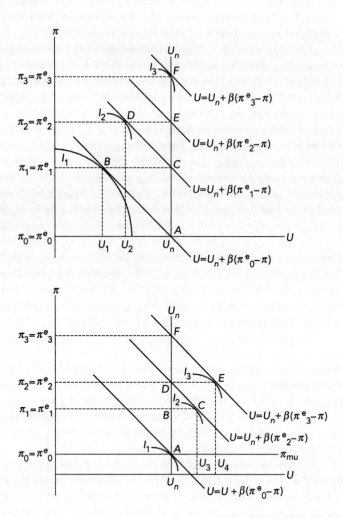

Fig. 9.3. The Phillips Curve: disinflation via an irrevocable currency peg or a single currency

Fig. 9.3a. Inflation

If inflation is correctly expected, unemployment is at its natural level (point A). The government could be tempted to lower U by inflating the economy (point B). The short-run trade-off vanishes, if $\pi^e = \pi_1$ (point C). At that moment, government has to inflate more (point D). The inflationary process comes to an end at point F. The exchange rate has to be adjusted according to the inflation differential.

Fig. 9.3b. Disinflation

The economy is at point F and the government opts for a disinflation policy. A gradual policy would imply the adjustment path FECA. A radical policy (the immediate adjustment from F to A) has to realize $\pi^e = \pi^e_0$ via an irrevocably fixed peg or via a common currency.

The reason for this peculiar performance is the assumption that government is short-sighted and, thus, does not care about the long run.[9] For the authorities, the policy of zero inflation is 'time inconsistent' if the welfare of the far distant future is not taken into account. By considering only the short end of the time horizon, they only look for better short-term outcomes (for instance, point *B* compared to point *A*). According to Rogoff (1985), a policy implication of such absurd behaviour would be that monetary policy must be carried out by an independent central bank.

At point *F*, the government would be better off with a lower inflation rate (see Fig. 9.3*b*). We assume that its map of indifference curves has been changed, because, for instance, a new government has been elected. If it is wanted to follow a deflationary policy (for instance, point *E*), it could only do so with a higher rate of unemployment ($U_4 > U_n$). The reason for this is sticky inflation expectations ($\pi^e = \pi^e_3$). The public does not believe the anti-inflationary policy announcements. The public is surprised when point *E* is reached and notices that real wages, negotiated in the past and still valid until the older labour contracts run out, are too high and that the rate of unemployment is increasing.[10] For all new contracts, inflationary expectations are revised to the level of π^e_2 (point *D*).

The painful adjustment process ($F \rightarrow E \rightarrow C \rightarrow A$) could be avoided, if government could persuade the public that its anti-inflationary intentions are serious. Thus, at point *F*, the authorities have to make it crystal clear that the inflation rate in the near future will be at point *A*. This announcement could be made credible by pegging the exchange rate to the stable anchor currency. But, as exchange rates can also be adjusted, the exchange rate peg has to be 'irrevocable'. Unfortunately, in matters of fixed exchange rates, nothing is irrevocable—in particular, with full capital mobility—since some other countries may lack the commitment to the ultimate objective of a monetary union. From this perspective, the only really credible signal that the country's inflation rate will be reduced to that of the monetary union (π_{mu}) would be the introduction of a single common currency. This shock therapy in the form of monetary unification would constitute an enormous gain for the more inflationary countries in the currency area, since it would avoid the unemployment losses which arise from the less credible programme of gradual monetary unification.[11]

The Benefits of Irrevocably Fixed Exchange Rates

The ultimate target of an exchange rate peg is price stability. The selected anchor country must have a high score for price stability, while the satellite should have strong commercial links to the anchor country. Austria and the Netherlands are the best examples of this, with Germany as the anchor country (see Box 2.5). The benefits are in terms of the price stability 'imported' from the anchor country via the law of one price for tradable goods $(P_T = E_0 \, P^*_T)$.[12] The anchor country, in turn, must have a floating exchange rate to stabilize P^*_T.

The size of the benefits depends on various factors. One important consideration is the society's preference function for price stability, which could be influenced by its historical experience of high inflation and by the degree of consensus about the target of price stability among various groups in the society.

Another benefit could concern an improved allocation of resources through which the growth potential of the economy is increased. The distortions in the allocation of resources—and also in income distribution—arise mainly from erroneous inflation expectations as has already been shown in the previous section. In particular, when the government implements a deflationary policy, we have seen that *ex-post* real wages and interest rates tend to be higher because of the inertia of inflationary expectations. In this regard, the disinflation programme must be highly credible and this credibility could be brought about by the ('irrevocably') fixed exchange rate peg with the anchor currency.[13]

A monetary union (like that of the future European Monetary Union) implies more benefits for the satellite country than those enumerated so far. Since the implementation of irrevocably fixed exchange rates is decided by common agreement with all union members, additional rules such as a European Central Bank are introduced, which, in principle, tend to break the hegemony power of the anchor country so that the union works like a symmetrical currency area. These additional benefits accrue to the former satellite countries of the EMS which now become as 'independent' as the former anchor country. Of course, these specific benefits are more important for large countries than for small countries if the former have a more important say in decision-making on the board of the common central bank. On the other hand, the anchor country is now locked into the common central bank and its monetary independence is thus curtailed.

The Costs of Irrevocably Fixed Exchange Rates

The loss of the exchange rate as a policy tool is generally considered to be the most serious disadvantage for a country which joins the monetary union. The country may be faced with the necessity of having a real depreciation or a real appreciation. The questions we have to ask are whether other policy instruments are available which can bring about the necessary change in the real exchange rate, and whether the costs they involve are higher than those of a change in the nominal exchange rate. We are already familiar with this question from our various analyses of the monetary mechanism which brings about changes in the real exchange rate under the regime of fixed exchange rates.

The need for real depreciations and the cost of unemployment. We shall consider the case of a member country whose current account deficit is judged to be 'unsustainable'. It should be noted that, within the monetary union, there is perfect capital mobility and almost no difference in interest rates when the exchange rate margins are extremely narrow (like ± 0.11 per cent in the Austrian case). Thus, the deficit country has 'unlimited' access to credit markets. However, it considers its ratio of external debt to GDP as too high and decides to implement a stabilization programme.[14]

We shall interpret the real exchange rate as the internal terms of trade of tradable goods (e_2), assuming the law of one price for tradables within the monetary union ($e_1 = 1$). For some markets, this assumption may appear to be heroic (see Box 9.4). As discussed in Section 8.3, the main policy instrument for attaining external equilibrium is the reduction of expenditure (absorption).[15]

Box 9.4. The average price differentials (net of taxes) for tradables in the European Economic Community: the same automobile in 1986 and 1989 (Denmark = 100)

	1986	1989
Denmark	100	100
Belgium	121	123
Netherlands	123	130
Germany	129	137
France	130	132
Italy	144	148
United Kingdom	151	161

National markets were still very segmented in the European market for automobiles, at least in the 1980s. The reasons are price discrimination by car producers and dealers, and various national administrative regulations.
Source: de Grauwe (1992: 62).

We can now apply the analysis of Section 8.3. The reduction in public expenditure—implying either a lower budget deficit or even a budget surplus—could arise exclusively from buying fewer tradable goods. The current account balance would be improved without any change in the real exchange rate being necessary. However, when the reduction in public expenditure also includes non-tradable goods, an excess supply of non-tradable goods emerges and the only adjustment mechanism is a decline in P_N (real depreciation), also involving a decline in the general price level P.

In Fig. 9.4a we have reproduced our frequently used diagram of the money market in the space $P_T P_N$. It stands for the money market of a member country of the EU. The Union's level of P_T—say that the union represents the future European Monetary Union (EMU)—is linked to the international level—which is that of America (P^{USA}_T)—via the (floating) exchange rate

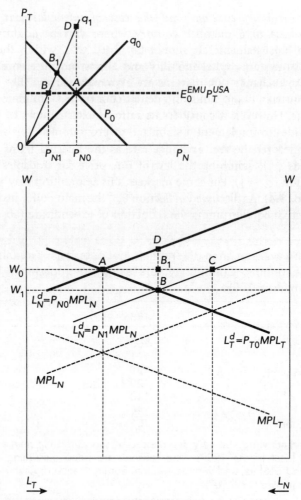

Fig. 9.4. EMU: The need for a real depreciation of a member country and the repercussions on its money and labour markets

Fig.9.4a. The money market

The real depreciation (q_1) is brought about by the movement from A to B.

Fig. 9.4b. The labour market

The decline of P_N shifts the demand for labour in the N-sector from D to B. With wage rigidities, unemployment is equal to AC.

which is supposed to be $E^{EMU}{}_0$. Monetary equilibrium of the member country is at point A. The initial real exchange rate (q_0) is illustrated by the ray Oq. The real depreciation required (q_1) is indicated by the movement from A to B, which is brought about by the restrictive fiscal policy causing a decline of P_N

from P_{N0} to P_{N1}, combined with an accommodating deflationary monetary policy which shifts the P_0 schedule to the left through point B. Thus, there will also be a decline in the general price level.

The more important diagram is that of Fig. 9.4b, which is a reproduction of Fig. 8.9b, and which describes the impact of the decline in P_N on the labour market. The initial equilibrium in the labour market is at point A. The fall of P_N from P_{N0} to P_{N1} shifts the schedule $L^d_N = P_{N0} MPL_N$ downwards through point B by the amount of the price decline in P_N. After labour has migrated from N to T, nominal wages in both sectors have to fall to the level W_1.

High costs of irrevocably fixed exchange rates appear when there are rigidities in the labour market. If trade unions are opposed to the fall of wages, unemployment equal to AC would emerge.[16] Conversely, if the country revokes its 'irrevocable' fixed exchange rate peg, it could devalue and avoid the unemployment AC. Two kinds of devaluation are conceivable.

With the first (a rise of P_T and a fall of P_N at point B_1 in Fig. 9.4a), the value component of the marginal product of L_T increases and, correspondingly, the value component of the marginal product of L_N falls, so that the general price level *and* the nominal wage level remain constant (point B_1 in Fig. 9.4b). The potential increase in W_T resulting from ΔP_T is compensated by the decline in MPL_T due to labour migration to T. Similarly, W_N should fall when $-\Delta P_N$, but rising labour productivity in N compensates the potential decline in W_N.

The other kind of devaluation would be from A to D (Fig. 9.4a), implying an unchanged P_{N0} and a rising P_T. This would have shifted the schedule ($L^d_T = P_{T0} MPL_T$ upwards through point D (Fig. 9.4b). There would be no unemployment. However, nominal wages would have risen to correspond to a higher general price level (at point D in Fig. 9.4a).

These results meet Robert Mundell's (1961a) criteria of optimal currency areas exactly. In the case of rigidities in national labour markets, the exchange rate is an essential tool. Rigidities can consist of labour immobility and downward wage inflexibility. Since Mundell worked with the real exchange rate as the relative price of domestic and foreign tradable goods, labour mobility involves the migration of unemployed labour to other member countries. However, in our context of the real exchange rate as the relative price of tradable and non-tradable goods, there are no barriers to internal labour migration and labour could move from N to T within the national economy, provided that wages in T and N do decline and that wage earners accept lower wages. With wage rigidities, the tool of the nominal exchange rate would avoid unemployment by devaluating the domestic currency (point B_1 in Fig. 9.4).

The need for real appreciations and the cost of inflation. So far we have considered two types of countries. There were inflationary countries, which want to get rid of high inflation rates and which would gain credibility with an irrevocably fixed exchange rate peg. On the other hand, there were countries which had already opted for such a peg, and which may face an unsustainable current account deficit at some future time. With wage rigidities, the cost of having joined the monetary union may be very high in terms of higher unemployment which results from the re-establishment of external equilibrium. There is still a third type of country, the former anchor country, and its cost may be higher inflation.

In a two-country model (discussed at the end of Chapter 7.5), the real exchange rate is defined as the ratio of two relative prices—the relative price of non-tradable goods in the domestic country (q) *and* the relative price of non-tradables in the foreign country (q^*).[17] Over the long run, and under certain conditions, there is a need for a change, even a continuous change, in the real exchange rate. One such condition is the existence of a growth differential between two countries. Other conditions relate to the supply and demand side of tradable and non-tradable goods, productivity differentials, biased in favour of tradable goods, and higher income elasticities of the demand for non-tradable goods.

Box 9.5. Inflation and productivity growth in industrialized countries during the Bretton-Woods period, 1950–71 (annual compound rates)

	USA	Germany	Japan
Productivity Growth 1950–71			
Services	1.4	2.8	4.0
Industry	2.2	5.6	9.5
Inflation 1950–60	2.6	2.8	5.3
Inflation 1960–71	3.4	4.1	5.5

During the Bretton-Woods regime, inflation rates among industrialized countries (United States, Germany, and Japan), differed. Given the world inflation rate for tradables, international and intersectoral productivity growth differentials pushed the domestic inflation rate up in the countries with higher growth rates. Japan accepted this trend, but Germany was reluctant to do so. Germany restrained inflation through sterilization policies, thus avoiding the need for real appreciations; Giersch (1984). The task became harder when capital account convertibility was introduced in the 1960s, and the deutschmark was revalued in 1961, 1969, and 1971.
Source: Obstfeld (1991).

Real exchange rate adjustments among industrial countries are shown for the future EMU, in particular for Germany. Rapidly growing countries may have a trend of real appreciations relative to countries that grow slowly. Thus, the dilemma of Germany—if its growth rate is high—will be that it can no longer use nominal appreciations as the tool of adjustment (see Box 9.5). Real appreciations could only be achieved by higher inflation rates relative to some other union members.

In Fig. 9.5, we illustrate the inflationary outcome for Germany, or, in more

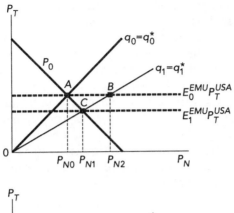

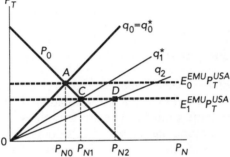

Fig. 9.5. EMU: the need for real appreciations in the rapidly growing member countries and their inflationary impact

Fig. 9.5a.

There is the same increase in the relative price of non-tradables in the member countries without an inflationary impact ($A \rightarrow C$), since there is a nominal appreciation of all currencies of the monetary union.

Fig. 9.5b.

There is a higher increase in the relative price of non-tradables in the home country ($q < q^*$). An inflationary impact takes place in the home country ($C \rightarrow D$).

general terms, for any other member country with relatively high growth rates. We shall assume that the EMU consists of two identical countries. The initial equilibrium is at point A. The home country is assumed to have the same relative price of non-tradables as the foreign country ($q_0 = q_0^*$). Two cases are examined. There is an identical increase in the relative price of non-tradables in both countries ($q_1 = q_1^*$ in Fig. 9.5a). The second case considers that the home country's non-tradables prices increase more sharply ($q_2 < q_1^*$ in Figure 9.5b). The third country is the rest of the world which could again be represented by the United States.

In the case of Figure 9.5a, there is no change in the real exchange rate between the two countries. Their economies could move to point B with an accommodating rise in the quantity of money for the EMU. The other possibility consists of maintaining price stability (P_0) by revaluing the European currency against the US dollar which would lower EMU's price level of tradables (P_T), which implies a movement from A to C. If we retain this latter option for interpreting Fig. 9.5b (where $q_2 < q_1^*$), the movement for Germany will be from A to D, while the other member country (assuming that it is France) moves from A to C. The European currency appreciates *vis-à-vis* the US dollar (point C), producing a lower price level for tradables within the EMU. Furthermore, the price level of non-tradables increases more sharply in Germany (point D) than in France (point C). Thus, Germany has neither the deutschmark nor lower inflation.

A Cost–Benefit Comparison

When the benefits of a monetary union exceed its costs, a monetary union in the sense of irrevocably fixed exchange rates would be the best outcome. This may be the case for some countries but not for others. A priori, one could notice that small open economies have a more favourable trade-off than large economies which are relatively closed; see de Grauwe (1992: 82–6).

On the horizontal axis of Fig. 9.6, the openness of the potential member country is measured by the ratio of trade over GDP. The volume of trade relates to the commercial transactions with all other members of the monetary union. The benefits are measured as a percentage of GDP. We assume that they are independent of the degree of openness. However, the benefits can be on a lower or higher level, depending on the described factors which determine their size of the benefits. For the anchor country, the benefits will be low if it continues to grow rapidly and can no longer use the tool of nominal appreciations to avoid the inflationary impact of a higher rise in P_N compared to that of P^*_N.[18]

The cost side is more ambiguous. The two alternative cost schedules indicate that costs are decreasing with more openness. The idea behind this particular *slope* is that the *cost of internal adjustment (in terms of expenditure reducing policies) for achieving some external equilibrium* is lower for open economies than for relatively closed economies. In an open economy—i.e. a small economy—the share of imported goods in the total of tradable goods (i.e. domestic plus imported tradables) is higher by far. Consequently, a restrictive fiscal policy aimed at improving the current account balance will be more successful, since the reduction in public expenditure will be more likely to affect imported goods than in a relatively closed (i.e. large) economy.[19]

The loss of the exchange rate tool influences the *position* of the cost schedules with respect to the origin. We have drawn two alternative schedules from the point of view of the labour market. The renouncement of the exchange rate policy can be considered as marginal to the extent that there

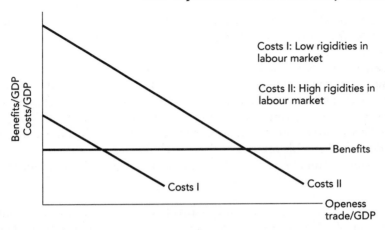

Fig. 9.6. A cost–benefit comparison of monetary unions

To the right of the intersection point of the schedules of costs and benefits, the country will opt for an irrevocably fixed exchange rate peg.

is high downward wage flexibility in the national labour market. Under the opposite assumption, the cost of the irrevocable exchange rate peg will be high.

From a purely formal point of view, a country will decide not to introduce the irrevocable exchange rate peg, when it is to the left of the intersection between the benefit and cost schedules. To the right of this point, it will be better off joining the monetary union. An additional consideration could be the point of view of highly inflationary countries whose anti-inflationary policies would become fully credible at a stroke as soon as they belong to the monetary union—provided the other member countries accept them.

9.3. A Cost–Benefit Analysis of Monetary Unions with a Single Currency

The Benefits of a Single Currency

We shall now evaluate the *additional* advantages and disadvantages which accrue to a member country of a monetary union which decides on currency unification.

The function of money as a *means of payment* refers to a generally acceptable means of payment. The general acceptability may differ between areas and between types of transactions. The latter concerns the technical question of which different kinds of the same currency unit (coins, bank notes, or sight deposits) are not complete substitutes, so that in many cases, one or other can be used more easily for certain types of payments. However, the real economic issue is related to the money circulation area. If there are many currencies within the area, the optimum number of currencies will be one, for the following reasons.

1. As Swoboda has shown,[20] the average holding of transaction balances will be more important, the higher the number of currencies. This result is based on the assumption that certain payments (for instance, intra-national ones) can be effected only in one money, and other types of payments (for instance, international ones) must be made in another money. This statement can be proved by the Baumol–Tobin model.

The Baumol–Tobin formula for the transactions demand for money (M) is:

$$M = \sqrt{(tT/2r)} \qquad\qquad (9.7)$$

where T is the value of transactions (payments), t the fixed costs per transaction 'selling bonds—buying money'[21] and r the interest rate. Let us assume the existence of n monies, expressed in the same numéraire. The transactions demand for the n monies will be:

$$\Sigma M_i = n \sqrt{(tT_i/2r)} \qquad \text{where } i = 1, \ldots n \qquad (9.8)$$

where T_i is the transaction volume in i's money and where t and r are supposed to be identical for all monies. Assume, for simplicity, that there is the same transaction volume in each money ($T_1 = T_2 = \ldots = T_n$) so that the total transaction volume is $T = n\, T_i$. Then, formula (9.7) for a country belonging to a monetary union with a single currency can be written as:

$$M = \sqrt{(tnT_i/2r)}. \qquad\qquad (9.7a)$$

Consequently, the transaction balances in a world of n currencies (9.8) are higher than in a single money world (9.7a) by:

$$\Sigma M_i - M = [n - \sqrt{n}] \sqrt{(tT_i/2r)} \qquad (9.8) - (9.7a)$$

The economies of transaction balances increase with a decreasing number of monies. If there is a currency unification of four countries ($n = 4$), the country would only need half of its former money holdings as transactions balances for international payments.

Box 9.6. EMS gains of a single currency

'The EC Commission has recently estimated these gains, and arrives at a number between 13 to 20 billion ECUs per year (one Ecu was approximately equal to one US dollar). This represents one-quarter to one-half of one per cent of the Community GDP. This may seem peanuts. It is, however, a gain to be added to the other gains from a single market.

It should be noted here that these gains that accrue to the general public have a counterpart somewhere. They are mostly to be found in the banking system. Surveys in different countries indicate that about 5% of the banks' revenue are the commissions paid to banks in the exchange of national currencies. This source of revenue for the banks will disappear with a monetary union.

The preceding should not give the impression that the gain for the public is offset by the loss of the banks. The transaction costs involved in exchanging money are a *deadweight* loss. They are like a tax paid by the consumer in exchange for which he gets nothing. Banks, however, will have a problem of transition: they will have to look for other profitable activities. When this has been done, society will have gained. The banks' employees, previously engaged in exchanging money, will now be free to perform more useful tasks for society.' de Grauwe (1992: 61–2).

2. Calculation costs are another item which reduces the optimum number of currencies to one. They are minimized when exchange rates are fixed at the rate of 1 : 1. In this case, these costs are approximately zero, because such a fixed exchange rate system resembles a one money world. But even in such a world, there are still transaction costs because one type of money has to be converted to another when payments have to be made in this other money; these costs are evaluated in Box 9.6. Another type of transaction cost is the opportunity cost of the average higher transaction balances individuals must hold which we analysed above.

Box 9.7. The analogy of monetary systems to telephone systems

The monetary quality of a single, universally accepted means of payment is the highest one in comparison with the existence of several monies. The existence of two monies can be compared with the existence of two telephone systems, T_1 and T_2. In the non-shaded section of the area $T_1(T_2)$, all telephone users can communicate with each other via the system $T_1(T_2)$; the monetary analogy would be that in this area section, the only money used is the money of type $T_1(T_2)$. In the shaded section, both systems are used.

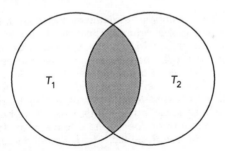

Fig. 9.C. Communication integration.

One possible (and most costly) type of organization would be that the inhabitants of the shaded area must have a second phone receiver. To eliminate the 'calculation costs', the phone number of each user should be the same in both telephone systems. Thus, the remaining costs—the 'transaction costs'—for the inhabitants of the shaded section consist of 'holding' two receivers. To merge the two systems into a single one (with only one phone receiver) implies a simple costless linking of the lines between the two telephone centres. Transaction and calculation costs are minimized when the area covers both circles so that they coincide in a single, but larger circle.

The Costs of a Single Currency

'Irrevocably' fixed exchange rates do not mean that they would always remain fixed for all member countries for all time. However, once a single currency is introduced, reneging on its membership to the monetary union becomes even more difficult for any member country. If we again take our example of a country with an unsustainable current account deficit and with high wage rigidities in its labour market, which has to implement a stabilization policy, this country may more easily opt out to avoid higher unemployment under irrevocably fixed exchange rates than if there is a unified currency. In this regard, the cost of currency unification must appear higher than the cost of 'irrevocably' fixed exchange rates.

Box 9.8. The French franc zone as a monetary union of 'irrevocably' fixed exchange rates

Thirteen African countries belong to the French Franc Zone (FFZ), namely the six member countries of the Bank of Central African States (BEAC): Cameroon, Central African Republic, Chad, Congo, Equatorial Guinea, and Gabon; and the seven member states in the West African Monetary Union (UMOA): Benin, Burkina Faso, Côte d'Ivoire, Mali, Niger, Senegal, and Togo.

These countries have pursued a fixed parity of 50 CFA francs for one French franc since 1948. The following rough data for 1990 may serve to characterize the zone: the population of the African member countries exceeded that of France by 25 per cent; their GDP corresponded to 4 per cent of the French GDP; and their M2 money supply was approximately 1.5 per cent of the French money supply.

There are important economic differences between the African member countries behind these global figures. The richest country is Gabon with an annual GDP per capita of $2,994 and the poorest is Chad, with a GDP per capita of $195 (both in 1988). The thirteen countries can be divided into three groups according to their level of development: the relatively prosperous oil-exporting countries of Cameroon, Congo, and Gabon; the former showcases of West Africa, Côte d'Ivoire and Senegal, which have been losing ground since the early 1980s; and the less advanced countries, which have been in a situation of permanent stagnation in terms of per capita income for the last 20 years (Benin, Burkina Faso, Central African Republic, Chad, Equatorial Guinea, Mali, Niger, and Togo).

Monetary policy for both the West and Central African zones is guided by a couple of rules. Concerning the external conduct of monetary policy, 65 per cent of foreign exchange reserves have to be converted into French francs and held in interest bearing accounts (called operations accounts) with the French Treasury providing an exchange rate guarantee in SDR terms. The French government guarantees the convertibility of the CFA franc into the French franc by allowing overdrafts from the French Treasury at a cost linked to the French rediscount rate. Changes in the exchange rate require the unanimous agreement of all member countries, including France. The conduct of internal monetary policy is governed by two principles. Government borrowing from the central bank cannot exceed 20 per cent of the previous year's tax revenues. If external reserves of the union's central bank fall below 20 per cent of the central bank's sight liabilities (reserve money, government deposits, and foreign liabilities) during three consecutive months, the central bank has to pursue restrictive monetary policy.[22]

The monetary adjustment mechanism of the FFZ is the same as in any other system of fixed exchange rates. If a member country pursues a highly expansionary monetary policy, it will be punished by a balance of payments deficit. The subsequent loss of international reserves constitutes the first danger signal for the conduct of its monetary policy. If reserves are nearly exhausted, the only option is a radical change in its monetary policy.

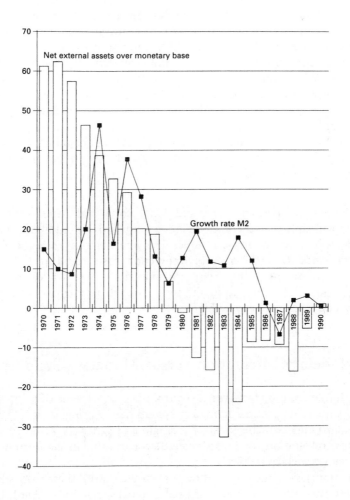

Fig. 9.D. The French franc zone: international reserves and money supply, 1970–1990.

These textbook rules of monetary adjustment are exactly what is institutiona-
lized in the FFZ, although the rules were not applied in the crisis years of the
1980s. During the 1970s, the average annual growth rate of M2 within the FFZ
was 20 per cent, but it fell to 8 per cent during 1980s. The statutes of the FFZ
prescribe a restrictive monetary policy if the ratio of net external assets to the
monetary base attains 20 per cent. That was precisely the case from 1978
onwards, but the growth rate of M2 remained relatively high until the mid-
1980s. Since 1979, net external assets have turned negative, but the growth
rate of M2 has remained positive except for 1987.

In Box 9.8, we have shown the case of the French Franc Zone. For forty-
five years, it was an area of 'irrevocably' fixed exchange rates, but not an
area with a single currency. In the African member countries, the French
franc was interchangeable with the CFA franc at the rate of 50 CFA francs
for one French franc. There was full convertibility between the two
currencies. When the current account deficits of the African countries
became 'unsustainable'—or, in other words, France refused to finance
them any longer—and when the internal adjustment costs in terms of
the required decline in the absolute level of prices and wages also became
unsustainable, the African countries and France could still revoke the
irrevocably fixed exchange rates and they did this in January 1994 (100
CFA francs for one French franc).

A cost–benefit comparison. The additional costs and benefits of a single
currency will shift the schedules of Fig. 9.6 upwards. In addition, the benefit
schedule will have an upward slope. The benefits rise with the degree of
openness, since the economies of transaction costs resulting from a single
currency will be more important in countries where trade, measured as
percentage of GDP—and, thus, the international payments—with the other
member countries is relatively high.

9.4. Monetary Integration versus Monetary Stability

As is well known, money serves two purposes: it is a means of payment and a
store of value. The optimal monetary system has to bring about (1) a perfect
means of payment in the form of a single and generally accepted currency
(monetary integration) *and* (2) a perfect store of value in the form of a stable
price level (monetary stability).

Each monetary constitution has (or should have) these two objectives:
monetary integration and monetary stability (Claassen 1984, 1986). Unfortunately, they cannot be realized simultaneously as they are, for certain (long)
periods, incompatible. Thus, for instance, higher monetary stability may be
attained by the introduction of a flexible exchange rate, which implies a lower

degree of monetary integration. Conversely, a higher degree of monetary integration, through a fixed exchange rate system or the formation of a currency area, may involve a lower level of monetary stability. It should be emphasized that the possibility of a trade-off relationship has to be seen from a long-run perspective (or, looking backwards, from a historical perspective). Consequently, the whole argument must be seen in terms of decades (or even centuries). Applied to the monetary scene in Europe, it could explain the different stages of a higher or lower degree of European monetary integration, in the past and probably also in the future.

The quality of money as a generally accepted means of payment is inherently linked to its store-of-value quality. Money is generally accepted as a means of payment when people have confidence in it, and this confidence is basically founded on its purchasing power value stability. Confidence belongs to the domain of information and information is based on past experience and future expectations. It follows that newly created and existing currencies have completely different degrees of confidence. Thus, for instance, a newly created money which lacks, by definition, any historical dimension of (good and/or bad) value stability has to be equipped with resources which create confidence. These resources may include backing the money with commodities, other currencies as reserves, reputable names in bank management, or various other techniques. Consequently, the money producer has the costs of selling (not only of producing) the money which are equivalent to the investment cost of building up a 'brand-name capital', as Klein (1974) calls it, which assures a certain degree of monetary confidence.

Under this aspect, certain past monetary experiences no longer constitute a puzzle for monetary theory. On the one hand, looking at the gold standard, gold was not necessarily a costly money for the economy compared with paper money, because the cost of constituting the brand-name capital in terms of the gold content of money was lower then than the investment cost of creating confidence in paper money.

A reasonable explanation of why credit money did not replace commodity money before it did may not be because someone did not happen to think of the credit money idea, but rather may be because commodity money was, at the time, the cheapest way to produce confidence; i.e. a forced movement from commodity to fiduciary money would have implied a negative social saving. (Klein 1974: 435). On the other hand, if looking at German (and other) hyperinflation, the German mark was still being used as a means of payment—at least for small change—even though there were certain amounts of unauthorized monies issued by municipalities and private organizations, which were denominated in the hyperinflating unit. Foreign currencies, which circulated domestically side-by-side at flexible exchange rates, were also used. Consequently, the costs of switching to a new money (foreign currencies, for instance) were too high in terms of information-transaction costs so that only a currency reform (as a means of restoring confidence) could induce such a switch.

Monetary history presents a large range of monetary experiments in the form of waves of monetary integration followed by monetary disintegration (several monies and flexible exchange rates). The latter always emerged with increasing monetary instability. Our contention is that there is no monetary constitution which permanently guarantees the optimum in terms of monetary integration and monetary stability. The targets of monetary integration and monetary stability may, at one time, be opposing, and, at another time, converging forces.

Appendix: The Geometry of the International Specialization of Savings and Investment

Capital movements are caused by differences in time preference or differences in capital productivity and they equalize either marginal time preferences or marginal productivities of capital among countries. Countries borrow and lend in the international capital markets either to optimize their intertemporal consumption stream or to take up profitable investment opportunities. Because both motives are likely to exist simultaneously, we shall analyse this more general case within the following geometrical framework of a two-country model. We assume identical production functions for the two countries, but different intertemporal utility functions.

Fig. 9.A1 assumes an identical production possibility curve, TT (i.e. the transformation curve between present and future consumption goods) for the home and foreign countries. Its slope indicates the marginal productivity of capital (MPC, or more precisely, $1 + MPC$). When both countries are closed with regard to the capital account, their own production and consumption points coincide. For the home (foreign) country this is at point A (A^*) at which its indifference curve (not drawn) is tangent. The interest rate of the domestic country is very high (r') reflecting its high marginal productivity of capital and its high marginal time preference. The opposite is true of the foreign country (r'^*). For the domestic country, present income amounts to y'_0 and its future income to y'_1. Conversely, the foreign country has a low present income or production (y'^*_0 and a high future income or production (y'^*_1).

When free capital movements take place, there will be one single interest rate in the world economy ($r_0 = r^*_0$). The production point in both countries will be at P, the domestic consumption point at E and the foreign consumption point will be situated at E^*. The domestic country, with its high productivity

	Domestic open economy	Foreign open economy
Production point	P	P
Consumption point	E	E*
Trade balance t_0	Deficit *DE*	Surplus *D*P*
Current acc. balance t_1	Surplus *DP*	Deficit *D*E**

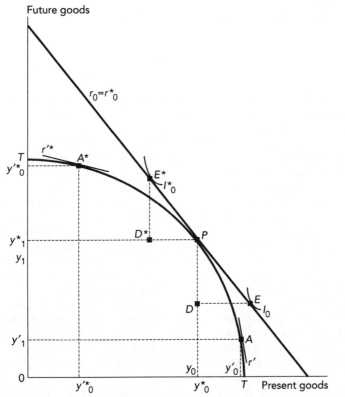

Fig. 9.A1. International specialization of savings and investment as a result of differences in time preference and productivity (a two-country model)

Both countries have an identical production possibility curve (*TT*) and the domestic (foreign) country has a high (low) preference for present consumption goods. When both economies are closed, their production/consumption point lies at A (A*) with the high (low) interest rate *r′* (*r′ **). With free capital movements, the new production/consumption points are indicated in the Box of Fig. 9.A1.

for future goods, will produce more of these and the foreign country less. The present and future incomes of the domestic country are now y_0 and y_1, respectively. For the foreign country, present income becomes higher ($y*_0$) and future income lower ($y*_1$). The domestic country borrows *DE*, equal to its trade balance deficit, and correspondingly, the foreign country lends *D*P* which is its trade balance surplus. In the following period, *DP* is the domestic current account surplus, equal to the foreign current account deficit *D*E**.

Capital mobility has equalized the marginal rates of capital productivity and time preference in the two countries and both are now on higher indifference curves, I_0 and I^*_0 (relative to points A and A^*, respectively). In the next period, the home country offsets its debt DP with a corresponding trade balance surplus, while the foreign country dissaves by the amount D^*P, which corresponds to its trade balance deficit.

Notes

1. It is assumed that both countries produce the same commodity. If products differ between the countries, the investment by the foreign country in the domestic country may improve the terms of trade for the foreign country if it can get imports at a lower price. The home country would have had a trade balance deficit of $(I > S)$ and the foreign country a trade balance surplus $(S^* > I^*)$.
2. However, this loss in world labour income does not always take place and it depends on the types of production function in the two countries.
3. The Appendix to the present chapter illustrates the case where capital productivity *and* time preference are different in the two countries.
4. For the equation $I/Y = a + b(S/Y)$, $b = 0$ and $b = 1$ would represent the extreme cases of perfect real capital mobility and immobility, respectively.
5. Another interpretation of the optimal sequencing would be that stage II should be preceded by stage III. In this scenario, a common and single currency would be the crowning cornerstone for achieving the monetary union.
6. At the micro level, each entrepreneur is considered to know the future evolution of the prices of the products he produces. The profit maximization of firms concerns the difference between their sales, evaluated at the *individual* product prices, and their costs, while trade unions have to predict the price level of consumption goods for the evaluation of workers' real wages. At the macro level, the correctly expected inflation rate by firms would be π.
7. If the authorities care far more about unemployment than inflation, the indifference curves will be steep. To reduce unemployment, they are willing to tolerate high rates of inflation. Conversely, if aversion to inflation is very large, the indifference curves are rather flat. They would be horizontal if government only cared about inflation.
8. At point A, government is on a 'higher' indifference curve (not drawn) which intersects the short-run Phillips curve.
9. See Kydland and Prescott (1977) and Barro and Gordon (1983).
10. Other contracts such as credit contracts also contribute to higher unemployment. Thus, the real *ex post* interest rate is higher than the real *ex ante* interest rate where $r_{ex\ post} = i - \pi$ and $r_{ex\ ante} = i - \pi^e$.
11. Furthermore, it must also be said that the low inflation countries, including the anchor country, may not show any interest in radical monetary unification, since their present benefits from a monetary union may not be great.
12. The exchange rate margins around the central parity should be very narrow (e.g. $\pm$ 0.11% for Austria instead of $\pm$ 2.25% within the former EMS).
13. The benefits listed above would also be received by a country which is not formally part of a monetary union, but which has chosen to have an irrevocably fixed

exchange rate peg with an anchor currency that is characterized by long-run price stability.

14. If the country is regarded as a dubious debtor, it has to pay a risk premium above the union's common interest rate. Another tricky question is whether the union has to bail out the debtor country when the latter becomes insolvent. This issue is treated by de Grauwe (1992: 166–7).

15. Restrictive monetary policy is excluded for the reduction of absorption, since the country must have the same interest rate as the other member countries. Consequently, fiscal policy becomes of primary importance for achieving external equilibrium.

16. In sect. 8.3 I also mentioned the case where unemployment could have been avoided, if there is a gain in labour productivity, equal to the distance BB_1 in Fig. 9.4b, in both production activities.

17. Remember (from Table 5.1) that $e = [EP^*_T/P_T] [q^b/q^{*b*}]$.

18. The benefit schedule can also be conceived of as downward-sloping for satellite countries if large former satellite countries with a small degree of openness have a greater influence on the union's common monetary policy than small countries have.

19. De Grauwe's (1992) cost analysis of irrevocably fixed exchange rates uses a Keynesian model. In a small open economy, the marginal propensity to import is rather high. An expenditure reducing policy implies a certain reduction in national income. The subsequent reduction in imports (and, thus, the improvement in the current account balance) is higher in a small economy than in a large one.

20. Swoboda (1968: 39–41). See also Canzoneri and Rogers (1990).

21. Since the alternative of money holding is the holding of bonds (for instance, time deposits).

22. For a description of the institutional arrangements of the FFZ, see Bhatia (1985), Honohan (1990), and Boughton (1991). The latter study also includes a discussion of the question of whether the FFZ constitutes an optimum currency area.

10

DEVELOPING AND POST-SOCIALIST COUNTRIES

....

Five issues are treated in this chapter:

1. *The causes of the long-run evolution—or deterioration—of the terms of trade and the macroeconomic impact of their short-run improvement; this subject is relevant not only to developing countries but also for those post-socialist countries which are important producers of primary products, such as nearly all states of the former Soviet Union. The specific mix of stabilization policies (fiscal, monetary, and exchange rate policy) for attaining internal equilibrium (price stability) and external equilibrium (current account balance) is considered for*
2. *developing countries and*
3. *post-socialist countries. The policy for developing countries differs from that for industrialized countries with respect to the issue of capital mobility, while the macroeconomic transition problem of post-socialist countries requires the elimination of the monetary overhang and the introduction of the world price structure for tradable goods.*
4. *Stabilization policies in hyperinflating and dollarized countries and*
5. *the debt problem are issues which are relevant for both developing countries and post-socialist countries.*

10.1. Similarities and Differences between the South and the East

The year 1989 was, in all probability, as significant for world history as was the year 1789. Political democratization and economic liberalization in the East are a challenge to any possibility of a third way between capitalism and socialism. Forty-five years on from the Second World War, fifty-five years after the establishment of the Nazi, and later, communist regimes in Central Europe, and seventy-five years on from the introduction of Marxism-Leninism in the

Soviet Union, it was finally recognized that democracy and the market are the least of all possible evils for the political and economic organization of society.

The countries of the Third World experienced a shorter painful period. Many of them (with the exception mainly of those in Latin America) became independent in the 1950s and then went through an experimental phase in which they tried out the third way preached in Oxford, Cambridge, and Paris in the 1950s. At the beginning of the 1980s, under pressure from twenty or thirty years of mismanagement, they began to try to liberalize their economies.

If one follows the World Bank's typology of developing countries (1992: 204–5), according to which middle-income countries are those with a GNP per capita (in 1989) between $580 and $6,000, some socialist countries would have belonged to the upper-middle-income economies with a GNP per capita above $2,335. Thus, Hungary, Czechoslovakia, or Yugoslavia were approaching the Portuguese level, and the former German Democratic Republic was above it.

The main difference between the Third and Second Worlds is probably the importance of the public sector and, more crucially, the organizing principle of the economy as a whole. The dream of the classical Soviet-type model was to run the whole economy like one huge factory. Even though in many developing countries the public sector, with all its accompanying distortions, is just as important, the main difference is in the way the economy is organized. In developing countries, important sectors are more likely to be run as a type of market economy. Consequently, liberalization efforts in the South, which take the form of structural adjustment measures, though extremely painful, are nevertheless milder than those associated with the transition of the Eastern countries to a rudimentary market economy.

The second difference, which is a corollary of the first, is that the socialist economies were closed economies and the developing countries are open ones. Of course, a distinction must be made between large and small economies— the Soviet Union and India, for instance, are naturally fairly closed. However, even the small Central European countries were tightly closed economies, because of the former bilateral (or barter) trade relationships in the Eastern bloc and the external inconvertibility of their currencies, not only with the industrialized countries but also among themselves. Exchange controls can also exist in the South, but their international trade is predominantly multilateral. The socialist economies were closed as a result of their refusal to take part in the international division of labour; their denial of its advantages implied the autarky principle. The most striking example was Albania.

There are, however, many similarities between the South and the East. Disguised unemployment is one common feature. Capital intensive production resulting from an extremely low artificial price for capital, is another. Unlike in the South, two of the basic particular characteristics of the economy in the former Eastern bloc related to the quality of their production factors, labour and capital. On the one hand, human capital is highly qualified, at least in Central Europe, due to the education system inherited from the pre-communist past. On the other hand, the investment ratio was rather high because inventory stocks were needed in a monetary system with limited domestic 'moneyness'. The term 'moneyness' is used by Hicks (1946: 163–6) and stands for the quality of money. Perfect moneyness would mean that money is a perfect means of payment and a perfect store of value. Since money could not buy goods, firms were forced to stock all kinds of primary and intermediate goods to maintain minimum production.

A final common element in the East and the South is the rudimentary structure of the financial system. Generally, in both types of economy, the only financial assets are currency, bank deposits, and sometimes treasury bonds. Financial repression is the usual cause of this phenomenon. In the case of the East, repressed inflation, the subsequent limited internal convertibility of the domestic currency into goods, and the lack of property rights were the main reasons. In the South, credit controls, credit selection, and interest ceilings are the main reasons for financial underdevelopment.

10.2. Terms of Trade

The Long-Run Evolution of the Terms of Trade

There has been a slight deterioration in DCs' terms of trade in recent decades, combined with a high short-run volatility (see Table 10.1). The main explanation is the change in the nominator which reflects the world prices of primary products—always expressed in terms of the US dollar—which are still the main exports of many DCs and PSCs, such as the states of the former Soviet Union. In a rather inflationary world economy, a long-run deterioration of the terms of trade would mean a smaller rise in the world prices of primary commodities than in those of industrial products.

Table 10.1 indicates two basic facts. First, the average terms of trade are significantly lower in the most recent period. Second, there is a sharp increase in the variance of the terms of trade, much pronounced in all the commodities and food groupings. The coefficient of variation increases considerably as the terms of trade become more volatile around a declining trend.

The explanation of such a trend relates to the developments in total demand and supply in the world market for primary products, generally only non-oil products. If the growth of the supply of primary products is greater than the growth in the demand, the long-run outcome would be a decline in 'real' commodity prices (see Borensztein and Carmen, 1994). Thus, a lower trend value of the growth rate of GDP observable in the industrialized countries could enhance a lower growth rate in the demand for primary products. This tendency may have increased since the late 1980s because of the fall in production in the PSCs. On the other hand, the stronger liberalization of the economies of DCs since the mid-1980s, together with a wave of real depreciations, may have had a strong output effect on primary commodities;

Table 10.1. Terms of Trade 1957:I–1993:II

Sample period	1957: I–1969: IV	1970: I–1979: IV	1980: I–1993: II
All commodities			
Mean	4.714	4.705	4.386
Variance	0.001	0.017	0.031
Coefficient of variation	0.789	2.806	4.036
Beverages			
Mean	4.573	4.668	4.203
Variance	0.018	0.112	0.199
Coefficient of variation	2.974	7.178	10.61
Food			
Mean	4.766	4.789	4.341
Variance	0.002	0.042	0.053
Coefficient of variation	0.839	4.280	5.300
Metals			
Mean	4.819	4.677	4.412
Variance	0.008	0.016	0.024
Coefficient of variation	1.868	2.737	3.490

Note: The terms of trade are commodity prices equal to the IMF all non-fuel commodity price index deflated by the IMF index of manufacturing export unit values (MEUV) of industrial countries. Both indices are in US dollars. Like other price indices of manufactured goods, the MEUV fails to capture quality improvements in manufactured goods. The data are logs. The coefficients of variation are based on a moving 15-year sample.
Source: Reinhart and Wickham (1994).

furthermore, the breakdown of the post-socialist economies may have set free primary products from internal production to increased exports.

Cyclical factors responsible for the price volatility can be found on both the supply and the demand sides. Seasonal factors and cyclical weather conditions are of course important for price formation of food and export crops. The business cycle in the industrialized countries constitutes another element in both the down-swings and up-swings of commodity prices. Finally, since the world prices of primary products are measured in dollars, a real appreciation of the US dollar with respect to many other currencies may imply a decrease in total demand for primary products, while a real depreciation would imply the reverse.

Favourable Terms of Trade and Real Appreciation

During the 1970s favourable terms of trade shocks occurred in many developing countries. They not only led to the beneficial effect of a sharp increase in revenues from raw material production, but also constituted a threat to the survival of the tradable goods industry making de-industrialization a possible result. This phenomenon is called the 'Dutch disease' because it was observed for the first time in the Netherlands after the discovery of the North Sea gas in the 1960s. The transmission link between prosperous exogenous shocks (the discovery of resources or favourable terms of trade) and de-industrialization is the real appreciation of the domestic currency in form of a rise in the relative price of non-tradables. This occurs when the country's increased prosperity is partly used to buy more non-tradable goods.

It should be noted that there was a wave of real appreciations in many developing countries in the mid-1970s. At that time there was a large boom in the prices of primary commodities in the range of 200 to 400 per cent. Most governments realized a big windfall gain in revenues, which were often spent immediately on huge public investment programmes using large quantities of non-tradables (such as construction, transport, and water dam projects). The price boom for primary products was only short-lived. When, after two or three years, the terms of trade returned to their original level, most governments continued their euphoric expenditure (see Box 10.1). This could no longer be financed as previously by extra export revenues. Large budget deficits occurred, which were mainly financed by external borrowing. The increase in foreign debt in the late 1970s created the debt problem of the 1980s for many developing countries.

Box 10.1. Morocco and the boom in phosphate prices and vast public investment programmes, 1974–80

'The first world-wide wave of adverse external shocks [increase in oil price] hit the Moroccan economy in a prosperous, but short-lived way: the quadrupling of the price of phosphates, Morocco's main export item, during 1974/5. . . . The boom of phosphate prices . . . was followed by expansionary domestic policies which, in 1976 and 1977, produced the country's worst ever budget deficit and, consequently, its worst current account deficit. . . . Government revenue also fell since the revenue from phosphate rock exports (which had constituted one-fourth of total government revenue in 1974) returned to roughly its original level. As a consequence of the external deterioration, Morocco reversed its domestic policies during 1978–80 with an austerity programme'

	Budget deficit/*GDP*	Current account deficit/*GDP*		Budget deficit/*GDP*	Current account deficit/*GDP*
1973	2.0	− 1.6	1977	15.3	16.0
1974	3.8	− 3.0	1978	10.7	9.9
1975	9.1	5.8	1979	9.8	9.3
1976	17.3	14.0	1980	10.1	7.8

Source: Claassen and Salin (1991: 191–3).

In the present section, we shall show the impact of the improvement in the terms of trade on the real exchange rate. We explicitly consider developing countries. In the following section, we describe the effect of the real appreciation on the tradables sector. We use the models developed by Corden and Neary (1982), Edwards and Aoki (1983) and Edwards (1984).

We now have three categories of goods instead of two: non-tradables (N) and two kinds of tradables, manufactures (T) and primary products, i.e. commodities (C). There are two relative prices: the real exchange rate, i.e. the relative price of tradables (manufactures) to non-tradables, $q = P_T/P_N$, and the terms of trade (TOT), defined as $TOT = P_C/P_T$. The terms of trade concern the price ratio of exported goods to imported goods. For most developing countries, the exported goods are mainly primary products and the imported goods are mainly industrial products. With three types of goods, there are two 'independent' relative prices, q and TOT. However, the terms of trade are given exogenously. Consequently, there is only one relative price to be determined— our real exchange rate. There is still a third relative price (q_C) we shall use. It is the relative price of primary commodities (P_C) to non-tradables (P_N): $q_C = P_C/P_N$. It is derived from the two first relative prices, since $q_C = q \times TOT$.

In nominal terms, total domestic income (Y) measured from the production side is equal to

$$Y = P_N S_N + P_T S_T + P_C \bar{S}_C \tag{10.1}$$

where S_C stands for the volume of primary products produced. For the moment, we assume a given output for primary products. We shall express real income (y) in terms of non-tradable goods by dividing (10.1) by P_N

$$y = S_N + q S_T + q_C \bar{S}_C \tag{10.2}$$

The increase in the world price of primary commodities (i.e. the improvement in the terms of trade) produces a real income effect ($\Delta y = \Delta q_C \times \bar{S}_C$). This generally involves an increase in total demand for tradables and non-tradables. While the additional demand for tradables could be supplied by international trade, the extra demand for non-tradables can only be satisfied by domestic production. If the non-tradables sector is at its full capacity, a real appreciation has to take place to make the production of non-tradables more attractive.

In Fig. 10.1 the slope of the $0T_0$ ray indicates the reciprocal value of the terms of trade, i.e. P_T/P_C (since $TOT = q_C/q = P_C/P_T$). An improvement in the terms of trade is illustrated by the $0T_1$ ray. The income effect resulting from the price rise of primary commodities is equal to $\Delta y = (\Delta q_C)\bar{S}_C$, where Δq_C is the distance AB. The increase in real income creates more demand for non-tradables. At point B, there is excess demand for non-tradables. The NN-schedule is sensitive both to real income from primary commodities (q_C) and to changes in the relative price of tradables and non-tradables (q). The excess demand for non-tradables is eliminated by the real appreciation from q_0 to q_1 (point C).

The NN-schedule corresponds to the equilibrium condition

$$S_N(q, q_C) = D_N(q, y, m) + G_N \tag{10.3}$$

We have differentiated between private and public demand for non-tradables (D_N and G_N, respectively). We assume that primary products are only

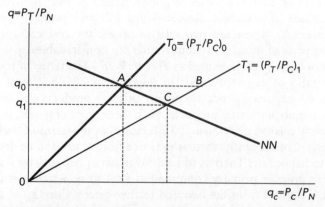

Fig. 10.1. An improvement in the terms of trade and real appreciation

The slope of the $0T$-ray indicates the size of the *TOT*. Their improvement is caused by Δq_c (*AB*). The increase in q_c involves higher income and higher demand for non-tradable goods. The subsequent excess demand for non-tradables (point *B*) is eliminated by a real appreciation.

demanded by foreign countries so that q_C does not enter as an argument in the demand function for non-tradables. We also abstract from the interest rate though it could alternatively be considered to be constant.[1]

The real appreciation (movement from *A* to *C*) is frequently associated with a considerable increase in demand for non-tradables which stems mainly from government. Two cases are conceivable (Fig. 10.2). One is that primary products are only produced by public enterprises (Fig. 10.2*a*), something also observable in developing countries. Assuming a given output of primary commodities and unchanged wage rates, a rise in q_C would not change the real income of the private sector. Consequently, the *NN*-schedule is horizontal. The whole additional revenue accrues to the government sector and is spent partly on non-tradables (G_{N1}). The real appreciation (q_1) is entirely due to the additional government demand (point *C*).

The alternative case is where primary products are produced in the private sector (Fig. 10.2*b*). A price rise for primary commodities considerably increases the industry's rent income which is partly taxed by government. The rise in private income leads to a higher demand for non-tradables (point *C*). Government revenues also increase and they are spent on tradables and non-tradables (G_{N1}). The additional demand for non-tradables by government could give rise to a stronger real appreciation (point *D*).

The Phenomenon of 'Dutch Disease'

The change in the relative prices of q and *TOT* causes, on the production side, resource movements between the three sectors: tradables in the form of

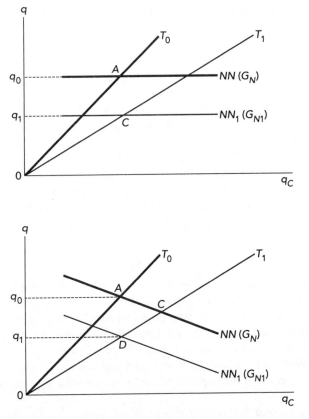

Fig. 10.2. An improvement in the terms of trade, fiscal expansion, and real appreciation

The improvement in the terms of trade gives rise to a policy of fiscal expansion mainly spent on non-tradable goods (G_{N1}). The result is again a real appreciation.

Fig. 10.2a.

The production of primary products by the public sector.

Fig. 10.2b.

The production of primary products by the private sector.

manufacturing goods (T) and primary commodities (C), and non-tradables (N). According to Corden and Neary (1982), there is an 'indirect resource movement effect' from the industrial tradables sector to the non-tradables sector as a consequence of higher terms of trade, increased real income, additional spending on non-tradables, and the subsequent real appreciation. There is also a 'direct resource movement effect' arising from higher profitability in the production of primary commodities, involving a shift of resources from the manufacturing tradables and non-tradables sectors to the primary products sector.

We shall assume that the resource movements consist entirely of labour movements. Capital already invested in the various production sectors is sector specific and cannot be moved elsewhere. The capital stock can only be depleted by not renewing the depreciated capital stock in the shrinking sector, while all new net investment can be directed towards the expansionary sectors.

In Fig. 10.3 we have illustrated the country's overall labour market under conditions of full employment. The various schedules show the marginal productivity of labour for the various production sectors. In each sector, the nominal wage (W) is equal to the marginal physical product of labour (MP) multiplied by the product price; furthermore, nominal wages are assumed to be equal in all sectors since labour skills are assumed to be homogeneous

$$W = P_N MP_N = P_T PM_T = P_C MP_C \tag{10.4}$$

$$\underset{L_N}{\longleftrightarrow} \quad \underset{L_T}{\longleftrightarrow} \quad \underset{L_C}{\longleftrightarrow}$$

The initial equilibrium is at point A.[2] The horizontal distance between ($L_T + L_C$) and L_T represents the labour demand in the primary products sector.

The real appreciation of Fig. 10.2 produces two kinds of labour movement. The first consists of a higher demand for labour in the non-tradables sector which shifts the demand for labour schedule upwards to L_{N1}. The new labour market equilibrium is at point B. There is an increase in the labour force in the non-tradables sector at the expense of the two other sectors (a movement from A to B).

There is a second labour movement effect from B to C arising from the increase in the value of the marginal product of labour in the primary products sector which shifts the ($L_T + L_C$) schedule to ($L_T + L_{C1}$). This labour movement takes place again at the expense of T, and also at the expense of N. Point C is the ultimate equilibrium situation in the labour market. The precise impact on labour allocation in the non-tradables sector is ambiguous. In Fig. 10.3 we assumed an overall increase in labour input for the production of non-tradables. However, the contrary is also conceivable if the primary products sector needs a large rise in labour input.

In contrast, the impact on labour input is very precise in the case of the manufactured tradables sector. Both the indirect and direct resource movement effects ($A_1 B_1$ and $B_1 C_1$, respectively) produce the fall in labour input from A_1 to C_1 and the subsequent de-industrialization.

It could be asked whether such a de-industrialization necessarily implies a fall in total welfare. If resources are not renewable, there may be some need for industry later on. Furthermore, as in our case of favourable terms of trade, the improvement in the terms of trade may only be temporary (as in the mid-1970s) while some part of industry has been permanently demolished. Finally, many of the exports may be manufactured products whose prices are generally more stable than those of primary products.[3]

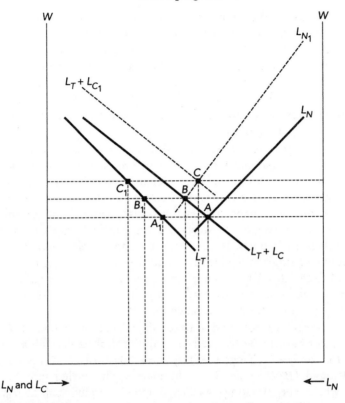

Fig. 10.3. An improvement in the terms of trade, real appreciation, and labour movements between production sectors

The initial equilibrium is at point A. The price rise of primary products increases the value of the marginal labour product in the C-sector (see L_{c1}) and in the N-sector as a consequence of the higher demand for N (see L_{N1}). The new equilibrium is at point C. The T-sector is less industrialized (lower labour input, A_1C_1) with the 'indirect' labour movement (A_1B_1) caused by Δq and the 'direct' labour movement (B_1C_1) caused by Δq_c.

10.3. Stabilization Policies for DCs

Foreign Exchange Controls

Stabilization policies in developing countries are mainly implemented in order to re-establish equilibrium in the current account. The deficit in the current account has become 'unsustainable' in the sense that the country has insufficient international reserves and does not obtain sufficient additional credit either from official or private sources. Since the typical deficit country is also a highly indebted one, it must achieve a trade balance surplus to be able to service the interest payments on its debt.

The overvaluation of the country's currency is another symptom of external disequilibrium. Any overvaluation implies that the country has a fixed exchange rate. Unlike industrialized countries, the developing country could live with this for a certain time since there are no massive capital outflows which would force the country to adjust the exchange rate as is the case with industrial countries characterized by a high degree of financial capital mobility. Furthermore, most DCs impose some kind of foreign exchange controls, at least as far as capital account transactions are concerned.[4]

When the currency is overvalued and there are foreign exchange controls, the emergence of a parallel foreign exchange market is fairly automatic. We have illustrated the workings of dual exchange rates in Fig. 10.4. There is a fixed official exchange rate (E_1) and a floating parallel exchange rate (E_0). We assume that foreign exchange transactions arise mainly from current account transactions. Their supply (S) stems predominantly from exports and their demand (D) from imports. In the absence of any foreign exchange controls, there would be a single exchange rate, E_0 in the case of floating rates, and E_1 in the case of fixed rates. Under the latter regime, the monetary authorities have to decrease their international reserves by the amount of AB to satisfy the excess demand in the foreign exchange market.

With exchange controls and a fixed official exchange rate at E_1, export revenues (OF) have to be transferred to the central bank, which rations the demand for foreign exchange (OG) by the amount of OF. Consequently, the excess demand $(EXD = D-S = AB)$ may be channelled into the parallel market, where the (floating) exchange rate is established at E_0. At the exchange rate E_0, the additional export revenues (AH) are sold on the black market. They satisfy the additional demand by importers for foreign exchange (AH).[5]

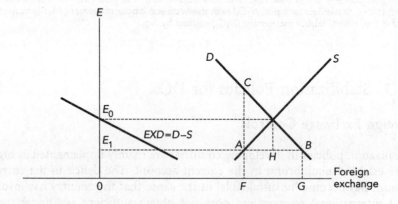

Fig. 10.4. The parallel market for foreign exchange

Without foreign exchange controls the market rate is above the official rate $(E_0 > E_1)$. With an excess demand of AB at the rate E_1, the export revenues (OF) have to be rationed.

Expenditure Reducing and Expenditure Switching Policies

One policy instrument of the total stabilization programme consists of devaluation, for instance, to the level of the parallel market rate.[6] However, a devaluation without any other policy instrument would only have an inflationary impact on the economy and would not improve the current account balance, that is, higher prices for tradable goods → higher prices for non-tradable goods as the consequence of the substitution effect → higher wage claims → permissive expansionary monetary policy.

We illustrate the ingredients of a successful stabilization programme within a simple theoretical framework of the Australian model (Fig. 10.5a) as shown in the Appendix to Chapter 7. The *TT* and *NN* lines are the partial equilibrium schedules of the markets for tradable and non-tradable goods, respectively. The two categories of goods are assumed to be gross substitutes. The slope of each schedule depends on the relative price of the two types of goods. Any point which is situated right to the *NN* line (*TT* line) represents an excess supply of non-tradables (excess demand for tradables which is equal to the trade balance deficit). The *MM*-line describes the equilibrium in the money market. For a given money supply, this line gives the general price level which is compatible with different combinations of the price levels of tradable and non-tradable goods, P_T and P_N. Internal and external equilibrium exists at the intersection point Q. The nominal equilibrium exchange rate is at the level E_0. The real equilibrium exchange rate ($q = P_T/P_N$) is indicated by the slope of the Oq ray.

One typical case of macroeconomic disequilibrium for developing countries is point A in Fig. 10.5b. There is an internal equilibrium (the economy is at the intersection point of the *NN*- and *MM*-schedules) accompanied by an external disequilibrium in the form of a trade balance deficit. The trade deficit is assumed to become unsustainable since there are no longer sufficient capital inflows, as was the case with many DCs after the outbreak of the Mexican debt crisis in August 1982. The position of *NN* could have been caused by budget deficits financed mainly by foreign sources. The expansionary fiscal policy could have had various origins. Thus, as in the case of Dutch disease, the favourable change in the terms of trade could have led to euphoric public investments which did not stop when the terms of trade reversed. A common denominator in all budget deficits was the fairly easy access DCs had to the international credit market in the 1970s. At that time, there was excess liquidity due to the recycling of oil revenues by the oil exporting countries and the slowdown of the economic activity in the OECD countries. The bulk of the external debt was mainly contracted with foreign banks.

One indispensable element of stabilization policies is the reduction or even elimination of the budget deficit. According to the absorption approach ($A - Y = Im - X$), total absorption has to be reduced in order to improve the trade balance. Of course, the reduction of absorption could also affect private absorption. Thus, for instance, the liberalization of the domestic credit

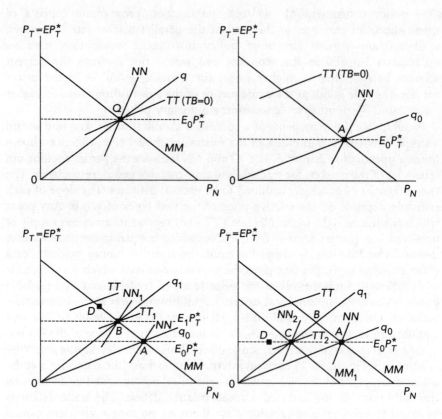

Fig. 10.5. Macroeconomic stabilization policies for developing countries

Fig. 10.5a. Internal and external equilibrium

The intersection point between the *NN*- and *MM*-schedules represents internal equilibrium. The corresponding real exchange rate is indicated by the slope of the O*q*-ray.

Fig. 10.5b. Internal equilibrium and external disequilibrium

The economy is at point *A*, where there is a trade balance deficit. Any point to the right of the *TT*-schedule represents situations of deficits in the trade balance..

Fig. 10.5c. Stabilization policy with nominal devaluation

Fig. 10.5d. Stabilization policy with a decline in the price level

In both cases reduction in expenditure on T ($TT \rightarrow TT_1$) and on N ($NN \rightarrow NN_1$) takes place. The real depreciation ($q_0 \rightarrow q_1$) occurs either through a devaluation with a constant price level (point *B*) or through a decline in the price level (point *C*).

market would generally lead to higher interest rates and higher savings (meaning lower consumption) if there had previously been credit controls and credit selection at arbitrarily low interest rates. The decline of absorption generally involves a decline in the absorption of non-tradables (a leftward shift of the *NN*-schedule) and tradables (a rightward shift of the *TT*-schedule). Furthermore, there is not only a need for a reduction in total absorption, but also for restructuring total absorption from fewer non-tradables to more tradables. This restructuring necessitates a real depreciation.

In Fig. 10.5*c* the reduction in total absorption shifts the *NN*–*TT*-schedules to the position of NN_1–TT_1. The real depreciation is indicated by the Oq_1 ray. It should be noted that, in general, the absorption policies affect both categories of goods. This is particularly the case when government expenditure is reduced, since they are also oriented towards non-tradables. However, another conceivable hypothesis is that the decline of absorption only concerns the demand for tradables. In that case, the *NN*-schedule would remain at *A* while the *TT*-schedule would shift through point *A* maintaining the real exchange rate at q_0.

There are two possible ways of realizing the real depreciation (q_1) if the developing country maintains a regime of a fixed exchange rate. The first method is to devalue by the rate E_1E_0/E_0 (Fig. 10.5*c*). This rate would also be established in a regime of floating exchange rates. The change in the relative price comes about through an increase in P_T and a decrease in P_N which are necessary in order to maintain price level stability indicated by the *MM*-schedule. The second method (Fig. 10.5*d*) consists of maintaining the parity (as in the case of the African countries of the French Franc Zone until the end of 1993; see Box 9.8). With this method, the whole adjustment burden has to be carried out by a decline in the price level of non-tradable goods (point *C*). A deflationary monetary policy has to be pursued which shifts the *MM*-schedule to the position MM_1.[7]

A final remark concerns the trade balance. As we have already mentioned several times, under certain circumstances, a heavily indebted developing country does need a surplus, and not just equilibrium, in the trade balance, in order to service its debt. In this case, a further reduction in absorption and a further real depreciation are indispensable. These cases are indicated by point *D* in Fig. 10.5*c–d*. Assuming a nominal devaluation (Fig. 10.5*c*), the further reduction of absorption shifts the TT_1-schedule downwards and the NN_1-schedule upwards where the new *NN*-schedule passes through point *D*. A similar shift takes place in the case of a fixed nominal exchange rate (Fig. 10.5*d*): point *D* would be the intersection point of the new *NN*- and *MM*-schedules.

Financial Liberalization and Real Appreciation

External financial liberalization (the abolition of any capital controls and full capital account convertibility) means that domestic interest rates are aligned to international ones, credit constraints become looser when expenditures exceed receipts, and the menu of portfolio allocation becomes richer. From the point of view of the international economy, financial liberalization profits from the international specialization of savings and investment. A young country, which is usually a deficit country with a higher investment than savings ratio is able to borrow from mature surplus countries (see Section 9.1).

Financial liberalization can produce a real appreciation of the domestic currency and an adverse effect on the trade balance (Claassen, 1992).[8] If we assume that the country implements external financial liberalization, and neglect the impact on the domestic interest rate, we can look at the effect of net capital imports as a possible outcome of financial liberalization. If net capital imports are used to increase demand for tradable and non-tradable goods, the TT and NN lines of Fig. 10.6 shift to TT_1 and NN_1. The new real exchange rate equilibrating the market for non-tradable goods is indicated by the slope of the Oq_1 ray (real appreciation). Under floating exchange rates, the real appreciation is brought about by a mix of nominal appreciation (E_1) *and* a rise in the price level of non-tradables, while the general price level remains constant (point B). In a regime of fixed exchange rates (E_0), the overall price level has to increase (point C) via an accommodating monetary policy, since the real appreciation can only be realized by a rise in P_N. Because of the higher general price level, both schedules (TT_1 and NN_1) shift upwards (not drawn) and the new NN-schedule has to pass through point C. For both exchange rate regimes, the internal equilibrium is accompanied by a trade balance deficit.

In Sections 10.2 and 10.3, we have become acquainted with two happy events which gave rise to a real appreciation of the domestic currency: favourable terms of trade and financial liberalization. In both cases, these caused excess demand for non-tradable goods, either via expansionary fiscal policies or via heavy capital inflows. Both cases could give rise—over the medium term—to an overvaluation of the domestic currency if the current account deficit becomes 'unsustainable'. The stabilization policies discussed above must then be adopted.

10.4. Stabilization Policies for PSCs

Sequencing and Timing

With rationing and price controls (repressed inflation), the domestic currency in any former socialist economy was deprived of its functions as a means of

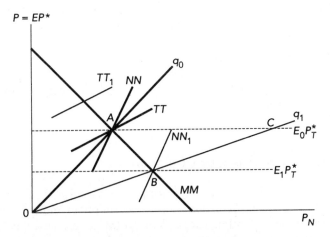

Fig. 10.6. Financial liberalization and real appreciation

The initial situation is at point A. Capital controls are abolished. By assuming net capital imports, there is an additional demand for T ($TT \rightarrow TT_1$) and ($NN \rightarrow NN_1$). A real appreciation takes place ($q_0 \rightarrow q_1$).

payment and a store of value. Consequently goods took over the functions of money. On the one hand, many domestic transactions took the form of barter. On the other, households and firms hoarded goods as a store of value.[9] Thus, we have the paradoxical situation that hoarded goods were abundant but purchasable goods were scarce, since only a limited amount of (soft) goods could be bought with the domestic currency.

The sequencing of the transition of the centralized socialist economies towards free market economies takes place in three steps which may sometimes overlap. The first is the implementation of stabilization policies. The second, privatization, may start at the same time as the macroeconomic stabilization measures, but will take much longer to complete. Finally, restructuring single enterprises and the whole economy will take up to five, ten, or even more years.

We are concerned here with the sequencing and timing of stabilization policies. As in the preceding section on DCs, stabilization policies are broadly defined as monetary, fiscal, and exchange rate policies. The sequencing of stabilization policies refers to the specific order in which monetary, fiscal, and exchange rate policies are introduced. Their timing refers to the speed with which the necessary adjustment policies are implemented.

The policy procedures of the former German Democratic Republic (GDR) provide a benchmark for sequencing and timing. The correct sequencing of stabilization policies could have been first, to liberalize prices liberalization and eliminate the monetary overhang via an adequate monetary and fiscal policy mix. The second phase could have been to introduce external convertibility in step with the liberalization of commercial transactions, followed later by the liberalization of capital transactions. As we know, these stabilization measures were introduced in the GDR on 1 July 1990. Other countries (like Poland) chose a more moderate sequencing, but the timing of their stabilization programme was still radical. For the GDR, there was a third phase on 1 July—not only an irrevocably fixed exchange rate with the deutschmark, but full currency unification.

Currency Reform versus Open Inflation

In the case of repressed inflation, the price level is fixed (in the form of price controls) and there is simultaneously an excess supply of money—monetary overhang—and a corresponding excess demand for goods. This phenomenon reflects the shortage of goods in the economy, or the imperfect 'convertibility' of the domestic currency into domestic goods.

In Figure 10.7 we have represented the money market where the demand for money (M^d) is proportional to nominal income, P_y (real income y is assumed to be given). The monetary overhang is measured by the distance GH, and the repressed inflation by the distance HJ, where P_1 is the artificially low price level.

The two extreme solutions for getting rid of the monetary overhang are

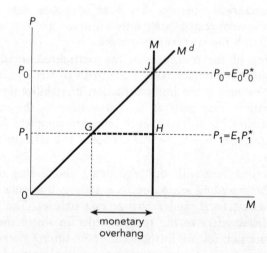

Fig. 10.7. The monetary overhang in socialist economies: open inflation versus currency reform.

At the price level P_1 goods are rationed and the monetary overhang amounts to the distance GH which is equal to the excess demand for goods. With price liberalization, the monetary equilibrium is established either at point J (open inflation with the corresponding exchange rate E_0) or at point G (direct confiscation of the money volume GH with an exchange rate of E_1).

given by the equilibrium situations at point *J* or point *G*. Solution *J* is 'open inflation' (i.e. a once-and-for-all increase in the price level) implying a corresponding fall in the real value of financial assets, in practice, the outstanding volume of M3. Solution *G* is to reduce the nominal quantity of money by the amount *GH*. There are two possible ways of doing this, either freezing parts of the money supply or implementing a currency reform. The freeze in deposits can be accompanied (at either the same time or later) by the forced conversion of the frozen deposits into a government loan or by a voluntary exchange of the frozen deposits for private property titles, which were formerly collective ones. In both cases, the deposits acquired are taken out of circulation. As far as the currency reform is concerned, either an existing currency is chosen (like the DM for the former GDR) or a new currency is created, as in the case of earlier currency reforms in Germany (Box 10.2).[10]

Box 10.2. Three former currency reforms in Germany

Rentenmark 1923
On 23 November 1923 bank notes of paper marks amounted to 224 quadrillion marks (= 224×10^{15} marks). One week earlier, a parallel currency, the rentenmark, had been introduced, which was backed by mortgage bonds denominated in gold marks and yielded an interest rate of 5 per cent. The exchange rate between the two currencies was fixed at 1 billion paper marks for 1 gold mark, with 4.2 gold marks equal to 1 dollar, implying that 4.2 billion paper marks = 4.2 rentenmarks = 1 dollar. The value of the outstanding amount of paper mark notes was only 224 million gold marks (equal to US $53m), because of the hyperinflation implying an extremely high velocity level of paper marks. The total stock of gold held by the Reichsbank was equal to 467 million gold marks. The total amount of the new currency issue was limited to 2.4 billion gold marks—an amount which was ten times higher than the real value of the outstanding volume of paper marks, since a big increase in the demand for gold marks was expected in the following months, which was indeed the case.

and the deutschmark 1948
Twenty-five years later, in June 1948, the second currency reform took place; this replaced reichsmarks (RM) with deutschmarks (DM) at an initial conversion rate of 10 : 1, but half of the outstanding demand deposits were frozen. The main difference between 1948 and 1923 was repressed inflation, resulting from a price and wage freeze, and the rationing of goods and foreign exchange. By the end of June, DM 4.4 billions were circulating in the economy. During the following months the general price level rose by approximately 15 per cent, implying that the former monetary overhang had not been cancelled completely. Consequently, in September 1948, 70 per cent of the frozen deposits were annulled. The conversion rate of RM into DM was finally 10 : 0.65. The stock of money had been cut by 93.5 per cent instead of the planned 90 per cent. In this context it is interesting to note that, in 1946, Lloyd Metzler (1979) calculated for the Colm-Dodge-Goldsmith Committee (whose plan was the basis of the 1948 currency reform) the adequate exchange rate for the deutschmark to be in the range of DM 2.8 and 4.2 per dollar. In June 1948 it was fixed at 3.3 DM and one year later, after the devaluation of the English pound, at DM 4.2, a rate identical to that of the rentenmark in 1923.

... and the ostmark 1948
The currency reform of the deutschmark was implemented on 20 June 1948 in
the three occupational zones of Western Germany. At the very beginning of the
West German currency reform, the Western Allies did not include West Berlin in
the DM area. Because they wished to retain the unified city government, a
uniform currency for Greater Berlin constituted an important condition for
avoiding a political division. On 23 June 1948, the Soviet Marshal Sokolovsky
announced a currency reform for the Soviet occupational zone and Greater
Berlin. The 'coupon mark'—the reichsmark but with a special coupon pasted
on—was introduced, which, some weeks later, was replaced by the 'deutschmark'. Consequently, the uniform currency area of the reichsmark had been split
into two separate currency areas, those of the deutschmark (West) and the
deutschmark (East). On 25 June 1948, the Western occupational authorities
integrated West Berlin into the currency area of Western Germany, but admitted
the ostmark as a restricted parallel legal tender for West Berlin. The immediate
reaction of the Soviets was the blockade of West Berlin (Claassen (1991b): 124–
9).

In the case of open inflation, rising prices do not lower the money supply,
but increase the money demand. The subsequent (hopefully short-lived)
hyperinflation (as in the Polish case) could also be regarded as a (silent)
confiscation of the monetary overhang, since its real value is reduced via the
price level increase. The inflation method ($-\Delta m = M_0/\Delta P$) is usually preferred
to the direct confiscation method ($-\Delta m = -\Delta M/P_0$), since it operates by
deceit on an unsuspecting public.[11]

The Issue of the Nominal Anchor

Among the lessons that could be drawn from open macroeconomics over the
last three decades is the recognition that policy-makers can only fix one
nominal variable, and the others become endogenous as long as markets
clear. According to Robert Mundell (1991), among the nominal variables
that can be chosen as the single exogenous one—which is nothing other
than the nominal anchor of the system—are the quantity of money, the
nominal exchange rate, the price level, and the nominal wage rate. In our
Western industrialized countries, we are normally used to choosing between
the first two variables, i.e. to targeting either the outstanding quantity of
money or the exchange rate.[12] The first monetary system involves a fixed
quantity of money or a fixed growth rate of the money supply (nominal
anchor) and a flexible exchange rate (as in the case of Germany). The second
system is just the contrary, a fixed exchange rate (nominal anchor) and a
flexible quantity of money (as in the case of France).

When the rate of growth of the money supply is fixed, all other nominal
variables have to adjust as endogenous magnitudes: the price level, the nominal
exchange rate, and the nominal wage rate. The money supply target can be

motivated by the ultimate goals of price level stability or low inflation rates. The three current monetary areas in the world economy (the dollar, deutsch mark, and yen areas) could be interpreted as areas where each country fixes the growth rate of its money supply according to what it wants the price level to be, and all other nominal variables float correspondingly.

The second monetary system has a fixed nominal exchange rate, and all other nominal variables float. Its ultimate goals could also be price level stability or the realization of low inflation rates. Since a country can only fix one exchange rate among the $(n\text{-}1)$ independent exchange rates (n representing the number of currencies in the world), it would choose the exchange rate of the country which is its most important trading partner *and* which succeeds relatively well in pursuing price level stability. The evolution of the European Monetary System (EMS) into a German Monetary Area is one striking example of this. The choice between a fixed and a floating exchange rate is not a matter of indifference, if the monetary authorities of the country lack credibility as a consequence of their past, inflation-prone, behaviour. Pegging to the deutsch mark involved following the monetary policy of the Bundesbank which had acquired a high level of credibility with regard to price level stability over the previous four decades.

In the context of the monetary overhang, the exchange rate peg should be established at the same time as the currency reform (E_1 in Fig. 10.7) or, as in the case of an open inflation, when the price level rise comes to an end (E_0 in Fig. 10.7). The exchange rate peg is only a necessary, but not a sufficient, condition for price stability. Inflationary sources other than the monetary overhang also have to be eliminated. The standard example is that of a budget deficit financed by money creation. Another condition concerns the existence of a sufficient volume of international reserves in order to be able to fend off any currency 'attack'.

If the nominal exchange rate is used as the nominal anchor for avoiding inflationary pressure, confidence in the newly convertible currency can only be built up if a future devaluation is absolutely excluded. The currencies of many post-socialist countries, in practice, were newly created ones, as their former status had no 'moneyness'. Their monetary authorities could not rely on any past monetary performance because there was none. Their credibility could only be based on future monetary policy. With a fixed and immovable exchange rate, they were able to take over the credibility of the currency to which they were pegged. This insight is valid, at least for the small open economies of Central Europe and Central Asia, but not necessarily for the big and relatively closed economy of Russia.

Whether the exchange rate (fixed exchange rate) or the growth of the money supply (floating exchange rate) is chosen as the nominal anchor, both cases assume full convertibility of the currencies concerned, at least for current account transactions. The convertibility issue is different from the anchor issue, the latter being raised for a credible anti-inflation policy. The current account convertibility concerns the inexistence of foreign exchange controls for current account transactions and it is independent from the question of fixed versus floating exchange rates. For countries in transition, it is not only important for their gains from international trade, but also for the immediate implementation of the international price structure of tradable goods on the national price structure at the moment when the monetary overhang is eliminated. Thus, the prices of essential consumption goods which were heavily subsidized in former times, will go up and the prices of other consumption goods, mainly of the durable type, which were virtually unavailable in former times, will go down.

The Case of the German Monetary Union

'Eins zu eins,
oder wir werden niemals eins.'

was a slogan heard in Leipzig and Berlin in early 1990.[13] It indicates that Germany's monetary union was an issue concerned with currency unification and country unification. The case of German monetary unification can be conceived of as three separate analytical stages (sequencing), which in reality took place at the same time, but which could have been introduced step by step (timing) as already mentioned. The first stage consisted of the elimination of the monetary overhang by avoiding open inflation. The second stage was to maintain the East German currency, and fix its exchange rate to the West German mark.[14] In the minds of many German economists, including the Council of Economic Advisers (Sachverständigenrat (1990*a*, 1990*b*)), this procedure was the preferred one, since it retained an additional policy instrument in case a change in the foreign exchange rate proved necessary. The third stage, which could have been undertaken several years later, was the conversion of eastmarks into deutschmarks.

The simultaneous adoption of all three actions on 1 July 1990 guaranteed the political unification which followed three months later without having to be passed by a German Confederation. The political unification, in turn, made possible the huge public transfers from West to East Germany which in the years that followed reached a level of about 50 per cent of East German GNP.[15] Without these transfers, the East German fiscal policy reforms, which were needed to avoid monetary financing of budget deficits, would have been more drastic than they were (as in the case of so many other post-socialist countries). The radical timing for the above three stages was to a large extent motivated by the threat of unemployment in West and East (see Box 10.3) if it were not possible to shift the MPL_e-schedule upwards via investment quickly enough.

Box 10.3. The gradual unification of Germany's labour markets

There were three possible outcomes for labour migration after the monetary and political unification. Before migration started, we assume that there was no unemployment in either of the countries—or, in other words, we only measure the unemployment resulting from the opening of both labour markets. The active population in the West (L_w) is measured from left to right and the active population in the East (L_e) from right to left. The marginal productivity of labour in each region is represented by the downward-sloping schedules, MPL_w and MPL_e. Before the fall of the Berlin wall, the distribution of the active population was at L, where labour productivity in the East (point B) was estimated to be one-third of that in West Germany (point A).

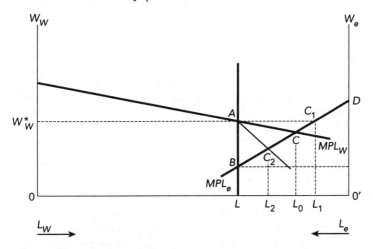

Fig. 10.A. Wage differential and labour migration.

Optimum solution: point C (no unemployment L_0). In opening the West German labour market to the Eastern part, the optimal migration level would have been determined by the intersection point C, at which the marginal labour productivities are equalized. The Eastern labour of LL_0 would have migrated to the West and the whole area would have had a net benefit in terms of an additional *GDP* equal to the triangle ABC. At the same time, a considerable number of Eastern firms which formerly produced BLL_0C of the total Eastern *GDP* would have closed. Eastern *GDP* shrinks to the level of $CL_0O'D$.

Disastrous solution: point C_1 (unemployment LL_1). However, the optimal solution of C was unlikely to happen. What is optimal for both regions taken together is not optimal from the point of view of West German trade unions. The West German level of real wages would have fallen from A to C (but, correspondingly, the real wage level of all East Germans would have risen from B to C). Let us assume that West German trade unions succeeded in maintaining their original real wage level at W^*_w. This outcome was even more likely to occur if it is considered that future West German real wages after taxes would probably decrease by the same amount as the tax burden had to rise to finance some of the public expenditure in the East. With an unchanged real wage rate of W^*_w situation C_1 would have occurred: massive unemployment in both regions (with or without migration) of LL_1, and a total net loss of *GDP* for both regions equal to the area BLL_1C_1.

Intermediate solution: point C_2 (unemployment LL_2). Fortunately, situation C_1 would not have occurred, since, when migrating, Eastern workers had to take the great risk of unemployment into account when seeking to enter the Western labour market. At this stage, we can resort to a model developed by Harris and Todaro (1970) for developing countries, which is concerned with labour migration from a low productivity rural sector to a high productivity urban sector. The main considerations for labour migration are wage differentials, but, in the Harris–Todaro framework, the wage differentials must be the expected, not the effective ones. Applying their model to the German economy, we find that the effective real wage differential is $W^*_w - W_e$ while the probable or expected wage differential is $pW^*_w - W_e$ where p represents the degree of probability of finding a job in the West German economy. The coefficient p can be represented by the ratio of West German employment (E_w) over the total active population in West Germany (L_w). The schedule AC_2 illustrates the evolution of $pW^*_w - W_e$ where p is assumed to fall increasingly with higher migration (the vertical L line shifts to the right in the direction of L_2). The vertical distance between AC and AC_2 represents the shrinking expected wage differential. The (potential) migration stops at point C_2 and unemployment amounts to LL_2. It has to be assumed that Western wages remain at the rigid level W^*_w and that Eastern wages rise from B to C_2. The net loss of GDP for the whole territory is the area BLL_2C_2. Furthermore, it was expected that the monetary and political unification would shift the MPL_e-schedule upwards via investment quickly enough.

The currency reform (stages one to three)—or better, currency reform plus currency unification—can be described as follows (see Table 10.2). East German *flow* magnitudes (prices of goods and incomes) were converted at the ratio of $1:1$, even though it was expected that the prices of most tradable goods would decline (which was the case except for subsidized 'essential' goods like food) and that incomes would remain constant or even fall (which was a pious hope). The monetary overhang eliminated was 93 bn. eastmarks from a total outstanding quantity of M3-money of 249 bn. eastmarks. The subsequent overall conversion rate for the money *stock* was 1.60 eastmark for one deutschmark. However, for social considerations, one-third of the money holdings by households was converted at the preferential rate of $1:1$. The remaining East German money holdings, including those of firms, were converted at the rate of $2:1$.[16]

Two considerations dominated the discussion about the appropriate conversion rate, the elimination of the monetary overhang and the elimination of the debt overhang. As far as the evaluation of the size of the monetary overhang is concerned, the same liquidity preference for East Germany as for West Germany was assumed (Box. 10.4). While the West German ratio of M3 over GDP would have increased the actual conversion rate of 1.60 to $1.85:1$, the West German ratio of M3 over disposable income would have resulted in a conversion rate of $1.66:1$, which was close to the actual one.[17]

Table 10.2. The conversion of eastmarks into deutschmarks (M3), July 1990

	Amount in billions of eastmarks	Conversion rate	Amount in billions of deutschmarks
Deposits (households)	167.9[a]	1.44:1	116.3
1. Deposits of 4,000 eastmarks per resident from age 14 to 60	40.4	1:1	40.4
2. Deposits of 2,000 eastmarks per child younger than 14	6.4	1:1	6.4
3. Deposits of 6,000 eastmarks per resident over 60	18.0	1:1	18.0
4. Remaining deposits of residents	100.8	2:1	50.4
5. Deposits of non-residents at 31.12.1989	2.1	2:1	1.0
6. Remaining deposits of non-residents at 1.7.1990	0.2	3:1	0.1
Cash (households)	13.6	2:1	6.8
M3 (households)	181.5	1.47:1	123.1
Deposits (firms)[b]	57.0	2.05:1	27.8
Deposits (government)	10.8	2:1	5.4
M3	249.3	1.60:1	156.3
Monetary overhang (total)	93.0		
Households	58.4		
Firms	29.2		
Government	5.4		

[a] Excludes deposits of households with life insurance companies (14.2 bn. marks).
[b] Additional deposits of firms accumulated since January 1990 were converted at the rate 3:1.
Sources: Deutsche Bundesbank (1990), no. 6 (June), no. 7 (July), and no. 10 (October). Schinasi *et al.* (1990: 144–7).

Box. 10.4. The calculation of required M3 DM-volume for East Germany, 1 July 1990

I. *Basis: Ratio M3 to GDP of West Germany*
  1. Ratio M3 to GDP of West Germany in 1989 (in DM bn.): 1,225.4/2,219.4 = 0.556.
  2. GDP of East Germany in 1990: 238.5 bn. eastmarks.
  3. Required M3 volume: 0.556 × 238.5 = DM 134.9 bn. which required the conversion rate: 249.3/134.9 = 1.85/1.
  4. Monetary overhang: 249.3 − 134.9 = 114.4 bn. eastmarks (instead of 93).

II. *Basis: Ratio M3 to Disposable Income of West Germany*
  1. Ratio M3 to disposable income of West Germany in 1989 (in DM bn.): 1,255.4/1,403.8 = 0.894.
  2. Disposable income in East Germany in 1989: 167.5 bn. eastmarks.
  3. Required M3 volume: 0.894 × 167.5 = DM 149.8 bn. which required the conversion rate: 249.3/149.8 = 1.66/1.
  4. Monetary overhang: 249.3 − 149.8 = 99.5 bn. eastmarks (instead of 93).

The position of the Bundesbank was mainly guided by the debt overhang of commercial banks. In fact, their loans were converted at the rate 2:1. However, the Bundesbank did not succeed in imposing the same conversion rate for the liability side. Consequently, banks' assets were less than their deposit liabilities, and public authorities provided DM 27 bn. to the banking system as 'equalization claims'.[18]

The most decisive argument for the German Monetary Union, and thus against all other solutions, was precisely its radical form as opposed to more gradual measures. It could be argued that the choice of a radical versus a gradual reform programme would be a matter of indifference if the results were identical except for timing. However, during the adjustment process, radical programmes may be more credible than gradual ones, since the latter, in particular in democracies, can always be altered, attenuated, and uncertain, so that their final outcome is less satisfactory. One of the ultimate economic reasons for Germany's radical timing of the stabilization policies was the unified labour market, which constituted an enormous threat of increasing unemployment in East and West.

Real Exchange Rate

The main argument against the German currency unification was that East Germany would lose an essential policy instrument, namely the foreign exchange rate whose existence would be required in the case of a necessary devaluation. The case for a devaluation can be made with the following typical scenario. There is a shock in the labour market in the form of an excessive rise in nominal wages which exceeds gains in labour productivity. The increase in real wages over productivity could only be neutralized by higher product prices. However, the rise in prices would have a lasting impact on the competitiveness of the domestic tradable goods sector with respect to foreign tradable goods and only a devaluation could avoid the loss in international competitiveness. This type of devaluation was used in the Polish case in May 1991 and also again later. East Germany was deprived of such an adjustment mechanism. The rise of East German wages from one-third to one-half of the West German wage level during 1990/1, and to 80 per cent by 1992/3, could not have been accommodated by higher inflation rates and a corresponding devaluation rate. The outcome was still higher unemployment in East Germany and more migration to the West.

What a devaluation can also achieve is a change in the real exchange rate, defined as the relative price of tradable and non-tradable goods. However, for all formerly socialist countries, this type of real exchange rate (e_2) necessitates rather a real appreciation and not a real depreciation which is of primary concern.

Thus, in early 1991, people from East Berlin who used the local transport system in West and East Berlin still paid one-tenth of the price paid by people from West Berlin. Similar ratios existed for postal services and energy prices.

For housing, rents diverged by one-tenth and one-twentieth. The price liberalization for non-tradable goods would have considerably lowered the real purchasing power of salaries within the tradables sector, bringing with it the danger of higher wage claims in this sector, and higher unemployment. This is why many governments in post-socialist countries postponed the price rise for non-tradables relative to tradables (a real appreciation).

In Fig. 10.8 we have again illustrated the price levels of tradable (P_T) and non-tradable goods (P_N). The relative price of the two categories of goods, which is the real exchange rate (q), is represented by the slope of the Oq_0 ray. The equilibrium schedule of the money market is MM. When we analysed the stabilization policies in terms of currency reform versus open inflation, the macroeconomic equilibrium was reached at point A for Eastern Germany (a currency reform with the new money stock MM_1) and at point B for countries like Poland which opted for open inflation. The real exchange rate (q_0) is still a disequilibrium one. A real appreciation (q_1) is needed which would change the production structure in favour of non-tradable goods.

In the case of East Germany, the price level of non-tradables has to rise by AD. Consequently, the quantity of money has to increase such that the new MM_1 schedule passes through point D. There are two ways for other countries that have pursued open inflation and maintained their proper currencies

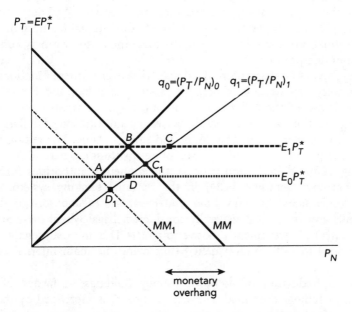

Fig. 10.8. Post-Socialist Countries: The need for real appreciation

The need for real appreciation means a gradual liberalization of certain prices of non-tradable goods. In the case of a currency reform, the real appreciation takes place from A to D (or to D_1). In the case of an open inflation, the adjustment takes place from point B to C (or to C_1).

(point *B*), to realize the real appreciation, namely point *C* or point C_1. Solution C_1 implies a fall in P_T via a nominal revaluation and an increase in P_N so that the general price level would remain unchanged. Solution *C* is analogous to the German case. The quantity of money has to increase and the new *MM*-schedule has to pass through point *C*.

10.5. Stabilization under Dollarization

Stylized Sequencing of Dollarization

The phenomenon of dollarization represents a particular type of currency substitution referred to as 'asymmetrical'. Residents hold domestic and foreign money simultaneously, and there is no demand for domestic money by non-residents. The reason for the asymmetry is the sharp difference of quality between the two currencies. The domestic money is a weak currency and often even inconvertible, whereas the foreign money is a hard currency.[19] Since World War II, the most common foreign currency used has been the US dollar.

The fundamental reason for the dollarization of an economy is the low degree of 'moneyness' for the domestic currency. It cannot be attributed to any hegemonic intentions coming from the United States. It is 'imposed' by the general public as a 'market-enforced monetary reform' (Melvin, 1988) and tolerated by the government. It is a response to the internal financial instability and high inflation which, in turn, are the outcome of the wrongly conducted macroeconomic policies.

In the process of dollarization, the dollar takes over all three functions of the domestic currency: as unit of account, a store of value, and a medium of exchange. However, the dollar-monetization process is a gradual one and, with increasing inflation rates, first mainly causes the substitution of dollars for the domestic currency as a unit of account and store of value. The reason for this particular sequencing is, in most cases, of an institutional nature. At the very beginning of the dollarization process, the monetary authorities forbid any foreign currency deposits (FCD) in the national banking system. Consequently, individuals can only hold dollar banknotes and foreign deposits with banks abroad. This is generally considered illegal where there are strict capital controls. Government's motive to ban FCD is the maintenance of the inflation-tax base—the budget deficit thus being the main internal cause of inflation.

Thus, the reduction of domestic money holdings in favour of dollar holdings, including those held with banks abroad, is motivated by the inflation hedge. Payment is made in the weak domestic currency and dollars are held as a store of value (Gresham's Law). Typically, at the early stage of dollarization, the exchange rate with the dollar remains fixed, and the monetary authorities lose international reserves. Over time, the exchange rate becomes more and more overvalued. Despite strict exchange controls, the public succeeds in increasing its dollar holdings either via official transactions (a decline in international reserves) or via unofficial transactions on the parallel market for foreign exchange, which give rise to an unofficial current account surplus.

As inflation continues at double-digit levels, a currency float (or a crawling peg) becomes necessary to avoid further reserve losses. At the same time (or when devaluation occurs), the ban on FCD is lifted, since government expects the conversion of dollar banknotes into (interest-bearing) FCD and the repatriation of at least some of foreign currency deposits abroad.[20] At that very moment, stage II of the dollarization process begins. Dollars are now also held as the medium of exchange for domestic transactions. Dollar quotations for key prices also become fairly general. Since the exchange rate regime with the dollar has become flexible, good money (dollars) will now drive out bad money and the dollarization process spreads faster (reversal of Gresham's Law).[21]

Stage III of the dollarization process concerns the stabilization phase of the dollarized economy. Figuring among the various policy measures is the choice of the nominal anchor. In principle, either the growth rate of the money supply or the exchange rate to the dollar could be fixed. Dollarization limits the option in favour of an exchange rate based stabilization programme. If the programme is successful, a process of de-dollarization may emerge provided that the domestic currency offers more advantages and that one is not confronted by the phenomenon of hysteresis (irreversibility).

Is Dollarization Inflationary?

It is probably this aspect which makes politicians and central bankers feel uneasy about the phenomenon of dollarizaton. On the one hand, an increase in the domestic component of the money supply is transmitted automatically to the foreign component via the exchange rate mechanism: a higher supply of pesos or roubles → higher domestic price level → depreciation of the domestic currency → higher domestic value of the outstanding volume of dollars. However, this money-supply-amplification impact does not necessarily mean an extra inflationary impact since the demand for the foreign component of the money supply rises by the same amount. This demand reaction, expressed in domestic currency, means nothing other than an unchanged demand for dollars.

Box 10.5. Dollarization in Russia

The dollar was already circulating in the various economies of Eastern Europe and the CIS when the transition to market economies began, and its use was intensified by open inflation. Since estimates of cash are vague, dollarization can only be measured when dollar currency deposits are tolerated by government, and when these can be used officially as a parallel means of payment.

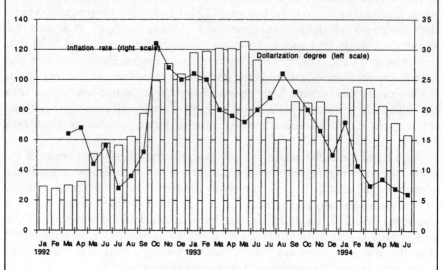

Fig. 10.B. Dollar deposits over rouble deposits and monthly inflation rates (CPI), January 1992–June 1994.
Sources: Claassen (1994*b*) and Granville (1995).

For Russia, the ratio of dollar deposits to rouble deposits rose from 30 per cent (January 1992) to the maximum of 120 per cent (first half of 1993) and then declined over time to 60 per cent in mid-1994 (Fig. 10.*B*). This rise and fall are rather symmetrical to the evolution of the monthly inflation rate. The initial jump of dollarization began mid-1992, when the exchange rates were unified. Its subsequent intensification may be explained by high negative monthly real interest rates on rouble deposits. On the other hand, as Fig. 10.*C* shows, the ratio of rouble deposits to GDP declined steadily, at least until March 1994, when monthly inflation rates began to be single digit.

No assessment can be made as to whether most of the dollars were held by enterprises or the urban population. Furthermore, one should expect that, for a given high inflation rate, the degree of dollarization is lower in a large country like Russia than in the small countries of Eastern Europe and the CIS. In a large country the exchange rate (or a foreign currency) plays a less important role than in a small country. An example is Brazil, where the economy was 'indexed' when Argentina or Bolivia were 'dollarized'. This difference can be important for exchange rate based stabilization policies. An exchange rate peg could be more successful in combating inflation in small countries than in a country like Russia.

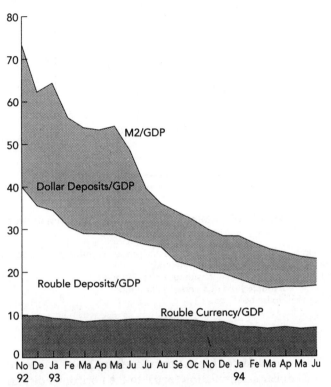

Fig. 10.C. Russia: Monetary aggregates as a percentage of GDP, November 1992–June 1994.
Note: M2 stands for FCD/MZ. M3 stands for (FCD + FCDA)/M3.
Source: Claassen (1994a) and Granville (1995).

On the other hand, the definite inflationary impact in a dollarized economy—for instance, the Russian economy (see Box 10.5) and, in particular, Fig. 10.C)—arises from the fact that the demand for real rouble holdings falls much more in a dollarized economy than in one without dollarization. Fig. 10.9 illustrates this point. The schedule d^d is the demand for real rouble holdings without dollarization and d^d_1 represents the demand for real rouble holdings under the regime of dollarization. The horizontal distance between d^d and d^d_1 indicates the inflationary impact of dollarization. Consequently, the additional price level push of a dollarized economy does originate on the demand side for roubles and not on the supply side.

There are two forces working on currency substitution in favour of dollar holdings (f^d). The first (f_1) is the replacement of rouble holdings by dollar holdings which is equal to the horizontal distance between d^d and d^d_1. However, because the nominal amount of roubles does not disappear, its real value declines (by the amount of f_1) through an additional jump in the

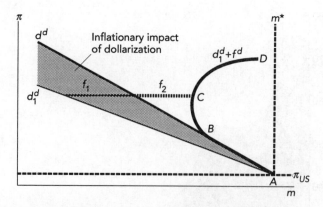

Fig. 10.9. The impact of dollarization on inflation and the demand for real dollar holdings

The inflationary impact of dollarization concerns the 'proper' currency substitution $d^d - d^d_1 = f_1$. The additional dollarization (f_2) is inflation-neutral.
d^d = demand for real rouble holdings without dollarization
d^d_1 = demand for real rouble holdings under dollarization
f^d = demand for real dollar holdings

price level. The second force (f_2), in operation from point B onwards, consists of an additional dollar accumulation (equal to the horizontal distance between BCD and d^d) to reconstitute part of the real cash balances m^*, which would have been held at a hypothetical domestic inflation rate equal to the US inflation rate π_{US}.[22] The additional real dollar holdings of f_2 are inflation-neutral (where $f^d = f_1 + f_2$).[23]

The usual and also correct view of dollarization's impact on inflation is that currency substitution reduces the inflation tax-base in terms of lower real rouble holdings. If the government cannot reduce its budget deficit, it is forced to increase the inflation rate to realize the same inflation tax revenue as before dollarization. Thus, dollarization may lead to higher inflation, even though the ultimate cause of the additional inflationary impulse is not dollarization but the unchanged budget deficit.[24]

Exchange Rate Overshooting in a Dollarized Economy

The phenomenon of overshooting can emerge in a dollarized economy, satisfying the value component of increasingly desired dollar holdings. By expressing the real value of the quantity of dollars (F) in terms of the domestic currency (f), we obtain:

$$f = \frac{EF}{P} = eF \qquad (10.6)$$

$$\Delta f = F\Delta e + e\Delta F \qquad (10.7)$$

where e is the real exchange rate.[25] The additional demand for real dollar holdings can be matched by the *value component* (Δe) implying a real depreciation of the rouble with respect to the dollar or by the *volume component* (ΔF).

There are several ways in which the public (i.e. the non-government, non-banking sector) could acquire ΔF.[26] One possibility would be to obtain them through the depletion of international reserves held by the central bank—a procedure implying currency convertibility. Another mechanism would be the indebtedness of the public with respect to foreign countries, which implies that the private sector has access to international credit markets. This assumption is rather bold for high inflationary countries. Finally, the third way, which we shall discuss in some detail, is the realization of a current account surplus within a floating exchange rate regime either in the official market or in the parallel market for foreign exchange.[27]

In principle, a current account surplus could be brought about by a reduction in absorption. When the additional demand for dollars 'financed' by the decline in absorption (for instance, a decline in consumption) first appears, the foreign exchange market will react with a real depreciation. The immediate impact of the real depreciation is an increase in the value component (Δe) of real dollar holdings, so that the additional demand for dollars is satisfied. However, subsequently, the real depreciation would also provide a current account surplus, which affects the volume component (ΔF) of real dollar holdings, and which would reverse the real depreciation. These two effects are limited in time. If the higher demand for real dollar holdings represents a stock adjustment from a lower to a higher desired level of real dollar holdings, the real depreciation will only occur during the stock adjustment process and will afterwards return to its initial level.

The argument is illustrated with the help of Fig. 10.10.[28] The equilibrium in the current account (line $CA = 0$) is established at the real exchange rate level e_0.[29] The second schedule, the curve f_0, is a rectangular hyperbola, indicating a constant level for f with different combinations of e and F. The level of the f_0 schedule reflects a given liquidity preference for real dollar holdings. It is drawn for a given inflation rate (π_0). The demand for real dollar holdings (f) depends on exchange rate expectations. At point A an equality between the expected and actual real exchange rates is assumed. Since f also depends on the inflation rate, the liquidity schedule will be at a higher level (f_1) when the domestic inflation rate increases ($\pi_1 > \pi_0$).[30]

At point A, and for the inflation rate π_0, the demand for real dollar holdings is satisfied ($f_0 = e_0F_0$) and the current account is in equilibrium. An increase in the domestic inflation rate from π_0 to π_1 shifts the dollar demand schedule

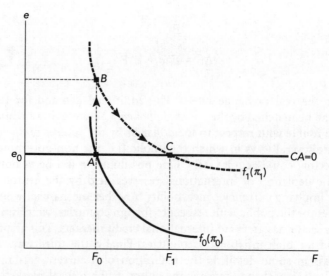

Fig. 10.10. The impact of dollarization on the real exchange rate

Any point above the line of the current account balance ($CA = 0$) represents a surplus. The liquidity preference curve for real dollar holdings (f_0) indicates a constant amount of real dollars ($f_0 = eF$) which is the desired one. The initial equilibrium is at point A. A higher liquidity preference for dollars as a consequence of a higher domestic inflation ratre π_1) shifts f_0 to f_1. The excess demand for dollars is satisfied immediately by the real depreciation (point b). The subsequent current account surplus (movement from B to C) increases the physical component of dollar holdings and diminishes their value component (real appreciation).

upwards to the position $f_1\,(\pi_1)$. The nominal exchange rate rises by $dE/E = dE/E)_1 + (dE/E)_2$ where $(dE/E)_1 = \pi_1$ (at point A) and $(dE/E)_2 = (de/e)$ (point B). The overshooting of the nominal exchange (above the domestic inflation rate) signifies the real depreciation of the domestic currency. This depreciation is necessary to satisfy the additional demand for real dollar holdings immediately via their value component ($\Delta f = F\Delta e$). Subsequently, the current account reacts to the real depreciation and produces a surplus. These additional 'physical' dollars create an excess supply of dollars so that the initial real depreciation of AB is slightly reversed by a nominal appreciation. The adjustment process comes to an end at point C, where $f_1 - f_0 = e_0\,(F_1 - F_0)$.

Exchange Rate Based Stabilization under Dollarization

In the present context, the targets of stabilization policies will be restricted mainly to the inflation issue. Among the various policy instruments—monetary or fiscal policies—particular attention will be given to the exchange rate instrument within a dollarized economy. The choice has to be made between two possible monetary anchors: the growth rate of the domestic money supply (which represents the single solution for a closed economy) and the exchange rate peg. An exchange rate peg with the US dollar would be the most credible outcome in a dollarized economy for reducing present and future inflationary expectations, provided that all other aggregates (budget, credit constraints, social safety net . . .) are under control. However, as we already mentioned in the context of Russia, one constraint in particular has to be taken into account. For a large country like Russia—unlike in small economies—it is not evident that the dollar is used by the majority of the population as a (parallel) unit of account, a store of value, and (whether tolerated by government or not) as a medium of exchange.

Box 10.6. Dollarization in Bolivia

Bolivia experienced two dollarization periods. the first one began in 1973 and ended in 1982 with forced conversion from foreign currency deposits (FCD) to domestic currency deposits (DCD) at a confiscatory exchange rate. The authorization of FCD holdings in October 1973 was aimed at repatriating capital outflows. It ended in November 1982 in order to stop capital outflows and the *official* dollarization plummeted to zero.

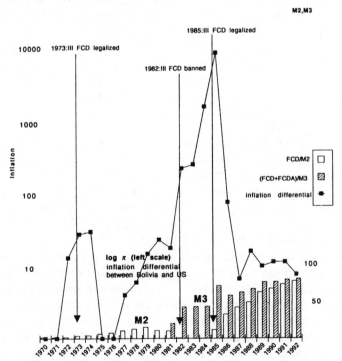

Fig. 10.D. Bolivia: foreign currency deposits (FCD) and foreign currency deposits abroad (FCDA), FCD/M2 and (FCD + FCDA)/M3, 1970–1992.
Source: Claassen and de la Cruz Martinez (1994).

The second dollarization episode was part of the stabilization programme implemented in September 1985. In August 1985 with an inflation rate above 10,000 per cent the official exchange rate was 67,000 pesos per dollar and the black market rate was at a monthly average of 1.1 million pesos per dollar. The black market rate shot up to 1.5 million pesos just before the announcement of the unification of the two exchange rates. When the rates were unified and fluctuated freely, the market exchange rate was at a level of about 1.1 million. The new peg was set officially at this rate and dollar holdings were authorized, but not as a means of payment. See Sachs (1986: 29). Towards the end of 1987, foreign currency checking deposits were also permitted. Thus, by 1987, the dollar was 'officialized' not only as a unit of account and store of value, but also as a means of payment. Despite extremely low inflation rates in the late 1980s and early 1990s, the dollarization was intensified.

In a small dollarized economy the exchange rate peg with the US dollar represents a stronger stability anchor than in a non-dollarized economy since everybody is acquainted with the parallel currency. Even if dollars were officially banned, they would continue to be used in the underground sector, with a corresponding parallel exchange rate. When the anti-inflationary programme is announced, it could be combined with legal dollarization and with fixing the exchange rate around the parallel market rate (as in Bolivia in September 1985; see Box 10.6). This fixed rate will probably be highly under-valued. However, there are still inflationary sources which are active and arise from the money expansion created in the months before the implementation of the stabilization programme. Consequently, prices will still rise over a couple of months making the currency less undervalued (as was the case in Poland in early 1990).

An exchange rate based stabilization programme can include a variety of commitments as credibility indicators for future exchange rate policy and, thus, for the success of an anti-inflation policy. If the commitment to a fixed exchange rate rule is very strong, the costs of deviating from it are very high, and the government will hesitate to modify the exchange rate. Consequently, the programme becomes more credible since the public knows the higher cost associated with reneging on the exchange rate rule.[31]

The weakest commitment (point A in Fig 10.11) consists of fixing the exchange rate with no promise to maintain the fixed exchange rate in future (see Brazil's Cruzado plan of 1986).[32] A stabilization programme with some minimum commitment (point B) would be a fixed exchange rate combined with fiscal reform, and the commitment not to finance the budget deficit through money creation any more (see Argentina's Austral plan of 1985). Such a programme would become even more credible, if an independent central bank were set up. A still stronger commitment (point C) would be a fixed exchange rate combined with the legal obligation that an increase of the monetary base is only the outcome of an increase in international reserves (as

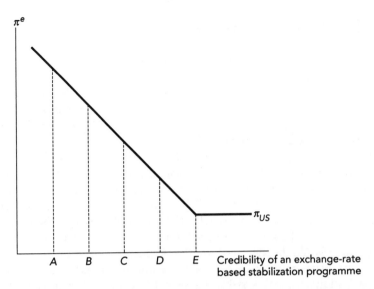

Fig. 10.11. Credibility of an exchange-rate based stabilization programme with and without dollarization

Commitment A: A fixed exchange rate
Commitment B: Legal exclusion of monetary finance of the budget deficit
Commitment C: Full backing of the monetary base by foreign assets and full convertibility
Commitment D: The US dollar as a parallel currency with legal tender
Commitment E: US dollar as a single currency
A price level stabilization programme opting for a fixed exchange rate can be accompanied by several other commitments in order to reduce credibly the expected inflation rate (π^e). The strongest commitment is dollarization in the form of the US dollar as a parallel currency or a fortiori as a single currency.

in Argentina's convertibility programme of 1991) or to fully back the monetary base with international reserves.[33]

The strongest commitment would be dollarization either in its weaker form (point D) of accepting the dollar as a parallel currency, possibly with legal tender, or in its stronger form (point E) of using the dollar as the single currency. If, at some future time, there are external shocks which necessitate the disposal of the exchange rate tool, government would be forced to resist the re-establishment of a domestic currency standard for a long time.[34] The option of full dollarization as a policy of price level stabilization was not chosen by the European hyperinflating countries after World War I and World War II[35] nor by any highly inflationary Latin American country recently.

Dollarization and De-dollarization

Views about the optimal degree of dollarization range from the extreme idea of 'full dollarization' to the extreme of the exclusive use of the domestic currency. Some economists consider that revenue from seigniorage is the main argument for maintaining the national currency.[36] Others argue that national pride and national self-preservation are an important factor (and probably they are) in maintaining monetary sovereignty.[37]

The optimum number of currencies for an economy would be one, under the condition that monetary policy provided price stability (see Section 9.3). With high price instability, stable parallel currencies will emerge and the optimum number of currencies will be two, the domestic currency and, in the case of Latin America or the CIS, the dollar. We exclude the option of a single currency in the form of a fully (100 per cent) dollarized economy since the country would be deprived of the exchange rate tool as an ultimate adjustment instrument for cases of adverse internal or external shocks.

Dollarization also bears risks. These risks relate to the possibility of an amplification of inflation. If a stabilization-cum-dollarization programme were introduced unsuccessfully, higher dollarization, as the combined result of higher inflation rates and lower demand for domestic real cash balances, would produce an additional jump in the price level. A very strong argument against dollarization concerns the vulnerability of the banking system.[38] Since the US central bank does not act as lender of last resort for foreign banks, any run on an individual bank can provoke a liquidity crisis for the total banking system and it can collapse.

There is some probability that even a successful stabilization programme will not lead to a de-dollarization process (see the case of Bolivia after 1987 in Box 10.6). This is the phenomenon of hysteresis (or irreversibility). Under these circumstances, the domestic currency has to become better than the dollar over a long period.[39] With a sounder national currency, even hysteresis may become reversible.

10.6. The Debt Problem

The Pattern of Indebtedness

A current account deficit can be financed by an increase in net foreign debt, ΔD (capital balance surplus), and/or by a decrease in international reserves (balance of payments deficit). If the international reserves of the debtor country remain unchanged, we have

$$\Delta D \qquad = \qquad Im - X \qquad + \qquad rD \qquad\qquad (10.8)$$

capital	trade	net factor
balance	balance deficit	payments deficit
surplus		

current account balance deficit

In the absence of any further increase in net foreign debt ($\Delta D = 0$ in equation (10.8)), the interest payments to foreigners (rD) have to be financed by a corresponding trade balance surplus ($X - Im$), as we already explained in Section 8.1, which means the net transfer of resources from the debtor country to the creditor countries. The above situation in the balance of payments also means that the national product (GNP) is lower than the domestic product (GDP) by the amount of net factor payments abroad.

Since the current account deficit ($Im - X + rD$) of equation (10.8) is also equal to the savings gap (investment minus national savings; see also Box 10.1), the evolution of investment and savings will determine the time path of foreign indebtedness.[40] Thus, the current account deficit must be equal to the domestic savings gap (in private and public sectors):

$$\Delta D = Im - X + rD = I - S_n \qquad (10.8a)$$

or

$$\Delta D/Y = I/Y - S_n/Y \qquad (10.8b)$$

S_n has to be interpreted as national savings.

In Fig. 10.12a we have illustrated the propensity to save (S_n/Y) and the propensity to invest (I/Y) as functions of the long-run level of income. Thus, a 'young country', which has high investment requirements and very low saving resources, will borrow heavily abroad. If the investment requirements are very high relative to the domestic saving resources, indebtedness will rise, and over a certain time, the growth rate of debt will exceed the growth rate of income (up to the point M in Fig. 10.12b, where the ratio D/Y has reached its maximum value, $(D/Y)_{max}$). With efficient investments, the growth rate of the domestic product will rise, involving an increasingly higher volume of domestic savings, and thus eventually closing the savings gap. The rise in foreign debt will then reach a maximum (point A in Fig. 10.12b) and decline if savings exceed investment. As soon as it has repaid all its outstanding (net) debt (point B), the country will become a 'mature country' acting as a net lender to foreign countries.

Steady State Limits to Indebtedness

In a growing economy (see Claassen, 1985b) the foreign debt can rise continuously provided that the (real) interest rate is less than, or equal to, the

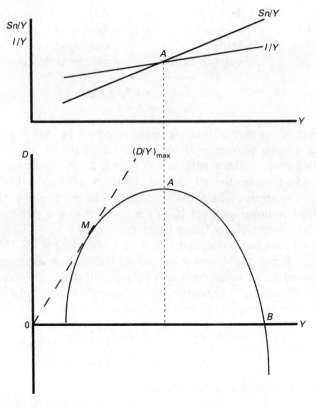

Fig. 10.12. The pattern of indebtedness

A 'young' country (i.e. a country with a low income level) has a low savings ratio and a high investment ratio which results in foreign indebtedness. From point A onwards, the country re-imburses its debt. At point B, the country becomes a net creditor.

Fig. 10.12a. The evolution of $\Delta D/Y = I/Y - S_n/Y$

Fig. 10.12b. The evolution of D and D/Y

marginal productivity of capital (MPK), and that the growth rate of foreign debt ($\Delta D/D$) is less than, or equal to, the growth rate of the domestic product (g):

$$\Delta D/D = (Im - X)/D + r \qquad (10.9)$$

No debt problem if $r \leqslant MPK$, $\Delta D/D \leqslant g$ and $r > g$.

Equation (10.9) corresponds to equation (10.8) but it has been divided by D. While the equality of the interest rate with the marginal productivity of capital represents the standard investment rule, the other two requirements, $\Delta D/D \leqslant g$ and $r > g$, must be discussed in further detail.[41]

If foreign debt grew at a faster rate than g, there would be a steadily rising D/Y ratio resulting in a debt explosion during the steady state. The outstanding volume of foreign debt would not only exceed the country's collateral, but national income would eventually become negative at an amount equal to the difference between *GDP* and the interest payments on debt.

Assuming that $\Delta D/D = g$ (implying a constant D/Y ratio), the equality of the real interest rate with the growth rate of real domestic income means that all interest payments due to foreigners are financed by additional foreign indebtedness ($\Delta D/D = r$ or $\Delta D = rD$). Consequently, the trade balance must be in equilibrium $[(Im - X)/D = 0)]$. Thus, the interest incomes are re-invested in the borrowing country, so that the country never pays back the principal or the interest. From the point of view of the creditor, a loan will never be granted if it is known that the debt service will never be honoured.[42] If $r > g$ and assuming again $\Delta D/D = g$, the debtor country pays one part of its interest service by a trade balance surplus.

The Emergence of a Debt Problem

From a purely economic point of view, a very high debt-income ratio would not harm the borrowing country, provided that the interest rate is not above the marginal productivity capital, and that the growth rate of foreign debt is not higher than the growth rate of domestic income, at least over a very long period. Thus, for instance, a debt-income ratio of 30 per cent is no more alarming than a lower debt-income ratio and no less alarming than a debt-income ratio of 100 per cent or 200 per cent. The essential prerequisite for any high debt-income ratio to be economically neutral would be that the foreign debt is used for productive domestic investment.

Assuming $\Delta D/D = g$ and ignoring the steady state, a debt problem arises when (*ex post*) the marginal productivity of capital is lower than the real interest rate. Assume further that, over a certain time period, the real interest rate may exceed the growth rate of real income. In this case the trade balance must be in surplus ($(Im - X) > 0$) according to equation (10.9)—at least at the moment when the international reserves are exhausted. Under these circumstances the new foreign debt (growing at the same rate as income) finances only some of the interest payments due to foreign countries. The rest must effectively be paid through an internal adjustment which produces a trade balance surplus.

For the very extreme case of a zero growth rate in real income, no additional foreign debt may be available to the debtor country. All interest payments must be covered by a corresponding trade balance surplus ($rD = X - Im$). It should be emphasized that (particularly in the case of zero income growth) the debt problem arises because of the internal adjustment burden, according to which the absorption has to be reduced by the amount of the interest payments due abroad. In this specific context, the most important indicator of a debt problem is the ratio of interest payments to income (*GDP*). It was 5 per cent or more for some Latin American countries in the early 1980s (see Box 10.7), involving a reduction in absorption by the same percentage (assuming the trade balance to be in equilibrium before the internal adjustment measures were implemented).

Box 10.7. The Latin American debt problem of the 1980s

This was not only explicable by the reduction of the real growth rate, but *a fortiori* by the evolution of the *ex post* real interest rate. The low real growth rate was an outcome of the low *ex post* marginal productivity of capital, since many investment programmes proved to be inefficient. For existing debts, which had been negotiated in the past, the relevant real interest rate—in an inflationary environment—became the *ex post* real interest rate ($r_{ex\ post}$) which is equal to the nominal market interest ($i = r + \pi^e$ where π^e represents the expected inflation rate) minus the actual inflation rate (π). Since most of the debt contracts were in terms of the US dollar, the relevant nominal interest rate was the US market interest rate (prime rate plus a country-risk premium). Consequently, the historically high level of the US interest rate, observable in the early 1980s, implied a corresponding increase in the interest service on the Latin American debt, at least for those credit contracts which were short term or had a variable interest rate clause. A high nominal interest rate on the one hand, and a relatively low actual inflation rate on the other hand, had pushed up the real burden of the interest service abruptly (and *a fortiori* of debt service) to an extremely high level since 1980–1 (see Sjaastad, 1983) so that $MPK_{ex\ post} < r_{ex\ post}$. The extremely high *ex post* real interest rate necessitated an enormous trade balance surplus with a corresponding reduction in absorption to pay the high real value of interest payments due to foreigners. Since such an internal adjustment was considered too harmful and as a possible cause of political and social unrest, a proper mix between external financing and internal adjustment (trade balance surplus) had to be found for each particular country.

   . . . and in the 1930s. Starting in 1931, many Latin American countries suspended their debt service and asked for their debts to be rescheduled. These negotiations stretched on as far as the 1940s. Some defaulted officially on part of their outstanding debt by repurchasing their own (partially or wholly unserviced) *bonds* which were exchanged at a discount in foreign markets. Whether this partial default resulted from the virtual impossibility of paying the debt service (i.e. the case of insolvency) or from a well calculated debt repudiation as there were no sanctions, is a question that remains open in the literature.[43]

Debt Repudiation

The debtor who defaults on foreign debt can be the government or one of the country's many government agencies (including nationalized enterprises) or private firms whose foreign debts are guaranteed by the government authorities. The default can result from debt confiscation. While internal government debt confiscation can take a variety of forms (open debt repudiation, permanent debt rescheduling with low interest charges, continuous erosion of the real value of fixed interest yielding debt through inflation), external government debt confiscation involves the repudiation of foreign debt. Debt repudiation refers to the borrower's *unwillingness* to service the debt, while illiquidity and insolvency imply his *incapacity* to do so (Aliber, 1980).

A government can repudiate its debt even when there is no problem of solvency and liquidity. As Eaton and Gersovitz (1981) and Sachs (1984) have shown, repudiation can be seen as resulting from cost–benefit analysis. The benefit consists of not having to pay the outstanding debt and the interest payments. The costs are the exclusion from the international credit market, at least for a certain time, confiscation of the debtor country's overseas assets (financial assets, physical assets like direct foreign investments, aircraft, ships, export shipments), exclusion from foreign trade, or limited bilateral foreign trade because trade credit will not be available. The debt repudiation will take place when the benefits exceed the present value of the expected costs. The declaration of default as a result of debt repudiation is made unilaterally, while the declaration of default as a result of a situation of insolvency may be negotiated with the creditors.[44]

Illiquidity versus Insolvency

A debtor country is illiquid when it cannot service its foreign debt in the present, but it can do so in the future. The situation of illiquidity and insolvency means that the country cannot pay its debt service either now or in the future. There is no doubt that there is some (or even much) ambiguity in the notion of insolvency of a country compared to insolvency of an individual or of a firm (see Claassen, 1985c and Box 10.8).

Box 10.8. Illiquidity versus insolvency of individual firms

Illiquidity of a firm has two distinct features. On the one hand, the net worth of the firm is positive, i.e. the value of its assets exceeds its liabilities. On the other hand, there is a shortage of liquidity, in the sense that the firm's cash flows are not sufficient to meet its contractual payments. The basic reason for this lack of cash flow is that the firm's liabilities are maturing faster than its assets. Consequently, a firm's liquidity problem (sometimes called also 'technical insolvency') is a maturity problem and not a value problem. The firm's illiquidity does not necessarily imply bankruptcy as long as the credit market correctly evaluates the firm's positive value as a going concern.

   Insolvency of a firm is a situation where its liabilities exceed the value of its assets so that the net worth of the firm is negative. Insolvency means bankruptcy. However, there is still the question of whether the bankrupt firm should be reorganized and allowed to operate during the reorganization, or whether it should be liquidated and thus disappear immediately. If the firm has a positive 'organization value' (goodwill), reorganization will be chosen, since the firm's

> anticipated cash flows could be sufficient to meet its liabilities. If, on the other hand, the liquidation value of the firm is greater than its value as a going concern, the liquidation of the firm's assets will be declared, and the firm will go out of business.

Insolvency of a debtor country means its (present and future) inability to service its debt. There is, however, a difference between an insolvent firm and an insolvent country. An insolvent firm has zero or negative net worth and it disappears (in the case of its liquidation). Unlike firms, countries do not disappear (especially when the government sector is the insolvent debtor) and they may continue to maintain full control of the assets acquired with their debts. However, from the point of view of creditors, they can become like bankrupt firms when they are incapable of servicing debt over a long period, and, as debtors, they 'disappear' economically.

The solvency criterion of a firm (in terms of its net worth) could be applied to a debtor country in the following formal way:

$$NEW_0 = R_0 + \sum_{t=0}^{\infty} TB_t/(1 + r_t)^t - D_0 \qquad (10.10)$$

$$= R_0 + \sum_{t=0}^{\infty} (Y_t - A_t)/(1 + r_t)^t - D_0 \qquad (10.11)$$

where

NEW_0 = net external wealth of the country today,
R_0 = international reserves today,
TB_t = current account balance in period t in today's value,
D_0 = net foreign debt today,
r = real interest rate,
Y_t = domestic product (*GDP*) in period t in today's value,
A_t = domestic expenditure (absorption) in period t in today's prices.

According to (10.10), the country is solvent when its net external worth is positive. The latter is positive if the amount of international reserves plus the present value of the country's future trade balance surpluses exceed the current volume of net foreign debt. A negative value for NEW_0 would indicate an insolvency case. According to (10.11), the capacity to generate sufficiently high future current account surpluses depends on the country's prospective gaps between domestic product and domestic absorption. Consequently, the net external worth depends positively on the future growth rates of domestic product, and negatively on the future growth rates of domestic absorption and on the real interest rate.[45]

The above analogy between the solvency criterion for an individual firm and for a country has been pushed too far, since there are two main constraints which set an upper limit to a country's net external wealth (Liviatan, 1984).

The first constraint—a liquidity constraint—fixes a minimum volume for international reserves (R') below which current reserves cannot fall. The second constraint—the standard-of-living constraint—sets a minimum value for absorption (A') below which absorption cannot fall. Consequently, the net external 'transferable' wealth (NETW) could be formulated as:

$$NETW_0 = (R_0 - R'_0) + \sum_{t=0}^{\infty} TB_t/(1 + r_t)^t - D_0 \qquad (10.10a)$$

$$= (R_0 - R'_0) + \sum_{t=0}^{\infty} (Y_t - A'_t)/(1 + r_t)^t - D_0 \qquad (10.11a)$$

The liquidity constraint $(R_0 \geqslant R'_0)$ indicates that there is a critical level of reserves necessary to maintain for motives like transactions (in the context of imports), speculation (in the context of the maintenance of the foreign exchange rate), security, and financial credibility abroad.[46] The standard-of-living constraint $(A_t \geqslant A'_t)$ shows that domestic spending cannot be reduced below a minimum tolerable level. Thus, the critical (i.e. lowest) level for consumption can be measured by some average of consumption per capita over the previous years. The minimum tolerable level of investment expenditure could be that of an unchanged capital stock per capita. The interpretation of the minimum level for government expenditure may be rather controversial with respect, for instance, to how much expenditure on education, welfare, and defence can be curtailed.[47]

Deterioration in the net external wealth position of debtor countries can be due to both internal and external factors. An external factor is a higher real interest rate determined in the world capital market. An internal factor is the deceleration, or even stagnation, of the growth rate of GDP, which is partly the result of investment plans which later turn out to have low, or even zero, productivity. Furthermore, if foreign debt served for consumption loans to smooth intertemporal consumption, prediction errors (by borrowers and lenders) about the future expansion of GDP may be another source of a debt problem.

If the country is only illiquid, its net external transferable wealth is positive, and there is only a maturity problem in relation to the debt service and the prospective foreign exchange revenues. If the situation of insolvency is clear-cut, the country, by agreement with its creditors, should declare itself to be in permanent default. It is in its own self-interest not to wait too long before making such a declaration, and to repay a part of its debt service determined by the trade balance surplus it could realize by 'tolerable' internal adjustment measures (see the next section on debt relief). The debtor country's self-interest is related to its future credit-worthiness, because its economy will also need access to the international credit market in the future.

In the past, only a limited number of debtor countries have opted for permanent default: the Soviet Union after World War I, and North Korea and Cuba after World War II. A country like Cuba, which defaulted completely on its total foreign debt, could no longer function in the free world economy and thus shifted into the communist bloc. However, the unilateral default declaration of the above countries took place after the political regime had changed. It could be argued that their permanent default took the form of debt repudiation rather than of insolvency.

Debt Relief

Debt rescheduling (lengthening and postponing repayment periods for interest payments and debt reimbursement) and new loans would be the rule for illiquid debtors, while debt relief would be the solution for insolvent creditors. A secondary market for bank claims on the debtor countries has emerged in the context of the debt problem since the early 1980s. Only banks have access to this market. Debts are exchanged at a discount rate. This discount rate reflects the countries' rate of insolvency (see Table 10.3).

Table 10.3 Secondary-Market Debt Prices, September, 1991 (%age of face value)

Chile	88.25	Yugoslavia	32.50
Argentina (Bonex 89)	79.20	Dominican Republic	28.00
Colombia	77.00	Ecuador	23.50
Philippines	71.25	Poland	23.00
Venezuela (Par-Bonds)	67.38	Panama	17.50
Mexico (Par-Bonds)	59.38	Zaire	16.50
Brazil (Investm. Bonds)	54.00	Peru	14.00
Morocco	52.62	Nicaragua	8.00
Costa Rica	51.50	Côte d'Ivoire	5.00
Nigeria	41.50	Cuba	5.00

Source: The Economist, 12 October 1991.

The theoretical rationale for debt relief is illustrated by the 'debt relief Laffer curve', a concept formulated by Krugman (1989) and illustrated by the curve OABC in Fig. 10.13a. The expected value (V) of a country's outstanding debt is drawn as a function of its contractual value (D). The degree of solvency is measured by the ratio V/D (Fig. 10.13b). The expected value is the market value in the secondary market. There is no default risk for the debt volume D_1 and the face value of the debt (D) corresponds to its expected value (V). For a debt volume larger than D_1, the debtor country has a 'debt overhang', since its nominal debt obligations exceed the amount it is expected to pay. The rate of solvency is measured by the slope of the ray OB (for D_2) or OC (for D_3).

The falling section BC of the debt relief Laffer curve is explained by the debtor's disincentive to service his debt. For section OA he is capable of and willing to repay his debt. For section AB he is incapable but willing. Finally, from point B onwards, he is incapable and *increasingly unwilling* to service the

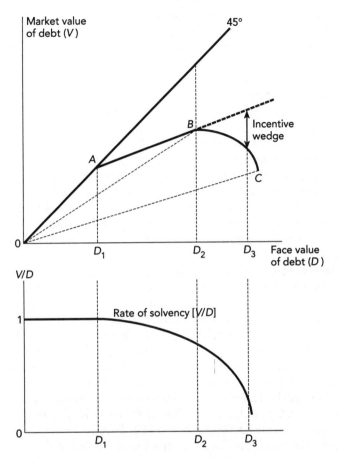

Fig. 10.13. Debt relief

For the debt volume D_1D_2, the borrower is willing but incapable to serve fully the debt service. From D_2 onwards, he is not only incapable but also increasingly unwilling. The debt relief of D_2D_3 is acceptable for the creditors since the market value of D_2 is higher than that of D_3.

Fig. 10.13a. Debt relief: The Laffer curve.

Fig. 10.13b. The rate of solvency.

debt. 'When the debt burden is large, a country has less incentive to make current sacrifices to improve its situation since a large part of the new income or resources generated will be captured by creditors' (Lessard, 1989: 302). The unwillingness (from the debt volume D_2 onwards) is translated into the deceleration of the necessary internal adjustment measures, since the increase in output or the decrease in absorption would go entirely to the creditor.

Debt relief can take the form either of debt forgiveness or 'buybacks' by debtor countries at secondary market prices (V). Debt forgiveness is a stronger form than debt buybacks and it creates a higher degree of 'moral hazard'. Both reward the bad debtors and punish the good debtors who effectively pay. In this respect, all debtors should be treated on even terms. If, for instance, forgiveness of 10 per cent is granted on the outstanding volume of debt, it should apply to all debtors to avoid the moral hazard phenomenon. However, such equal treatment is more onerous for the creditor.

The specific characteristics of the Krugman proposal (1989) for debt relief (also advocated by Sachs and Huizinga, 1987) concern the common interest debtors and creditors have in reducing the outstanding debt, when the debtor countries find themselves on the 'wrong side' of the Laffer curve, i.e. on the righthand section (BC), where debtors are unwilling to pay.[48] Box 10.9. uses Krugman's numerical example of debt relief through buybacks which are in creditors' interest. There is only a net gain in the market value of total debt for the creditor if the debtor makes additional efforts to improve future trade balance surplus.

Debt relief could be combined with liquidity relief. As Froot (1989) has shown, the disincentive effects of the debt burden can be decomposed into two factors: a liquidity disincentive and the debt overhang disincentive, which we have been discussing up to now. A country is 'liquidity constrained', if it is unable to attract voluntary new lending from abroad. As a result, investment declines or stops, because it is too costly in terms of foregone consumption. In Fig. 10.14 debt relief from D_3 to D_2 increases the creditor's expected value of the debt (V) from C to B. Subsequent liquidity relief in form of new loans (D_2D_4) could shift the Laffer curve to the position L_1. However, the liquidity relief will only be a benefit for the creditor if ΔV (the distance EG) exceeds the additional credit volume D_2D_4 ($= BG = FG$). It must be stressed that debt relief and liquidity relief must be a concerted action by *all* creditor banks. Any individual bank has an incentive to free-ride since it would profit from the action of the other banks.

Box 10.9. An example of profitable debt relief (buyback) for debtors and creditors

Outstanding debt volume $D = 100$. Outstanding volume of international reserves $R = 5$ reduces the net volume of external debt to 95. Present value of expected trade balance surplus: either $T = 110$ (exceeding the net external debt of 95 by 15) with the probability of $p = 1/3$ or $T = 20$ with the probability of $(1 - p) = 2/3$.

1. *Market value of debt (V_1) without debt relief*

$$V_1 = R + p(D - R) + (1 - p)T$$
$$= 5 + 1/3 \times 95 + 2/3 \times 20 = 50.$$

2. *Market value of debt (V_2) with debt relief*

Debtor country buys back $BB = 10$ at market value V_1 against $R = 5$. Reduction of D from 100 to 90. Probability p remains unchanged.

$$V_2 = R + p(D - BB) + (1 - p)T$$
$$= 5 + 1/3 \times 90 + 2/3 \times 20 = 48.3.$$

$R = 5$ remains in the formula since $D - BB$ has to be interpreted as $D - R$—debt relief (which is 5). Since V_2 (with debt relief) $< V_1$ (without debt relief), creditors do not gain from debt relief. Debtors gain 5, since they have exchanged $R = 5$ against $\Delta D = 10$. Assume that the gain of 5 makes the incentive higher for internal adjustment measures (increasing p) for realizing the trade balance surplus of 110.

3. *Determination of p for* $V_2 > V_1$

$$V_2 > V_1$$
$$R + p_2(D - BB) + (1 - p_2)T > R + p_1(D - R) + (1 - p_1)T$$
$$5 + p_2 \times 90 + (1 - p_2) \times 20 > 50$$
$$p_2 > 25/70 = 0.357.$$

4. *Market value of debt* (V_3) *with buyback (case 2) and higher probability:* $p = 2/5 = 0.4$

$$V_3 = R + p(D - BB) + (1 - p)T$$
$$= 5 + 0.4 \times 90 + 0.6 \times 20 = 53.$$

The debtor's gain is again 5 and the creditor's gain is 3.
Source: Krugman (1989).

10.7. First World, Second World, and Third World

There is not one economic theory for country A and another for country B, neither are there separate economic theories for the First, Second, and Third Worlds. There is only one economic theory, but its application may differ from country to country. We shall give three examples each of which covers an essential issue from Parts I, II, and III.

Capital mobility versus capital immobility (Part I). Assuming a floating exchange rate in a 'typical' country of the North, the East, or the South, there is no doubt that the determination of the exchange rate is more 'sophisticated' in an industrialized country than in a DC or PSC. The most important distinction that can be drawn here is between capital mobility and capital immobility. For industrialized countries, international financial capital movements are the dominant determinant of fluctuations in the exchange rate over the short run. For those countries in the Second and Third Worlds, which only have (limited) current account convertibility of their currencies, the exchange rate is determined mainly by commercial transactions (even though there will probably also be a parallel foreign exchange market because of capital controls). The modelling of the foreign exchange market for these countries would

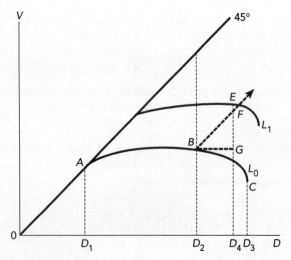

Fig. 10.14. Debt relief and liquidity relief

The debt relief is D_2D_3. The liquidity relief consists of additional loans equal to $BG = FG$, which give rise to a net incremental market value of EF.

follow the traditional lines in terms of demand and supply schedules derived mainly from commercial transactions. For an industrialized country the interest rate parity, coupled with some currency risk premium, should be used.

e_1 *versus* e_2 *(Part II).*　Over the short run, e_1 is the most relevant real exchange rate for industrialized countries. The reason for this is that the financial sector determines the movements in E and, thus, in EP^*_T so that EP^*_T can diverge considerably from a given P_T. For the longer run, e_2 is the relevant real exchange rate for all types of countries. In a system of fixed exchange rates, the most likely candidate for changes in the real exchange rate is e_2 via movements in P_N, and this again holds for all types of countries.

Stabilization policies (Part III).　Stabilization policies were defined as fiscal, monetary, and exchange rate policies—sometimes also wage policy—and their targets were price stability and a certain 'sustainable' current account balance. For all types of countries, price stability could be realized rather easily via a fixed exchange rate provided that the anchor country has a stable price level. Again, also for all kinds of countries, the ultimate cause of an external disequilibrium could be a budget deficit. Industrialized countries differ from others in terms of the financing of the budget deficit. In the former it can be financed by private credit markets but this is generally not the case for the Second and Third Worlds in which it is ultimately financed by money creation. For all types of countries, external equilibrium can be established by the policy mix of reducing the budget deficit and switching the expenditure from foreign goods to domestic goods via a real depreciation. The latter can be implemented by an appropriate change in the exchange rate (exchange rate policy), or by a lower domestic price level (monetary policy). Any adverse repercussions on employment could be avoided by moderate and disciplined wage behaviour.

Notes

1. The function $S_N(q, q_C)$ will be explained in the section on the Dutch disease.
2. By dividing formula (10.4) by P_N, we obtain the wage equalization in real terms (w), where real wages are measured in terms of non-tradable goods

$$w = MP_N = qMP_T = q_C MP_C \qquad (10.5)$$

3. An extreme case of a non-industrialized country is represented by the Gulf emirates. There is no industry at all, except for the production of petrol. All tradables are imported and the high demand for non-tradables is satisfied by local production using imported labour.
4. In 1990 there was restricted access to the official foreign exchange market in the form of foreign exchange controls in seventy member countries of the IMF (Burton and Gilman, 1991).
5. There are two aspects to the simplification of Fig. 10.4. On the one hand, we have assumed that those importers who are willing to pay the highest prices for foreign exchange (i.e. those who are located above point C of the demand curve) obtain the import licences. In reality, the selection process may be arbitrary (and corrupt). On the other hand, if transactions on the parallel market are illegal, buyers and sellers run the risk of punishment. Consequently, the sellers will ask a higher price and the buyer a lower price as compensation for the risk premium.
6. In reality, the width between the official and parallel rate is about ten or fifteen percentage points. Any larger difference would cause the official export revenues to drift increasingly to the parallel market. On the other hand, it could be assumed that the domestic prices of tradables are already valued at the parallel foreign exchange rate; see Pinto (1991). In that case, there would still be a current account deficit.
7. Since the slopes of the NN-TT system are *dependent only on relative prices*, $NN_1 - TT_1$ of Fig. 10.5c (and not reproduced in Fig. 10.5d) shifts downwards along the Oq_1 line towards NN_2-TT_2 in Fig. 10.5d. However, as we have stressed on several occasions, the deflationary option will only be a solution if wages are not rigid downwards; otherwise, external equilibrium will be accompanied by increasing unemployment.
8. Another unfavourable impact of financial liberalization is the constraint on domestic stabilization policies, which become far less autonomous with an open capital account. A monetary-fiscal policy mix which diverges from that of the outside world may have immediate repercussions on the balance of payments (for fixed exchange rates), on the foreign exchange rate (under floating exchange rates), or on both (managed float). These repercussions may be undesirable in that they bring in the well-known external constraints on domestic stabilization policies.
9. Ronald McKinnon (1991) has estimated that the inventories of firms for the Soviet Union in 1985 amounted to 82 per cent of national income, whereas the US firms accumulated inventories equal to 31 per cent in the same year.

10. As Robert Mundell (1991) has emphasized, a monetary overhang cannot be eliminated by cancelling one or two zeros for the outstanding quantity of money and by lowering prices by the same proportion, since the excess supply of money would continue, expressed now by another numéraire. Examples are the new French franc or the new peso.

11. There are still other potential sources of inflation during the transition phase. This aspect has been demonstrated by Ronald McKinnon (1991) for the case of the Soviet Union, but it is equally applicable to other Eastern countries. In the absence of an advanced fiscal system, the main government revenue of socialist countries was formerly provided by the surpluses of enterprises. The central planning authorities fixed prices according to cost (labour, intermediaries) plus the so-called surplus which was transferred to government. When the first price deregulation occurred and certain enterprises were allowed to set prices freely, these surpluses disappeared. The Soviet budget deficit rose from 1.8 per cent of GNP in 1985 progressively to 10 per cent in 1989.

There was also a third inflationary source in many Eastern countries where the banking system had not been reformed. In the planned economies, firms had full access to bank credits at zero or low interest rates to finance the purchase of the inputs needed to fulfil the plans. In the terminology of the Hungarian economist Kornai, enterprises had 'soft' budget constraints. This specific lack of financial constraint constitutes another source of inflation, if bank reforms are retarded.

12. Pegging the price level is probably the most inconvenient method since it would not only imply the price control of thousands, if not millions, of goods, but would primarily result in the distortion of relative prices. The choice of nominal wages ('income policy') is the *ultima ratio* in the Keynesian case of wage rigidities.

13. 'One for one [currency] or we will never be one [country].'

14. It also needed to obtain a stabilization fund of foreign exchange from West Germany in order to effectively guarantee convertibility, at least with respect to the current account, the capital account convertibility could follow later.

15. Deutsches Institut für Wirtschaftsforschung, *Wochenbericht*, various issues, 1991, 1992, and 1993.

16. The exact conversion rate of money holdings by *households* was 1.47 : 1 and the monetary overhang was 58.4 billion marks (Table 10.2). It could be argued, with respect to the households' money holdings, that the conversion rate of 1.47 : 1 was equivalent to the conversion rate of 1 : 1 combined with frozen deposits of the amount of DM 58.4 bn. These frozen deposits could be converted, in the future, into property claims on the former state-owned wealth, administered by the Treuhand Anstalt. 'According to paragraph 10.6 of the Treaty of May 18, 1990, eventual situations should be envisaged that, at some future date, savers are granted property titles on the people-owned wealth for the loss of deposits which were converted at the rate 2 : 1.' *Einigungsvertrag*, 31 August 1990, para. 25.6. However, the Treuhand had a total net deficit of DM 209 bn. by the end of 1994 when its activity was completed, out of which DM 73 bn. were used for past bad loans; see Hornef (1995).

17. However, since the West German velocity of circulation has a long-run downward trend, the conversion rate might have been even higher if some long-run average of the M3 ratio over the past had been chosen. Furthermore, East Germany's GDP and disposable income were overestimated.

18. Furthermore, until state enterprises were privatized (or liquidated), the Treuhand

continued to pay the interest on most old bank loans and guaranteed new bank credits for working capital ('liquidity credits'), to prevent enterprises from failing.

19. Symmetrical currency substitution refers to the case where both residents and non-residents simultaneously hold domestic and foreign money (McKinnon, 1982). Both monies are hard currencies. This type of currency substitution is relevant for developed countries. However, the issue is controversial since the substitution may be concentrated in foreign financial assets other than (non-interest bearing) currency. The return on foreign money holdings would consist only of the expected appreciation of the foreign currency. See Cuddington (1983).

20. With this procedure, the central bank can only gain international reserves indirectly through the reserve requirements (in dollars) on FCD. But, more importantly, the central bank loses fewer reserves, since the source of foreign exchange to the public becomes the foreign exchange market.

21. See Bernholz (1989), and Guidotti and Rodriguez (1992). 'In the post-World War I European hyperinflations, the lack of a stable domestic means of payments was a serious inconvenience in trade and production, and foreign currencies therefore came to be desired not merely as a store of value but actually as a means of domestic payment . . . Thus, in advanced inflation, Gresham's Law was reversed: good money tended to drive out bad, and not the other way round: the reason being the irreducible need for a serviceable medium of exchange in any modern economy based on division of labor and interchange of goods and services.' League of Nations (1946: 48).

22. Implicitly, we assume that dollarization is legalized.

23. The amplification of desired dollar holdings from point C to point D, involving an accelerating degree of the economy's monetization, could be explained by the public good character of money holdings. The quality of money—or its moneyness—as a medium of exchange rises with the use of money. At the beginning of the dollarization process (AB and BC) the marginal 'productivity' of dollars as a domestic means of payment is rather modest, since there is only a limited number of people who use the same medium of exchange. In this situation, the dominant return element of dollar holdings may be provided mainly by their quality as a store of value. However, over time, and under pressure from high inflation rates, more and more people may use the dollar as a medium of exchange involving positive 'transaction cost externalities'. The marginal return on dollar holdings increases as the group of dollar users becomes larger so that their total demand for dollars shifts upwards. The more the dollar is used, the lower the costs of switching into it. From a critical level of the inflation rate onwards (point C), the use of the dollar spreads ever faster with rising inflation.

It could legitimately be asked why there is still a positive demand for real rouble holdings (d^d_1) at high inflation rates. One of the answers concerns the various denominations of domestic cash balances (Rostowski, 1992: 99–101). Money is not necessarily a homogeneous good. Money as a store of value and means of payment for large transactions (e.g. real estate and automobile sector) will be held in bank deposits and large denomination banknotes. The substitution of the inflating domestic currency will begin with those large denominations of the money stock which are held for a longer time. Notes and coins held for small transactions very often resist the currency substitution process since the amount of money involved is not high and it is held for a fairly short time. It should come as no surprise that the demand for domestic currency as small change is maintained even with very high inflation rates. Thus, in a highly dollarized economy, the domestic currency may collapse into small change.

24. See Calvo and Vegh (1992: 14–15).

25. The term e is defined as EP^*/P so that $F = P^*F^*$ in order to be consistent with Box 8.1 in ch. 8.1. We assume that $P^* = 1$. If we had an (almost) fully dollarized economy in which the unit of account is predominantly the dollar, the domestic price level would refer to domestic dollar prices.

26. The quantity of money is generally measured as the volume of money held by the 'public', that is, the non-government and the non-banking sectors.

27. In the literature, this issue for economies with currency substitution was raised by Calvo and Rodriguez (1977). They provoked a series of controversial papers discussed in Calvo and Vegh (1992: 11–13).

28. The construction of Fig. 10.10 is a simplified version of that by Calvo and Frenkel (1991: 275–8).

29. The equation for the current account is

$$CA = X_T (e, \ldots),$$

where X_T stands for the excess supply of tradable goods in the domestic market for tradables. In contrast to Fig. 8.2, the CA-schedule is not upward sloping. We assume that there is no wealth effect on absorption.

30. The demand for real dollar holdings can be written as

$$f = L(dE/E, i_m \ldots) \text{ where } dE/E = de/e + \pi.$$

The term i_m stands for interest payments on domestic currency deposits, which we shall neglect in our subsequent discussion. A higher i_m would decrease f.

31. See Cukierman *et al.* (1992).

32. The following description is contained in Bruno *et al.* (1991) and in Cukierman *et al.* (1992).

33. The British Currency Board system would be another type of the 100 per cent backing of domestic high powered money. It should be emphasized that the use of sterling as the local currency was not required. The local banknotes were fully backed by sterling reserves. Financial liberalization in the sense of full convertibility (including capital account convertibility, as in the case of the last plan in Argentina) does not necessarily increase the credibility of maintaining the fixed exchange rate in the future or, at least, it is a controversial issue. If it implies large net capital inflows, and a subsequent increase in total expenditure, then real appreciation could be the outcome, along with a deteriorating current account balance (see the end of Sect. 10.3). This latter development may feed the expectation of a future devaluation. Consequently, for policy-makers it could seem easier to realize the exchange rate commitment with some restrictions on capital account convertibility.

34. The case of the German Monetary Union (July 1990) which preceded political unification (October 1990) is the most extreme case of dollarization where a return to a proper exchange rate tool is completely excluded for the five eastern *Länder*. The shocks in the East German economy in the form of excessive wage claims cannot be absorbed by devaluation, since there is no longer an East German currency, and high unemployment (open or disguised) is the consequence, as we have already analysed in Sect. 10.4.

35. On this subject see Dornbusch and Fischer (1986), Dornbusch (1992), Garber and Spencer (1992) and Santaella (1993).

36. See Fischer (1982).

37. Holtfrerich remarks with respect to the German hyperinflation of 1923: 'the stabilization of the currency was necessary in Germany because of a crisis of the state rather than of the economy. The economy had widely changed to a foreign currency standard, with which it could have lived . . . The crisis originated since the Reich would and could not tolerate the use of foreign currency for domestic transactions wanted by the economy because of reasons of national self-preservation and especially as long as the inflation was needed as a source of revenues.' Holtfrerich (1980: 310).

Panamanian experience (the freezing of deposits of Panamanian banks by the USA in the late 1980s) demonstrates how vulnerable a dollarized country could be to US interference. Another example was the forced resignation of the finance minister of Israel when he proposed dollarization to the Knesset in 1983.

38. See Calvo and Vegh (1992).

39. Like the Singaporean currency, which was deliberately managed to be stronger than the US dollar to avoid the dollarization of the Singaporean economy: see Claassen (1992).

40. For a debtor country, we have $GNP = GDP - rD$. The current account deficit (CAD) always exceeds the trade balance deficit (TBD) since $CAD = TBD + rD$. The current account deficit is equal to the savings gap $I - S_n$ where S_n stands for national savings defined as domestic savings (S) minus net interest payments to foreigners: $S_n = S - rD$. Consequently, we have $CAD = TBD + rD = I - S_n = I - S + rD$ and $TBD = I - S$. We have disregarded the government sector. Capital inflows could also be used to accumulate international reserves (R). Such a case would imply that ΔR has to be added to the right-hand side of equation (10.8).

41. If inflation is taken into account, the nominal D has to be deflated by P, so that the condition $\Delta D/D \leqslant g$ becomes $(\Delta D/D - \Delta P/P) \leqslant g$.

42. The same is true *a fortiori* for the case $g > r$, where the foreign debt grows at rate g and where the country never honours its debt service. The consequence of $g \geqslant r$ is that the debtor would be excluded from the international credit market. Another possibility is that the interest rate rises above g (higher country-risk premium) so that the debtor country will again have access to the credit market.

43. Eaton and Gersovitz (1981: 26) conclude that this partial default was 'a chosen strategy rather than an uncontrollable event'. Diaz Alejandro (1983: 29–31) suggests that the worldwide protectionism in the 1930s changed the international rules. The suspension of German reparations and the partial default of the Latin American debt would have been defensible, even necessary, as a result of the Great Depression.

44. A unilateral declaration of debt repudiation (by one debtor country or many countries forming a debt cartel) implies that the country's import volume will shrink to the level of its export volume for some extended future period during which it has no access to the international credit market. Debt repudiation only makes sense when the three following conditions hold (Schäfer, 1984: 26). First, the present and future trade balance surpluses are used exclusively for the debt service. Secondly, the trade balance surpluses are realized, *inter alia*, by a reduction of imports to a level equivalent to that which would hold in the case of debt repudiation. Thirdly, the smaller import volume jeopardizes the prospective growth of the country's GDP so that its output per capita may be stagnant or may even decrease; foreign lenders are not willing to grant any new credit, even if the country honours its debt service through a corresponding trade balance

surplus. Under these three conditions, a country could opt for debt repudiation because resources equal to the future cumulative trade balance surpluses are saved for internal use.

45. Remember that, in the whole future, the cumulative trade balance surplus (*TB*) has to exceed the cumulative current account surplus since $CA = TB - rD$.

46. Triffin (1960: 46) defines the critical level of international reserves as 20 per cent of annual imports.

47. Furthermore, the ambiguity in understanding an insolvent situation consists of the probabilistic nature of the evolution of Y_t, A_t, and r_t, and of the length of the future time horizon for the insolvency.

48. Remember that section *AB* is irrelevant for debt relief from the point of view of creditors, since debtors are willing to service the debt.

REFERENCES

Aghevli, B. B. and Montiel, P. J. (1991), 'Exchange Rate Policies in Developing Countries', in Claassen (1991a): 205–37.

Aliber, R. Z. (1980), 'A Conceptional Approach to the Analysis of Developing Countries', Staff Working Paper no. 421, Washington, DC: World Bank, Oct.

Archibald, G. C. and Lipsey, R. G. (1958), 'Monetary and Value Theory: A Critique of Lange and Patinkin', *Review of Economic Studies*, 26(1): 1–26.

Aukrust, O. (1970), 'PRIM I: A Model of the Price and Income Distribution Mechanism of an Open Economy', *Review of Income and Wealth*, 16(1): 51–78.

Balassa, B. (1964), 'The Purchasing Power Parity Doctrine: A Reappraisal', *Journal of Political Economy*, 72(6): 584–96.

Baltensperger, E. (1992), 'Monetäre Aussenwirtschaftstheorie', *Zeitschrift für Wirtschafts- und Sozialwissenschaften*, 112(4): 505–65.

Barro, R. J. (1974), 'Are Government Bonds Net Wealth?', *Journal of Political Economy*, 82(6): 1095–1117.

———— and Gordon, D. (1983), 'Rules, Discretion, and Reputation in a Model of Monetary Policy', *Journal of Monetary Economics*, 12(1): 101–21.

Baxter, M. and Crucini, M. J. (1993), 'Explaining Saving-Investment Correlations', *American Economic Review*, 83(3): 416–36.

Bernholz, P. (1989), 'Currency Competition, Inflation, Gresham's Law and Exchange Rate,' *Journal of Institutional and Theoretical Economics*, 145(1): 149–64.

Bhagwati, J. N. (1984), 'Why Are Services Cheaper in the Poor Countries?', *Economic Journal*, 94(374): 279–86.

———— (1989), 'The Pass-Through Puzzle: the Missing Prince from Hamlet', *Rivista di Politica Economica*, 89 (June): 103–13.

Bhatia, R. J. (1985), *The West African Monetary Union: An Analytical Review*, Occasional Paper 35, Washington, DC: International Monetary Fund, May.

Blanchard, O. (1979), 'Speculative Bubbles, Crashes, and Rational Expectations', *Economic Letters*, 386–89.

Bordo, M. D. and Schwartz, A. J. (1990), 'What Has Foreign Exchange Market Intervention Since the Plazza Agreement Accomplished?', National Bureau of Economic Research, Working Paper no. 3562, Dec.

Borensztein, E. and Reinhart, C. M. (1994), 'The Macroeconomic Determinants of Commodity Prices', Working Paper no. 94/9, Washington, DC: International Monetary Fund, Jan.

Boughton, J. M. (1991), 'The CFA Franc Zone: Currency Union and Monetary Standard', Working Paper no. 91/133, Washington, DC: International Monetary Fund, Dec.

Branson, W. H. (1968), *Financial Capital Flows in the U.S. Balance of Payments*, Amsterdam: North-Holland.

—— (1979), 'Exchange Rate Dynamics and Monetary Policy', in A. Lindbeck (ed.), *Inflation and Employment in Open Economies*, Amsterdam: North-Holland: 189–224.

—— (1986), 'The Limits of Monetary Coordination as Exchange Rate Policy', *Brookings Papers on Economic Activity*, no. 1: 175–94.

—— and Henderson, D. W. (1985), 'The Specification and Influence of Asset Markets', in R. W. Jones and P. B. Kenen (eds.), *Handbook of International Economics*, vol. 2, Amsterdam: North-Holland: 749–805.

—— and Myhrman, J. (1976), 'Inflation in Open Economies. Supply-Determined versus Demand-Determined Models', *European Economic Review*, 20.

Bruno, M. (1990), 'High Inflation and the Nominal Anchors of an Open Economy', National Bureau of Economic Research, Working Paper no. 3518, Nov.

——, Fischer, S., Helpman, E., and Liviatan, N. (eds.) (1991), *Lessons from Stabilization and Its Aftermath*, Cambridge: MIT Press.

Buiter, W. H. (1985), 'A Guide to Public Sector Debt and Deficits', *Economic Policy*, 5(1): 14–79.

Burda, M. and Wyplosz, C. (1993), *Macroeconomics. A European Text*, Oxford: Oxford University Press.

Burton, D. and Gilman, M. G. (1991), 'Exchange Rate Policy and the IMF', *Finance and Development*, 28(3): 18–19.

Calvo, G. A. and Frenkel, J. A. (1991), 'From Centrally Planned to Market Economy,' *IMF Staff Papers*, 38(2): 269–99.

—— and Rodriguez, C. A. (1977), 'A Model of Exchange Rate Determination under Currency Substitution and Rational Expectations,' *Journal of Political Economy*, 85: 617–25.

—— and Vegh, C. A. (1992), 'Currency Substitution in Developing Countries: An Introduction,' *Revista de Analisis Economico*, 7(1): 3–27.

Camen, U. and Genberg, H. (1990), 'Over- and Undervalued Currencies: Theory, Measurement, and Policy Implications', in E. M. Claassen (1990): 15–39.

Canzoneri, M. B. and Rogers, C. A. (1990), 'Is the European Community an Optimal Currency Area? Optimal Taxation versus the Cost of Multiple Currencies', *American Economic Review*, 80(3): 419–33.

Caves, R. E., Frankel, J. A., and Jones, R. W. (1990), *World Trade and Payments*, 5th edn., New York: Harper Collins.

Choudhry, T., McNown, R., and Wallace, M. (1991), 'Purchasing Power Parity and the Canadian Float in the 1950s', *Review of Economics and Statistics*, 73(3): 558–63.

Claassen, E. M. (1974), 'The Role of Economic Size in the Determination and Transmission of World Inflation', in H. Frisch (ed.), *Inflation in Small Economies*, Berlin: Springer-Verlag: 91–120.

—— (1984), 'Monetary Integration and Monetary Stability: The Economic Criteria of the Monetary Constitution', in P. Salin (ed.), *Currency Competition and Monetary Union*, The Hague: 47–58.

—— (1985a), 'Wechselkurseffekte von Devisen- und Offenmarktoperationen', in H. Milde and H. G. Monissen (eds.), *Rationale Wirtschaftspolitik in komplexen Gesellschaften*, Stuttgart: Kohlhammer: 230–39.

—— (1985b), 'The Latin American Debt Problem and the Lender-of-Last-Resort Function', in M. Connolly and J. McDermott (eds.), *The Economics of the Carribean Basin*, Praeger, New York: Praeger: 27–67.

—— (1985c), 'The Lender-of-Last-Resort Function in the Context of National and International Financial Crises', *Weltwirtschaftliches Archiv*, 121(2): 217–37.

―――― (1986), 'The Optimum Monetary Constitution: Monetary Integration and Monetary Stability', in: W. Maihofer (ed.), *Noi si mura*, Florence: European University Institute: 399–429.

―――― (1989a), 'IMS, EMS, and the (N-1) Problem', *Economic and Social Review*, 20(2): 91–96.

―――― (1989b), 'The Real Exchange Rate Under Alternative Nominal Exchange Rate Regimes', *Rivista di Politica Economica*, 79 (June): 63–81.

―――― (1990), *International and European Monetary Systems*, New York: Praeger.

―――― (1991a), *Exchange Rate Policies in Developing and Post-Socialist Countries*, San Francisco: ICG Press.

―――― (1991b), 'Gradual versus Radical Transformation: The Case of the German Monetary Union', in E. M. Claassen (1991a): 123–43.

―――― (1992), 'Financial Liberalization and Its Impact on Domestic Stabilization Policies: Singapore and Malaysia', *Weltwirtschaftliches Archiv*, 128(1): 36–67.

―――― (1994a), Stabilization under Dollarization: Russia, IIASA-Conference on International Trade Issues of the Russian Federation, Laxemburg (Austria), 5–7 May.

―――― and de la Cruz Martinez, J. (1994b), *Dollarization and Its Impact on the Economy: Bolivia, Uruguay, Argentina*, Working Paper Series 168, Washington, DC: Inter-American Development Bank.

―――― and Salin, P. (1991), *The Impact of Stabilization and Structural Adjustment Policies on the Rural Sector. Case-Studies of Côte d'Ivoire, Senegal, Liberia, Zambia and Morocco*, Rome: FAO.

―――― and Wyplosz, C. (1985), 'Capital Controls: Some Principles and the French Experience', in J. Melitz and C. Wyplosz (eds.), *The French Economy. Theory and Policy*, Boulder, Colo.: Westview Press: 237–78.

Clinton, Kevin (1988), 'Transactions Costs and Covered Interest Arbitrage: Theory and Evidence', *Journal of Political Economy*, 96(2): 358–70.

Connolly, M. B. (1983), 'Optimum Currency Pegs for Latin America', *Journal of Money, Credit, and Banking*, 15(1): 56–72.

Corden, W. M. (1986), 'Fiscal Policies, Current Accounts and Real Exchange Rates: In Search of a Logic of International Policy Coordination', *Weltwirtschaftliches Archiv*, 122(3): 423–38.

―――― and Neary, P. (1982), 'Booming Sector and De-Industrialization in a Small Open Economy', *Economic Journal*, 92(368): 825–48.

Cuddington, J. (1983), 'Currency Substitution, Capital Mobility and the Demand for Money,' *Journal of International Money and Finance*, 2(1): 111–13.

Cukierman, A., Kiguel, M. A., and Liviatan, N. (1992), 'How Much to Commit to an Exchange Rate Rule? Balancing Credibility and Flexibility,' *Revista de Analisis Economico*, 7(1): 73–89.

Cumby, R. E. and Obstfeld, M. (1981), 'A Note on Exchange-Rate Expectations and Nominal Interest Rate Differentials: A Test of the Fisher Hypothesis', *Journal of Finance*, 36(3): 697–703.

―――― (1984), 'International Interest-Rate and Price Level Linkages Under Flexible Exchange Rates: A Review of Recent Evidence', in J. O. F. Bilson and R. C. Marston (eds.), *Exchange Rate Theory and Practice*, Chicago: University of Chicago Press.

De Grauwe, P. (1990), 'Fiscal Policies in the EMS: A Strategic Analysis', in E. M. Claassen (1990): 121–140.

―――― (1992), *The Economics of Monetary Integration*, Oxford: Oxford University Press.

De Grauwe, P., and Fratianni, M. (1985), 'Interdependence, Macro-economic Policies and All That', *World Economy*, 8(1): 63–76.

Deutsche Bundesbank (1990), *Monatsberichte*, no. 6 (June), no. 7 (July), no. 10 (Oct.), Frankfurt: Deutsche Bundesbank.

—— (1995), *Geschäftsbericht 1994*, Frankfurt: Deutsche Bundesbank.

Diaz Alejandro, C. F. (1983), 'Stories of the 1930s for the 1980s', in P. Aspe Armella, R. Dornbusch, and M. Obstfeld (eds.), *Financial Policies and the World Capital Market: The Problem of Latin American Countries*, Chicago: University of Chicago Press: 5–35.

Dominguez, K. M. and Frankel, J. A. (1993), *Does Foreign Exchange Intervention Work? Consequences for the Dollar*, Washington, DC: Institute for International Economics.

Dooley, M. P. and Isard, P. (1980), 'Capital Controls, Political Risk, and Deviations from Interest-Rate Parity', *Journal of Political Economy*, 88(2): 370–84.

—— (1982), 'A Portfolio-Balance Rational-Expectations Model of the Dollar-Mark Exchange Rate', *Journal of International Economics*, 12(3/4): 257–76.

Dornbusch, R. (1973), 'Devaluation, Money and Nontraded Goods', *American Economic Review*, 63(5): 871–80.

—— (1974), 'Real and Monetary Aspects of the Effects of Exchange Rate Changes', in R. Z. Aliber (ed.), *National Monetary Policies and the International Financial System*, Chicago: University of Chicago Press.

—— (1975), 'Exchange Rates and Fiscal Policy in a Popular Model of International Trade', *American Economic Review*, 65(5): 859–71.

—— (1976a), 'Capital Mobility, Flexible Exchange Rates, and Macroeconomic Equilibrium', in E. M. Claassen and P. Salin (eds.), *Recent Developments in International Monetary Economics*, Amsterdam: North-Holland: 261–78.

—— (1976b), 'Expectations and Exchange Rate Dynamics', *Journal of Political Economy*, 84(6): 1161–76.

—— (1980), *Open Economy Macroeconomics*, New York: Basic Books.

—— (1982), 'Equilibrium and Disequilibrium Exchange Rates', *Zeitschrift für Wirtschafts- und Sozialwissenschaften*, 102(4): 573–99.

—— (1983), 'Real Interest Rates, Home Goods, and Optimal External Borrowing', *Journal of Political Economy*, 91(2): 141–53.

—— (1986), 'Flexible Exchange Rates and Excess Capital Mobility', *Brookings Papers on Economic Activity*, no. 1: 209–26.

—— (1988), 'Real Exchange Rates and Macroeconomics: A Selective Survey', National Bureau of Economic Research, Working Paper no. 2775.

—— (1992), 'Monetary Problems of Post-Communism: Lessons from the End of the Austro-Hungarian Empire,' *Weltwirtschaftliches Archiv*, 128(3): 391–424.

—— and Fischer, S. (1980), 'Exchange Rates and the Current Account', *American Economic Review*, 70(5): 960–71.

—— and Fischer, S. (1986), 'Stopping Hyperinflations Past and Present,' *Weltwirtschaftliches Archiv*, 122(1): 1–47.

Driskill, R. A. (1981), 'Exchange-Rate Dynamics: An Empirical Investigation', *Journal of Political Economy*, 89(2): 357–71.

Eaton, J. and Gersovitz, M. (1981), *Poor-Country Borrowing in Private Financial Markets and the Regulation Issue*, Princeton Studies in International Finance no. 47, Princeton NJ., June.

Edgren, G., Faxén, K. O., and Odhner, C. E. (1973), *Wage Formation and the Economy*, London: Macmillan.

Edison, H. J. (1993), *The Effectiveness of Central Bank Interventions: A Survey of the Post-1982 Literature*, Princeton Essays in International Finance no. 18, Princeton NJ, July.

Edwards, S. (1984), 'Coffee, Money, and Inflation in Colombia', *World Development*, 12(11/12).

—— (1989a), *Real Exchange Rates, Devaluation, and Adjustment: Exchange Rate Policy in Developing Countries*, Cambridge, Mass.: MIT Press.

—— (1989b), 'Real Exchange Rates in the Developing Countries: Concepts and Measurement', National Bureau of Economic Research, Working Paper no. 2950, Apr.

—— and Aoki, M. (1983), 'Oil Export Boom and Dutch-Disease: A Dynamic Analysis', *Resources and Energy*, Sep.

Fama, E. F. (1984), 'Forward and Spot Exchange Rates', *Journal of Monetary Economics*, 14(3): 319–38.

Feldstein, M. and Horioka, C. (1980), 'Domestic Saving and International Capital Flows', *Economic Journal*, 90(358): 314–29.

Fischer, S. (1982), 'Seigniorage and the Case for a National Money', *Journal of Political Economy*, 90: 295–313.

Fleming, M. (1962), 'Domestic Financial Policies Under Fixed and Floating Exchange Rates', *IMF Staff Papers*, 9(4): 369–79.

Flood, R. P. and Taylor, M. P. (1995), 'Exchange Rate Economics: What's Wrong with the Conventional Macro Approach?', in J. A. Frankel, G. Galli, and A. Giovannini (eds.), *The Microstructure of Foreign Exchange Markets*, Chicago: University of Chicago Press.

Frankel, J. A. (1982), 'In Search of the Exchange Risk Premium: A Six-Currency Test Assuming Mean-Variance Optimization', *Journal of International Money and Finance*, 1(3): 255–74.

—— (1983), 'Monetary and Portfolio-Balance Models of Exchange Rate Determination', in J. S. Bhandari, B. H. Putnam, and J. H. Levin (eds.), *Economic Interdependence and Flexible Exchange Rates*, Cambridge, Mass.: MIT Press.

—— and Froot, K. A. (1986), 'Understanding the Dollar in the Eighties: The Expectations of Chartists and Fundamentalists', *Economic Record*, 62 (supplement): 24–38.

—— and Froot, K. A. (1990), 'Chartists, Fundamentalists, and Trading in the Foreign Exchange Market', *American Economic Review, Papers and Proceedings*, 80(2): 181–85.

—— and MacArthur, A. T. (1988), 'Political vs. Currency Premia in International Real Interest Differentials: A Study of Forward Rates for 24 Countries', *European Economic Review*, 32(4): 1083–1112.

Fraser, P. and Taylor, M. P. (1990), 'Some Efficient Tests of International Real Interest Parity', *Applied Economics*, 22 (Aug.): 1083–92.

Frenkel, J. A. (1976), 'A Monetary Approach to the Exchange Rate: Doctrinal Aspects and Empirical Evidence', *Scandinavian Journal of Economics*, 78 (2): 200–24.

—— (1978), 'Purchasing Power Parity: Doctrinal Perspective and Evidence from the 1920s', *Journal of International Economics*, 8(2): 169–91.

—— (1981a), 'The Collapse of Purchasing Power Parity During the 1970s', *European Economic Review*, 16(1): 145–65.

—— (1981b), 'Flexible Exchange Rates, Prices and the Role of "News"', *Journal of Political Economy*, 89(4): 665–705.

Frenkel, J.A. (1985), 'Commentary on "Causes of Appreciation and Volatility of the Dollar"', in Federal Reserve Bank of Kansas City (ed.), *The U.S. Dollar—Recent Developments, Outlook, and Policy Options*, Kansas City: Federal Reserve Bank of Kansas City: 53–63.

────── and Johnson, H. G. (1976), *The Monetary Approach to the Balance of Payments*, Toronto: University of Toronto Press.

────── and Levich, R. M. (1975), 'Covered Interest Arbitrage: Unsupported Profits?', *Journal of Political Economy*, 83(2): 325–38.

────── and Levich, R. M. (1977), 'Transaction Costs and Interest Arbitrage: Tranquil Versus Turbulent Periods', *Journal of Political Economy*, 85(6): 1209–26.

────── and Razin, A. (1987), *Fiscal Policies and the World Economy*, Cambridge, Mass.: MIT Press.

Friedman, M. and Schwartz, A. J. A. (1964), *A Monetary History of the United States: 1867–1960*, Princeton: Princeton University Press.

Froot, K. A. (1989), 'Buybacks, Exit Bonds, and the Optimality of Debt and Liquidity Relief', *International Economic Review*, 30(1): 49–70.

Frydman, R., Wellisz, S., and Kolodko, G. (1991), 'Stabilization in Poland: A Progress Report', in E. M. Claassen (1991a): 89–115.

Garber, P. M. and Spencer, M. G. (1992), 'The Dissolution of the Austro-Hungarian Empire: Lessons for Currency Reform', Working Paper no. 92/66, Washington, DC: International Monetary Fund, July.

Genberg, H. (1984), 'On Choosing the Right Rules for Exchange-Rate Management', *World Economy*, 7 (3): 391–406.

Giavazzi, F. and Giovannini, A. (1987a), 'Models of the EMS: Is Europe a Greater Deutsche-Mark Area?', *European Economic Review*, 31.

────── (1987b), 'The EMS and the Dollar', in: R. C. Bryant and R. Porter (eds.), *Global Macroeconomics: Policy Conflict and Cooperation*, New York: 237–65.

Giersch, H. (1984), 'Real Exchange Rates and Economic Development', Kiel Working Papers no. 218, Nov.

Goldsbrough, D. and Teja, R. (1991), 'Globalization of Financial Markets and Implications for Pacific Basin Developing Countries', Working Paper no. 91/34, Washington, DC: International Monetary Fund, Mar.

Graham, F. D. (1925), 'Germany's Capacity to Pay and the Reparation Plan', *American Economic Review*, 15(3): 209–227.

Granville, B. (1995), *Ending High Inflation: The Case of Russia versus Poland and the CSFR*, PhD dissertation, Florence: European University Institute.

Guidotti, P. E. and Rodriguez, C. A. (1991), 'Dollarization in Latin America: Gresham's Law in Reverse?', Working Paper no. 91/117, Washington, DC: International Monetary Fund, Dec.

Harris, J. R. and Todaro, M. P. (1970), 'Migration, Unemployment and Development: A Two-Sector Analysis', *American Economic Review*, 60(1): 126–42.

Hayek, F. A. (1976a), *Choice in Currency: A Way to Stop Inflation*, Occasional Paper no. 48, London: Institute of Economic Affairs, Feb.

────── (1976b), *Denationalisation of Money*, Hobart Paper Special no. 70, London: Institute of Economic Affairs, Oct.

Helliwell, J. F. (1990), 'Fiscal Policy and the External Deficit: Siblings, But not Twins', National Bureau of Economic Research, Working Paper no. 3313, Apr.

Hicks, J. R. (1946), *Value and Capital*, 2nd edn., Oxford University Press: Oxford.

Hodrick, R. J. (1978), 'An Empirical Analysis of the Monetary Approach to the

Determination of the Exchange Rate', in J. A. Frenkel and H. G. Johnson (eds.), *The Economics of Exchange Rates*, Reading, Mass.: Addison-Wesley: 97–128.

———— and Srivastava, S. (1986), 'The Covariation of Risk Premiums and Expected Future Spot Exchange Rates', *Journal of International Money and Finance*, 5 (supplement): 5–22.

Holtfrerich, C. L. (1980), *Die Deutsche Inflation*, Berlin: de Gruyter.

Honohan, P. (1990), 'Monetary Cooperation in the CFA Zone', Policy Research and External Affaires Working Paper no. 389, Washington, DC: World Bank, Mar.

Hornef, Heinrich (1995), 'Die Treuhand-Finanzen – eine Investition in den Aufbau Ost', *Deutsche Bundesbank. Auszüge aus Presseartikeln*, no. 48, 3 July: 16–18.

Ito, T. (1990), 'Foreign Exchange Rate Expectations: Micro Survey Data', *American Economic Review*, 80(3): 434–49.

Isard, P. (1991), 'Uncovered Interest Parity', Working Paper no. 91/51, Washington: International Monetary Fund, May.

Johnson, H. G. (1962), 'The Balance of Payments', *Pakistan Economic Journal*, June, repr. in H. G. Johnson, *Money, Trade and Economic Growth*, Cambridge, Mass.: Havard University Press.

———— (1972a), *Inflation and the Monetarist Controversy*, Amsterdam: North-Holland.

———— (1972b), 'The Monetary Approach to Balance of Payments Theories', *Journal of Financial and Quantitative Analysis*, Mar.

Kearney, C. and MacDonald, R. (1992), 'Tests of Efficiency in the Australian Foreign Exchange Market', *Economic Record*, 68.

Kenen, P. B. (1985), *The International Economy*, Englewood Cliffs, NJ: Prentice Hall.

Keynes, J. M. (1923), *A Tract on Monetary Reform*, London: Macmillan.

———— (1930), *Treatise on Money*, London: Macmillan.

Kindleberger, C. P. (1978), *Manias, Panics and Crashes. A History of Financial Crises*, London.

———— and Laffargue, J. P. (eds.), (1982), *Financial Crises*, Cambridge.

Klein, B. (1974), 'The Competitive Supply of Money', *Journal of Money, Credit and Banking*, 6(4).

———— (1978), 'Competing Monies, European Monetary Union and the Dollar', in M. Fratianni and T. Peters (eds.), *One Money for Europe*, London: Macmillan.

Kouri, P. J. K. and Porter, M. (1974), 'International Capital Flows and Portfolio Equilibrium', *Journal of Political Economy*, 82(3): 443–67.

Kravis, I. B. (1986), 'The Three Faces of the International Comparison Project', *Research Observer*, 1(1).

————, Kenessy, Z., Heston, A., and Summers, R. (1975), *A System of International Comparisons of Gross Product and Purchasing Power*, Baltimore: Johns Hopkins.

———— and Lipsey, R. G. (1983), *Toward an Explanation of National Price Levels*, Princeton Studies in International Finance, no. 52, Nov.

Krugman, P. (1989), 'Market-Based Debt-Reduction Schemes', in J. A. Frenkel, M. P. Dooley, and P. Wickham (eds.), *Analytical Issues in Debt*, Washington: International Monetary Fund.

Kydland, F. and Prescott, E. (1977), 'Rules rather than Discretion: The Inconsistency of Optimal Plans', *Journal of Political Economy*, 85: 473–90.

Lavigne, M. (1991), 'Intraregional Convertibility in Eastern Europe: Is it Still an Issue?', in E. M. Claassen (1991a): 175–202.

League of Nations (1946), *The Course and Control of Inflation: A Review of Monetary*

Experience in Europe After World War I, Geneva: League of Nations: Economic, Financial and Transit Department.

Levich, R. M. (1985), 'Empirical Studies of Exchange Rates: Price Behavior, Rate Determination, and Market Efficiency', in R. W. Jones and P. P. Kenen (eds.), *Handbook of International Economics*, vol. II, Amsterdam: North-Holland.

—— and Thomas, L. R. (1993), 'The Significance of Technical Trading-Rule Profits in the Foreign Exchange Market: A Bootstrap Approach', *Journal of International Money and Finance*, 12(5): 451–74.

Lessard, D. R. (1989), 'Beyond the Debt Crisis: Alternative Forms of Financing Growth', in Ishrat Husain and Ishac Diwan (eds.), *Dealing with the Debt Crisis*, Washington, DC: World Bank: 294–306.

Lindbeck, Assar (1979), 'Imported and Structural Inflation and Aggregate Demand: The Scandinavian Model Reconstructed', in A. Lindbeck (ed.), *Inflation and Employment in Open Economies*, Amsterdam: North-Holland: 13–40.

Liviatan, N. (1980), 'Anti-Inflationary Monetary Policy and the Capital-Import Tax', Warwick Economic Research Papers no. 171.

Liviatan, O. (1984), 'A Macro-Absorption Approach for Estimating the Foreign Debt Burden', *Economic Development and Cultural Change*, 32(4): 803–18.

Loopesko, B. E. (1984), 'Relationships Among Exchange Rates, Intervention, and Interest Rates: An Empirical Investigation', *Journal of International Money and Finance*, 3 (Dec.): 257–78.

Lothian, J. R. and Taylor, M. P. (1995), 'Real Exchange Rate Behavior: The Recent Float from the Perspective of the Past Two Centuries', *Journal of Political Economy* (forthcoming).

MacDonald, R. (1995), 'Long-Run Exchange Rate Modeling: A Survey of the Recent Evidence', *International Monetary Fund Staff Papers*, 42(3): 437–89.

—— and Taylor, M. P. (1992), 'Exchange Rate Economics: A Survey', *International Monetary Fund Staff Papers*, 39(1): 1–57.

McKinnon, R. I. (1982), 'Currency Substitution and Instability in the Dollar World Standard', *American Economic Review*, 72(3): 320–33.

—— (1991), 'The Problem of Internal Convertibility', in E. M. Claassen (1991a): 59–87.

McNown, R. F. and Wallace, M. (1989), 'National Price Levels, Purchasing Power Parity and Cointegration: A Test of Four High Inflation Economies', *Journal of International Money and Finance*, 8 (4): 533–45.

Marston, R. C. (1980), 'Cross-Country Effects of Sterilization, Reserve Currencies and Foreign Exchange Intervention', *Journal of International Economics*, 10(1): 63–78.

Mastropasqua, C., Micossi, S., and Rinaldi, R. (1988), 'Interventions, Sterilization and Monetary Policy in European Monetary System Countries, 1979–87', in F. Giavazzi, S. Micossi, and M. Miller (eds.), *European Monetary System*, Cambridge: Cambridge University Press.

Meade, J. E. (1951a), *The Theory of International Economic Policy*, vol. 1: *The Balance of Payments*, London: Oxford University Press.

—— (1951b), *The Theory of International Economic Policy*, vol. 2: *The Balance of Payments (Supplement)*, London: Oxford University Press.

Meese, R. A. and Rogoff, K. (1983), 'Empirical Exchange Rate Models of the Seventies: Do They Fit Out of Sample?', *Journal of International Economics*, 14(1): 3–24.

—— (1984), 'The Out-of-Sample Failure of Empirical Exchange Rate Models:

Sampling Error or Misspecification?', in J. A. Frenkel (ed.), *Exchange Rates and International Macroeconomics*, Chicago: University of Chicago Press.

Melitz, J. (1985), 'The Welfare Case for the European Monetary System', *Journal of International Money and Finance*, 4(4): 485–516.

Melvin, M. (1988), 'The Dollarization of Latin America as a Market-Enforced Monetary Reform: Evidence and Implications', *Economic Development and Cultural Change*, 36(3): 543–58.

Menkhoff, L. and Schlumberger, M. (1995), 'Persistent Profitability of Technical Analysis on Foreign Exchange Markets?', *Banca Nazionale del Lavoro. Quarterly Review*, 48(193): 189–216.

Metzler, L. A. (1951), 'Wealth, Saving and the Rate of Interest', *Journal of Political Economy*, 59(2), 93–116.

—— (1979), 'The Colm-Dodge-Goldsmith Plan (1946). Appendix N: Considerations Regarding the Foreign Exchange Rate for the Deutsche Mark', *Zeitschrift für die Gesamte Staatswissenschaft*, 135 (Sep.).

Mishkin, F. S. (1984), 'Are Real Interest Rates across Countries Equal? An Empirical Investigation of International Parity Conditions', *Journal of Finance*, 39 (Dec.): 1345–57.

Mundell, R. A. (1961a), 'Flexible Exchange Rates and Employment Policy', *Canadian Journal of Economics and Political Science*, 27(4): 509–17.

—— (1961b), 'A Theory of Optimal Currency Areas', *American Economic Review*, 51(4): 657–65.

—— (1968), 'Appendix to Chapter 18: The World Economy', in: R. A. Mundell, *International Economics*, New York: Macmillan.

—— (1971), *Monetary Theory: Inflation, Interest and Growth in the World Economy*, Pacific Palisades, Calif.: Goodyear.

—— (1991), 'Stabilization Policies in Less Developed and Socialist Countries', in E. M. Claassen (1991a): 21–51.

Murphy, R. G. (1984), 'Capital Mobility and the Relationship between Saving and Investment in OECD Countries', *Journal of International Money and Finance*, 3(4): 327–42.

Mussa, M. (1981), *The Role of Official Intervention*, Occasional Paper no. 6, New York: Group of Thirty.

—— (1984), 'The Theory of Exchange Rate Determination', in J. F. O. Bilson and R. C. Marston (eds.), *Exchange Rate Theory and Practice*, Chicago: University of Chicago Press: 13–58.

—— (1986), 'Nominal Exchange Rate Regimes and the Behavior of Real Exchange Rates: Evidence and Implications', in K. Brunner and A. H. Meltzer (eds.), *Real Business Cycles, Real Exchange Rates and Actual Policies*, Amsterdam: North-Holland: 117–214.

Niehans, J. (1978), 'Metzler, Wealth and Macroeconomics: A Review', *Journal of Economic Literature*, 16(1): 85–95.

Obstfeld, M. (1982), 'Can We Sterilize? Theory and Evidence', *American Economic Review. Papers and Proceedings*, 72(2): 45–50.

—— (1983), 'Exchange Rates, Inflation and the Sterilization Problem: Germany 1975–81', *European Economic Review*, 21(1): 161–89.

—— (1987), 'Fiscal Deficits and Relative Prices in a Growing World Economy', Working Paper, Philadelphia: University of Pennsylvania, May.

Obstfeld, M. (1991), 'The Adjustment Mechanism', National Bureau of Economic Research, Working Paper no. 3943, Dec.

Ohlin, B. (1929), 'Transfer Difficulties, Real and Imagined', *Economic Journal*, 39 (June): 172–78.

Oppenheimer, P. (1974), 'Non-Traded Goods and the Balance of Payments: A Historical Note', *Journal of Economic Literature*, 12(3): 882–88.

Papell, D. H. (1988), 'Expectations and Exchange Rate Dynamics After a Decade of Floating', *Journal of International Economics*, 25(3/4): 303–17.

Patinkin, D. (1965), *Money, Interest and Prices*, New York: Harper and Row.

Pearce, I. F. (1961), 'The Problem of the Balance of Payments', *International Economic Review*, 2(1): 1–28.

Penati, A. (1987), 'Government Spending and the Real Exchange Rate', *Journal of International Economics*, 22(3/4): 237–56.

Pennant-Rea, R. (1994), 'Dances with Elephants: The International Monetary System and Domestic Economic Policy', Speech at the Third Bank of England/London School of Economics Lecture, 7 Dec.

Pinto, B. (1991), 'Unification of Official and Black Market Exchange Rates in Sub-Saharan Africa', in E. M. Claassen (1991a): 327–51.

Purvis, D. D. (1985), 'Public Sector Deficits, International Capital Movements, and the Domestic Economy: The Medium-Term is the Message', *Canadian Journal of Economics*, 18(4): 723–42.

Reinhart, C. M. and Wickham, P. (1994), 'Commodity Prices: Cyclical Weakness or Secular Decline?', Working Paper no. 94/7, Washington, DC: International Monetary Fund, Jan.

Rogoff, K. (1984), 'On the Effects of Sterilized Intervention: An Analysis of Weekly Data', *Journal of Monetary Economics*, 14(2): 133–50.

——— (1985), 'Can Exchange Rate Predictability be Achieved without Monetary Convergence? Evidence from the EMS', *European Economic Review*, 28(1): 93–115.

Rostowski, J. (1992), 'The Benefits of Currency Substitution during High Inflation and Stabilization', *Revista de Analisis Economico*, 7(1): 91–107.

Sachs, J. D. (1984), *Theoretical Issues in International Borrowing*, Princeton Studies in International Finance, July.

——— (1986), 'The Uneasy Case for Greater Exchange Rate Coordination', *American Economic Review, Papers and Proceedings*, 76(2): 336–41.

——— and Huizinga, H. (1987), 'U.S. Commercial Banks and the Developing-Country Debt Crisis', *Brookings Papers on Economic Activity*, no. 2: 555–601.

——— and Larrain, F. (1993), *Macroeconomics in the Global Economy*, New York: Harvester Wheatsheaf.

——— and Wyplosz, C. (1984), 'La Politique Budgétaire et le Taux de Change Réel', *Annales de l'INSEE*, no. 53.

Sachverständigenrat (1990a), *Sondergutachten vom 20. Januar 1990. Zur Unterstützung der Wirtschaftsreform in der DDR: Voraussetzungen und Möglichkeiten*, Bonn: Deutscher Bundestag.

——— (1990b), *Jahresgutachten 1990/91 des Sachverständigenrates zur Begutachtung der gesamtwirtschaftlichen Entwicklung*, Bonn: Deutscher Bundestag.

Salter, W. E. (1959), 'Internal and External Balance: The Role of Price and Expenditure Effects', *Economic Record*, 35(71): 226–38.

Salemi, Michael K. (1984), 'Comment on Meese and Rogoff', in J. A. Frenkel (ed.),

Exchange Rates and International Macroeconomics, Chicago: University of Chicago Press.

Samuelson, P. (1964), 'Theoretical Notes on Trade Problems', *Review of Economics and Statistics*, 46(2): 145–154.

Santaella, J. A. (1993), 'Stabilization Programs and External Enforcement: Experience from the 1920s', Working Paper no. 93/3, Washington, DC: International Monetary Fund, Jan.

Schäfer, H.-B. (1984), *Jenseits des Krisenmanagements. Internationale Schuldenkrise und IWF-Kredite*, Bonn.

Schinasi, G. J., Lipschitz, L., and McDonald, D. (1990), 'Monetary and Financial Issues in German Unification', in L. Lipschitz and D. McDonald (eds.), *German Unification. Economic Issues*, Occasional Paper no. 75, Washington, DC: International Monetary Fund, Dec.: 144–54.

Sjaastad, L. A. (1983), 'The International Debt Quagmire: To Whom Do We Owe It?' *The World Economy*, 6(3): 305–24.

Smith, P. and Wickens, M. (1990), 'Assessing Monetary Shocks and Exchange Rate Variability with a Stylized Econometric Model of the U.K', in A. S. Courakis and M. P. Taylor (eds.), *Private Behavior and Government Policy in Interdependent Economies*, Oxford: Oxford University Press.

Stiglitz, J. E. (1990), 'Symposium on Bubbles', *Journal of Economic Perspectives*, 4 (Spring): 13–18.

Stockman, A. C. (1983), 'Real Exchange Rates under Alternative Nominal Exchange-Rate Regimes', *Journal of International Money and Finance* 2(2): 147–66.

—— (1988), 'Real Exchange Rate Variability under Pegged and Floating Nominal Exchange Rate Systems: An Equilibrium Theory', National Bureau of Economic Research, Working Paper no. 2565.

Summers, R. and Heston, A. (1988), 'A New Set of International Comparisons of Real Product and Price Levels: Estimates for 130 Countries, 1950–85', *Review of Income and Wealth*, 34(1): 1–25.

—— (1991), 'The Pen World Table (Mark 5): An Extended Set of International Comparisons, 1950–88', *Quarterly Journal of Economics*, 106(425): 327–68.

Swan, T. (1960), 'Economic Control in a Dependent Economy', *Economic Record*, 36(73): 51–66.

Swoboda, A. K. (1968), *The Euro-Dollar Market: An Interpretation*, Essays in International Finance no. 64, Princeton, NJ: Princeton University: Feb.

Taylor, M. P. (1987), 'Risk Premia and Foreign Exchange: A Multiple Time Series Approach to Testing Uncovered Interest Parity', *Weltwirtschaftliches Archiv*, 123(4): 579–91.

—— (1990), *The Balance of Payments: New Perspectives on Open Economy Macroeconomics*, London: Edward Elgar.

—— (1995), 'The Economics of Exchange Rates', *Journal of Economic Literature*, 33(1): 13–47.

—— and Allen, H. L. (1992), 'The Use of Technical Analysis in the Foreign Exchange Market', *Journal of International Money and Finance*, 11(3): 304–14.

Tesar, L. S. and Werner, I. M. (1992), 'Home Bias and the Globalization of Securities Markets', National Bureau of Economic Research, Working Paper no. 4218, Nov.

Tobin, J. (1982), 'A Proposal for Monetary Reform', in J. Tobin (ed.), *Essays in Economic Theory and Policy*, Cambridge, Mass.: MIT Press.

Triffin, R. (1960), *Gold and the Dollar Crisis*, New Haven, Conn.: Yale University Press.

Tryon, R. (1983), 'Small Empirical Models of Exchange Market Intervention', Staff Studies no. 134, Washington, DC: Board of Governors of the Federal Reserve System.

Turner, P. and Van't dack, J. (1993), *Measuring International Price and Cost Competitiveness*, Economic Paper no. 39, Basle: Bank for International Settlements, Nov.

Ungerer, H., Evena, O., and Young, P. (1986), *The European Monetary System*, Occasional Paper no. 48, Washington, DC: International Monetary Fund.

Van Germert, H. and Gruijters, N. (1994), 'Patterns of Financial Change in the OECD Area', *Banca Nazionale del Lavoro Quarterly Review*, 48(190): 271–94.

World Bank (1987), *World Development Report 1987*, Oxford: Oxford University Press.

——— (1991), *World Development Report 1991. The Challenge of Development*, Oxford: Oxford University Press.

INDEX

N.B. Page references to boxes, figures and tables are printed in italic.